ENCYCLOPEDIA OF AMERICAN INDIAN CIVIL RIGHTS

Edited by
JAMES S. OLSON

Associate Editors:
Mark Baxter, Jason M. Tetzloff,
and Darren Pierson,

Greenwood Press
Westport, Connecticut • London

Library of Congress Cataloging-in-Publication Data

Encyclopedia of American Indian civil rights / edited by James S.
   Olson ; Mark Baxter . . . [et al.] associate editors.
      p.   cm.
   Includes bibliographical references and index.
   ISBN 0–313–29338–4 (alk. paper)
      1. Indians of North America—Civil rights—Encyclopedias.
   2. Civil rights—United States—Encyclopedias.   I. Olson, James
   Stuart, 1946–   .   II. Baxter, Mark.
   KF8210.C5E53   1997
   323.1'197073'03—dc20   96–35352

British Library Cataloguing in Publication Data is available.

Library of Congress Catalog Card Number: 96–35352
ISBN: 0–313–29338–4

First published in 1997

Greenwood Press, 88 Post Road West, Westport, CT 06881
An imprint of Greenwood Publishing Group, Inc.

Printed in the United States of America

The paper used in this book complies with the
Permanent Paper Standard issued by the National
Information Standards Organization (Z39.48–1984).

10 9 8 7 6 5 4 3 2 1

Cover photo: Wounded Knee, S.D., March 8, 1973. (AP/Wide World Photos)

CONTENTS

Photo essay follows page 204.

PREFACE

In 1959, when I was 13 years old, I spent the summer living with my Navajo friend, Jerry Pete, on the reservation near Parker, Arizona. Placed in a white family's home by a church social service agency when he was 6 years old, Jerry spent the school year in Paramount, California, and then returned to his own family during summer vacation. In California, we were next-door neighbors and became fast friends, riding bicycles, hitting baseballs, and mowing lawns for extra change together. At school he was quiet and shy, but not here at home on the reservation. When we got off the Greyhound bus in Parker, Arizona, that summer of 1959, he peeled off his California identity like layers of crusty onion skin. Beneath the guarded exterior I had seen so often was a bright, animated Navajo-speaking boy who greeted his family with all the love I had for my own. The Navajo reservation was life for him and suburban Los Angeles only an artificial, temporary reality.

Over the centuries Indian civil rights law, like Jerry Pete's life, was caught between those two distinct worlds. Native Americans have often been caught between the confusing and sometimes inconsistent competing jurisdictions of local, state, federal, and tribal governments, as well as the demands of the U.S. Constitution. In the *Encyclopedia of American Indian Civil Rights* I have tried to provide brief descriptions of the major concepts, court decisions, congressional acts, and individuals involved in the history of Native American civil rights. I am grateful to my associate editors and each contributor to the encyclopedia, and to the librarians at Sam Houston State University who have made my research task easier.

Readers should note that I am aware of existing controversies over the use of "Indian," "American Indian," and "Native American." Each term, of course, carries its own cultural and political baggage. Many Native Americans resent the term "Indian" because it was given to them by an ignorant European who thought he had sailed all the way from Spain to the East Indies. The term "American Indian" is not much better, for the same reason. "Native American" implies people native to the New World, but it can be confusing because non-Indian people born in the New World can also be identified by it. The best policy would be to identify Indians by the tribal name in their own language, but that approach too is complicated by the large numbers of Indian people who can claim multitribal ancestry and by the problem of what to do when talking about Native Americans generically. Throughout the *Encyclopedia of American Indian Civil Rights* I have used the terms "Indian," "American Indian," and "Native American" interchangeably, moving back and forth between them for variety's sake and as stylistic reasons have dictated. Entries are cross-referenced with asterisks.

James S. Olson

MAJOR LANDMARKS IN THE HISTORY OF AMERICAN INDIAN CIVIL RIGHTS

1781	The Articles of Confederation go into effect.
1785	Congress passes the Land Ordinance.
1787	The U.S. Constitution is drafted.
	Congress passes the Northwest Ordinance.
1789	The Constitution goes into effect.
1790	Congress passes the Indian Trade and Intercourse Act.
1791	The Bill of Rights, or first ten amendments to the Constitution, is ratified and goes into effect.
1793	Congress passes the Indian Trade and Intercourse Act.
1796	Congress passes the Indian Trade and Intercourse Act.
1800	Congress passes the Land Act.
1802	Congress passes the Indian Intercourse Act.
1803	The U.S. Senate approves the Louisiana Purchase.
1804	Congress passes the Land Act.
1810	The Supreme Court decides the *Fletcher v. Peck* case.
1812	The Supreme Court decides the *New Jersey v. Wilson* case.
1819	Congress establishes the Civilization Fund.
1820	Congress passes the Land Act.
1823	The Supreme Court decides the *Johnson's and Graham's Lessee v. M'Intosh* case.
1824	Congress establishes the Bureau of Indian Affairs.
1830	Congress passes the Indian Removal Act.
1831	The Supreme Court decides the *Cherokee Nation v. State of Georgia* case.
1832	The Supreme Court decides the *Worcester v. Georgia* case.
	Congress passes the Land Act.

1834	Congress passes the Indian Intercourse Act.
1848	The U.S. Senate ratifies the Treaty of Guadalupe Hidalgo.
1861	The Civil War breaks out.
1862	Congress passes the Homestead Act.
1864	The Sand Creek massacre takes place in Colorado.
1866	The Supreme Court decides *The Kansas Indians* case.
1867	The Indian Peace Commission is established after Congress passes the Peace Commission Act.
1868	The Fourteenth Amendment is ratified.
1869	The federal government's new "Peace Policy" goes into effect.
1870	The Supreme Court decides the *McKay v. Campbell* case.
1875	The Indian Hope Association is founded.
1876	The Supreme Court decides the *United States v. Joseph* case.
	June 25: Custer's Seventh Cavalry is destroyed at the Little Bighorn Valley in Montana.
1877	Chief Joseph unsuccessfully tries to lead his Nez Percé people to Canada.
1878	Chief Dull Knife unsuccessfully tries to lead his Northern Cheyenne people out of Indian Territory back to their indigenous homeland in the northern plains.
1879	The Supreme Court decides the *Standing Bear v. Crook* case.
1880	The Bureau of Indian Affairs bans the Sun Dance religious ceremony in the United States.
1881	Helen Hunt Jackson's *A Century of Dishonor* is published.
1882	The Indian Rights Association is founded.
	The Supreme Court decides the *McBratney v. United States* case.
1883	The Supreme Court decides the *Ex Parte Crow Dog* case.
	The first of the Lake Mohonk conferences of the Friends of the Indians is held.
1884	The Supreme Court decides the *Elk v. Wilkins* case.
1885	Congress passes the Major Crimes Act.
	The National Indian Defense Association is founded.
1886	The Supreme Court decides the *United States v. Kagama* case.

1887	Congress passes the Dawes Severalty Act and launches the allotment campaign.
1890	The Wounded Knee, South Dakota, massacre takes place.
	The Oklahoma Territory is created out of a portion of the Indian Territory.
1892	Congress passes the Intoxication in Indian Country Act.
1894	The Supreme Court decides the *Missouri, Kansas and Texas Railway Co. v. Roberts* case.
1896	The Supreme Court decides the *Talton v. Mayes* case.
1897	The Atoka Agreement is signed in Oklahoma Territory.
	The Supreme Court decides the *United States v. Wong Kim Ark* case.
1898	Congress passes the Curtis Act.
1902	Congress passes the Dead Indian Land Act and amends the Dawes Act.
1903	The Supreme Court decides the *Lone Wolf v. Hitchcock* case.
1904	Congress passes the Pipelines Act.
1905	The Supreme Court decides the *United States v. Winans* case.
1906	Congress passes the Burke Act and amends the Dawes Act.
	Congress passes the Alaska Allotment Act.
1907	The Supreme Court decides the *Kansas v. Colorado* case.
	Indian Territory is incorporated into the new state of Oklahoma.
1908	The Supreme Court decides the *Quick Bear v. Leupp* case.
	The Supreme Court decides the *Winters v. United States* case.
1910	The Department of the Interior reiterates its prohibition on the Sun Dance ceremony.
1911	The Society of American Indians is established.
1912	The Alaska Native Brotherhood is founded.
1913	The Supreme Court decides the *United States v. Sandoval* case.
1916	The Supreme Court decides the *United States v. Nice* case.
1919	Congress passes the Indian Veteran Citizenship Act.
1920	Congress passes the General Leasing Act.
	The North Dakota Supreme Court decides the *Swift v. Leach* case.

1921   A federal district court decides the *Skeem v. United States* case.

1922   The American Indian Association is established.

            The Association on American Indian Affairs is established.

            Congress fails to pass the Bursum Bill.

            The Eastern Association on Indian affairs is established.

1923   The Committee of One Hundred is founded.

            John Collier founds the American Indian Defense Association.

1924   Congress passes the Synder Act awarding citizenship to all Indians born in the United States.

            A California court decides the *Piper v. Big Pine School District* case.

1925   Congress passes the Osage Guardianship Act.

1926   The Indian Defense League of America is established.

            The National Council of American Indians is founded.

1928   The Brookings Institution issues the Meriam Report.

1933   The National League for Justice to American Indians is established.

1934   Congress passes the Indian Reorganization Act and ends allotment.

            Congress passes the Johnson-O'Malley Act.

            The American Indian Federation is established.

            Congress passes the U.S. Citizenship for Metlakatla Indians Act.

1935   Congress passes the Indian Arts and Crafts Board Act.

1936   Congress passes the Alaska Reorganization Act.

            Congress passes the Oklahoma Indian Welfare Act.

1938   The Supreme Court decides the *United States v. Klamath Indians* case.

            Congress passes the Indian Lands Mining Act.

1941   The Supreme Court decides the *Seminole v. United States* case.

1944   The National Congress of American Indians is established.

            The Supreme Court decides the *Green v. United States* case.

1946   Congress passes the Indian Claims Commission Act and begins the compensation program.

1948   Congress passes the Assimilative Crimes Act.

The Supreme Court decides the *Harrison v. Laveen* case.

1950   Congress passes the Navajo-Hopi Long-Range Rehabilitation Act.

1952   The House of Representatives passes House Resolution 698.

The House of Representatives passes House Concurrent Resolution 108.

1953   Congress formally launches the termination program.

1954   A federal district court decides the *Toledo et al. v. Pueblo de Jemez et al.* case.

1955   The Supreme Court decides the *Tee-Hit-Ton Indians v. United States* case.

1956   The Supreme Court decides the *Iron Crow v. Oglala Sioux Tribe*, the *Ahtanum Irrigation District v. United States*, and the *Squire v. Capoeman* cases.

1958   The Supreme Court decides the *Williams v. Lee* case.

1959   A federal district court decides the *Native American Church v. Navajo Tribal Council* case.

1961   The National Indian Youth Council is formed.

February 12: The Mohawks demand that construction of Kinzua Dam be stopped.

June 13–20: The American Indian Chicago Conference is held.

1962   *March 5:* The Supreme Court decides the *Metlakatla Indian Community v. Egan* case.

1963   *June 3:* The Supreme Court decides the *Arizona v. California* case.

1964   The Survival of American Indians Association is founded.

1965   *February 15:* The Nisqually Indians stage a fish-in in Washington State to protest state laws requiring only hook and line fishing.

1966   The Alaska Federation of Natives is formed.

1967   The American Law Center is established.

1968   *March 6:* The National Council on Indian Opportunity is founded.

April 11: Congress passes the Indian Civil Rights Act.

May 27: The Supreme Court decides the *Puyallup Tribe v. Department of Game* (Puyallup I) case.

July 18: The American Indian Movement is founded in Minneapolis.

December 18: The Mohawk Blockade of the Cornwall Bridge in upstate New York takes place.

1969   The American Indian Movement for Equal Rights is founded.

The Kennedy Report on Indian education is released.

The Supreme Court decides the *United States v. Oregon* case.

April 29: Paiute Stanley Smart protests Nevada state game laws.

October 10: AMERIND, Inc. is established.

October 12: Dartmouth College drops its Indian mascot.

October 29: Congress passes the Indian Health Care Act.

November 9: Indians of All Tribes occupy Alcatraz Island in San Francisco Bay.

November 12: The National Indian Education Association is founded.

1970   *March 8:* Lehman Brightman leads a group of Indians in a march on the state capitol in Sacramento, California, to protest the fatal shooting of a Hoopa Indian.

March 8: United Indians of All Tribes invade Fort Lawton to demand their right to take title to surplus federal lands.

March 14: Indian activists stage protest demonstrations at Bureau of Indian Affairs offices throughout the country to demand fair employment practices.

March 16: Indian activists demonstrate at Ellis Island to claim the abandoned immigration building as an Indian commune.

March 22: Various Indian groups stage sit-ins at Bureau of Indian Affairs offices in Denver, Cleveland, Minneapolis, Sacramento, and Santa Fe.

April 13: Congress passes the Indian Elementary and Secondary Education Act.

April 27: Various AIM groups picket the opening of the film *A Man Called Horse*.

April 27: The Supreme Court renders its decision in *Choctaw Nation et al. v. Oklahoma et al.*

May 17: Mohawk demonstrators try to drive non-Indian campers off Loon Island in the St. Lawrence River of New York.

June 6: Pit River Indians stage a protest demonstration to claim ownership of Lassen National Forest.

June 10: Pomo Indians occupy and claim as their own a 64-acre tract of land they claim is sacred near Clear Lake, California.

July 15: Oglala Sioux demonstrators seize an area on Sheep Mountain, North Dakota, and demand that the federal government return it to the tribe.

August 1: Puyallup Indians stage fish-ins in Washington State to demand their treaty fishing rights on the Puyallup River.

September 18: A group of fifty Indians from various tribes occupies Mount Rushmore in South Dakota and demands its return to Native Americans.

Early October: Sioux Indians establish a protest encampment at the Badlands National Monument in South Dakota.

October 10: Pit River Indians occupy a site near Burney, California, and claim it as their own.

October 15: Taos Indians protest federal policies over ownership of Blue Lake in New Mexico.

November 22: Pomo Indians begin imposing tolls on motorists driving through the reservation.

November 23: The American Indian Movement holds its *Mayflower II* demonstration.

December 15: Congress passes the Taos Blue Lake Act.

1971

The Institute for the Development of Indian law is established.

The National Tribal Chairmen's Association is founded.

The National American Rights Fund is established.

January 21: Fishing rights activist Hank Adams is shot while staging a fish-in on the Puyallup River in Washington State.

March 11: Congress passes the Alaska Native Claims Settlement Act.

May 16: Indian activists occupy an abandoned naval air station near Minneapolis and demand that it be turned into an Indian cultural center.

May 26: A group of Pit River Indians occupies the Toyon Job Corps Center near Redding, California, and demands return of the site to the tribe.

June 6: Sioux activists establish a camp at the top of the Mount Rushmore National Memorial and demand the return of Sioux lands.

June 11: The nineteen-month occupation of Alcatraz Island by the Indians of All Tribes comes to an end.

June 14: Indians of All Tribes occupy abandoned Nike missile sites.

August 15: AIM protestors seize an abandoned Coast Guard lifeboat station in Milwaukee, Wisconsin.

August 18: Iroquois Indians protest the widening of Interstate 81 in New York State.

1972   Congress passes the Indian Education Act.

March 2: Stanford University abandons use of an Indian as its athletic mascot.

April 23: AIM holds a protest demonstration at the Fort Totten Indian Reservation in North Dakota to highlight the problem of police brutality.

June 11: Lumbee Indian students at Pembroke State University in North Carolina protest a decision to demolish an ancient Indian historic site on campus.

September 13: John Trudell leads a group of Oklahoma Indians in taking over a federal office in Pawnee, Oklahoma, to protest improper use of educational funds.

November 2: The Trail of Broken Treaties demonstration takes place in Washington, D.C. More than 600 Indians barricade themselves in the BIA offices.

1973   The Oglala Sioux Civil Rights Organization is founded.

The Supreme Court decides the *McClanahan v. Arizona State Tax Commission* case.

February 6–8: AIM protestors clash with police in Custer, South Dakota, over a local judge's decision to grant bail to a white man accused of murdering an Indian.

February 27–May 8: Wounded Knee, South Dakota, is the scene of a standoff involving AIM protestors, the FBI, and Pine Ridge reservation officials.

March 27: The Supreme Court decides the *Mescalero Apache Tribe v. Jones* case.

March 27: Marlon Brando refuses to accept his Best Actor Award at the Academy Awards ceremony because of the industry's treatment of Indians on film and television.

August 13: The Civil Rights Division of the Department of Justice establishes an Office of Indian Rights.

November 19: The Supreme Court decides the *Puyallup Tribe v. Department of Game* (Puyallup II) case.

December 22: The Menominee Indians regain full federal recognition and protection, ending termination.

1974   The Women of All Red Nations is formed.

February 12: The Supreme Court decides the *United States v. Washington* case.

April 12: Congress passes the Indian Finance Act.

May 13: Mohawk militants begin a three-year occupation of a 612-acre campsite in the Adirondack Mountains of New York.

June 17: The Supreme Court reaches its decision in the *Morton v. Mancari* case.

December 22: Congress passes the Hopi and Navajo Relocation Act.

1975   *January 1:* Forty-five Menominee Indians seize a Roman Catholic convent in Gresham, Wisconsin, and demand return of its 225 acres to the Indians.

January 4: Congress passes the Indian Self-Determination and Education Assistance Act.

February 25: AIM activists occupy the Fairchild Camera and Instrument Corporation Electronics Plant at Shiprock, New Mexico, to protest the company's decision to lay off 140 Navajo workers.

June 26: Leonard Peltier is charged with the murder of two FBI agents in Pine Ridge, South Dakota.

1976   The Council of Energy Resource Tribes is formed.

The Supreme Court decides the *Puyallup Tribe v. Department of Game* (Puyallup III) case.

March 2: The Supreme Court makes its decision in *Fisher v. District Court*.

April 27: The Supreme Court decides the *Moe v. Confederated Salish & Kootenai Tribes* case.

May 29: Congress passes the Indian Crimes Act.

June 15: The Supreme Court decides the *Bryan v. Itasca* case.

September 16: Congress passes the Indian Health Care Improvement Act.

October 31: Puyallup protestors occupy the Cascadia Juvenile Diagnostic Center in Tacoma, Washington.

1977   *March 21:* Menominee activists occupy the courthouse in Keshena, Wisconsin, demanding punishment of the individuals responsible for beating up two Indian women.

April 28: Leonard Peltier is convicted on two counts of first-degree murder (see 1975).

1978   *February 11:* The American Indian Movement begins its Longest Walk demonstration.

March 6: The Supreme Court decides the *Oliphant v. Suquamish Indian Tribe* case.

March 22: The Supreme Court decides the *United States v. Wheeler* case.

May 15: The Supreme Court decides the *Santa Clara Pueblo v. Martinez* case.

May 17: Approximately twenty-five Chumash Indians protest construction of a natural gas depot in Little Cohu Bay near Point Conception, California.

August 11: Congress passes the American Indian Religious Freedom Act.

October 1: The Federal Acknowledgement Project formally begins operation.

November 8: Congress passes the Indian Child Welfare Act.

1979   *June 13:* The U.S. Court of Claims awards $122.5 million to the Lakota Sioux for the loss of the Black Hills of South Dakota. The tribe refuses to accept the money, insisting on the return of the land.

October 5: Two thousand Indian activists protest the decision to develop uranium mines in the Black Hills of South Dakota.

October 31: Congress passes the Archaeological Resources Protection Act.

1980   *June 27:* The Supreme Court decides the *White Mountain Apache Tribe v. Bracker* case.

June 30: The Supreme Court decides the *United States v. Sioux Nation of Indians* case.

October 11: Congress passes the Maine Indian Claims Settlement Act.

1981   *May 2:* The Supreme Court decides the *Seminole Tribe of Florida v. Butterworth* case.

May 29: The Supreme Court decides the *Montana v. United States* case.

1982   *January 8:* Congress passes the Indian Mineral
                    Development Act.

                    January 12: Congress passes the Federal Oil and Gas
                    Royalty Management Act.

                    January 14: Congress passes the Indian Tribal Government
                    Tax Status Act.

                    January 25: The Supreme Court decides the *Merrion v.
                    Jicarilla Apache Tribe* case.

1983   *January 25:* The Supreme Court decides the *Lac Courte
                    Oreilles Band of Lake Superior Chippewa Indians v.
                    Voight* case.

                    June 13: The Supreme Court decides the *New Mexico v.
                    Mescalero Apache Tribe* case.

                    June 24: The Supreme Court decides the *Nevada v. United
                    States* case.

                    July 15: The Supreme Court decides the *Arizona et al. v.
                    San Carlos Apache Tribe* case.

1984   *July 22:* Indian militants protest the state of Connecticut's
                    decision to assume police jurisdiction on reservations.

1985   *March 4:* The Supreme Court decides the *County of
                    Oneida v. Oneida Indian Nation* case.

                    April 16: The Supreme Court decides the *Kerr-McGee
                    Corporation v. Navajo Tribe* case.

                    June 3: The Supreme Court decides the *Montana v.
                    United States* case.

1986   *August 27:* The Klamath Indians are restored to full federal
                    recognition, ending termination.

1987   *February 25:* The Supreme Court decides the *California v.
                    Cabazon Band of Mission Indians* case.

1988   *April 19:* The Supreme Court decides the *Lyng v.
                    Northwest Indian Cemetery Protective Association*
                    case.

                    April 28: Congress passes the Repeal of Termination Act.

                    June 2: Mohawk militants in New York protest attempts by
                    New York to restrict free movement across the Mercier
                    Bridge at the Canadian border.

                    July 8: The Supreme Court decides the *Oklahoma Tax
                    Commission v. Muscogee (Creek) Nation* case.

                    October 17: Congress passes the Indian Gaming Regulatory
                    Act.

1989   *March 3:* The Supreme Court renders its decision in the
            *Lac Courte Oreilles Band of Lake Superior Chippewa
            Indians et al. v. State of Wisconsin* case.

            April 3: The Supreme Court decides the *Mississippi Band
            of Choctaw Indians v. Holyfield et al.* case.

            April 23: More than 100 Wisconsin Indians protest to
            protect the fishing rights of northern Wisconsin
            Indians.

            July 21: The Supreme Court decides the *Brendale v.
            Confederated Tribes and Bands of the Yakima Indian
            Nation* case.

            August 13: The state of New York agrees to return twelve
            wampum belts to the Onondoga Nation of New York.

            November 2: Congress passes the National Museum of the
            American Indian Act.

1990   The Indian Nations at Risk Task Force is established.

            April 17: The Supreme Court decides the *Employment
            Division, Department of Human Resources of Oregon
            et al. v. Alfred L. Smith et al.* case.

            May 29: The Supreme Court decides the *Duro v. Reina*
            case.

            August 18: Congress passes the Indian Law Enforcement
            Act.

            October 30: Congress passes the Native American
            Languages Act.

            November 16: Congress passes the Native American Graves
            Protection and Repatriation Act.

            November 29: Congress passes a new version of the Indian
            Arts and Crafts Board Act.

1991   Congress renames the Custer Battlefield National
            Monument in southeastern Montana the Little Bighorn
            Battlefield National Monument.

1993   *September 8:* Congress passes the Religious Freedom
            Restoration Act.

1994   *February 11:* Dennis Banks of the American Indian
            Movement begins the "Walk for Justice" protest
            march.

1996   The Clinton administration proposes new federal adoption
            programs that will reduce tribal influence over the
            placement of Indian children.

Mohican tribes try to stop the construction of a Wal-Mart store on what they consider to be sacred ground in Leeds, New York.

The attorney general of New Mexico orders the closing of several reservation casinos.

INTRODUCTION

Ever since Columbus set foot on New World soil in 1492, Euroamericans have been trying to figure out the place of Native Americans in the larger society. Europeans and their descendants have consistently approached the indigenous people from one of two perspectives. On the one hand, the Europeans have lusted after Indian economic resources. They created powerful negative stereotypes about the Indians, justifying the conflict necessary to drive them off the land. If the Indians really were blood-thirsty savages, they argued, society was better off without them. Over the centuries the Europeans' and Euroamericans' desires for particular resources have changed. But whether it was the brazilwood of the sixteenth century in Brazil or the coal of today in the Four Corners region of the American Southwest, Euroamericans are continually trying to push Indians off the land.

If the Indians had peaceably relocated to other, less valuable areas, most Europeans would have been willing to leave them alone, but the key was getting them off the valuable land. If violence was necessary, so be it. All over the New World, these notions led to genocidal assaults on the Indian tribes. Ironically, time, technology, and population expansion eventually render all the land valuable. The penetration of Yanomami land in northwestern Brazil today by gold prospectors is just the latest chapter in a long history of exploitation and invasion.

The second approach to indigenous people seems more humane (superficially, at least) and grew out of a combination of liberal guilt and missionary zeal. Dismayed about the violence inflicted on indigenous people, some Europeans wanted to protect them, to insulate them from the more aggressive, less morally restrained settlers. But they also wanted to change the indigenous people. These Europeans accepted the natives' humanity—as well as what they saw as their cultural inferiority—but instead of annihilating them to clear the land, liberals and missionaries sought to assimilate them into European culture and society. That is, they sought to remake Indian society, transforming Native Americans into "law-abiding" farmers who would accept the notions of private property, nuclear families, individual aggrandizement, and Jesus Christ. The pattern is the same, whether promoted by Jesuits of the sixteenth century or Protestant evangelicals of the 1990s. Ironically, although the methods of the assimilationists were far more benign than the genocidal ravages of Indian haters, the results were the same: the virtual elimination of indigenous civilizations.

In the United States, Indian law has evolved in the context of those two Euroamerican approaches to Native Americans. Over the last two centuries, three questions have driven the development of Indian law. First, to what extent do Indian tribes enjoy political sovereignty and the right to self-government? Second, are individual Indians citizens of their tribes or of the United States or both, and what civil rights accrue to them because of such citizenship[s]? And third, what is the legal relationship between federal, state, and local governments and Indian tribes? American policymakers have tried, again and again, to answer each of these questions ever since the day George Washington took the oath of office in 1789.

Although the three concepts seem simple and clear enough, they have been the source of endless controversy as the body of Indian law has evolved. There is a subtle but powerful tension between notions of individual rights and tribal sovereignty,* and that tension has generated bitter, ongoing jurisdictional disputes between various state governments, state governments and the federal government, state governments and tribal governments, tribal governments and the federal government, individual Indians and their own tribal governments, and Indians and non-Indians. Each of these entities has made Indian civil rights law a rich but often confusing area of American jurisprudence.

The history of American Indian civil rights can be divided into five chronological stages since the U.S. Constitution* went into effect in 1789.

THE AGE OF SOVEREIGNTY, 1789–1870

The Europeans came to the New World convinced that they were on a mission from God, but they were also a legalistic people who worried about property rights, land title, and conquest.* The European states agreed that whoever "found" an area first gained all the rights to the region against any other European nation. This is called right of discovery. Natives in the areas claimed by the European empires were to be dealt with by the discovering power only, and other nations had no right to negotiate with the affected indigenous peoples. The question of which European power could claim sovereignty over an area was resolved diplomatically. In the Treaty of Tordesillas of 1494, which the pope recognized, Spain and Portugal divided up the New World, cutting the South American continent in half, which explains why Brazilians today speak Portuguese and not Spanish. By right of discovery and papal recognition, the Spanish and Portuguese argued, these lands were exclusively reserved to them.

England, France, and the Netherlands, whose imperial ventures did not really begin until the late sixteenth and early seventeenth centuries, disputed the claim. English diplomats cited the doctrine of "effective occupation," claiming that nations could claim only those regions that they had "effectively occupied and administered." They argued for decades with Spain about the doctrine of effective occupation, but it became operational with the Treaty of Madrid of 1670, in which Spain effectively extended recognition of English sovereignty to the territories that England had already occupied. Portugal, France, and the Netherlands tacitly recognized the arrangement as well.

However, resolving the issue of Indian property rights, land title, and sovereignty proved far more difficult. Soon after the first discoveries, debate raged in the royal courts of Europe about the nature of indigenous peoples. Were Indians human beings? Did they possess souls? If so, what rights did they have to their lands? Could the Spanish legitimately come among them, for any purpose? Finally, could they be conquered in the name of Christianity, or must they be left alone if they resisted conversion? Eventually the philosophical debate ended up in favor of the Indians, in theory at least. They were human beings with eternal souls who should be treated with equity and fairness. They enjoyed title to their lands as long as they agreed to convert to Christianity. If they resisted conversion, their lands were fair game for the conquering powers. In practice, of course, the European settlers eventually managed to take the land whether or not the Indians converted.

By the seventeenth century the view evolved that Indian tribes were sovereign nations enjoying title to their land, and that if the European powers wanted the land, they would have to negotiate its purchase through treaties. Spain, Portugal, France, the Netherlands, and Great Britain engaged in the practice of treaty-making. The United States, in dealing with Native Americans, claimed that the discovery rights of Great Britain had been passed on to the United States after the American Revolution.* Therefore, the United States had clear title to the Indian lands, superseding any other country.

The U.S. Constitution then established the legal groundwork for the supremacy of the federal government over state and local governments in dealing with Indian affairs. In 1789, when the U.S. Constitution went into effect, Indians were not considered citizens of the United States. During the years of the Articles of Confederation* (1781–1789), state governments had tried to assert their authority over Indian lands within their boundaries, as had the central government. The result was a confused, haphazard, and often contradictory set of federal and state policies. State assertions of power also constituted a threat to tribal legal sovereignty. The framers of the Constitution were convinced that having a consistent federal policy, not thirteen different state policies, was the best way to handle Indian affairs. The Constitution stipulates that Congress enjoys the exclusive power to "regulate commerce with foreign nations, among the several states, and with the Indian tribes."

Over the course of the next eighty years, Indian law developed within a legal framework that recognized tribes as sovereign entities, Indian individuals as citizens of the tribe, and the federal government as the supreme governmental power in dealing with the tribes. The United States entered into treaties with Indian tribes, and the Senate had to ratify those treaties before they went into effect. During the 1820s and 1830s, a series of congressional laws and Supreme Court decisions upheld that point of view. In *Johnson's and Graham's Lessee v. M'Intosh** (1823), *Cherokee Nation v. State of Georgia** (1831), and *Worcester v. Georgia** (1832), the Supreme Court under Chief Justice John Marshall* argued that although the Indian tribes were not truly sovereign and independent nations, they were "domestic, dependent nations" subject to federal, not state, jurisdiction. When the Indian Removal Act* of 1830 precipitated the mass movement of Native Americans to reservations* west of the Mississippi River, Congress had to deal with the question of criminal jurisdiction. If an Indian traveling through a state committed a crime, did it constitute a federal or a state offense? In 1834, Congress responded with the Indian Country Crimes Act,* which gave the federal government exclusive criminal jurisdiction over Indians.

Nor was there any question during these years that Indians were not citizens of the United States. In 1870, the case of *McKay v. Campbell** made that abundantly clear. The Supreme Court ruled that any Indian born within "tribal allegiance" had not been born within the United States and was therefore not a citizen of the United States. Indian tribes, the Court reasoned, are "distinct and independent political communities, retaining the right to self-government."

THE AGE OF ASSIMILATION, 1871–1934

But the Supreme Court had barely rendered its decision in *McKay v. Campbell* when Congress began to pursue an assimilationist policy that continued for more than a half-century and all but destroyed the foundations of Indian law. In 1871, Congress passed the Indian Appropriations Act,* which contained a legal clause of enormous significance. The federal government would no longer deal with Indian tribes as sovereign or domestic dependent nations deserving treaty rights. Henceforth, Congress would legislate for the tribes, and the federal government would administer programs through the Department of the Interior, not through negotiated, ratified treaties.

The great irony of the Indian Appropriations Act, however, revolved around the fact that it took away from tribes their status as sovereign nations without awarding U.S. citizenship* to individual Indians. In a prominent Supreme Court decision—*Elk v. Wilkins** (1884)—the justices ruled that Indians born into a tribal entity were not U.S. citizens and therefore did not enjoy the right to vote.* Native Americans now occupied a legal no man's land in the United States; they were subject to the law but not protected by the rights of citizenship. The decision enraged Indian reformers and played a central role in Senator Henry Dawes's decision to promote Indian citizenship through allotment.*

The term "allotment" describes a process of breaking up reservation land and redistributing it in small parcels to individual members of the tribe, who then held title to those parcels. White reformers believed that the continued existence of reservations, with Indian tribes concentrated on them, would only perpetuate the cultural distinctiveness of Native Americans, and white economic interests would continue to apply concerted pressure to take Indian land. Over time, under allotment, tribes would control less and less land and individual Indians more and more, until tribes no longer existed as political or economic entities. In 1881, the reservations totaled 155 million acres and were controlled by only 300,000 or so Indians. Simple arithmetic made it clear that if each head of family were given 160 acres, only 50 million acres would be allotted.

That would open up more than 100 million acres to white development. In the Dawes Act* of 1887, the Curtis Act* of 1898, and the Alaska Allotment Act* of 1906, Congress implemented the allotment program.

Once the president of the United States decided a tribe was ready for allotment, each Indian head of family would receive 160 acres. Single adults and orphans would get 80 acres each. Single youths under the age of 18 would receive 40 acres. Each Indian had four years to select his or her individual allotment; for those who had not made a selection by that time, the federal government would choose a parcel for them. Once every member of a tribe had accepted an allotment, the tribe ceased to exist as a legal entity. The federal government could then sell surplus lands to whites. Upon accepting a piece of allotted land, an individual Indian became a citizen of the United States. In *United States v. Wong Kim Ark** (1897) and *Swift v. Leach** (1920), the Supreme Court upheld the citizenship of allotted Indians. And in 1924, with passage of the Snyder Act,* all Native Americans became citizens of the United States.

Nor was there much equivocation about the rights associated with citizenship. A number of states, for example, refused to admit Indian children into the public schools. Long before the Supreme Court ordered the integration of whites and blacks in public schools, it issued such orders for American Indian children. In *Crawford v. School District No. 7* (1913), *Piper v. Big Pine School District** (1924), and *Grant v. Michaels* (1933), the states of Oregon, California, and Montana were ordered to admit Indian children into the public schools. Eventually the federal courts applied the same logic to voting rights. Although the Snyder Act of 1924 conferred U.S. citizenship on all American Indians, several states—including Utah, Arizona, Idaho, New Mexico, Washington, and North Carolina—built obstacles to Indians voting. They justified denial of voting rights on the grounds that (1) Indians were exempt from state taxes, or (2) because reservations were not state property, Indians were not legally state residents. The Supreme Court resolved the issue in 1948 with its decision in *Harrison v. Laveen*, granting Arizona Indians the right to vote in all state and local elections.

Allotment was a gradual process that consumed more than fifty years. Some tribes were allotted immediately; others waited for decades. During the transition period, until the allotment process was complete and a tribe no longer existed, the federal government had to maintain a special trust* relationship with the tribe. A number of federal court decisions and congressional laws—*McBratney v. United States** (1882), the Major

Crimes Act* of 1885, *United States v. Kagama** (1886), *Talton v. Mayes** (1896), *Lone Wolf v. Hitchcock** (1903), and *United States v. Sandoval** (1913)—established the principle that since non-allotted Indians were not citizens of the United States, and since tribes were no longer sovereign entities, the federal government had a special trust, or guardianship,* responsibility to them. Indian tribes were defined as "dependent Indian communities." Criminal jurisdiction remained with the federal and tribal governments, not state governments, until the allotment process had been completed for a tribe. Also, as made clear in *The Kansas Indians** (1866) case and *Trapp v. Choate* (1912), Indians with allotted land, Indians living on reservations, and Indian tribes were exempt from state taxation.

The federal government also had a special charge to protect Indian water rights. In the arid sections of the West, where many Indian reservations were established in the nineteenth century, water was a scarce commodity. But during the late nineteenth and early twentieth centuries, when large numbers of non-Indians settled there, competition for the precious resource became intense. In a series of federal court decisions, the law came to recognize that the Indian right to water was "senior" to the non-Indian right. In *Kansas v. Colorado** (1907), *Winters v. United States** (1908), *Skeem v. United States** (1921), and a host of other decisions, the Supreme Court decided that Indian water rights* were reserved* by "necessary implication." The "Winters Doctrine" argued that if the federal government placed a tribe on a reservation so that tribal members would become farmers, it also implied that the Indians would have all the water necessary to farm. It made no sense for the federal government to adopt a reservation policy that required tribes to become farmers if it did not intend that the tribes had priority or senior rights that superseded any white claim to available water supplies.

By the 1930s, after a half-century of assimilation through allotment and citizenship, it appeared on paper that Congress and the federal courts had developed a consistent, logical approach to Indian individual and tribal rights. Supposedly, Indians were abandoning tribal economies and governments for the larger commercial economy and legal system of non-Indians. Between 1887 and 1934, more than 100 million acres of land had changed hands from Indians to whites. But reservation reality told a different story. After a half-century of the federal government's assimilationist crusade, the Native American population had dropped to only 250,000 people. Poverty, unemployment, and alcoholism afflicted many Indians. Reformers looked to allotment as the real culprit. It had not worked. Indians were not assimilating. They were poor, landless, and dying instead.

THE INDIAN NEW DEAL, 1934–1945

When Franklin D. Roosevelt became president in 1933, federal Indian policy did an about-face. During the Great Depression and World War II, a brief interlude interrupted the assimilationist crusade. The term "Indian New Deal"* has been commonly used to describe those years. Convinced that allotment was responsible for the loss of tens of millions of acres of Indian land and for Indian poverty, Congress passed a series of laws designed to end the program, increase the Indian land base, restore self-government to tribes, and improve education and economic life among Native Americans.

The so-called Indian New Deal consisted of three major pieces of legislation: the Indian Reorganization Act* of 1934, the Johnson-O'Malley Act* of 1934, and the Indian Arts and Crafts Board Act of 1935. The Indian Reorganization Act ended allotment, restored to tribes surplus reservation lands that the Dawes Act of 1887 had created, established a government fund to purchase additional lands, and provided for the establishment of constitutions to govern the tribes and tribal corporations to control economic development. Once again, the federal government began dealing with tribal governments as semi-sovereign entities. The Johnson-O'Malley Act was designed to improve Indian education* and reverse the centuries-old policy of using federal Indian schools as a front for attacking Indian cultures and promoting assimilation. The Indian Arts and Crafts Board Act established the Indian Arts and Crafts Board* to promote reservation economic self-sufficiency by strengthening arts and crafts operations. The board consisted of five commissioners serving four-year terms. To improve the market for authentic Indian crafts, the board established government trademarks for Indian-made products to ensure their authenticity. Many Native American leaders hailed the Indian New Deal as a new day in Indian affairs.

ASSIMILATION REVISITED, 1945–1969

The new day did not last long. When World War II began, the Indian New Deal lost much of its political momentum. Its emphasis on community rather than private property, tribal rather than individual values, and ethnic autonomy rather than assimilation and national unity seemed suspect, especially in a world where authoritarianism and ethnic holocausts were norms. A new drive to "reform" federal policy was under way. But in this case, "reform" was just a euphemism for "assimilation." Congress resumed its assimilation crusade with the compensation,* termination,* and relocation* programs.

The federal government, once and for all, was determined to "get out of the Indian business" and see to it that Indians disappeared into the larger society. Compensation was a first step. Many Indian tribes still had unsettled financial claims against the federal government for lands that had been seized illegitimately during the late eighteenth and nineteenth centuries. Before it could be finished with Indian affairs, Congress hoped to settle each of those claims and eliminate any lingering resentments and injustices. The Indian Claims Commission Act of 1946 established the Indian Claims Commission* to hear all those claims and decide on monetary compensation.

Hand in hand with compensation came the relocation program. Assimilationists were convinced that the continued existence of reservations as homes to hundreds of thousands of American Indians would only serve to perpetuate poverty and cultural alienation. One solution was to move Indians into large cities, where they would work in industrial jobs and send their children to public schools. Between 1947 and 1952, the Bureau of Indian Affairs* (BIA) implemented a relocation program that provided funds to relocate thousands of Indians to cities. The BIA provided job training, moving expenses, housing location assistance, and a thirty-day subsistence allowance to Indians willing to leave the reservations. The third leg of the assimilationist tripod after World War II was the termination program, in which Congress passed legislation ending the special trust relationship between individual tribes and the federal government and turning over the Indians to state jurisdiction. Ostensibly, Congress would not terminate a tribe until the tribe "was ready" for assimilation.

During the heyday of compensation, relocation, and termination in the 1950s, 1960s, and 1970s, the federal government maintained the trust relationship with nonterminated tribes. In such cases as *Oliphant v. Suquamish Indian Tribe** (1978), *United States v. John** (1978), and *United States v. Wheeler** (1978), the Supreme Court maintained federal jurisdiction over state jurisdiction in dealing with the criminal acts of Indians. Indian tax exemptions also survived in *Squire v. Capoeman** (1956), *Warren Trading Post Co. v. Arizona Tax Commission** (1965), *McClanahan* *v. Arizona State Tax Commission** (1973), and *Mescalero Apache Tribe v. Jones** (1973). Voting rights were upheld as well. In *Allen v. Merrill** (1957), the Supreme Court overturned a new attempt by the state of Utah to restrict Indian voting, and in *Montoya v. Bolack** (1962), the Supreme Court ordered New Mexico to allow Indians to vote in state and local elections.

None of the assimilationist programs, however, achieved its objective of helping Indians disappear into American society. Compensation became hopelessly bogged down in intertribal, intratribal, and interracial legal squabbling. Nor did relocation succeed. City life had little appeal to many Indians. Its materialism, anonymity, and emphasis on individual aggrandizement proved to be a cultural shock, and most relocated Indians soon found themselves caught in a different cycle of poverty. Moreover, Indian leaders bitterly resisted termination because they felt that only the trust relationship with the federal government could protect them from aggressive non-Indian interests at the state and local levels.

THE AGE OF SELF-DETERMINATION, 1969–1996

Late in 1969, President Richard M. Nixon decided to end the termination program. Compensation had already run out of steam, and the Indian Claims Commission still had nearly twenty years of litigation ahead of it. But well in advance of Nixon's announcement, the Red Power* movement had emerged in the United States, with such groups as Indians of All Tribes* and the American Indian Movement* demanding the recognition of treaty rights* and the restoration of tribal sovereignty. Most Indians did not want to be subject to state fish and game laws because their original treaties with the federal government had preserved those rights even while transferring land to non-Indians. Much as whites might reserve mineral rights on a parcel of land they have sold, Indians claim similar fishing* and hunting* rights. Indian activists staged "fish-in" demonstrations to protest local fish and game regulations and took their cases to the federal courts. For the most part during the 1960s—in such cases as *Kake v. Egan* (1962), *Puyallup Tribe v. Department of Game** (Puyallup I) (1968), and *United States v. Oregon** (1969)—the Supreme Court upheld Indian fishing and hunting rights. It did so as well in the 1970s and 1980s in such cases as *Puyallup Tribe v. Department of Game** (Puyallup II) (1973), *Antoine v. Washington** (1974), *Kimball v. Callahan** (1974), *United States v. Washington* (1974), *Sohappy v. Smith* (1976), *Puyallup Tribe v. Department of Game** (Puyallup III) (1977), *Washing-*

ton v. Washington State Commercial Passenger Fishing Vessel Association* (1979), and *New Mexico v. Mescalero Apache Tribe** (1983).

During the 1970s and 1980s, Congress tried to restore the notion of tribal sovereignty in such legislation as the Indian Education Act* of 1972, the Indian Finance Act* of 1974, the Indian Self-Determination and Education Assistance Act of 1975, the Indian Child Welfare Act* of 1978, and the Repeal of Termination Act of 1988, which collectively prohibited termination without the express permission of the tribe, gave Indian parents and tribal leaders direct control over adoption policies and school curricula, and allowed tribal entities, instead of the BIA, to subcontract out reservation social services.

The self-determination* movement provided new support for tribal sovereignty, the trust relationship with the federal government, and Indian insulation from state and local taxation and criminal jurisdiction. *White Mountain Apache Tribe v. Bracker** (1980), *Central Machinery Co. v. Arizona State Tax Commission** (1980), *Kerr-McGee Corp. v. Navajo Tribe** (1985), *Oklahoma Tax Commission v. Citizen Band Potawatomi Indian Tribe** (1991), and *Department of Taxation and Finance of New York State v. Milhelm Attea & Bros.** (1994) maintained Indian tax exemptions; *Oliphant v. Suquamish Indian Tribe** (1978), *United States v. John** (1978), *United States v. Wheeler** (1978), *Duro v. Reina** (1990), and *Gerber v. United States** (1993) all preserved federal criminal jurisdiction over Indians.

Self-determination and restoration of the federal-tribal trust relationship, when combined with cuts in BIA appropriations in the 1980s, gave rise to the Indian gaming* movement in the 1980s. In order to raise badly needed money, many tribes claimed the right to initiate legal gambling businesses on reservations, even if state law prohibited it. The tribes claimed to be sovereign entities, independent of state authority, and therefore free to develop whatever economic enterprises they chose on their own reservations. In *Cabazon Band of Mission Indians et al. v. California* (1987) and *Seminole Tribe of Florida v. Butterworth** (1981), the Supreme Court upheld the right of tribal governments to develop casinos, off-track betting facilities, and commercial bingo parlors on reservations. In the Indian Gaming Regulatory Act* of 1988, Congress established a federal agency to monitor and regulate Indian gaming operations.

But the restoration of tribal sovereignty inspired a new set of civil rights questions. If Indians are citizens of the United States and protected—under the First,* Fourth, Fifth,* Sixth,* Eighth, and Fourteenth* amendments of the U.S. Constitution—from the arbitrary actions of federal, state, and local governments, are they also protected from such practices by sovereign, tribal governments? A number of court cases after World War II precipitated the debate over the relationship between individual Indian civil rights and tribal sovereignty.

In 1940, for example, the Navajo Tribal Council outlawed the importation, sale, and use of peyote* on the reservation. When Navajo tribal police, without search or arrest warrants, raided a peyote ceremony in 1957, the Native American Church sued the tribe, claiming violations of First and Fourteenth Amendment rights. In 1959, the Tenth Circuit Court decided *Native American Church v. Navajo Tribal Council*,* upholding the tribe's right to outlaw the use of peyote. A similar case was *Toledo et al. v. Pueblo de Jemez et al.** (1954). The tribal leaders of the Jemez Pueblo in New Mexico had declared Roman Catholicism the official religion of the tribe and outlawed other ceremonies on the reservation. Six tribal members who were Protestants sued, claiming violation of their right to freedom of religion.* The federal district court in New Mexico, however, decided against the Protestants in 1954, refusing to hear the case and essentially upholding the power of the tribal leaders.

Congress conducted a special investigation in 1962 to evaluate complaints of civil rights misconduct by tribal officials, and several congressmen concluded that individual Indians needed "some guaranteed form of civil rights protection against the actions of their own governments." In 1968, Congress passed the Indian Civil Rights Act,* which conferred certain rights on all persons who are subject to the jurisdiction of a tribal government and empowered federal courts to enforce these rights. Congress did deny some individual rights, which it felt were inherently dangerous to the survival of tribal self-government. The legislation guarantees to tribal members, against the actions of their own tribal governments, all but a few of the fundamental rights enumerated in the U.S. Constitution. Tribal governments are not subject to the establishment clause of the First Amendment, do not have to provide legal counsel free of charge to indigent defendants, need not provide a trial by jury in civil cases, and do not have to issue grand jury indictments in criminal cases.

Many activists protested the Indian Civil Rights Act of 1968 as a blatant affront to tribal sovereignty and self-determination, but the federal courts upheld the law. In *Dodge v. Nakai** (1969), the Supreme Court argued that tribal governments were not completely independent, self-governing entities and did not enjoy sovereign immunity from the Bill of Rights,* except in those limited areas outlined by the Indian Civil Rights Act of

1968. Because of the First, Fourth, Fifth, Sixth, Eighth, and Fourteenth amendments to the Constitution, as well as the Indian Civil Rights Act of 1968, individual Indian civil rights are protected from arbitrary actions by federal, state, local, and tribal governments.

However, the federal courts have generally established limits to Indian religious rights when they conflict with land development. Historically, Native Americans viewed their tribal-landed estate as sacred, linked inextricably to their sense of deity, origin, and destiny. Non-Indians, however, have tended to view land as an economic commodity to be bought, sold, and developed for commercial advantage. In *Sequoyah v. Tennessee Valley Authority** (1980), the Cherokee tribe filed suit against the federal government, arguing that the development of dams and water reservoirs in the Tennessee Valley had permanently flooded sacred lands. *Badoni v. Higginson** (1980) was a similar case. The U.S. Army Corps of Engineers built a hydroelectric dam on the Colorado River in and around the environs of a Navajo holy site. Navajo medicine men, seeking to preserve the integrity of their sacred tribal grounds at the nearby Rainbow Bridge National Monument in southern Utah, sought a lowering of water levels and the imposition of restrictions on tourism in the area. In *Wilson v. Block** (1983), Hopis and Navajos tried to stop construction of a ski resort on the San Francisco Peaks in Arizona, which they considered sacred. That same year, in *Fool's Crow v. Gullett*,* several Plains tribes tried to stop, on similar religious grounds, the federal government from building viewing areas, trails, gutters, and parking lots in the Bear Butte region of South Dakota. And in *Lyng v. Northwest Indian Cemetery Protective Association** (1988), the Yurok, Tolowa, and Karuk tribes tried to secure an injunction against the U.S. Forest Service, which planned to construct a road through the Six Rivers National Forest in northern California. The road, they argued, would violate a sacred burial site. In each of these cases the federal courts found in favor of the federal government, not the Indian tribes.

EPILOGUE

The last word on Indian civil rights law has certainly not been written, and conflicts between individual rights and the powers of federal, state, local, and tribal governments will no doubt continue long into the future. A contemporary case provides a good example. Early in 1996, the attorney general of New Mexico ordered the closing of more than a dozen commercial casino and bingo operations on Indian reservations in the state, precipitating bitter protests from Indian groups throughout the country. Under the Indian Gaming Regulatory Act of 1988, Congress had authorized Indian tribes to negotiate official gambling compacts with state governments, after which they could open commercial gaming operations on their reservations. Tribes could file suit against any state that did not negotiate in good faith. Eight years later, however, in *Seminole Tribe v. Florida*,* the federal court of appeals for the Eleventh Circuit overturned that portion of the Indian Gaming Regulatory Act allowing lawsuits against state governments, arguing that it was an intrusion on state authority and a violation of the Eleventh Amendment to the Constitution. The Supreme Court later upheld the decision. On those grounds, the New Mexico attorney general decided to close down the gambling operations that had been established in the absence of a state compact. He found substantial support from white economic-interest groups who resented the volume of tourist dollars finding their way into Indian coffers.

The decision produced a storm of protest in Indian country.* Such activist groups as the American Indian Movement threatened a peaceful march on the state capitol in Albuquerque; if that did not work, they intended to set up roadblocks on Interstate highways 10, 25, and 40 in New Mexico, creating a traffic jam of epic proportions until the state backed down. The tribes claimed that the attorney general's order constituted a blatant violation of the long-recognized principle of tribal sovereignty. Richard Hughes, an attorney for several of the tribes, told a reporter, "The tribes have long memories. They have a very distinct sense that whenever they find something that looks too good to the white man—land, water, minerals, whatever it happens to be—there's going to be a backlash, and somebody's going to find a way to grab it." By late 1996, the dispute had moved to the federal courts, where years of litigation are anticipated.

THE ENCYCLOPEDIA

A

ABINATI, ABBY. An advocate for Native American children's issues, Abby Abinati, a Yurok Indian, was born in San Francisco, California, in 1947. She received a law degree from the University of New Mexico in 1973 and specialized in questions involving tribal development and social services. After passage of the Indian Child Welfare Act* of 1978 she focused much of her attention on children's issues, publishing her book *The Indian Child Welfare Act* in 1981 and working to protect the cultural heritage of Indian children. Abinati currently practices law in Eureka, California.

Suggested Reading: Duane Champagne, ed., *The Native North American Almanac*, 1994.

JAMES S. OLSON

ACKNOWLEDGEMENT PROJECT. See **FEDERAL ACKNOWLEDGEMENT PROJECT.**

ADAMS, HANK. An American Indian of Sioux and Assiniboine descent, Hank Adams was born on the Fort Peck Indian Reservation in Montana in 1947. A gifted athlete and student leader during high school, Adams moved to California after graduation and became involved in politics. He actively supported the John F. Kennedy administration, and in 1964 he refused induction into the U.S. Army until the federal government made good on all treaties with American Indians. That same year he worked diligently to stage Marlon Brando's protest march to the Washington State capitol in Olympia to demand Indian fishing rights.* In April 1964 Adams went into the army. When he left the military, Adams became director of the Survival of American Indians Association,* a group dedicated to Native American fishing rights. He focused his attention in 1968 on the Nisqually River near Franks Landing, Washington, where he protested state attempts to limit Indian net fishing. In January 1971, Adams was shot on the shore of the Puyallup River near Tacoma, where he had intentionally set an illegal fishing trap. Since that time, he has continued his struggle to exempt Indians from state fish and game regulations.

Suggested Reading: Duane Champagne, ed., *The Native North American Almanac*, 1994.

JAMES S. OLSON

ADOPTION. Historically, Native American children were raised in the presence of large, extended families; but U.S. government policies, beginning in the nineteenth and continuing into the twentieth centuries, had a deleterious effect on Indian family life. The reservation policy, which forced periodic relocations of Indian tribes to new reservations, undermined Indian economic life and in the process destabilize family life as well. The allotment policy, launched in 1887 with passage of the Dawes Act,* was supposed to strengthen Indian nuclear families by breaking up the tribal estate and distributing small farms to individual heads of families, who supposedly would then bring their own families into the modern commercial economy. Allotment* proved to be a failure, as did the termination* and relocation* programs of the 1950s and 1960s. Poverty,* disease,* and family instability steadily worsened over the years.

Misguided federal educational and social policies only made matters worse. Convinced that Indian children were certain to inherit the social pathologies of their parents, Bureau of Indian Affairs* (BIA) officials launched programs designed to remove Indian children from their homes. Off-reservation and reservation boarding schools took thousands of Indian children away from their own homes for years at a time, because reformers believed this was the only way to "civilize" them. In 1958 the BIA joined hands with the Child Welfare League of America and established a program to accelerate the adoption of Indian children. Under the adoption program, Indian parental rights were terminated—often without their full participation, understanding, or consent—and children were legally adopted by non-Indian families, usually through the sponsorship of various Christian churches. During the late 1950s and 1960s, more than 1,000 Indian children were adopted under the program.

But during the 1970s, Indian activists delivered bitter criticisms of the program, describing it as fundamentally racist and contrary to the needs of Indian families. Congress responded in 1978 with the Indian Child

Welfare Act,* a law that made it much more difficult for non-Indian families to adopt Indian children. In 1989 the Supreme Court rendered its decision in *Mississippi Band of Choctaw Indians v. Holyfield* et al.,* which upheld the right of Indian tribal governments to exercise control over the adoption process.

Suggested Reading: William Byler, *The Destruction of Indian Families*, 1977; Linda A. Marousek, "The Indian Child Welfare Act of 1978: Provisions and Policy," *South Dakota Law Review* 25 (Winter 1980), 98–115; Gaylene J. McCartney, "The American Indian Child-Welfare Crisis: Cultural Genocide or First Amendment Preservation?" *Columbia Human Rights Law Review* 7 (Fall–Winter 1975–1976), 529–51; Robert Ryan, *The American Indian Family: Strengths and Stresses*, 1980.

JAMES S. OLSON

AFFIRMATIVE ACTION. The term "affirmative action" refers to a series of rules and regulations that evolved throughout the 1960s, 1970s, and 1980s in an attempt to counteract the effects of historical discrimination against certain designated minority groups. With the Civil Rights Act* of 1964, most forms of formal, legal discrimination had been eliminated, but civil rights advocates soon realized there were a host of other practices and traditions, such as seniority rights and aptitude tests, that continued to militate against the hiring and promoting of minority workers. On September 24, 1965, President Lyndon B. Johnson responded to that problem by issuing an executive order requiring all federal contractors to use "affirmative action" in making sure that minority workers were hired in numbers consistent with their proportion in the population. In *Griggs v. Duke Power Company* in 1971, the Supreme Court invalidated the use of intelligence tests that had the effect of limiting minority hiring and promotion. Companies began to use a variety of criteria, not just intelligence tests, in making their hiring decisions. The Equal Employment Act of 1972 then extended affirmative action requirements to educational institutions.

Critics charged, however, that in many instances affirmative action requirements rigidified into hiring and promotion quotas and then constituted *reverse discrimination* against white males, violating their Fourteenth Amendment* right to equal protection under the law. Those claims became politically significant in the mid-1970s when the American economy stagnated. A number of cases protesting affirmative action wound their way through the federal courts. In 1978, the Supreme Court heard the *Regents of the University of California v. Bakke* case. Allan Bakke had been denied admission to the University of California at Davis medical school. But because of the school's quota system for admission, several minority students with lower grade point averages and lower test scores had been admitted. Bakke claimed that the practice constituted reverse discrimination. The Court ruled that rigid, special-preference admission programs were unconstitutional. After the *Bakke* decision, quotas were dead, although affirmative action programs that actively sought to hire or admit minority workers were still legal.

During the Reagan years of the 1980s, affirmative action continued to be a divisive political issue, with minority groups charging President Reagan with gutting civil rights programs and conservative whites praising him for ending reverse discrimination. The real meaning of affirmative action continued to be muddled. In *Fullilove v. Klutznick* in 1980, the Supreme Court upheld federal legislation requiring that 10 percent of all federal public works projects be reserved for minority contractors, regardless of whether they were low bidders on a project. By the early 1990s, with the American economy in a recession, criticisms of affirmative action programs surfaced again, generally with Democrats defending them and Republicans opposing them.

Tribal governments enjoyed some insulation from the anti–affirmative action laws. The Civil Rights Act of 1964, the foundation of President Lyndon B. Johnson's Great Society programs, prohibited discrimination on the basis of race, religion, color, national origin, and sex in employment, education, and access to public facilities. The law did, however, provide an exemption to American Indian tribes. Under the authority of Section 12 of the Indian Reorganization Act* of 1934, the federal government allowed the Bureau of Indian Affairs* to give preferential employment treatment to Indians.

The civil rights movement, of course, had specifically campaigned against preferential treatment because state and local governments in the South, and the federal government for decades, had hired only whites. However, non-Indian employees claimed racial discrimination based on the Civil Rights Act of 1964 and the 1972 Equal Employment Act, which required equal treatment in federal employment. They filed a lawsuit charging civil rights violations. But Indian tribal governments did not want to be forced to establish racially blind hiring policies, since they wanted to give as many jobs as possible to their own members. To accommodate their wishes, Congress exempted them from those provisions of the Civil Rights Act of 1964. The case—*Morton v. Mancari*—reached the Supreme Court in 1974. The Court held that Congress could give preference to Native Americans in hiring. The Court determined that federal statutes were not race-based but instead were the result of the "special relationship" between the U.S. government and the Indians.

Suggested Reading: Katharine Greene, *Affirmative Action and Principles of Justice*, 1990; Stephen L. Pevar, *The Rights of Indians and Tribes: The Basic ACLU Guide to Indian and Tribal Rights*, 1992.

JAMES S. OLSON

AHTANUM IRRIGATION DISTRICT v. UNITED STATES (1956). The lack of protection provided by the U.S. government for Indian water rights* is notorious. The Indian rights established in *Winters v. United States** (1908) were largely unenforced by a government that was intent on encouraging white settlement of the arid lands of the West. It is only since the 1970s that tribes have been able to assert their rights under *Winters*. The *Ahtanum* case (1956) addressed the question of whether and to what extent the water rights of Native Americans can be transferred to a non-Indian who acquires the land to which the water rights pertain. Non-Indian transferees' rights were judged subordinate to Indian rights but not nonexistent.

Although the decision allows non-Indians to exercise federal trust rights, sometimes in competition with Indians, the advantage to Indians of the decision is that it allows Indians to sell their allotments* to non-Indians and deed their allotments to non-Indian heirs at full value. The court awarded 75 percent of the natural flow of Ahtanum Creek, which forms a boundary of the Yakima Indian Reservation, in the state of Washington, to whites and 25 percent to Indians. Any excess over the natural flow was deemed solely for the use of the Indians. To qualify for water usage both parties must demonstrate that they are putting the water to beneficial use.* In case of loss of water between the north and south gauging stations on the creek, the Indians would receive their full 25 percent and the whites the remainder. The 75 percent/25 percent split was based on the water needs of the non-Indians who were parties to the original agreement of 1908. Should the water needs of these individuals ever be reduced below the 1908 level, the water rights of the Indian users would be correspondingly increased.

Suggested Reading: Lloyd Burton, *American Indian Water Rights and the Limits of the Law*, 1991; William C. Canby Jr., *American Indian Law in a Nutshell*, 1988; William L. Kahrl, *Water and Power: The Conflict Over Los Angeles' Water Supply in the Owens Valley*, 1982; 236 *Federal Reporter* 2d 321, 342 (1956); 320 *Federal Reporter* 2d 897 (1964).

J. JEFFERSON MACKINNON

AKIN CASE. See *COLORADO RIVER WATER CONSERVATION DISTRICT v. UNITED STATES* (1976).

ALASKA ALLOTMENT ACT OF 1906. In 1906, as part of its continuing commitment to the assimilation of American Indians through the allotment* of tribal lands, Congress passed the Alaska Allotment Act, which extended the terms of the Dawes Act* of 1887 to Alaskan natives. It was a misguided attempt. Soil quality in Alaska was so poor that no Alaskan native could make a living on a 160-acre farm. White demand for Indian land at that time in Alaska was quite limited, and the law ultimately had little effect.

Suggested Reading: Robert D. Arnold, *Alaska Native Land Claims*, 1978; David S. Case, *Alaska Natives and American Laws*, 1984; James S. Olson and Raymond Wilson, *Native Americans in the Twentieth Century*, 1984.

JAMES S. OLSON

ALASKA FEDERATION OF NATIVES. The Alaska Federation of Natives was formed in 1966 by more than four hundred representatives of Alaskan native groups from across the state. Their original purpose was to organize in order to promote settlement of their land claims against the state and federal governments. They achieved their primary objective in 1971 when Congress passed the Alaska Native Claims Settlement Act.* In subsequent years, the Alaska Federation of Natives became a powerful lobbying group representing Alaska Native demands and needs before state and federal officials. It has focused its efforts on public health, civil rights, educational, and environmental issues.

Suggested Reading: Robert D. Arnold, *Alaska Native Land Claims*, 1978; Mary B. Davis, ed., *Native Americans in the Twentieth Century*, 1994.

JAMES S. OLSON

ALASKA NATIVE BROTHERHOOD. Beginning in 1910 the Bureau of Indian Affairs,* as well as Presbyterian missionaries in southern Alaska, began encouraging the formation of a self-help Alaskan native organization. Tlingit and Haida natives of the region acted on the proposal and established the Alaska Native Brotherhood (ANB) in 1912. A similar organization for women—the Alaska Native Sisterhood—was established in 1915. Both organizations were composed primarily of Tlingit and Haida peoples. Even though the groups were composed of only two Alaskan peoples, federal and state officials tended to view the Alaska Native Brotherhood as the quasi-official representative of all Alaskan natives. Beginning in 1920, under the leadership of Tlingit William Lewis Paul, the Alaska Native Brotherhood began promoting federal citizenship for Alaskan natives on the grounds that the Fourteenth Amendment* to the Constitution so qualified them. Paul and the Alaskan Native Brotherhood also campaigned for the elimination of salmon trap fishing by commercial fishermen because it threatened salmon stocks. In addition, the Alaskan Native Brotherhood crusaded for an end to segregated schools and settlement of indigenous land claims. During the 1950s the ANB opposed statehood for Alaska until native land claims were guaranteed, and in recent years the organization has focused its resources on land claim issues.

Suggested Reading: Robert D. Arnold, *Alaska Native Land Claims*, 1978; David S. Case, *Alaska Natives and American Laws*, 1984; Philip Drucker, *The Native Brotherhoods*, 1991.

JAMES S. OLSON

ALASKA NATIVE CLAIMS SETTLEMENT ACT OF 1971. From the time of the Alaska purchase in 1867, the federal government had maintained a rather ambiguous relationship with Alaska's often neglected native inhabitants. However, the discovery of vast oil reserves and untapped mineral wealth on the frozen land mass during the middle decades of the twentieth century changed all that. Soon the quest for profit produced a steady influx of whites, which increased the population to such an extent that Alaska attained statehood in 1959. With their ancient way of life in peril, the indigenous peoples banded together to form the Alaska Federation of Natives.* By mounting an effective lobbying campaign in Congress, the Alaska Federation of Natives influenced the passage of the Alaska Native Claims Settlement Act of 1971, which affected some 50,000 Indian, Eskimo, and Aleut peoples.

The act constituted a signal victory for Indian rights advocates. In exchange for 40 million acres in federal land grants, an immediate $462 million cash settlement, and another $500 million in future payments for mineral rights, Alaska's indigenous peoples relinquished all outstanding land claims and acquiesced in the elimination of existing reserves. A total of 4 million acres was set aside for Native American corporations in cities, cemeteries, historic sites, and reserves. At the same time, the Alaska Allotment Act* was rescinded.

Under the provisions of the new law, Alaskan natives were awarded shares in newly created regional economic corporations that were divided into twelve distinct geographical regions. Nonresident natives received shares in a thirteenth region set aside for their benefit. On the local level, the village corporations held surface rights and dispensed federal benefits. The regional corporations wielded authority over subsurface or mineral rights, parceled out dividends, and invested much of the remainder of the proceeds in various economic ventures.

However, despite the favorable terms of the agreement, its half-hearted implementation by the Department of the Interior worried many Indian rights advocates, who voiced their concern that the measure merely supplanted traditional tribal authority with the money-oriented corporations. Joe Upickson of the Arctic Slope Native Association charged that the legislation would destroy indigenous cultures. The legislation resulted in the loss of millions of acres of land, as well as hunting and fishing rights, and greatly stimulated the economic development of the region. Millions of acres also ended up in national parks and forest reserves.

Suggested Reading: Robert D. Arnold, *Alaska Native Land Claims*, 1978; David S. Case, *Alaska Natives and American Laws*, 1984; Arthur Lazarus Jr. and W. Richard West Jr., "The Alaska Native Claims Settlement Act: A Flawed Victory," *Law and Contemporary Problems* 11 (Winter 1976), 132–65; James S. Olson and Raymond Wilson, *Native Americans in the Twentieth Century*, 1984.

MARK BAXTER

ALASKA NATIVE REVIEW COMMISSION. In 1971, Congress passed the Alaska Native Claims Settlement Act,* but in the wake of the legislation, many Alaskan natives were concerned that cash settlements would deprive them of their lands and that the corporations set up to control the land would not reflect their interests. In 1983, the Inuit Circumpolar Conference established the Alaska Native Review Commission, headed by Canadian jurist Thomas R. Berger, to review the political, social, cultural, and environmental impact of the Alaska Native Claims Settlement Act. The commission held sixty-two village hearings and took testimony from nearly 1,500 Alaskan natives, almost all of whom expressed deep concerns about the loss of land and the impact of such a loss on indigenous cultures. They also demanded direct control of land use and related fish and game issues, independent of state control. Berger eventually recommended transferring title over native lands from the corporations set up under the Alaska Native Claims Settlement Act to tribal governments, as well as jurisdiction over land and water use. In general, Alaskan natives received the Berger report (published in 1985 as *Village Journey*) with enthusiasm.

Suggested Reading: Robert D. Arnold, *Alaska Native Land Claims*, 1978; Thomas R. Berger, *Village Journey: The Report of the Alaska Native Review Commission*, 1985; David S. Case, *Alaska Natives and American Laws*, 1984.

JAMES S. OLSON

ALASKA NATIVE SISTERHOOD. See **ALASKA NATIVE BROTHER-HOOD.**

ALASKA REORGANIZATION ACT OF 1936. Under the positive influence of Indian Affairs Commissioner John Collier* and the policy shift of the Indian New Deal,* the United States embarked on a more enlightened approach toward Native Americans. The government's new policy of tolerance was predicated on a proper respect for Indian culture, a sincere drive for Indian self-determination* and self-government, and a calculated push to develop a viable Indian economy. Under the auspices of the Indian Reorganization Act* of 1934, the United States initiated a program of federal funding for Indian activities, preferential hiring practices for prospective Indian employees, and the promulgation of Indian constitutions and bylaws. Although Section 17 of the Indian Reorganization Act gave Alaskan natives access to a federal revolving credit fund, it did not allow them to receive corporate charters, which effectively cut them off from the funds. Thus these tribal groups had no authorization to form constitutions, and the tribal corporations were denied access to federal credits.

In order to rectify the situation, Congress passed the Alaska Reorganization Act (Alaskan Indian Welfare Act) of 1936. The new legislation, which was virtually identical to the Indian Reorganization Act, amended the earlier oversight and empowered the secretary of the interior to set aside reservation land for Alaskan tribes when armed with the popular consent of Alaska's indigenous communities. As a result of the legislation, sixty-six of Alaska's tribal groups embraced a constitution and acquired a charter before the Indian New Deal had run its course.

Suggested Reading: Terry I. Anderson, *Property Rights, Constitutions and Indian Economies*, 1992; Theodore H. Haas, *Ten Years of Tribal Government under the I.R.A.*, 1947; James S. Olson and Raymond Wilson, *Native Americans in the Twentieth Century*, 1984; Francis Paul Prucha, *The Great Father*, Vol. 2, 1984.

MARK BAXTER

ALASKAN INDIAN WELFARE ACT OF 1936. See **ALASKA REORGANIZATION ACT OF 1936.**

ALCATRAZ ISLAND. On November 9, 1969, a group of American Indian college students and urban Indian people from the San Francisco Bay area set out in a chartered boat to circle Alcatraz Island and symbolically claim the island for Indian people. On November 20, 1969, this symbolic occupation of Alcatraz Island turned into a full-scale occupation when Indian students from San Francisco State University, the University of California at Berkeley, the University of California at Santa Cruz, and the University of California at Los Angeles joined with urban Indian people from the greater San Francisco Bay area and reoccupied the island, claiming title by "right of discovery."

The newly formed Alcatraz organization, Indians of All Tribes,* Inc., demanded clear title to Alcatraz Island, the establishment of an American Indian University, an American Indian Cultural Center, and an American Indian Museum. The Indian occupiers on Alcatraz Island kept Americans aware of the occupation and their demands by publishing a newsletter, *Rock Talk*, and by starting their own radio program, "Radio Free Alcatraz." As a result, letters and telegrams began to pour in to government officials, including President Richard M. Nixon. The mood of the public could be summed up in a telegram sent to Nixon on November 26, 1969, that read: "For once in this country's history let the Indians have something. Let them have Alcatraz."

The Indian occupiers successfully held the island until June 11, 1971, and Alcatraz soon became a rallying cry for the new American Indian activism that would continue into the mid-1970s under the names of Red Power* and the American Indian Movement.* This activism included the 1972 occupation of the Bureau of Indian Affairs* headquarters in Washington, D.C., which lasted for seven days, and the occupation of Wounded Knee* in 1973, which lasted for seventy-one days. The occupation of Alcatraz Island represents the longest continuous occupation of a federal facility by a minority group in the history of the United States, and it is on Alcatraz that modern activism finds its roots. Alcatraz set in motion a wave of overtly nationalist Indian militancy that ultimately resulted in abandonment of the termination* program and the adoption of a policy of Indian self-determination.*

The nineteen-month occupation of Alcatraz Island was a watershed event in the American Indian protest and activist movement. The occupation brought together hundreds of Indian people who came to live on the island and thousands more who identified with the call for self-determination, autonomy, and respect for Indian culture. The Indian people who organized the occupation and those who participated either by living on the island or working to solicit donations of money, water, food, clothing, or electrical generators came from all walks of life. As the occupation gained international attention, Indian people came from Canada, from South America, and from Indian reservations across the United States to show support for those who had taken a stand against the federal government. Thousands came, some stayed, and others carried the message home to their reservations that Alcatraz was a clarion call for the rise of Indian activism.

Today Alcatraz Island remains a strong symbol of Indian activism and self-determination, and a rallying point for unified Indian political activities. On February 11, 1978, Indian participants began the "Longest Walk"* to Washington, D.C., to protest the government's ill treatment of Indian people. That walk began on Alcatraz Island. On February 11, 1994, American Indian Movement leaders Dennis Banks,* Clyde Bellecourt,* and Mary Wilson met with Indian people to begin the nationwide "Walk for Justice."* That walk also began on Alcatraz Island. On Thanksgiving Day of each year since 1969, Indian people have gathered on Alcatraz Island to honor those who participated in the occupation and those who share in the continuing struggle for Indian self-determination. The 1969 occupation of Alcatraz Island stands out as the most symbolic, the most significant, the most successful Indian protest action of the modern era.

Suggested Reading: Peter Blue Cloud, *Alcatraz Is Not an Island*, 1972; Troy R. Johnson, *The Occupation of Alcatraz Island: Indian Self-Determination and the Rise of Indian Activism*, 1996.

TROY JOHNSON

ALCOHOL. For more than two centuries, stereotypes of the "drunken Indian" have dominated many non-Indians' view of Native Americans in the United States. The stereotype has taken many forms, from the crudest examples of racial epithet to sophisticated intellectual notions. Some anthropologists, for example, have speculated that Indians consciously drink to live up to the stereotype as a way of confirming their own "Indianness" in a society that is trying to wipe out their culture. Since white people expect Indians to have an alcohol problem, public drunkenness becomes a way of asserting ethnic identity. Alcohol use, in other words, is a form of ethnic rebellion.

During the heyday of the Indian reform movement of the late nineteenth century, many whites began to believe that before Indians could be assimilated into the larger society, the issue of alcohol abuse would have to be successfully addressed among them. Using alcohol as bait, greedy whites had for decades been able to exploit Indians politically, socially, and economically; and by the 1880s, reformers were convinced, the problem of alcoholism on the reservations had become a serious block to assimilation. In 1892, Congress passed the Intoxication in Indian Country Act to deal with the problem. The legislation prohibited the sale and transportation of alcoholic beverages anywhere in Indian country.*

A century later, the problem was still prevalent. News stories in the 1990s about fetal alcohol syndrome created the impression that large numbers of Indian babies were being born with the disease. In recent years, in spite of no scientific evidence supporting the idea, many well-educated non-Indians have reinforced the stereotype by claiming that Indians carry a genetic flaw, an inability to properly metabolize alcohol, making them unable to "hold their liquor." Such a genetic characteristic may be true for individuals—Indian and non-Indian alike—but it is not true for groups of people, including Indian tribes. Alcohol abuse is certainly a problem in many Native American communities, as it is among other subgroups where poverty,* isolation, and low educational attainment are common. Most studies indicate that the number of American Indian adults who drink is no higher than the national average for alcohol consumption. In most tribes, the number of women who abstain from alcohol is higher than the national average.

Why, then, is the rate of fetal alcohol syndrome among Indian babies twice the national average? Why are there high arrest rates for public drunkenness and driving while intoxicated (DWI), as well as serious rates of cirrhosis of the liver, among Indians? What sociologists and ethnologists have concluded is that although the number of Indians who drink alcohol is the same as for non-Indians, the number who drink heavily and engage in risk behaviors is higher than the national average. It is not at all uncommon for certain individuals to be arrested a dozen or more times a year, skewing statistics and giving the impression that most Indians are abusers of alcohol.

Suggested Reading: Jerrold E. Levy and Stephen J. Kunitz, *Indian Drinking: Navajo Practices and Anglo-American Theories*, 1974; Nancy O. Lurie, "The World's Oldest On-Going Protest Demonstration: Native American Drinking Patterns," *Pacific Historical Review* 40 (August 1971); Jack O. Waddell and Michael W. Everett, eds., *Drinking Behavior among Southwestern Indians: An Anthropological Perspective*, 1980; Thomas D. Watts and Roosevelt Wright, eds., *Alcoholism in Minority Populations*, 1989.

JAMES S. OLSON

ALL INDIAN PUEBLO COUNCIL. Soon after the Spaniards reached the Pueblo communities in the 1590s, Pueblo leaders formed the All Indian Pueblo Council (AIPC) to deal unitedly with the crisis they were facing. During the next several centuries, the AIPC continued to meet periodically as a political organization. In the twentieth century, the AIPC emerged as an important Indian interest group when Senator Holm Bursum of New Mexico proposed legislation recognizing the land claims of non-Indians who had squatted on Pueblo land.

On November 21, 1922, a group of 121 Pueblo delegates assembled in a meeting of the All Indian Pueblo Council at Santo Domingo, New Mexico, to protest the legislation. A number of prominent Americans, including writers Carl Sandburg and Zane Grey, sided with the Pueblos and launched a national crusade against the bill. The Bursum Bill* died, and Congress instead passed the Pueblo Lands Act of 1924, which established the Pueblo Lands Board to determine title and arrange for compensation of aggrieved parties. More than 3,000 families had squatted on 60,000 acres, approximately 10 percent of the Pueblo landed estate. Although the government eventually paid less than $1 million to Pueblos for the loss of thousands of acres, the incident demonstrated the ability of AIPC to organize Indian peoples politically. During the 1950s, AIPC protested termination* and relocation* policies, and in 1965 it organized itself as a nonprofit corporation under New Mexico law. Today, a nineteen-person board of governors controls the All Indian Pueblo Council, and it contracts with the Bureau of Indian Affairs* to provide a number of services to Pueblo peoples.

Suggested Reading: Armand S. La Potin, *Native American Voluntary Organizations*, 1986; James S. Olson and Raymond Wilson, *Native Americans in the Twentieth Century*, 1984.

JAMES S. OLSON

***ALLEN v. MERRILL* (1957).** In 1955 the state of Utah disenfranchised (took away the voting rights of) an Indian because he lived on a reservation* and therefore did not meet the residency requirements for voting in state elections. The plaintiff argued that such exclusionary methods violated the protective guarantees set down in the Fourteenth* and Fifteenth Amendments. Justice J. Allen Crockett averred that Utah's Indians had been justly denied the right to vote because of their cultural and linguistic alienation from mainstream society and their purported inability to understand the American political process. Crockett contended that because the Indians had not accepted the responsibility for land owner-ship and were not subject to taxation, they were effectively wards of the U.S. government and, as such, had forfeited any claims to political par-ticipation in the state of Utah. Ultimately, the Supreme Court counter-manded the lower court's findings on appeal, but not before the Utah state legislature had already repealed the statute. Utah therefore became the last state to grant the franchise to Native Americans.

Suggested Reading: Russel Lawrence Barsh and James Youngblood Hender-son, *The Road: Indian Tribes and Political Liberty*, 1980; H. Barry Holt and Gary Forrester, *Digest of American Indian Law: Cases and Chronology*, 1990; Stephen L. Pevar, *The Rights of Indians and Tribes: The Basic ACLU Guide to Indian and Tribal Rights*, 1992; Wilcomb E. Washburn, *Red Man's Land, White Man's Law*, 1971; Charles F. Wilkinson, *American Indians, Time and the Law*, 1987; John R. Wunder, *"Retained by The People": A History of American Indians and the Bill of Rights*, 1994.

MARK BAXTER

ALLOTMENT. The term "allotment" describes a process of breaking up reservation* land and redistributing it in small parcels to individual mem-bers of the tribe, who then held title to those parcels. The idea of dis-solving tribal lands and alloting small farms to individual Indians had its advocates in the colonial period, but the first real allotment program began in 1839, when the federal government divided the lands of the Brotherton Indians in Wisconsin. Similar programs were later tried out on the Chippewas, Shawnees, Wyandots, Omahas, Ottawas, and Pota-watomies. In each case the law provided that once the allotment process was complete, the Indians would become citizens of the United States. Only then, the reformers believed, would land-hungry whites end their violence against Indians.

White reformers believed that the continued existence of reservations, with Indian tribes concentrated on them, would only perpetuate the cul-tural distinctiveness of Native Americans and that white economic inter-ests would continue their pressure to take Indian land. Convinced that allotment would protect the Indians from further white encroachments, white liberals in such groups as the Indian Rights Association* and the Conference of the Friends of the Indians supported a national allotment program. Congress began moving on proposals to end tribal sovereignty* in the 1870s, and in the 1880s the allotment programs finally triumphed.

In 1881 the reservations totaled 155 million acres and were controlled by only 300,000 or so Indians. Simple arithmetic made it clear that if each head of family were given 160 acres, only 50 million acres would be allotted. That would open up more than 100 million acres to white development. Land-hungry speculators began supporting the reform movement. After all, if the reservations were broken up into individual holdings, it would be easier to purchase land from the Indians. What was to become of the other 100 million acres? Greedy land lobbyists saw a windfall in the making. Breaking up the reservations and parceling out the land to individual owners would free up millions of acres for development.

Congress passed an allotment measure in 1880 that affected the Ute Indians of Colorado and Utah. Each Ute head of family was given 160 acres, and surplus land reverted to the federal government. A number of other bills successfully made their way through Congress between 1879 and 1887, by which time the government had allotted a total of 584,423 acres. In 1887, backed by such reformers as Richard Henry Pratt, Lyman Abbott, and Alice Fletcher, and such groups as the Indian Rights Association, Senator Henry L. Dawes successfully pushed through Congress what became known as the Dawes Act,* or the General Allotment Act.

The legislation provided for gradual allotment. Once the president of the United States decided a tribe was ready for allotment, each Indian head of family would receive 160 acres; single adults and orphans, 80 acres; and single youths under age 18, 40 acres. Each Indian had four years to select his or her individual allotment; for those who had not made a selection by that time, the federal government would choose a parcel for them. To prevent allotted Indians from selling their parcel, the land was held in trust by the federal government for a period of twenty-five years. Indians receiving an allotment also received U.S. citizenship.* The federal government could then sell surplus lands to whites. Because of several tribes' intense opposition to the law, the following groups were exempted from its provisions: the Senecas of New York; the Sioux in Nebraska; and the Creeks, Cherokees, Chickasaws, Choctaws, Seminoles, Osages, Miamis, Peorias, and Sacs and Foxes of Indian Territory.*

The prophets of doom proved correct: predictions that Indians would lose their land were tragically fulfilled. The most valuable land was first to go. Whites went after the rich grasslands of Kansas, Nebraska, and the Dakotas; the dense, black soil forests of Minnesota and Wisconsin; and the wealthy oil and natural gas lands of Texas and Oklahoma. In all, the Native American tribes lost more than 60 million "surplus" acres under the allotment law.

By the 1890s and early 1900s, the pressure to allot Indian land accelerated. In 1898, Congress passed the Curtis Act,* which forced the tribes of the Indian Territory to accept allotment. The Five Civilized Tribes (Creeks, Cherokees, Choctaws, Chickasaws, and Seminoles) lost most of the land they owned in the Indian Territory. In their bitterness toward the federal government after the removals of the 1830s and 1840s, some had sided with the Confederacy during the Civil War; in retaliation, the government opened their land to white homesteaders in 1889. The subsequent discovery of oil in Oklahoma unleashed new pressures on the land as excited wildcatters and large oil corporations, supported by county politicians, systematically took much of the remaining land from the Creeks, Cherokees, Choctaws, Chickasaws, and Seminoles. Between 1887 and 1924 the land of the Five Civilized Tribes declined from approximately 30 million to less than 2 million acres.

Still the land hunger continued. In 1902 the federal government began voiding the trust period of twenty-five years that was originally designed to prevent the sale of allotted lands. The Dead Indian Land Act* of 1902 permitted Native Americans to sell land they had inherited from deceased relatives, and the Burke Act* of 1906 authorized the secretary of the interior to declare Indian adults competent to manage their own affairs and sell their allotted lands. The Alaska Allotment Act of 1906* extended the provisions of the Dawes Act to Alaskan natives.

Between 1906 and 1917 the secretary of the interior cautiously issued competency patents to only 9,984 Indians, but then the pace quickened and more than 20 thousand Indians received patents between 1919 and 1924. Greedy real estate salesmen, corrupt government agents, land speculators, and white merchants all began buying allotted land from Indians, usually at greatly deflated prices. The Sisseton Sioux lost another 200,000 acres, leaving them with little more than 100,000 of the 918,000 acres they had owned in 1887. Under the Burke Act more than 27 million acres were sold to whites by Indian farmers, and by 1924 Native Americans held only 48 million of the 138 million acres they had owned in 1887, half of it arid and of marginal value. When allotment came to an end in the early 1930s, the Native American landed estate had dropped below 50 million acres. Some historians have described allotment as a sincere albeit misguided attempt to assist Indians; others have called it a cynical land grab. Nevertheless, allotment did succeed in alienating American Indians from more than 100 million acres of their own land.

Suggested Reading: Leonard A. Carlson, *Indians, Bureaucrats, and Land: The Dawes Act and the Decline of Indian Farming*, 1981; James S. Olson and Raymond Wilson, *Native Americans in the Twentieth Century*, 1984; D. S. Otis, *The Dawes Act and the Allotment of Indian Lands*, 1973; Francis Paul Prucha, *The*

Great Father, Vol. 2, 1984; Wilcomb E. Washburn, *The Assault on Indian Tribalism: The General Allotment Law (Dawes Act) of 1887*, 1975.

JAMES S. OLSON

AMERICAN INDIAN ASSOCIATION. The American Indian Association (AIA)—not to be confused with the American Indian Association that evolved into the Society of American Indians*—was established in 1922 by Joseph Strong Wolf, a Chippewa, and Sherman Coolidge, an Arapahoe. The American Indian Association was committed to the granting of U.S. citizenship* to American Indians and the protection of their legal and civil rights. It also called for federal programs to provide land to homeless Indians and government pensions for the elderly. AIA chapters developed in many cities (but especially in New York City) and eventually established urban centers, which became forerunners of the post–World War II urban cultural centers for American Indians. During the 1930s and 1940s the American Indian Association increasingly changed its focus from legal and civil rights programs to social, fraternal, and educational activities.

Suggested Reading: Duane Champagne, ed., *The Native North American Almanac*, 1994; Armand S. La Potin, *Native American Voluntary Organizations*, 1986.

JAMES S. OLSON

AMERICAN INDIAN CHICAGO CONFERENCE. The American Indian Chicago Conference of 1961 proved to be a milestone in the history of Native American activism. During the 1950s the National Congress of American Indians* (NCAI) became internally divided between a younger generation of primarily urban Indians and an older generation of more traditionally oriented reservation leaders. The younger activists resented the fact that the older traditionalists dominated the NCAI and began to express their discontent. Urban-born, university-educated, and imbued with a pan-Indian* spirit, the younger Indians felt the NCAI had capitulated to white control through the Bureau of Indian Affairs.* The depth of their discontent became abundantly clear at the American Indian Chicago Conference.

Sol Tax, a professor of anthropology at the University of Chicago, assisted the NCAI in organizing the conference. Its purpose was to present the new John F. Kennedy administration with a comprehensive Indian policy package. More than five hundred Indians from sixty-seven tribes attended. Although the NCAI adopted resolutions demanding the pres-

ervation of Indian land rights and cultural traditions, the younger delegates—led by Clyde Warrior, a Ponca; Melvin Thom, a Paiute; and Herbert
Blatchford, a Navajo—criticized the conference as too accommodationist,
too cautious, and too patient. They called for a formal condemnation of
American racism, ethnocentrism, and paternalism. When their demands
went unfulfilled, they formed the National Indian Youth Council,* a far
more strident group of American Indian activists.

Suggested Reading: James S. Olson and Raymond Wilson, *Native Americans
in the Twentieth Century*, 1984.

JAMES S. OLSON

AMERICAN INDIAN DEFENSE ASSOCIATION. At the end of World
War I, attitudes toward American Indians improved throughout the general American public. However, when President Warren G. Harding appointed Albert Fall of New Mexico as secretary of the interior and Charles
Burke of South Dakota as commissioner of Indian affairs, a major controversy erupted between the administration supporters, often called obscurantists, and reformers called Red Progressives.* The obscurantists
wanted to crush Indian culture, particularly dances and peyote, a hallucinogenic drug used for religious purposes, as a way of promoting assimilation; the progressives supported the Indians' right to learn and practice
their native culture.

Out of disputes over Pueblo Indian land ownership in the early 1920s,
two new civil rights groups, the Eastern Association of Indian Affairs and
the New Mexico Association on Indian Affairs, joined the older Indian
Rights Association.* When orders forbidding many native dances, including the Pueblo Sun dance, were issued by the Bureau of Indian Affairs*
in 1921 and 1923, the New Mexico group (consisting originally of writers
and artists in the Taos area) broadened in 1923 into a national organization called the American Indian Defense Association. Funding by the
General Federation of Women's Clubs assisted the organization's move
to national status. Soon, its leader was John Collier,* a New York sociologist and supporter of community organizations who had moved to
Taos in the early 1920s. Already believing in protecting traditional communities against western industrialization, Collier took up the Pueblo
cause. An energetic but often abrasive man of strong views, Collier was
an excellent lobbyist, organizer, and publicist.

His personal views were the themes of the Defense Association. They
stressed cultural pluralism and self-determination* and advocated citizenship* for all Indians, the end of allotment,* reestablishment of tribal gov-

ernments, improved education* and health services, and allowing the freedom of Indian religion and culture. This caused a split with the older Indian Rights Association, which supported Indian property rights and citizenship but opposed cultural preservation. The AIDA published *American Indian Life* with Collier as its editor for the first seven years; it often ran articles by Collier, George W. Schultz, Mary Austin, and others in the *New York Times*, *Sunset Magazine*, and the *Nation* as well.

The American Indian Defense Association became one of the most successful of all Indian civil rights groups. In the 1920s it achieved congressional recognition of Pueblo land ownership and congressional granting of equal legal status for executive order reservations with treaty reservations. In 1925 the Osage Guardianship Act* forced much more equitable land handling by Oklahoma judges. The AIDA also backed the Meriam Report's* devastating comments on the Bureau of Indian Affairs. The association's greatest triumph, achieved with all the Red Progressives, was the granting in 1924 of U.S. citizenship to the remaining Indians who had not yet gained it.

In 1933, President Franklin Roosevelt appointed Harold Ickes, a charter member of the AIDA, as his secretary of the interior, and after considerable political maneuvering Ickes named John Collier as his commissioner of Indian affairs. The two were convinced that the Indians had suffered as greatly in the economic downturn of the Great Depression as any other group and insisted that they were as deserving of federal relief as any group in the country. Immediately many emergency relief measures were adopted, including the Indian Civilian Conservation Corps, which provided for families as well as young male workers. With AIDA support the Johnson-O'Malley Act* of 1934 established federal grants to the states to provide for expanded educational, health, and social welfare services for American Indians.

The influence of the AIDA was most seen in the Indian Reorganization Act,* which was introduced into Congress in February 1934 and aimed at completely restructuring the relationship between the federal government and the American Indians. This bill split the reformers, with the AIDA strongly in support of and the Indian Rights Association* in opposition to many of its provisions. What emerged on June 18, 1934, as the Indian Reorganization Act was a compromise. The hand of the American Indian Defense Association can particularly be seen in the inclusion of constitutional guarantees of religious freedom for native religions and the scrupulous protection of Indian civil rights. The AIDA was also highly pleased by the provisions for formal tribal governments, although John

Collier was not particularly happy with the fact that Indian tribes were not required to establish them. On the matter of assimilation* versus cultural perservation, the Indian New Deal* was ambiguous, but its strong support of Indian education practically called for the teaching of Indian culture, thereby moving the country toward toleration if not active encouragement of Indian culture and civilization. In 1936, the American Indian Defense Association merged with the National Association on Indian Affairs to become the American Association on Indian Affairs. The AIDA was one of the most successful of all Indian civil rights groups in achieving its aims.

Suggested Reading: John Collier, *From Every Zenith*, 1963; Lawrence C. Kelly, *The Assault on Assimilation: John Collier and the Origins of Indian Policy Reform*, 1983.

FRED S. ROLATER

AMERICAN INDIAN FEDERATION. The American Indian Federation (AIF) was established in 1934 by Indians opposed to the Indian Reorganization Act* of 1934 and the so-called Indian New Deal.* The moving force behind the AIF was Joseph Bruner, a well-to-do Creek. Most of its members were Oklahoma Indians. Comprised of avowed assimilationists bent on integrating all Indians into the larger society and settling all Indian land claims against the federal government through cash payments, the American Indian Federation was extremely suspicious of the New Deal's emphasis on communal Indian property. The AIF set as its goals the removal of John Collier* as commissioner of Indian affairs; repeal of the Indian Reorganization Act, which it believed would perpetuate Indian ethnicity; and abolition of the Bureau of Indian Affairs.*

Not surprisingly, the American Indian Federation attracted the support of conservative, anti–New Deal politicians. By the late 1930s many AIF leaders were actually flirting with fascist groups such as the Silver Shirts, a pro-Hitler organization. The American Indian Federation disintegrated in the mid-1940s, just when Congress began dismantling the Indian New Deal. Many AIF proposals, however, eventually found expression in the termination* and compensation* movements of the late 1940s and 1950s.

Suggested Reading: Laurence M. Hauptman, "The American Indian Federation and the Indian New Deal: A Reinterpretation," *Pacific Historical Review* 52 (November 1983), 378–402; Kenneth R. Philp, *John Collier's Crusade for Indian Reform 1920–1954*, 1977.

JAMES S. OLSON

AMERICAN INDIAN LAW CENTER. The American Indian Law Center was established in 1967 by the law school of the University of New Mexico. Under the direction of Philip S. Deloria the center became independent of the university in 1977, although it is still housed in the law school and its staff members work closely with law school students and faculty. During its almost thirty-year history the American Indian Law Center has focused its activities on the analysis of federal, state, and local policies affecting Indian people, assisting tribal governments with legal issues, improving relationships between tribal and state governments, and helping to prepare Indian undergraduate students for law school.

Suggested Reading: Nell Jessup Newton, "American Indian Law Center," in Mary B. Davis, ed., *Native America in the Twentieth Century: An Encyclopedia*, 1994.

JAMES S. OLSON

AMERICAN INDIAN MOVEMENT. The American Indian Movement (AIM) was established in Minneapolis, Minnesota, in 1968 by a group of Anishinabes (Chippewas) protesting police brutality. Among its founders were Dennis Banks,* Mary Jane Williams, and George Mitchell. They used the Black Panthers as a model for their organization. In urban areas of the United States, where police forces were composed overwhelmingly of whites who lived in the suburbs, relationships between police officers and minority communities were usually tense and hostile. Indian people, the AIM leaders claimed, were often harassed and beaten by police. AIM also wanted to lobby for improved city services for urban Indians. In one of its first acts, it established an "Indian patrol" to monitor police activities.

Using insurgent political tactics, AIM soon established chapters in major American cities and participated in the 1969 occupation of Alcatraz Island* by Indians of All Tribes.* (Federal law said that abandoned U.S. government property should revert to its previous owners, and the Indian group claimed that Alcatraz, an abandoned federal penitentiary, belonged to Indians.) Russell Means,* an Oglala Sioux raised in Oakland, California, became active in AIM in the early 1970s. On July 4, 1971, he led a protest at Mount Rushmore; later in the year, on Thanksgiving Day, an AIM group occupied Plymouth Rock in Massachusetts and painted it red in symbolic protest. In February 1972, Means led a "caravan" of more than 1,000 Indians into Gordon, Nebraska, to protest the murder of Raymond Yellow Thunder, an Oglala, and the community's refusal to indict the killers. The protest succeeded in securing the indictments and eventual convictions of the white men involved in the crime.

AIM leaders actively participated in "fish-ins" in the Pacific Northwest to protest state fish and game laws, and in 1972 they organized the "Trail of Broken Treaties"* caravan to Washington, D.C., and the occupation of the Bureau of Indian Affairs* building. In 1973, AIM orchestrated the 71-day occupation of Wounded Knee,* South Dakota. The occupation began as a symbolic protest of Oglala Sioux politics, but once the FBI sent in 250 agents to surround the protestors, it became a broad-based protest of the plight of American Indians. When it was over, the occupation had become the symbol of the Red Power* movement.

Soon after the occupation of the BIA building in 1972, several hundred AIM members traveled to Rapid City, South Dakota, to protest the murder of Wesley Bad Heart Bull, an Oglala. Darold Schmitz, a white man, was charged with manslaughter in the case, but AIM protestors demanded an indictment of first-degree murder. On February 6, 1973, more than two hundred AIM protestors fought with police in Custer, South Dakota, over the incident.

By that time, trouble had erupted as well at the Pine Ridge reservation. Oglala traditionalists resented the leadership of Richard Wilson, who headed the federally backed tribal government. When they protested his leadership, the government dispatched sixty federal marshals to Pine Ridge. The traditionalists asked AIM for support. AIM protestors arrived at Pine Ridge, and on February 28, 1973, an armed confrontation began in the village of Wounded Knee. The standoff lasted for seventy-one days, with AIM committed to the notion of tribal sovereignty* and the federal government committed to the destruction of the American Indian Movement. The federal government then brought hundreds of charges against AIM leaders for their participation in the standoff; but of the 562 indictments, only fifteen convictions resulted, and these were for minor offenses. In the campaign for the tribal presidency of the Pine Ridge reservation in 1974, AIM nominated Russell Means for the office. Wilson won the election by a narrow margin, and although the Civil Rights Commission recommended decertification of the election because of voting irregularities, the Bureau of Indian Affairs let it stand.

In 1975, AIM established a protest encampment at Jumping Bull near the Oglala village. Federal agents joined forces with Richard Wilson's Guardians of the Oglala Nation and attacked the encampment. During the confrontation, a firefight took place. One AIM member and two federal agents were killed. Three AIM members—Bob Robideau, Darrel Butler, and Leonard Peltier*—were brought to trial. Robideau and Butler were acquitted by an all-white jury, but Peltier was convicted of murder and given two life sentences.

After Wounded Knee, AIM membership gradually declined. AIM tended to be overrepresented by Sioux and Chippewas and failed to significantly broaden its tribal representation. The end of the Vietnam War took a great deal of steam out of protest movements in general, and the civil rights movement entered a long period of decline in the 1970s. With the passage of the Indian Self-Determination Act of 1974, many Indian peoples felt they had succeeded, at least temporarily, in reversing the direction of government policy toward Indians. In 1974, Russell Means emerged as national chairperson of AIM. He promoted the International Indian Treaty Council* movement in the late 1970s. In 1978, Dennis Banks organized the "Longest Walk"* demonstration, which memorialized the Trail of Broken Treaties protest of 1972. Since then, AIM has functioned more at the local than the national level, promoting Indian civil rights.

Suggested Reading: Ward Churchill and Jim Vander Wall, *Agents of Repression: The FBI's Secret Wars against the Black Panther Party and the American Indian Movement*, 1988; Rex Weyler, *Blood of the Land: The Government and Corporate War against the American Indian Movement*, 1982.

JAMES S. OLSON

AMERICAN INDIAN MOVEMENT FOR EQUAL RIGHTS. The American Indian Movement for Equal Rights (AIMFER) was founded in 1969 by the National Indian Youth Council.* It was a civil rights advocacy group. One of its first targets was the Bureau of Indian Affairs,* which had relatively few Indian people in management positions. Eventually AIMFER wanted to create an all-Indian Bureau of Indian Affairs completely separate from the federal government. During their most vocal period in the 1970s and early 1980s, AIMFER members worked as watchdog groups in BIA offices trying to promote the hiring and advancement of American Indians.

Suggested Reading: Armand S. La Potin, *Native American Voluntary Organizations*, 1986.

JAMES S. OLSON

AMERICAN INDIAN POLICY REVIEW COMMISSION. In the wake of the Wounded Knee* incident, protests over termination* and relocation,* and Indian demands for self-determination,* Congress established the American Indian Policy Review Commission in 1975. Senator James

Abourezk of South Dakota was its primary sponsor. Congress directed the commission to undertake a full review of the relationship between Indians and the federal government and to make recommendations for the reform of existing Indian policy. Senator Abourezk chaired the commission, which also included senators Mark Hatfield of Oregon and Lee Metcalf of Montana; congressmen Lloyd Meeds of Washington, Sidney Yates of Illinois, and Sam Steiger of Arizona; and such Indian leaders as John Borbridge (Tlingit), Louis Bruce (Mohawk-Sioux), Ada Deer* (Menominee), Adolf Dial (Lumbee), and Jake Whitecrow (Quapaw-Seneca-Cayuga). The commission eventually investigated a wide variety of issues dealing with federal government–Indian relations, tribal government, health, education, recognition, alcohol and drug abuse, human resources, and economic development. The commission submitted its final report to Congress in 1977.

In its final report, the commission contended that Indian tribes are sovereign nations whose relationship with the federal government should be based on international law, and as such should be able to determine their own membership standards and pass and enforce their own laws on reservation* property. Eventually the Indian Self-Determination Act of 1975, the American Indian Religious Freedom Act* of 1978, and the Indian Child Welfare Act* of 1978 emerged out of the commission's recommendations.

Suggested Reading: *American Indian Policy Review Commission, Final Report,* 1977.

JAMES S. OLSON

AMERICAN INDIAN RELIGIOUS FREEDOM ACT OF 1978. Religious freedom is and has been an important element of Indian culture. Natives, however, were excluded from constitutional guarantees of freedom of religion, an exclusion reinforced by a federal court in the decision *Native American Church v. Navajo Tribal Council,** 272 F.2d 131 (10th Cir. 1959). According to this ruling, only Congress can protect Indians in the free expression of their religious beliefs. The American Indian Religious Freedom Act of 1978 prescribed that Native Americans should come under the "free exercise" clause of the First Amendment to the U.S. Constitution. No earlier legislation provided such protection, including the Indian Reorganization Act.* That act confirmed and protected Indians' right to freedom of religion but did not place that protection under the First Amendment clause. The California Supreme Court in *People v.*

Woody* (1964) gave constitutional freedom of religion only to California Native Americans.

However, as Robert S. Michaelson pointed out in 1985, the American Indian Religious Freedom act was toothless, saying only what should be done. Because it was in the form of a joint resolution of Congress, it possessed no provisions. A survey of cases revealed that the most important decisions had come when Indians sued to protect sacred sites from development or federal encroachment.

Indian religion is often more about place than person. For many Indian peoples, religion revolves around notions of sacred geography. Those places are frequently located where developers or recreationists wish to build. The American Indian Religious Freedom Act does not specifically address that issue, but the courts since 1978 have protected many sacred places from development. That protection has not been universal, for courts have on occasion refused to protect a site. Courts seem to be reluctant to provide tests of protection for sites. So the effects of the act have been mixed for Indians.

Suggested Reading: Vine Deloria Jr. and Clifford M. Lytle, *American Indians, American Justice*, 1983; Arrell Morgan Gibson, *The American Indian: Prehistory to the Present*, 1980; Robert S. Michaelson, "Civil Rights, Indian Rites," in Roger L. Nichols, ed., *The American Indian: Past and Present*, 1985.

TIMOTHY MORGAN

AMERICAN REVOLUTION. The colonial wars fought in America during the seventeenth and eighteenth centuries posed impossible challenges to Native American peoples, because the warring powers often vied for Indian support, forcing tribes to choose sides. The American Revolution was no exception. In 1775 the Continental Congress established the Committee on Indian Affairs, and representatives visited the major tribes either to enlist their support or to convince them to remain neutral in the conflict. Most tribes, however, convinced that a colonial victory was a long shot, eventually sided with the British. When the war ended, Great Britain acknowledged the independence of the United States but neglected to include any protection provisions in the peace treaty for its Indian allies. The results for Indian peoples were disastrous. Having defeated the British, Americans believed that they had also defeated the Native American allies, and to the victor went the spoils. The United States paid little heed to Indian claims of sovereignty* and ownership. By choosing the losing side in the American Revolution, many Indian tribes guaranteed the loss of their ancestral lands during the 1790s and early 1800s.

Suggested Reading: Colin B. Calloway, *The American Revolution in Indian Country: Crisis and Diversity in Native American Communities*, 1995; Bernard W. Sheehan, *Seeds of Extinction: Jeffersonian Philanthropy and the American Indian*, 1973.

JAMES S. OLSON

AMERICANS FOR INDIAN OPPORTUNITY. In 1970, LaDonna Harris* founded Americans for Indian Opportunity to promote cultural, economic, and political self-sufficiency for American Indians. Harris has served as president of Americans for Indian Opportunity ever since its founding. The group has played key roles in creating the Council of Energy Resource Tribes,* in assisting Indian tribes in protecting their tribal estate, and in promoting sound environmental management of Indian land. The group was especially influential in assisting the Taos Indians of New Mexico in their recovery of Blue Lake.* The $500,000 annual budget of Americans for Indian Opportunity is raised from private and public sources.

Suggested Reading: LaDonna Harris, "Americans for Indian Opportunity," in Mary B. Davis, ed., *Native Americans in the Twentieth Century*, 1994.

JAMES S. OLSON

AMERICANS FOR NATIVE DEMOCRACY. Americans for Native Democracy was founded in March 1985 by Bernice Muskrat, a Jicarilla Apache. A bitter opponent of the Bureau of Indian Affairs,* Muskrat dedicated Americans for Native Democracy to ending all federal control over Indian reservations.* Only then, she believed, could tribal councils and Native American political institutions function freely and independently. Decades of federal assistance and control had done nothing to improve reservation economies and address the problems of disease,* alcohol* abuse, poverty,* and unemployment.

Suggested Reading: Armand S. La Potin, *Native American Voluntary Organizations*, 1986.

JAMES S. OLSON

AMERIND. In 1969, the leaders of the National Indian Youth Council* established AMERIND, Inc., to fight employment discrimination against Native Americans. A number of Bureau of Indian Affairs* (BIA) employees had filed employment discrimination suits against the federal government, especially in the BIA's Gallup and Albuquerque, New Mexico, offices. AMERIND's stated objective has been to fight employment discrimination against Indian workers in the Bureau of Indian Affairs, the

U.S. Public Health Service, and other federal agencies serving Native Americans.

Suggested Reading: Duane Champagne, ed., *Chronology of Native North American History*, 1994.

JAMES S. OLSON

ANIMAL RIGHTS. For thousands of years, American Indians functioned in subsistence economies in which survival was closely associated to their relationship with the natural environment. The environment was so central to Indian economic life that it also occupied, for most tribes, a central position in their religious theology. In recent decades Indian activists have had to fight to preserve their fishing* and hunting* rights, usually from the interests of sport hunters and sport fishermen who fear that Indian commercial harvesting practices will deplete the supply of fish and game. State fish and wildlife departments represent the sportsmen and have worked to bring Indians into compliance with existing fish and game laws. For their part, Indians have argued that treaty rights and tribal sovereignty* protect their hunting and fishing rights. They also claim that whites, not Indians, have primarily been responsible for the destruction of game supplies in U.S. history. They mostly cite the near-annihilation of the buffalo herds as proof of their contention.

In the 1980s and 1990s, however, Indians have faced new challenges from a variety of animal rights and environmental groups, who argue that many Indian religious and ceremonial practices violate the rights of animals. Environmental groups insist that Indians as well as non-Indians be subject to the Endangered Species Act of 1973 as well as to other legislation designed to stave off the extinction of a particular species of animal life. In 1940 and 1962, Congress extended protection to eagles, outlawing the hunting of the bird. Yankton Sioux Dwight Dion, however, claimed the right to hunt bald eagles on the reservation as an act of religious freedom. When he was convicted of violating the Eagle Protection Act, he sued in federal court. Eventually, in *United States v. Dion,** the Supreme Court upheld his conviction, claiming that Congress had specifically and legitimately superseded his hunting rights to maintain the species.

Animal rights groups believe that animal species are also protected in their right to life and should be protected from ceremonial practices that result in the death of the animal. In southern Florida, for example, animal rights activists have protested the Santería religion's sacrificial slaughtering of animals as part of weekly communion. In 1996, animal rights groups tried, but failed, to put a stop to the Pueblo Indians' *gallo* practice. For centuries, various Pueblo tribes have engaged in *gallo*—an athletic event in which roosters are buried up to their heads in sand and Indians on horseback race by and try to pull them up. Animal rights groups demonstrated against the activity, and the Pueblos claimed that tribal sovereignty protected the practice. Disputes between animal rights activists and Native Americans are certain to become civil rights issues in the future.

Suggested Reading: H. Barry Holt and Gary Forrester, *Digest of American Indian Law: Cases and Chronology*, 1990; *New York Times*, June 24, 1996; Stephen L. Pevar, *The Rights of Indians and Tribes: The Basic ACLU Guide to Indian and Tribal Rights*, 1992; Wilcomb E. Washburn, *Red Man's Land, White Man's Law: A Study of the Past and Present Status of the American Indian*, 1971; Charles F. Wilkinson, *American Indians, Time and the Law*, 1987; John R. Wunder, *"Retained by The People": A History of American Indians and the Bill of Rights*, 1994.

JAMES S. OLSON

ANTOINE v. WASHINGTON (1974). The *Antoine* case revolved around deer hunting rights on the Colville reservation in eastern Washington state. In 1891 the United States and the Colville tribe had negotiated a formal agreement awarding the Indians year-round hunting rights.* The agreement was not a formal treaty, because the practice of negotiating treaties between the U.S. government and Indian tribes had ended in 1871. Early in the 1970s, Washington fish and game authorities tried to put an end to out-of-season deer hunting by Indians on the Colville reservation. The Washington Supreme Court first heard the case and decided that the state had the power to nullify the 1891 agreement, because it had not been a formal treaty and the state had not been a party to the agreement. On appeal, the U.S. Supreme Court overturned the decision, arguing that the difference between a treaty and an agreement between the United States and the tribe was not substantial and that the Indians enjoyed sovereign hunting rights.

Suggested Reading: Russel Lawrence Barsh and James Youngblood Henderson, *The Road: Indian Tribes and Political Liberty*, 1980; Vine DeLoria Jr. and Clifford M. Lytle, *American Indians, American Justice*, 1983; H. Barry Holt and Gary Forrester, *Digest of American Indian Law: Cases and Chronology*, 1990; Stephen L. Pevar, *The Rights of Indians and Tribes: The Basic ACLU Guide to Indian and Tribal Rights*, 1992; Wilcomb E. Washburn, *Red Man's Land, White Man's Law: A Study of the Past and Present Status of the American Indian*, 1971; Charles F. Wilkinson, *American Indians, Time and the Law*, 1987; John R. Wun-

der, *"Retained by The People": A History of American Indians and the Bill of Rights*, 1994.

JAMES S. OLSON

AQUASH, ANNA MAE. Anna Mae (Pictou) Aquash, a Micmac Indian whose murder remains unresolved, was born near Shubenacadie in Nova Scotia, Canada, in 1945. After finishing school in Nova Scotia, she moved to Boston and became involved in the movement to improve the lives of urban Indians. There she met Nogeeshik Aquash, a Chippewa Canadian artist, and in 1973 they joined the American Indian Movement* and moved to the Pine Ridge reservation in South Dakota. They were married there in April 1973. She became a vocal supporter of the American Indian Movement's campaign to impeach Richard Wilson, tribal chairman of the Oglala Sioux at Pine Ridge. In 1975, Anna Mae Aquash was found shot to death on the reservation. Her murderers were never apprehended.

Suggested Reading: Duane Champagne, ed., *The Native North American Almanac*, 1994.

JAMES S. OLSON

ARCHAEOLOGICAL RECOVERY ACT OF 1974. In recent decades, Native American activists have targeted archaeological remains as one focus for the Red Power* movement. Throughout U.S. history, economic developers and scientists often plundered Indian archaeological sites and burial grounds, and Indian people could do little to protect what they considered to be sacred. In 1960, Congress passed the Reservoir Salvage Act to require notification of the secretary of the interior if dam construction could lead to the loss of significant historic sites; and amendments to the law in 1974—known as the Archaeological Recovery Act—strengthened the provisions of the law concerning archaeological sites. The legislation provided money for the protection, recovery, or relocation of such sites, as well as the publication of information about such sites. The Archaeological Recovery Act was a major step in the campaign to protect Native American cultural resources.

Suggested Reading: Michael M. Ames, *Cannibal Tours and Glass Boxes: The Anthropology of Museums*, 1992; Douglas Cole, *Captured Heritage: The Scramble for Northwest Coast Artifacts*, 1985; George P. Horse Capture, *The Concept of Sacred Materials and Their Place in the World*, 1989; Phyllis Mauch Messenger, ed., *The Ethics of Collecting Cultural Property: Whose Culture? Whose Property?* 1989; H. Marcus Price, *Disputing the Dead: U.S. Law on Aboriginal Remains and Grave Goods*, 1991.

JAMES S. OLSON

ARCHAEOLOGICAL RESOURCES PROTECTION ACT OF 1979. One of the most important pieces of federal legislation in the movement to protect Indian archaeological sites and burial grounds was the Archaeological Resources Protection Act of 1979. The law provided fines and prison sentences for individuals caught removing artifacts from federal lands without permission. Subsequent amendments to the law, particularly in 1988, required all federal agencies to carry out archaeological surveys of all lands under their jurisdiction and to conduct public awareness campaigns to stop the looting of archaeological sites. The law, however, did nothing to protect Indian archaeological sites on private land.

Suggested Reading: Michael M. Ames, *Cannibal Tours and Glass Boxes: The Anthropology of Museums*, 1992; Douglas Cole, *Captured Heritage: The Scramble for Northwest Coast Artifacts*, 1985; George P. Horse Capture, *The Concept of Sacred Materials and Their Place in the World*, 1989; Phyllis Mauch Messenger, ed., *The Ethics of Collecting Cultural Property: Whose Culture? Whose Property?* 1989; H. Marcus Price, *Disputing the Dead: U.S. Law on Aboriginal Remains and Grave Goods*, 1991.

JAMES S. OLSON

ARIZONA v. CALIFORNIA **(1963).** Although the state of Arizona filed this suit in an effort to secure water rights* for itself on the Colorado River, the 1963 Supreme Court decision set important precedents for Indian water rights. The case dealt with the Colorado River Compact (1922), which divided water along the Colorado River among seven states and Mexico. Arizona alone chose not to participate in the compact, but by 1944 the state realized it needed its share of Colorado River water. Arizona brought the suit in 1952 to determine if its compact rights had been forfeited by prior appropriation of other users.

The Supreme Court decided in favor of Arizona but noted that water rights of Indians along the river superseded those of the states and individual users. The Court reiterated and clarified a precedent set in its 1908 *Winters v. United States** decision, arguing that when the federal government created an Indian reservation,* it reserved the right to water for that reservation from the date of its creation. This argument applied particularly to reservations created by executive order or act of Congress; the status of reservations created by treaty remained unclear. Presumably, Indians on treaty reservations had water rights by prior appropriation that predated the treaty.

The Court also established a means for measuring how large a right a given reservation would have. It developed the "irrigable acreage" standard: reservations had reserved rights* to the water reasonably needed to irrigate whatever portion of the reservation was practically irrigable. As Norris Hundley Jr. notes, "[Under *Arizona v. California*,] the standard for determining the quantity of the Indian water right is the size and irrigable character of a reservation; it is not the number of Indians on a reservation nor the wishes of those Indians about how a reservation should be developed." But other Supreme Court decisions indicate that water rights may extend to new and unforeseen uses, creating room for larger rights than those measured by irrigable acreage.

Suggested Reading: Lloyd Burton, *American Indian Water Rights and the Limits of the Law*, 1991; Felix S. Cohen, *Felix S. Cohen's Handbook of Federal Indian Law*, 1982; Norris Hundley Jr., "The Dark and Bloody Ground of Indian Water Rights," *Western Historical Quarterly* (October 1978), 455–82.

DARREN PIERSON

ARIZONA ET AL. v. SAN CARLOS APACHE TRIBE **(1983).** In the *Winters v. United States** case of 1908, the Supreme Court upheld Indian water rights* by agreeing that whenever the United States had created an Indian reservation,* there was an implied assumption that sufficient water would be available to fulfill reservation purposes. Non-Indian landowners protested the decision, but the federal government stood its ground. During the next fifty years, however, the federal government also constructed a series of vast reclamation projects that delivered large volumes of ostensibly Indian water to non-Indian customers. In 1963, the Supreme Court once again confirmed a broad interpretation of Indian water rights in the *Arizona v. California** case. It was not until 1983 that the Supreme Court began to back away from its expansive interpretation of Indian water rights. In *Arizona et al. v. San Carlos Apache Tribe* (1983), the Court agreed that tribes could be forced to adjudicate water rights disputes in state courts rather than in federal courts. This was a defeat for the tribes, since federal courts had always been more sympathetic to Indian needs than state courts. The *San Carlos* decision was a harbinger of many subsequent federal court decisions in the 1980s and 1990s, which upheld a states rights judicial philosophy and tended to look unfavorably on Indian water rights demands.

Suggested Reading: Russel Lawrence Barsh and James Youngblood Henderson, *The Road: Indian Tribes and Political Liberty*, 1980; Lloyd Burton, *American Indian Water Rights and the Limits of the Law*, 1991; H. Barry Holt and Gary Forrester, *Digest of American Indian Law: Cases and Chronology*, 1990; Stephen L. Pevar, *The Rights of Indians and Tribes: The Basic ACLU Guide to Indian and Tribal Rights*, 1992; Wilcomb E. Washburn, *Red Man's Land, White Man's Law*, 1971; Charles F. Wilkinson, *American Indians, Time and the Law*,

1987; John R. Wunder, *"Retained by The People": A History of American Indians and the Bill of Rights*, 1994.

JAMES S. OLSON

ARMED FORCES. See **SELECTIVE SERVICE.**

ARROW, INC. In 1949, Will Rogers Jr. and Robert Bennett established Arrow, Inc., a group dedicated to raising money to assist Native Americans suffering from the economic and geographic effects of the winter of 1948–1949. It was a subsidiary of the National Congress of American Indians.* Since then Arrow, Inc., has broadened its mission to include educational assistance, public relations guidance, and technical training to individual Native Americans and to tribal organizations. Since the late 1960s Arrow, Inc., has also provided management training for Indian judges presiding over tribal courts. To promote that activity, Arrow, Inc., founded the National American Indian Court Judges Association.

Suggested Reading: Armand S. La Potin, *Native American Voluntary Organizations*, 1986; Theodore W. Taylor, *American Indian Policy*, 1983.

JAMES S. OLSON

ARTICLES OF CONFEDERATION. When the American Revolution broke out in 1775, the American rebels immediately began a relationship with the American Indians. On July 12, 1775, a congressional committee including Patrick Henry of Virginia and Philip Schuyler of New York had Congress adopt a resolution stating that preserving the friendship of the Indian tribes was of extreme importance. In May 1776 the Continental Congress formed a standing committee on Indian affairs as part of an increasing tendency to organize an administration to run an emerging new nation. Losing the war for Indian allegiance to the British, Thomas Jefferson would write in the Declaration of Independence that George III had "endeavored to bring on the inhabitants of our frontiers the merciless Indian savages."

The Articles of Confederation, the first U.S. Constitution, stated in Article 9 that the Congress had the exclusive right of "regulating trade and managing all affairs with Indians, not members of any of the states, provided that the legislative right of any state within its own limits be not infringed or violated." With the adoption of the Articles in 1781, American Indians came under two jurisdictions, state and federal, a difficulty that would continue to plague Indians and governments alike until the present era. In 1783, jurisdiction over Indian affairs was placed under the Department of War, where it would remain until the establishment of the Department of the Interior in 1849.

On October 15, 1783, James Duane, chairman of the Committee on Indian Affairs, led Congress to adopt a convention that all lands ceded to the United States by the Treaty of Paris were exclusively under congressional control, and that because most Indians had sided with the British during the revolution, they had forfeited all their rights to previously owned lands. However, gradualists argued successfully that expelling all Indians from the boundaries of the United States would not be possible at the time. Consequently, a series of four treaties were made between Indians in the Ohio country and the United States between 1784 and 1789. Other treaties were made with southern tribes, freeing some land for white settlement.

A basic change in U.S. policy came about in the Northwest Ordinance* of July 13, 1787. Influenced by the inability of the government to forcibly seize the lands of the Northwest, Article 3 stated that "The utmost good faith shall always be observed towards the Indians, their lands and property shall never be taken from them without their consent." Further, their land was to be invaded only in "just and lawful wars authorized by Congress," and just and humane laws would be made to prevent wrongs to the Indians and to maintain "peace and friendship with them." Acting on this authorization, the Fort Harmar conferences negotiated two treaties in January 1789, one with the Six Nations (Iroquois) and the other with the Wyandots, Delawares, Ottawas, and Chippewas. In both, the principle of purchasing Indian lands was restored.

The governments of the United States from 1775 to 1789 fought many wars with Indians but also set much of the future Indian policy and federal administrative structure. In April 1789, the new government took over the administration of Indian affairs and the difficult civil rights problems that had already surfaced in the nation's early years.

Suggested Reading: Merrill Jensen, *The Articles of Confederation*, 1940.

FRED S. ROLATER

ASSIMILATION. The question of whether Native Americans should or even could be assimilated into the larger American society has influenced Indian policy for generations, often to the detriment and disempowerment of Indian people themselves. Religious impulses tell much about European expansion to the New World, and the English, French, Dutch, Spanish, and Portuguese explorers and settlers were all interested in converting Indians to Christianity. That attempt to wean Indians, violently and peacefully, away from their indigenous traditions and convert them to European values has affected relations between Indians and non-Indians from the colonial period until today.

The issue of assimilation has been particularly powerful during the past century. In the years following the Civil War,* when violence against the Indians of the Great Plains and the Southwest became particularly intense, reformers decided that the only way to prevent future violence was to see that Indians were assimilated into the larger society. Programs to assimilate Indians economically took the form of allotment,* compensation,* termination,* and relocation.* In 1887, Congress passed the Dawes Act,* which provided for the alloting of tribal lands: tribal estates were subdivided into small farming plots and distributed to individual heads of family. Reformers hoped to train Indians to become farmers selling their crops in a commercial economy. Allotment, the reformers believed, would weaken tribal power and enhance the authority of individualism. Commissioner of Indian Affairs T. J. Morgan best summarized assimilation by allotment in 1889 when he said that Indians should be "individualized and conform to the white man's ways, peaceably if they will, forcibly if they must." The allotment program continued for nearly a half-century, coming to an end when the "Indian New Deal"* went into effect in 1934.

After World War II, however, the pressures to assimilate Indians intensified again. Three federal government programs—compensation, termination, and relocation—were designed to bring about assimilation. The federal government intended first to settle all outstanding Indian claims against the United States for losses of land. The Indian Claims Commission Act of 1946 established the Indian Claims Commission* to evaluate those claims. At the same time, Congress began working on the termination program—to end the special legal status of Indian tribes as wards of the federal government and to turn them over to state jurisdiction. Finally, the Bureau of Indian Affairs* tried to relocate tens of thousands of Indians from their reservations* to city apartments, where they supposedly would mix in with other Americans. The compensation, termination, and relocation programs dominated federal Indian policy during the 1950s and 1960s and died out only when the self-determination* movement appeared in the 1970s and 1980s.

The granting of U.S. citizenship* to American Indians was also seen by reformers as a way of assimilating them legally and politically into American society. In 1871, Congress ended the legal sovereignty* of Indian tribes and ceased dealing with them as independent nations. The allotment program guaranteed citizenship to each American Indian who took ownership of a parcel of land. The next major step in the citizenship crusade took place after World War I when Congress granted citizenship to Indian veterans. In 1924, Congress passed the Snyder Act,* granting citizenship to all Native Americans. The termination program of the 1950s and 1960s, which attempted to turn all Indians over to state and local police and taxing jurisdictions, was a final attempt to assimilate Native Americans legally.

Although the federal government has largely abandoned its heavy-handed attempts to assimilate American Indians, the threat of assimilation still remains. Now, however, it is not government policy as much as larger social, economic, and cultural trends in American society that are promoting assimilation. The increasing number of Indians living in urban areas, the development of mass media, the rapid decline in the number of Indians speaking their native language, and improved Indian education are all working against the maintenance of specific tribal identities, leaving many Native Americans deeply troubled about their cultural future.

Suggested Reading: Robert E. Berkhofer Jr., *The White Man's Indian*, 1978; Sandra A. Cadwalader and Vine Deloria Jr., eds., *The Aggressions of Civilization: Federal Indian Policy since the 1880s*, 1984; Henry Fritz, *The Movement for Indian Assimilation, 1860–1890*, 1963; Frederick Hoxie, *A Final Promise: The Campaign to Assimilate the Indians, 1880–1920*, 1984; James S. Olson and Raymond Wilson, *Native Americans in the Twentieth Century*, 1984.

JAMES S. OLSON

ASSIMILATIVE CRIMES ACT OF 1948. In the decade after World War II, the retreat from the "Indian New Deal"* policies of John Collier* accelerated in the United States. Assimilationists, who wanted to end the separate trust status of Indian tribes and incorporate Native Americans into the existing legal system, gained the upper hand in Congress. Eventually the assimilationists promoted the termination* and relocation* programs to achieve their objectives. In 1947, the Hoover Commission* recommended ending all special activities by the federal government in behalf of Indians. The next year, Congress passed one of the first so-called termination laws—the Assimilative Crimes Act. For years, federal and state authorities had argued about how to treat Indians accused of criminal activity. Since the federal government had legal jurisdiction over reservations,* did federal law prevail in criminal cases? State authorities charged that Indian criminals could often defy state statutes and then retreat to the jurisdiction of the reservations, where federal laws prevailed. The Assimilative Crimes Act addressed that problem by allowing the Department of Justice to prosecute Native Americans accused of felonies in federal courts but under state laws. Tribal leaders and Indian rights advocates protested the law, but the assimilationists prevailed.

Suggested Reading: James S. Olson and Raymond Wilson, *Native Americans in the Twentieth Century*, 1984; Stephen L. Pevar, *The Rights of Indians and Tribes: The Basic ACLU Guide to Indian and Tribal Rights*, 1992.

JAMES S. OLSON

ASSOCIATION ON AMERICAN INDIAN AFFAIRS. The Association on American Indian Affairs was established in 1936 as the American Association on Indian Affairs after a merger of the National Association on Indian Affairs and the American Indian Defense Association.* During the 1930s the association campaigned for Indian land rights and religious freedom. In 1946 the association changed its name to the Association on American Indian Affairs. Oliver LaFarge served as its president from 1937 to 1942 and again from 1945 to 1963. During the late 1940s and 1950s the association opposed the termination* and relocation* movements, and then became a lobbying group to make sure that government Indian programs were properly funded. During the 1970s the association played a central role in passage of the Indian Child Welfare Act* of 1978. Since that time the association has been active in promoting Indian water rights,* religious freedom, reservation economic development, tribal self-determination,* federal recognition of various Indian peoples, and Indian control of education* programs. In 1989 Gary Kimble, a Gros Ventre, became director of the Association on American Indian Affairs.

Suggested Reading: Robert Hecht, *Oliver LaFarge and the American Indian: A Biography*, 1991; Theodore W. Taylor, *American Indian Policy*, 1983.

JAMES S. OLSON

ATOKA AGREEMENT. When Congress passed the Dawes Act* in 1887, many non-Native Americans hoped the legislation would accelerate the process by which American Indians were assimilated into the larger society. By breaking up tribal estates, distributing land to individual owners, and awarding citizenship to members of allotted tribes, reformers believed they could bring an end to the violence against Native Americans and absorb them into a modern economy and body politic. A number of tribes, however, vigorously protested the legislation, especially the Creeks, Cherokees, Choctaws, Seminoles, Osages, Miamis, Peorias, and Sacs and Foxes, all of whom lived in the Indian Territory.* Those tribes hired lobbyists in Washington, D.C., to represent their interests during the legislative process, and in the end Congress exempted those tribes from the allotment* provisions of the Dawes Act.

Advocates of assimilation,* however, resented the exemption. Many white reformers believed the tribes of the Indian Territory were the peoples *most* ready for assimilation, and the congressional exemption seemed to make no sense. In 1893, Congress established a commission to negotiate allotment agreements with the exempted tribes. President Grover Cleveland hired retired senator Henry Dawes to head the commission. Generally, full-bloods within the tribes opposed allotment, whereas mixed-bloods favored it. In 1896, Congress ordered the Dawes Commission to make a list of the members of each tribe. One year later, in 1897, the Choctaw and Chickasaw tribes signed the Atoka Agreement with the Dawes Commission, accepting allotments of 320 acres each.

Suggested Reading: D. S. Otis, *The Dawes Act and the Allotment of Indian Lands*, 1973.

JAMES S. OLSON

B

BADONI v. HIGGINSON (1980). In the late 1970s, the U.S. Army Corps of Engineers built a hydroelectric dam on the Colorado River in and around the environs of a Native American holy site. Navajo medicine men, seeking to preserve the integrity of their sacred tribal grounds at the nearby Rainbow Bridge National Monument in southern Utah, sought a lowering of water levels and the imposition of restrictions on tourism in the area. At issue was whether or not the maintenance of American Indian religious freedoms outweighed the claims of the local electric power and tourist industries. The Court of Appeals for the Tenth Circuit determined that government intervention to accommodate Indian religious observances would constitute a violation of the Establishment Clause in the First Amendment. Because the Navajos still had access to the site, it was ruled that the status quo should be maintained.

Suggested Reading: Russel Lawrence Barsh and James Youngblood Henderson, *The Road: Indian Tribes and Political Liberty*, 1980; Vine Deloria Jr. and Clifford M. Lytle, *American Indians, American Justice*, 1983; H. Barry Holt and Gary Forrester, *Digest of American Indian Law: Cases and Chronology*, 1990; Stephen L. Pevar, *The Rights of Indians and Tribes: The Basic ACLU Guide to Indian and Tribal Rights*, 1992; Kenneth R. Philp, ed., *Indian Self-Rule: First-Hand Accounts of Indian-White Relations from Roosevelt to Reagan*, 1986; Howard Stambor, "Manifest Destiny and American Indian Religious Freedom: *Sequoyah, Badoni*, and the Drowned Gods," *American Indian Law Review* 10 (1982), 59–89; Charles F. Wilkinson, *American Indians, Time and the Law*, 1987; John R. Wunder, *"Retained by The People": A History of American Indians and the Bill of Rights*, 1994.

MARK BAXTER

BANKS, DENNIS. Dennis Banks (Anishinabe Native American), a nationally known Indian activist, was born in 1930 on the Leech Lake Indian reservation in northern Minnesota. In 1968 with Clyde Bellecourt* and other Indian community members, Banks organized the American Indian Movement* (AIM) to protect the traditional ways of Indian people, improve government-funded social services, and prevent the harassment of Native Americans by police. On Thanksgiving Day, 1970, while attempting to extend its activism to a national audience, Banks and other members of AIM seized the *Mayflower II,** the replica of the original ship that carried the Pilgrims to the North American continent. AIM members proclaimed Thanksgiving Day a national day of mourning in protest against the seizure of Indian lands by the early white colonists.

In February 1973, Banks and other AIM members led a protest in Custer, South Dakota, after the mother of murder victim Wesley Bad Heart Bull was pushed down a flight of stairs following a meeting with officials. Banks was arrested as a result of his involvement in the 71-day occupation of Wounded Knee,* South Dakota, later in 1973. Acquitted of charges related to the occupation of Wounded Knee, Banks was convicted of assault with a deadly weapon without intent to kill and rioting while armed, charges stemming from the Custer incident. Jumping bail, Banks fled to California. Governor Jerry Brown refused to honor extradition requests from South Dakota, citing the strong hostility there against AIM members in general and Banks in particular. In March 1983 the Onondaga Nation, located south of Syracuse, New York, granted Banks asylum. Later in the year, after nine years as a fugitive, Banks surrendered to state authorities in Rapid City, South Dakota. He served approximately one year of a three-year sentence.

In the late 1980s, Banks actively protested the disturbance of Native American ancestral burial grounds by collectors and archaeologists. Due in part to Banks's efforts, the Smithsonian Institution agreed to return 25,000 Indian bones and other artifacts for reburial. Banks organized ceremonies for over 1,200 reinternment efforts. In 1988 Banks published his autobiography, *Sacred Soul*, in Japanese rather than English, citing English as the language of the conquerors. Banks played important roles in the movies *The Last of the Mohicans* (1992) and *Thunderheart* (1992).

Suggested Reading: Arlene Ehrlich, "The Right to Rest in Peace," *Sun* (Baltimore, Maryland), October 22, 1989; David Holmstrom, "Oglala Sioux: Up from Wounded Knee, Parts 1–3," *Christian Science Monitor*, October 16–18, 1989; Stanley David Lyman, *Wounded Knee, 1973: A Personal Account*, 1991; Kenneth Stern, *Loud Hawk: The United States versus the American Indian Movement*, 1994; Theodore W. Taylor, *American Indian Policy*, 1983; Rex Weyler, *Blood of the Land: The Government and Corporate War against the American Indian Movement*, 1982.

DAVID RITCHEY

BANYACYA, THOMAS, SR. He is a Hopi traditionalist convinced that American society is on a fast track to self-destruction unless it gains more respect for the environment. Born in the New Oraibi village of Hopi people in 1910, Banyacya came to public attention in the early 1970s when he began to protest government plans to relocate 10,000 Navajo people from Hopi land. The Navajo-Hopi dispute originated from the fact that Navajo herders had settled on sparsely populated Hopi land, but Navajo population growth far outpaced that of the Hopis. Although many Hopis wanted the Navajos removed, Banyacya worried that the relocation plan was a government ruse to clear Hopi land and then open it up to private corporations anxious to exploit local coal, oil shale, and uranium deposits. He has also been a vocal advocate of a return to traditional customs, the revival of ancient religions, the use of tribal chiefs and tribal councils selected by traditional means instead of elections supervised by the Bureau of Indian Affairs,* and the abandonment of majority rule politics in favor of traditional consensus politics.

Suggested Reading: Duane Champagne, ed., *The Native North American Almanac*, 1994.

JAMES S. OLSON

BARKER v. HARVEY (1901). Also known as the Cupeño case, *Barker v. Harvey* revolved around the land claims of several bands of Kumeyaay Indians. Before the Mexican War, the Kumeyaay occupied lands north and south of the border between Mexico and the United States, and between the California coast and the Colorado River. With the Treaty of Guadalupe Hidalgo,* which ended the Mexican War and transferred California to U.S. jurisdiction, four bands of the Kumeyaay found themselves under American sovereignty. More than a half-century later the descendants of those Kumeyaay bands sued in federal court, claiming that since their rights to the land had been guaranteed by Mexican law before the treaty, the United States and the state of California were constitutionally bound to continue those guarantees. *Barker v. Harvey* moved through the federal courts, and in 1901 the Supreme Court rendered its decision. The Court denied any obligation on the part of the United States to honor Mexican constitutional guarantees and ordered the eviction of the Kumeyaay bands.

Suggested Reading: Russel Lawrence Barsh and James Youngblood Henderson, *The Road: Indian Tribes and Political Liberty*, 1980; Vine Deloria Jr. and Clifford M. Lytle, *American Indians, American Justice*, 1983; H. Barry Holt and Gary Forrester, *Digest of American Indian Law: Cases and Chronology*, 1990;

Stephen L. Pevar, *The Rights of Indians and Tribes: The Basic ACLU Guide to Indian and Tribal Rights*, 1992; Wilcomb E. Washburn, *Red Man's Land, White Man's Law*, 1971; Charles F. Wilkinson, *American Indians, Time and the Law*, 1987; John R. Wunder, *"Retained by The People": A History of American Indians and the Bill of Rights*, 1994.

JAMES S. OLSON

BEATTY, WILLARD. Willard Beatty, director of Indian education in the Bureau of Indian Affairs* (BIA) from 1936 to 1951, was a leading education reformer. Born in California on September 17, 1891, he was awarded a B.S. degree from the School of Mechanical Arts of the University of California in 1913 and soon began his lifelong career in education. Beatty worked very closely with major Progressive Era educators and quickly became a leading figure in the call for reform in educational techniques and practices.

In January 1936 Beatty began serving in the BIA. He took over an agency that was responsible for the education of 80,000 Indian children. Beatty met this challenge by shifting the focus of Indian education away from boarding schools to day schools, a major change in how Indian children were educated. He also initiated innovative new curriculum designed to complement features of John Collier's* Indian Reorganization Act.* For example, some of this curriculum was bilingual, and Beatty encouraged the teaching and preservation of tribal culture and language. Previously, Indian students were often punished for even speaking a native tongue at school.

Beatty's innovations were almost wiped out after World War II, as budget cuts reduced the resources of his department. In addition, new BIA leadership increased efforts at assimilating Indian youth into white culture. Bilingual and cultural education virtually disappeared. Beatty fought these changes, but when his powers were further diminished in 1951, he resigned. Until his death in 1961, Beatty held a variety of jobs in government and in the private sector. Though he had critics, Beatty played an important role in the development of Indian education. Beatty was perhaps ahead of his time, for his work on bilingual and cultural education reappeared in the 1970s, when a more culturally sensitive approach to Indian education was again adopted.

Suggested Reading: Willard W. Beatty, *Education for Action: Selected Articles from Indian Education, 1936–43*, 1944; Willard W. Beatty, *Education for Cultural Change: Selected Articles from Indian Education, 1944–51*, 1953; Margaret C. Szasz, *Education and the American Indian*, 1977.

JASON M. TETZLOFF

BELLECOURT, CLYDE. Co-founder, with Dennis Banks* and other Native American community leaders, of the American Indian Movement* in Minneapolis, Minnesota, in July 1968. An Ojibway Native American, Bellecourt was born in 1939 on the White Earth reservation in Minnesota. His activism has spanned four decades.

The American Indian Movement (AIM) was originally formed to improve government-funded social services to urban neighborhoods and to prevent the harassment of Native Americans by police. During the 1972 occupation of the Bureau of Indian Affairs* building in Washington, D.C., Bellecourt helped draft the twenty-point document presented to the government. Although AIM demands were ignored, the government did establish a task force that met with movement leaders and promised to make no arrests in connection with the occupation. Bellecourt also worked extensively to raise funds for AIM-sponsored projects and was briefly associated with militant black activist Stokely Carmichael.

Increasingly confrontational, Bellecourt and other AIM leaders implemented an armed occupation of the tiny South Dakota hamlet of Wounded Knee* on February 27, 1973. Bellecourt was elected to the council of the AIM-declared "Nation of Wounded Knee" and eventually cosigned the peace agreement that ended the confrontation. Not long after Wounded Knee, Bellecourt was wounded when shot in the stomach by Carter Camp, another occupation leader.

In the 1990s, Bellecourt lobbied energetically on behalf of the Mille Lac Chippewa during their struggle to maintain traditional walleye pike harvests along the shores of Flathead Lake in Minnesota. (Earlier successes in Wisconsin had allowed Native Americans there to continue their treaty-guaranteed right to maintain a traditional subsistence fishing economy.) Powerful opposition in Minnesota, led by former Minnesota Viking football coach Bud Grant, persuaded the state legislature to reject an agreement that would have allowed the tribe to harvest about half of the walleye pike in Flathead Lake.

Suggested Reading: Margaret L. Knox, "The New Indian Wars: A Growing Movement Is Gunning," *Los Angeles Times*, November 7, 1993; Edward Lazarus, *Black Hills, White Justice: The Sioux Nation versus the United States, 1775 to the Present*, 1991; Stanley David Lyman, *Wounded Knee, 1973: A Personal Account*, 1991; Kenneth Stern, *Loud Hawk: The United States versus the American Indian Movement*, 1994; Rex Weyler, *Blood of the Land: The Government and Corporate War against the American Indian Movement*, 1982.

DAVID RITCHEY

BENEFICIAL USE DOCTRINE. See **WATER RIGHTS.**

BENNETT, RAMONA. A Puyallup Indian, Ramona Bennett has become a prominent advocate for Indian fishing rights,* Indian health and education,* and the rights of Indian children and their families. Bennett was born in Seattle, Washington, on April 28, 1948. After receiving an undergraduate degree from Evergreen State College in Washington, she earned a master's degree in education from the University of Puget Sound. From 1971 to 1978 she served as chair of the Puyallup Tribal Council, and today she is a director of the Survival of American Indians Association.*

Suggested Reading: Duane Champagne, ed., *The Native North American Almanac*, 1994.

JAMES S. OLSON

BENNETT, ROBERT. Indian rights activist and commissioner of Indian affairs from 1966 to 1969. Bennett, an Oneida Indian, was born in 1912 in Oneida, Wisconsin. He attended the Haskell Institute in Kansas and then earned a law degree at Southeastern University in Washington, D.C. With his law degree in hand, Bennett accepted a position with the Bureau of Indian Affairs* (BIA), where he worked as an administrative assistant on the Navajo reservation in New Mexico. With the outbreak of World War II, Bennett took a leave of absence from the BIA and served honorably in the Marine Corps. After the war he returned to the Bureau of Indian Affairs, and in 1966 he was named commissioner of Indian affairs, only the second Native American to hold the position. He headed the BIA until his resignation in 1969 when the Nixon administration took office. During his tenure with the BIA, Bennett was an indefatigable proponent of self-determination.* Since his retirement he has remained active in promoting Indian rights.

Suggested Reading: Duane Champagne, ed., *Chronology of Native North American History*, 1994.

JAMES S. OLSON

BILINGUAL EDUCATION. See *LAU v. NICHOLS.*

BILL OF RIGHTS. The Bill of Rights comprises the first ten amendments to the U.S. Constitution.* They were ratified and added to the Constitution in 1791. Included in the ten amendments are statements outlining the rights of American citizens and restrictions on the powers of the federal government. From the very beginning, the Bill of Rights raised serious questions and controversies about the individual rights of American Indians. Because federal law at the time considered them citizens of their tribes, not of the United States, Indians did not enjoy the protections of the Bill of Rights. Even when, by treaty, certain tribes had ceded their lands to the United States, that citizenship status did not change.

But in 1871 the United States stopped dealing with Indian tribes as sovereign nations and began legislating and negotiating agreements with them. The days of formal treaties were over. That decision rendered the issue of Indian tribal citizenship* less relevant, but they were still not considered citizens of the United States. In fact, Indians were neither citizens nor foreign aliens. Gradually, between 1887 and 1924, Congress extended citizenship to all American Indians; once an individual had accepted citizenship, he or she theoretically gained the protection of the Bill of Rights.

After World War II, controversy erupted over the relationship between the Bill of Rights and tribal sovereignty.* The Bill of Rights, and later the Fourteenth Amendment* to the Constitution, guaranteed that no American could have his or her rights denied by federal, state, or local governments. Whether or not that included tribal governments became a source of intense debate. It was argued that if tribes truly enjoyed sovereignty on the reservations, then they could impose on all tribal members their own definition of personal rights. But what if those definitions were not consistent with the Bill of Rights guaranteed to each American citizen? Could Indians sue their own tribal governments for civil rights violations? If not, did they really enjoy rights as American citizens? If so, were their tribes really sovereign? The major result of the debate was the Indian Civil Rights Act* of 1968.

Suggested Reading: Russel Lawrence Barsh and James Youngblood Henderson, *The Road: Indian Tribes and Political Liberty*, 1980; Vine Deloria Jr. and Clifford M. Lytle, *American Indians, American Justice*, 1983; Stephen L. Pevar, *The Rights of Indians and Tribes: The Basic ACLU Guide to Indian and Tribal Rights*, 1992; Kenneth R. Philp, ed., *Indian Self-Rule: First-Hand Accounts of Indian-White Relations from Roosevelt to Reagan*, 1986; Howard Stambor, "Manifest Destiny and American Indian Religious Freedom: *Sequoyah, Badoni*, and the Drowned Gods," *American Indian Law Review* 10 (1982), 59–89; Charles F. Wilkinson, *American Indians, Time and the Law*, 1987; John R. Wunder, *"Retained by The People": A History of American Indians and the Bill of Rights*, 1994.

JAMES S. OLSON

BLACK ELK. Black Elk was an Oglala Lakota (Sioux) medicine man and religious leader. Together with poet John G. Neihardt, Black Elk created *Black Elk Speaks* (1932), an account of his life that has become a classic text in both Native American and mainstream American culture. His lifetime spanned the Lakotas' transition from relative independence (he had heard of but not seen *wasichus* [whites] as a young boy) to reservation life. Late in life he also witnessed the resurging interest in Native American life and culture, which led him to collaborate on projects with Neihardt and with anthropologist Joseph Epes Brown (*The Sacred Pipe*, 1953).

Black Elk measured his own life in terms of his failure to fulfill the great vision he had as a boy. In the vision he received songs and instructions from six grandfathers, who gave him the task of helping his nation through the difficulties ahead. They showed him a glimpse of a future in which his nation's hoop was broken and his people were starving.

At age 16, Black Elk finally shared his vision with medicine men, who instructed him to enact the vision. He did so with the aid of family and other tribespeople. Thereafter, he directed his life toward curing, receiving training from older medicine men. Later he traveled with Buffalo Bill's Wild West show in England. After he returned to the reservation he participated in the Ghost Dance, which he believed was his vision coming true. He witnessed the subsequent massacre at Wounded Knee,* which left him convinced that the dream of his people had died and he had failed to fulfill his vision.

Black Elk converted to Catholicism in 1904, and scholars continue to debate what this meant for his practice of traditional Lakota religion. A recent examination argues that Black Elk probably maintained his involvement in traditional religion.

Suggested Reading: Raymond J. DeMallie, ed., *The Sixth Grandfather*, 1984; Clyde Holler, *Black Elk's Religion: The Sun Dance and Lakota Catholicism*, 1995; Michael Steltenkamp, *Black Elk: Holy Man of the Oglala*, 1993.

EMILY GREENWALD

BLACK HILLS CONTROVERSY. In 1868 the Fort Laramie Treaty* ended hostilities between the Lakota people and the U.S. government and delineated the boundaries for the Great Sioux Nation reservation, a tract of land that would allegedly be free of white intrusion forever. However, within a few months of the signing of the treaty, the discovery of gold in the Black Hills brought a veritable flood of white miners. Eventually the federal government confiscated 7.7 million acres of the reservation, without compensating the Indians for their land.

For the Lakota people the Black Hills region is sacred geography, "the Mother's heart and pulse" of their people. Restoration of the Black Hills, which today remains largely the public domain property of the federal government, is considered by Lakota traditionalists to be essential to the preservation of their heritage and identity. In 1923 the Sioux filed suit with the Court of Claims, arguing that their land had been taken in violation of the Fifth Amendment* to the Constitution.* The case remained in litigation in the Court of Claims, the federal courts, and the Indian Claims Commission for the next fifty-seven years. In 1979 the Court of Claims agreed that the U.S. government had violated the Fifth Amendment in taking Lakota land and awarded the Indians $17.5 million plus interest. One year later, in *United States v. Sioux Nation of Indians** (448 U.S. 371, 1980), the U.S. Supreme Court held for the Indians, rejecting the government's appeal of the Court of Claims decision.

However, the Sioux peoples were not about to accept a cash settlement. They wanted restoration of the Black Hills, not a monetary payment. Each of the eight participating Sioux tribes—Oglala, Rosebud, Cheyenne River, Standing Rock, Lower Brule, Nebraska Santee, Montana Fort Peck, and South Dakota Crow Creek—formally rejected the cash settlement. In 1986 several congressmen sponsored the Sioux Nation Black Hills Act, which would have restored more than 1.3 million acres to the Indians, but concerted opposition from the South Dakota delegation blocked passage. The controversy still rages today.

Suggested Reading: Edward Lazarus, *Black Hills, White Justice: The Sioux Nation versus the United States, 1775 to the Present*, 1991.

JAMES S. OLSON

BLACK KETTLE. The life story of Black Kettle, a Southern Cheyenne chief, is one of the classic Indian examples of violation of individual and corporate civil rights by the United States. Born around 1803, he grew up and came to prominence in his tribe before the arrival of American settlers on the southern Great Plains. By 1865, Black Kettle, along with the great majority of the Southern Cheyenne leaders, were known as peace chiefs.

In 1863, Black Kettle joined a delegation of plains chiefs that visited President Abraham Lincoln in Washington. However, the Civil War reached all regions of the country, including the southern plains. In April 1864 a rancher reported a raid by Cheyenne warriors who stole horses and cattle from his property. White retaliation followed, including an attack by Lieutenant George Eayre's militia on Black Kettle's camp in which Lean Bear was killed under a flag of truce by the whites, who were routed thereafter. Warfare spread into Colorado and Kansas through the summer and fall.

In the fall, Black Kettle represented six Cheyenne and Arapaho bands at the Camp Weld conference. He offered peace and, through a mistranslation, thought the whites had agreed, although Governor Evans of Colorado had extended no such offer. Acting on this misunderstood "assurance," Black Kettle moved his group to the Sand Creek reservation in southeastern Colorado for the winter. At dawn on November 29, 1864, Colonel J. M. Chivington and the First and Third Colorado Volunteers struck the sleeping encampment, over which fluttered Black Kettle's giant American flag and a white flag. The younger men were away hunting. Encircling the camp, the Volunteers entered firing. Some 200 of the 500-person band were massacred. Men were shot and castrated. Pregnant women were ripped open, and both mother and baby allowed to die. Children were shot or had their heads bashed. Black Kettle and his wife both survived, although she was struck by as many as twelve bullets. This massacre was popular in Colorado but created a storm of protest throughout much of the rest of the United States. The Congressional Joint Committee on the conduct of the war said that Chivington had "deliberately planned and executed a foul and dastardly massacre which would have disgraced the veriest savage among those who were the victims of his cruelty."

The Southern Cheyenne were kept moving, but Black Kettle and others agreed to the Little Arkansas Treaty, which moved them south of the Arkansas River along the Cimarron River. Two years later Black Kettle and the Southern Cheyenne and Arapahos agreed to the Medicine Lodge Treaty, which created a more formal reservation* in the area seized from the pro–Southern Cherokees in northwestern Indian territory.*

Black Kettle settled his people in the spring of 1868 along the Washita River on the western edge of the reservation. During the summer, renegade warriors raided and hunted off the reservation in Kansas. By November they had come back to the reservation, even into Black Kettle's camp. Knowing that the U.S. Army, under the leadership of General Philip Sheridan, was hunting those renegades in a winter campaign, Black Kettle made a quick trip south to Fort Cobb to ask protection of General William Hazen, who refused and sent him back to his own camp. A few hours later, in the early morning of November 27, 1868, Colonel George Custer's Seventh Cavalry struck from all sides of the camp. Black Kettle and his wife both managed to mount their horses but were shot and fell dead in the cold Washita River. In all, 103 Southern Cheyenne died and 53 were captured. Almost all of the 875-horse remuda was massacred also.

The United States had attacked Black Kettle's camp three times, and on the third try killed one of the leading peace chiefs on the southern plains.

Suggested Reading: Donald J. Berthrong, *The Southern Cheyennes*, 1963.

FRED S. ROLATER

BLACK MESA DEFENSE FUND. Many Indian traditionalists were at the forefront of the environmental movement* in the 1960s. Indian religious values often revolved around the land and the environment, and they frequently viewed technological and economic development as sacrilegious. Hopi and Navajo traditionalists in Arizona and New Mexico were especially concerned about the future of their ancient homeland in the high deserts. Desert environments are particularly fragile and very slow to recover from environmental damage. In 1969 these traditionalists organized the Black Mesa Defense Fund to lobby for an end to strip mining on reservation* land. Representatives from the fund appeared before the United Nations Conference on the Human Environment in 1972, creating enormous publicity against the project and successfully stalling it.

Suggested Reading: Marjane Ambler, *Breaking the Iron Bonds: Indian Control of Energy Development*, 1990; Hurst Hannum, *Autonomy, Self-Determination and Sovereignty: The Accommodation of Conflicting Rights*, 1990.

JAMES S. OLSON

BLUE LAKE. Blue Lake in northwestern New Mexico has become a symbol of Indian land claims and a rejection of the notion that cash settlements can make up for assaults on Indian culture. To the Taos Indians, it is an ancient holy place. They view it as a religious shrine, the source of life and a manifestation of the great spirit of the universe. Economically and spiritually, Blue Lake has been the center of their lives. But in 1906 the federal government incorporated Blue Lake and the surrounding 48,000 acres into the Kit Carson National Forest. Later the U.S. Forest Service opened the area to non-Indian hunters, fishermen, and campers. Taos Indian leaders began demanding return of the lake, and in 1965 the Indian Claims Commission* offered the tribe $10 million and 3,000 acres near the lake. Paul Bernal, a Taos leader, rejected the offer, telling the Indian Claims Commission, "My people will not sell our Blue Lake that is our church, for $10 million, and accept 3,000 acres, when we know that 50,000 acres is ours. We cannot sell what is sacred. It is not ours to sell." In 1970 President Richard M. Nixon came to support the Taos claim, and Congress passed the Taos Blue Lake Act, returning the lake and 48,000 acres to the tribe.

In 1996, however, Blue Lake and the Taos Indians were once again in the headlines. Although they had won the return of much of their land in 1970, the Taos people soon became concerned about the number of non-Indian vacation homes that were sprouting up near the reservation.* In order to generate the revenue needed to purchase neighboring land and get the non-Indians out, the tribe secured approval from the Department of the Interior in 1995 to open a gambling casino. The tribe purchased $10 million of nearby ranch land, made a down payment of $1 million, and took out a mortgage on the rest. But early in 1996, U.S. Attorney General John Kelly ordered the Taos Indians to shut down the casino because they did not have approval from the state of New Mexico to keep it open. Nine other New Mexico tribes were likewise ordered to close their casinos. The Taos Indians are concerned that if they lose gambling revenue, they will have to default on the mortgage and lose the land. The other tribes have similar concerns about land purchases and tribal services.

Closing ranks, the Indians refused to obey the order and filed suit in district court. They also approached the state legislature, asking for specific legislative authorization to continue operating; but non-Indian business owners in Santa Fe and Albuquerque oppose the casinos because they drain off tourists' discretionary spending. By the spring of 1996 the tribes affected by the decision were threatening to block Interstate highways 10, 20, and 25, disrupting transportation and commerce, if the casinos were shut down. The dispute remains in litigation late in 1996.

Suggested Reading: Vine Deloria Jr. and Clifford Lytle, *American Indians, American Justice*, 1983; *Houston Chronicle*, January 13, 1996; *New York Times*, February 11, 1996; James S. Olson and Raymond Wilson, *Native Americans in the Twentieth Century*, 1984.

JAMES S. OLSON

BOARD OF INDIAN COMMISSIONERS. In 1869, President Ulysses S. Grant established the Board of Indian Commissioners to supervise Indian programs within the Department of the Interior. The board was composed of private citizens appointed by the president. Over time, the board came to see its primary responsibility as the protection of reservation* Indians through relief, health, and education* programs, hoping to bring about the assimilation* of Indian peoples through economic improvement. Gradually the Board of Indian Commissioners became closely associated—too closely, in the minds of many critics—with the Bureau of Indian Affairs.* Early in the 1920s the Board of Indian Commissioners refused to speak out against the Bursum Bill,* which would have alienated Pueblo lands in northern New Mexico, and sided with the recommendations of the Bureau of Indian Affairs that certain Indian religious and tribal dance practices be banned. Critics charged the board with being an accomplice in the drive to destroy Indian culture. When John Collier* became commissioner of Indian affairs in 1933 and began to implement what became known as the Indian New Deal,* the Board of Indian Commissioners was doomed as an anachronism. The board ceased to function after 1933.

Suggested Reading: Henry Fritz, *The Movement for Indian Assimilation, 1860–1890*, 1963; Kenneth R. Philp, *John Collier's Crusade for Indian Reform, 1920–1954*, 1977.

JAMES S. OLSON

BOLDT DECISIONS. In 1974, Federal District Judge George Boldt presided over what may be one of the most important hunting and fishing rights* cases ever adjudicated. Presiding over *United States v. Washington*, Boldt ruled that recognized Indian tribes of the Pacific Northwest had the right to one-half of the allowable or harvestable off-reservation catch of salmon. Judge Boldt further ruled that the authority to regulate tribal fishing on and off the reservation* was reserved for the tribes. In addition, later phases of the original court case mandated that Washington State negotiate a co-management plan for all Washington State fisheries and negotiate the complicated environmental issues raised by the first phase of the case. When Washington refused, Boldt himself directed the state's efforts.

The impact of the Boldt Decisions has been dramatic. The acknowledgment that the recognized tribes were entitled to one-half of the allowable catch revitalized tribal fishing enterprises but had a negative effect on non-Indian fishermen in the state. As a result, the tribes that have exercised these rights have at times faced considerable and sometimes violent white backlash.

Perhaps the most important impact of the decisions has been the inclusion of the recognized tribes as equal partners with state, federal, and international organizations responsible for managing the catch. The tribes have taken this responsibility seriously and have devoted considerable resources to meeting their responsibilities. They have increased the number of fish raised at tribal hatcheries and have worked cooperatively to push for habitat improvements. In addition, they have been active litigants in the courts to both protect the salmon and its habitat and to make sure that they receive their share of the catch.

Suggested Reading: Fay G. Cohen, *Treaties on Trial: The Continuing Controversy over Northwest Indian Fishing Rights*, 1986; Donald L. Parman, *Indians and the American West in the Twentieth Century*, 1994; Charles F. Wilkinson, *American Indians, Time and the Law*, 1987.

JASON M. TETZLOFF

BONNIN, GERTRUDE SIMMONS. A leading campaigner for assimilation,* Gertrude Simmons was born as Aitkala-Sa, or Red Bird, on the Yankton Sioux agency in South Dakota on February 22, 1876. Her mother was full-blood Sioux, and her father was white. At the age of 8 she left the reservation* for White's Indiana Manual Labor Institute in Wabash, Indiana, a Quaker school. She excelled there and then earned an undergraduate degree at Earlham College. Simmons taught for two years at the Carlisle Indian School and then studied at the Boston Conservatory of Music, specializing in the violin. She took up writing there and in 1901 published her first book, *Old Indian Legends*. In 1902 she returned to South Dakota and married Raymond Bonnin, a Sioux who worked for the federal government. They moved to the Uintah and Ouray reservation in Utah, where she taught school again. After 1911, Gertrude went to work for the Society of American Indians,* where she campaigned for assimilation and for settlement of Indian claims against the federal government. She was elected secretary of the society in 1916 and moved to Washington, D.C. There she edited the society's journal, *American Indian Magazine*. When the Society of American Indians disintegrated in 1929, she founded the National Council of American Indians* and served as its president until her death in 1938.

Suggested Reading: Duane Champagne, ed., *The Native North American Almanac*, 1994.

JAMES S. OLSON

BRANCH OF ACKNOWLEDGEMENT AND RESEARCH. See **FEDERAL ACKNOWLEDGEMENT PROJECT.**

BRENDALE v. CONFEDERATED TRIBES AND BANDS OF THE YAKIMA INDIAN NATION (1989). Establishing the limits of tribal political authority has been an ongoing, and evolving, issue in the history of Indian law. The authority of tribal governments over non-Indians and non-Indian property on the reservations has been especially controversial. One such case was *Brendale v. Confederated Tribes and Bands of the Yakima Indian Nation*. The issue involved whether the Yakima Nation could pass zoning ordinances for an area of the reservation* inhabited primarily by non-Indians. Certain portions of the reservation consisted of more than 80 percent non-Indians. The Yakimas wanted the authority to pass such ordinances. The Supreme Court decided the case in 1989, holding that the Yakimas could not zone the land where non-Indians predominated unless their activities threatened the tribe's political integrity, health, or economic security. Indian activists considered the decision a backward step in the movement for self-determination.*

Suggested Reading: Stephan L. Pevar, *The Rights of Indians and Tribes: The Basic ACLU Guide to Indian and Tribal Rights*, 1992.

                                                                    JAMES S. OLSON

BRITISH COLONIAL POLICY. Great Britain did not inaugurate a general Indian policy for the North American colonies until 1763. Until that time, British administrators had permitted each colony the freedom to develop and carry out its own Indian policy. During time of war, Great Britain supplied the colonies with arms and ammunition to fight Indian or European enemies. British armies might come to the English colonial mainland to fight on behalf of the colonies during wartime, but generally the English government allowed colonial governments to deal with natives on their own.

Colonial governments looked out for their own interests in their pursuit of Indian policy, often to the detriment of their colonial neighbors. Colonial governments licensed traders and sent negotiators to treat with Indians in the over one and one-half centuries of British settlement on the mainland. Great Britain's administrators desired unified policy regarding Indian peoples; the colonial governments worked in their own interests. The most important element of Indian policy was trade—the exchange of furs, hides, and other Indian products for inexpensive British trade goods such as cloth, coats, iron tools and utensils, alcohol, and guns. Colonial governments wanted to advance their own trade interests at the expense of their neighbors, resulting in confusion among Indian peoples.

Diplomacy was another important area in which colonial governments worked at cross purposes with each other. Confusion over trade and diplomacy frequently stirred Indian hostility and aggression, as leaders of one Indian faction dealt with one colonial government and leaders of another with a second colonial government, each government giving the natives opposing goals. Colonies did occasionally unite—as in the New England Confederation of 1644, which sought to unify New England Indian policy during the rest of the seventeenth century. But the conflicting and competing interests of individual New England colonies frequently prevented the Confederation from carrying out its goals. England sometimes made noises about unifying Indian policy during the seventeenth and early eighteenth centuries, but it was not until the French and Indian War* that a concerted effort was made.

That war began in the Ohio River Valley in 1754 and then spread to the rest of the world. British efforts at presenting a united front were frustrated during the first four years of warfare by colonial jealousies and infighting. The Albany Congress of 1754, called by British officials, sought to forge a colonial union to make common Indian policy. Failure of the Albany Plan of Union to stir any interest among the colonies reminded British officials of the lack of common purpose among colonial governments. Each colonial government regarded its neighbors as simply more competition for English rewards.

In 1755 Edmond Atkin, an Indian trader, a member of South Carolina's council, and a businessman in that colony, drafted a report calling for creation of a common Indian policy. He pointed out the benefits of Indian trade and alliance, especially the use of Indians as barriers to other European peoples' expansion. He suggested that the time had come to end the competitive free-for-all in Indian policy formation that had gone on for a century and a half. He argued that French centralization of Indian policy gave the French clear superiority over the English in trade and diplomacy. He pointed out that the French knew all too well that the English had permitted the colonies to direct Indian affairs on their own, creating great confusion and ill will among Indian peoples.

In 1755 the British government announced the creation of the Indian superintendency system, with Sir William Johnson as superintendent of the Northern Department (the region north of the Ohio River and west of the Appalachian Mountains) and Atkin as superintendent of the Southern Department (the region south of the Ohio and west of the Appalachians). By 1762, John Stuart had replaced Atkin in the Southern Department. Each superintendent had agents (called commissaries) who lived with the separate tribes, representing the Crown and superintendent, not an individual colony.

The end of the French and Indian War in 1763 brought Great Britain an enormous accretion of territory, from the Appalachians westward to the Mississippi River and all of modern-day Canada. In 1763 the British government assumed control of all Indian relations, thereby completing its transformation of Indian policy. The British government considered each tribe a separate, independent nation and treated it accordingly. Indian citizens were seen as subjects of their respective tribal law, not British or colonial law. By this principle, the British government rejected assimilation* and acculturation of Indian peoples.

The British government sought to separate Indian and white peoples through the Proclamation Line of 1763, but British policy did not evolve much further as the American Revolution* and independence approached in the decade after 1765.

Suggested Reading: George Louis Beer, *British Colonial Policy, 1754–1765*, 1931; Arrell Morgan Gibson, *The American Indian: Prehistory to the Present*, 1980; Wilbur R. Jacobs, *Indians of the Southern Colonial Frontier: The Edmond Atkin Report and Plan of 1755*, 1954.

TIMOTHY MORGAN

BUREAU OF INDIAN AFFAIRS. In 1786 the Continental Congress ordered the creation of an Indian Department within the War Department. The newly created U.S. Congress followed the same practice in 1789 when it authorized a War Department and assigned administration of Indian affairs to the secretary of war. Responsibilities of the Indian Department steadily grew as the United States acquired territory, and problems of inadequate staff and funding soon arose. In 1824 the Bureau of Indian Affairs (BIA) was created as a separate branch of the War Department, and Congress gave the new branch legal status in 1834. The commissioner of Indian affairs, who headed the BIA, oversaw a wide range of employees. (By the 1870s these included reservation agents, school superintendents, clerks, inspectors, doctors, field nurses, teachers, farmers, and Indian police.) The commissioner reported annually to the secretary of the Interior, supplying policy recommendations as well as updates from each of the reservation agents. The Bureau steadily assumed more control over Indians' lives.

However, tension between the military and civil responsibilities of the BIA led Congress to transfer authority over Indians to the new Department of the Interior in 1849. The reassignment did not eliminate competition over control of Indian affairs, and several BIA commissioners called for a return to the War Department. The United States pursued both military and civil programs with regard to Indians, fighting some of its most famous wars during the tenure of the "Peace Policy,"* which placed reservations* in the hands of Christian missionaries. But the federal government recognized the fact that Indian lands were by then internal to the United States and increasingly regarded tribes as "domestic, dependent nations" rather than foreign powers. By the 1880s the civil program finally prevailed.

The BIA tried twice to abolish itself, through the assimilation* policy of the 1880s and the termination* policy of the 1950s. On both occasions the BIA pursued policies designed to render Indians self-supporting, which would ultimately eliminate federal expenditures for Indian affairs. Both strategies failed, creating more bureaucracy than they dissolved.

Following the failures of the assimilation policy the BIA came under severe attack, which culminated in the 1928 Meriam Report* critiquing every aspect of Indian administration. Congress subsequently passed the Indian Reorganization Act* of 1934; this legislation placed more authority in the hands of tribal governments, which were restructured under its guidelines. Americans, both Indian and non-Indian, continue to debate whether the BIA should exist, but ongoing treaty obligations seem to require a federal presence in Indian affairs.

After the termination debacle of the 1950s and 1960s, the focus of the BIA began to change. In 1966 Robert Bennett,* an Oneida Indian, was appointed commissioner of Indian affairs, a move that established the precedent of Indians heading the agency. Between 1969 and 1980 the percentage of BIA employees who were Indians increased from 48 to 78 percent. The Indian Self-Determination and Education Act of 1975 gave Indian tribes the power to contract out BIA services. The legislation gave the tribes much greater control over those programs. Although today the BIA remains committed to self-determination,* budget cuts and the inherent tension between the BIA's dual missions of promoting self-determination while protecting the Indian trust* status have made it only a limited success.

Suggested Reading: Curtis E. Jackson and Marcia J. Galli, *A History of the Bureau of Indian Affairs and Its Activities among Indians*, 1977; Robert M. Kvasnicka and Herman J. Viola, eds., *The Commissioners of Indian Affairs, 1824–1977*, 1979; Theodore W. Taylor, *The Bureau of Indian Affairs*, 1984.

EMILY GREENWALD

BURKE ACT OF 1906. Framed by South Dakota congressman Charles Burke, this legislation declared Native Americans competent to dispose of their own affairs provided that any Indian wishing to do so first acquired the approval of the Department of the Interior. After reviewing the petition of each Indian applicant on an individual case-by-case basis, the secretary of the interior was empowered to grant permission for the sale of Indian land. Thus the act of 1906 effectively removed the limited safeguards emplaced by the foregoing 25-year trust period for allotted land as prescribed in the Dawes Act* of 1887. Although occasional allowances were made to extend the trust period beyond 25 years, the congressional measure linked each Indian's receipt of federal citizenship* to the prior acquisition of a fee simple title.* Possession of said title automatically qualified American Indians to divest themselves of their allotted tracts of land without government consent.

Although mining, timber, ranching, and agricultural interests viewed the Burke Act as an instrument by which the Indians could be further dispossessed, liberal reformers hoped the permission clause within the new law would slow the wholesale liquidation of Indian land that many expected to occur on the expiration of the 25-year trust period in 1912. However, in actual practice the Burke Act of 1906 accelerated the dizzying pace of despoliation and alienation of Native American land that had long since been under way.

Suggested Reading: James S. Olson and Raymond Wilson, *Native Americans in the Twentieth Century*, 1984; Francis Paul Prucha, *The Great Father*, Vol. 2, 1984.

MARK BAXTER

BURSUM BILL. With the Treaty of Guadalupe Hidalgo* in 1848, the Pueblo Indians of New Mexico became part of the United States of America. As stipulated in the treaty, the Pueblos chose to renounce their Mexican citizenship for American citizenship.* But the method of entry into the United States of the Pueblos caused confusion for the U.S. government. No treaties had been signed with the Pueblos, as they had been treated like all other Mexican citizens under the Treaty of Guadalupe Hidalgo. As such, the Pueblos had never been treated as Indians by the United States.

If the Pueblo Indians now were citizens and had rights that were equal to those of all other Americans, then they should have the right to dispose of their property as they saw fit. In *United States v. Joseph** (1876), the U.S. Supreme Court ruled that the Pueblos were unique and did indeed have the same rights as all other citizens of New Mexico. Additionally, the Court declared the Pueblos to be more advanced than all other Indian nations and not in need of supervision. This ruling was overturned in 1913 by *United States v. Sandoval*,* in which the Supreme Court decided that the Pueblos were "inferior" like all other Indians in the United States. As such, the Pueblos were to be treated like the other Indian nations and put under congressional control.

Senator Holm O. Bursum of New Mexico introduced a bill into the U.S. Senate in 1922 that would ease the ability of whites to gain title to Pueblo lands. The Bursum Bill would restrict the rights of the Pueblos to fish at will and to control their property without any federal influence. The administration of President Warren Harding supported the bill, but it faced strong opposition from New Mexican Indian associations and national women's groups. The Bursum Bill was defeated and later replaced by the Pueblo Land Act of 1924.

Suggested Reading: Wilcomb E. Washburn, *Red Man's Land, White Man's Law*, 1971; John R. Wunder, *"Retained by The People": A History of American Indians and the Bill of Rights*, 1994.

JAMES S. OLSON

C

CABAZON BAND OF MISSION INDIANS v. CALIFORNIA (1987). The *Cabazon Band of Mission Indians v. California* case revolved around Indian gambling. The state of California prohibited the Mission Indians from establishing gaming operations on the Cabazon and Morongo reservations,* arguing that such operations violated federal Public Law 280, the termination law that gave California criminal jurisdiction in Indian country,* as well as the Organized Crime Control Act of 1970, which rendered violations of state gambling laws federal offenses. The Mission Indians sued in the federal courts, and in 1987 the Supreme Court decided in favor of the Indians, forbidding the state of California from regulating bingo and gambling on the reservations.

Suggested Reading: Duane Champagne, ed., *Chronology of Native North American History*, 1994.

JAMES S. OLSON

CADDO TRIBE OF OKLAHOMA, ET AL. v. UNITED STATES (1961). Under the Indian Claims Commission Act of 1946, the Caddo Indians of Oklahoma sued for compensation for the loss of their ancestral lands in Texas. In 1835 the Caddos had signed a treaty with the United States surrendering title to all of their lands east of the border between the United States and Mexico. Early in 1836, on the eve of the Texas Revolution, the Caddos left Louisiana and crossed over into Texas, which at the time was Mexican territory. Between 1836 and 1845 the Republic of Texas refused to recognize any Caddo right of occupancy. Considerable white violence against the Caddos took place during the 1850s, and in 1859 the Caddos were sent to a reservation* in Oklahoma. In 1961, however, the Indian Claims Commission* denied their claim, arguing that the

Caddos had no title to the land or right of occupancy because the Republic of Texas, before its annexation in 1845 by the United States, had never recognized such right or title. The United States, therefore, did not inherit any obligation to compensate the Indians. But in 1968, one year after the Court of Claims decision in *Lipan Apache Tribe, etc., Mescalero Apache Tribe, etc., and the Apache Tribe of the Mescalero Reservation, etc. v. the United States,** the Commission changed its 1961 decision in favor of the Caddos.

Suggested Reading: Russel Lawrence Barsh and James Youngblood Henderson, *The Road: Indian Tribes and Political Liberty*, 1980; Vine Deloria Jr. and Clifford M. Lytle, *American Indians, American Justice*, 1983; H. Barry Holt and Gary Forrester, *Digest of American Indian Law: Cases and Chronology*, 1990; Stephen L. Pevar, *The Rights of Indians and Tribes: The Basic ACLU Guide to Indian and Tribal Rights*, 1992; Wilcomb E. Washburn, *Red Man's Land, White Man's Law*, 1971; Charles F. Wilkinson, *American Indians, Time and the Law*, 1987; John R. Wunder, *"Retained by The People": A History of American Indians and the Bill of Rights*, 1994.

JAMES S. OLSON

CAREY ACT OF 1894. The Carey Act, passed by Congress on March 3, 1894, was part of the budding conservation movement in the United States. For years, John Wesley Powell of the U.S. Geological Survey had called for the preservation of American grasslands. In the 1890s Frederick Haynes Newell demanded similar attention to irrigation and reclamation. The Carey Act was the modest beginning of federal conservation programs. It authorized the federal government to grant up to one million acres of public land to states in arid regions. The states would then develop the irrigation potential of the land through private enterprise. The land was to be sold for 50 cents an acre and the water rights for $30 to $40 an acre, to be paid in ten annual installments. The states were to use the proceeds to finance subsequent irrigation and reclamation projects. The impact of the Carey Act on Indian people was to increase the pressures of white settlement and the alienation of Native American property.

Suggested Reading: B. H. Hibbard, *A History of Public Land Policies*, 1924.

JAMES S. OLSON

CENTRAL MACHINERY CO. v. ARIZONA STATE TAX COMMISSION (1980). The case of *Central Machinery Co. v. Arizona State Tax Commission* involved the issue of state taxing jurisdiction over federal Indian reservations.* The Central Machinery Company sold farm equipment on several Arizona reservations and claimed an exemption from the state gross proceeds tax. The state of Arizona argued that the company was liable for those taxes because it did not maintain an office on the reservations and had not licensed itself to do business under required Indian commercial statutes. However, the Supreme Court agreed with the company, arguing that business done in Indian country* between Indians and non-Indian interests was subject only to federal tax jurisdiction.

Suggested Reading: Russel Lawrence Barsh and James Youngblood Henderson, *The Road: Indian Tribes and Political Liberty*, 1980; H. Barry Holt and Gary Forrester, *Digest of American Indian Law: Cases and Chronology*, 1990; Stephen L. Pevar, *The Rights of Indians and Tribes: The Basic ACLU Guide to Indian and Tribal Rights*, 1992; Charles F. Wilkinson, *American Indians, Time and the Law*, 1987; John R. Wunder, *"Retained by The People": A History of American Indians and the Bill of Rights*, 1994.

JAMES S. OLSON

CHEROKEE NATION v. STATE OF GEORGIA (1831).

In *Cherokee Nation v. State of Georgia* of 1831, the Cherokee nation sued the state of Georgia to prevent it from enforcing state laws that the Cherokee felt threatened their people and their sovereignty.* Georgia had executed a Cherokee for murder while his appeal was still before the U.S. Supreme Court. The Cherokees sued Georgia to force its representatives to appear at a hearing before the Supreme Court.

Chief Justice John Marshall* made it clear that his sympathies were with the Cherokees, but he ruled that the U.S. Supreme Court did not have original jurisdiction over the case. The Supreme Court could hear cases involving foreign nations and American states, but Marshall ruled that Indian nations were not truly foreign nations. As such, the Cherokees could not begin a suit against the state of Georgia in the U.S. Supreme Court. Marshall did admit that the Cherokee were a unique nation, but their dependency on the United States prevented them from being an actual foreign nation as meant by the U.S. Constitution.*

The dissenting opinions in this case showed the controversial nature of the issue before the Court. How should Indian nations be treated within the United States? Justice Baldwin argued that the Cherokees were not a nation at all and should not be allowed to be plaintiffs in the Supreme Court. Baldwin was rejecting Marshall's suggestion that the Cherokees, although not a foreign nation, were a unique nation. Justice Thompson argued that a study of Georgia statutes clearly showed that Georgia treated the Cherokee nation as a foreign state.

Suggested Reading: Monroe E. Price, *Law and the American Indian: Readings, Notes and Cases*, 1973; John R. Wunder, *"Retained by The People": A History of American Indians and the Bill of Rights*, 1994.

DARREN PIERSON

CHOATE v. TRAPP **(1911).** In 1910 Congress passed the so-called Omnibus Act, which tried to rationalize all the amendments to the Dawes Act* since 1887. The hopes of assimilationists were high in 1910 that the federal government would be able to get out of the "Indian business" as soon as assimilation* became complete. The state of Oklahoma decided to jump the gun and tax the allotments* of the Choctaw and Chickasaw Indians. The Indians appealed the taxation plans through the federal court system, and in 1911 the Supreme Court rendered its decision in *Choate v. Trapp*. Claiming that the Indians were still wards of the federal government, the Supreme Court denied Oklahoma's taxing authority over allotted land.

Suggested Reading: Russel Lawrence Barsh and James Youngblood Henderson, *The Road: Indian Tribes and Political Liberty*, 1980; H. Barry Holt and Gary Forrester, *Digest of American Indian Law: Cases and Chronology*, 1990; Stephen L. Pevar, *The Rights of Indians and Tribes: The Basic ACLU Guide to Indian and Tribal Rights*, 1992; Charles F. Wilkinson, *American Indians, Time and the Law*, 1987; John R. Wunder, *"Retained by The People": A History of American Indians and the Bill of Rights*, 1994.

JAMES S. OLSON

CITIZENSHIP. Until it was finally granted in the Snyder Act* of 1924, the question of extending U.S. citizenship to American Indians stirred up decades of controversy. Liberal reformers in the late nineteenth and early twentieth centuries supported citizenship because they felt the Indians deserved it under the Fourteenth Amendment* by virtue of their birth in the United States. Those who promoted assimilation* often demanded the extension of citizenship to American Indians as the first step in integrating them into the larger body politic. Presumably the granting of citizenship would simultaneously end the special legal status, or trust* relationship, enjoyed by many tribes as wards of the federal government. With citizenship would also come legal responsibility; Indians would be subject to the same laws and taxes as other citizens of the United States. Some whites opposed citizenship because they believed American Indians were not ready for such responsibilities. Racists opposed citizenship because they were convinced that Indians were savages. Many Native Americans, especially full-bloods, often fought citizenship because they felt it implied the loss of tribal sovereignty.*

The drive for citizenship began indirectly in 1871, when Congress formally ended the sovereignty of individual Indian tribes. Until 1871 Congress had dealt with Indian tribes as sovereign nations, negotiating treaties with them and sending ambassadors and emissaries rather than legislating for them. The end of sovereignty, however, placed individual Indians in a unique legal position. By definition, they were not citizens in a nation because their tribe no longer enjoyed sovereign status; but at the same time they were not citizens of the United States either. Liberal reformers and assimilationists began promoting U.S. citizenship for Indians as a way of resolving that legal limbo as well as bringing about an integration of Indians into the larger legal system—a first step toward assimilation. In 1881, Congress opted to take a gradual approach to the issue.

The case of John Elk jump-started the drive for assimilation. Election officials in Omaha, Nebraska, denied Elk, an English-speaking Indian, the right to vote in municipal elections on the grounds that he was not a U.S. citizen. In 1884 the U.S. Supreme Court upheld the Omaha decision, arguing that Elk had neither been born under U.S. jurisdiction nor naturalized by an act of Congress. Liberal reformers were outraged by the decision and launched a campaign for the granting of citizenship. They merged the citizenship issue with the allotment* program when Congress passed the Dawes Act* in 1887. Each Indian who took an allotment of land under the law also received U.S. citizenship and became subject to the laws of the state in which he or she resided. By 1889, only 3,349 Native Americans had taken allotments and become U.S. citizens. By 1900 that number had jumped to 53,168. In 1901, Congress awarded citizenship to the 101,506 Indians living in the Indian Territory.* More than half of all Native Americans had become U.S. citizens by 1905.

After World War I, support for Indian citizenship grew dramatically. Senator Homer Snyder of New York was a powerful advocate of citizenship, which, he believed, would integrate Native Americans into the larger society. In 1919 he decided that all Native Americans who had served in the U.S. military during World War I should be entitled to citizenship. The logic was simple: those who fight for their country and risk their lives should be eligible for all the rights afforded to citizens. Snyder drafted the Indian Veteran Citizenship Act,* and Congress passed the measure in 1919. All Indian veterans of World War I who applied for citizenship would receive it. Five years later, Snyder sponsored the legislation (Snyder Act) that finally awarded U.S. citizenship to all American Indians.

Suggested Reading: Arrell Morgan Gibson, *Between Two Worlds*, 1986; R. Alton Lee, "Indian Citizenship and the Fourteenth Amendment," *South Dakota History* 4 (Spring 1974); James S. Olson and Raymond Wilson, *Native Americans in the Twentieth Century*, 1984; Gary C. Stein, "The Indian Citizenship Act of 1924," *New Mexico Historical Review* 47 (July 1972); John R. Wunder, *"Retained by The People": A History of American Indians and the Bill of Rights*, 1994.

JAMES S. OLSON

CIVIL RIGHTS ACT OF 1964. The Civil Rights Act of 1964, the foundation of President Lyndon B. Johnson's Great Society program, prohibited discrimination on the basis of race, religion, color, national origin, and sex in employment, education, and access to public facilities. However, the law provided an exemption to American Indian tribes. Back in 1935 during the heyday of the Indian New Deal,* the federal government had allowed the Bureau of Indian Affairs* to give preferential employment treatment to Indians, and in *Morton v. Mancari** (1974) the Supreme Court had upheld the practice. Of course, the civil rights movement had specifically campaigned against preferential treatment because state and local governments in the South, as well as the federal government for decades, had hired only whites. But Indian tribal governments did not want to be forced to establish racially blind hiring policies, since they wanted to give as many jobs as possible to their own members. To accommodate their wishes, Congress exempted them from those provisions of the Civil Rights Act of 1964.

Suggested Reading: William C. Canby Jr., *American Indian Law in a Nutshell*, 1988; Stephen L. Pevar, *The Rights of Indians and Tribes: The Basic ACLU Guide to Indian and Tribal Rights*, 1992.

JAMES S. OLSON

CIVIL WAR. The outbreak of the Civil War had a dramatic effect on Native Americans and on Indian-white relations in the United States. After the firing on Fort Sumter in the spring of 1861, the United States of America and the Confederate States of America began mobilizing for the conflict. Most regular army units were withdrawn from frontier forts in the western territories and relocated to battle areas in the East. The withdrawal of federal troops appeared to many Indians to be an opportunity to repossess territory that had been lost in the past. In 1862, for example, the Santee Sioux rebelled in Minnesota, and in 1864 a number of Plains tribes revolted. Apache and Navajo rebellions occurred in the Southwest.

To fill the military void, state governments in the North and the South began organizing local militia units to deal with Native Americans.

During the Civil War the westward movement continued, particularly in the Dakotas and the intermountain West. The arrival of settlers and miners triggered new hostilities with local Indian tribes, and the recently organized volunteer forces had to deal with the conflicts. Native to the West and less professional than the regular army units, the volunteer regiments had little sympathy for the Indians and often proved to be unnecessarily violent in their military control activities. Events like the Sand Creek* massacre of 1864, in which Colorado volunteer forces murdered several hundred Cheyenne women and children, became common. In most cases, local authorities used the Indian rebellions as justification for seizing even more Indian land.

As they had done in previous conflicts on the North American continent since the seventeenth century, Indians were forced to choose sides during the Civil War. Elements of the Five Civilized tribes—Cherokees, Choctaws, Chickasaws, Creeks, and Seminoles—in the Indian Territory* sided with the Confederacy. When the Union triumphed, charges of "disloyalty" and "treason" were leveled against the Five Civilized tribes and were used to justify further alienations of tribal land in the Indian territory.

Suggested Reading: M. Thomas Bailey, *Reconstruction in Indian Territory: A Story of Avarice, Discrimination and Opportunism*, 1972; H. Craig Miner and William E. Unrau, *The End of Indian Kansas: A Study of Cultural Revolution, 1854–1871*, 1978; Loring Benson Priest, *Uncle Sam's Stepchildren: The Reformation of United States Indian Policy, 1865–1887*, 1942; Francis Paul Prucha, *American Indian Policy in Crisis: Christian Reformers and the Indian, 1865–1900*, 1976.

JAMES S. OLSON

CIVILIZATION FUND. A law that provided for the civilization of Indian tribes living in proximity to frontier settlements was enacted on March 3, 1819. Later called the Civilization Fund, this act appropriated $10,000 to be used at the president's discretion to employ people of good character to teach the Indians agriculture and to teach their children reading, writing, and arithmetic. Rather than use a portion of the money to create a new bureau, President James Monroe and Secretary of War James Calhoun decided it would be more efficacious to spend the appropriation through those agencies already in the field engaged in teaching the Indians.

In 1824 the House Committee on Indian Affairs noted that there were then twenty-one Indian schools in existence, only three of those being extant prior to establishment of the fund. Missionary societies extended the government's largesse by adding their own money to the pool. Although there were detractors to the policy, none took a position on the apparent violation of the First Amendment's Establishment Clause prohibiting such intermingling of public and parochial monies. This may have been because the program continued to be, at least, statistically successful. By November 1824 there were thirty-two schools in operation, involving 916 Indian children. The number of schools and the population of Indian children attending them continued to rise, which encouraged the missions to proffer more of their funds.

However, even though attendance statistics might indicate that the program was an overwhelming success, these numbers represented a small sample in relation to the Indian population that the fund sought to educate. Conversions in such small numbers could have no appreciable effect on the tribes. Those Indians who completed the course of study often returned to traditional ways of living. In addition to the Civilization Fund, the cause of Indian education* was furthered by special treaty provisions with various tribes. Treaties with the Chippewas, Potawatomis, Winnebagos, Menominees, Kickapoos, Creeks, and Cherokees all provided for education.

Suggested Reading: Francis Paul Prucha, *The Great Father: The United States Government and the American Indians*, 1984.

PHILIP HUCKINS

COLLIER, JOHN. Commissioner of Indian affairs from 1933 to 1945, John Collier was the father of the "Indian New Deal."* Born in Atlanta, Georgia, on May 4, 1884, Collier was the fourth child in a family of seven children. His father, a baker and politician, was instrumental in shaping Collier's belief that only through cooperative, communal efforts could social ills be reformed. Although he never received a formal degree, Collier was well educated, studying at Columbia University and at the Collège de France. He became secretary of the People's Institute in New York City in 1907, where he worked on behalf of immigrants and came to the conclusion that rejecting one's heritage was not necessary to the process of Americanization.

Collier resigned from the People's Institute in 1919 after federal support for the program evaporated, and he became director of adult education in California. But the state legislature eliminated the position in 1920, fearing that Collier's approach was too "bolshevik." Mabel Dodge, a friend of Collier's from New York, learned of his misfortune and invited him to Taos, New Mexico, where he viewed firsthand the problems confronting the Pueblo Indians. After living among them for several months, Collier realized that these people still maintained a sense of unity—a community spirit—in spite of generations of attacks on their culture. Collier saw them as a symbol of his philosophy. He had discovered his "Red Atlantis."

Convinced that he could help the American Indians, Collier became research agent for the Indian Welfare Committee of the General Federation of Women's Clubs in 1922. There he gained national attention in blocking the Bursum Bill,* which threatened Spanish land grants to the Pueblo Indians. In 1923 he organized and became executive director of the American Indian Defense Association,* a group that called for termination of the Dawes Act,* preservation of Indian cultures, and certain guarantees of political and economic rights for all Native Americans. For the next ten years Collier continued his efforts to help Indian people. In April 1933 he became commissioner of Indian affairs, a position he held until 1945.

As Indian commissioner, Collier promised Indian America a "New Deal." For example, he secured enactment of the Pueblo Relief Bill to give compensation to the Pueblo Indians for land lost to non-Indian settlers, channeled millions of dollars from New Deal relief agencies to help destitute Indians, and canceled Indian debts to the federal government for irrigation projects and highways. Collier's "Indian New Deal" further resulted in passage of the Johnson-O'Malley Act* of 1934, which gave the federal government the power to make contracts with states to provide for Indian educational, medical, and social welfare services. Also in 1934, the cornerstone of the "Indian New Deal" was passed in the form of the Indian Reorganization Act.* Although it was not as comprehensive as Collier envisioned, this measure ended the policy of land allotments* in severalty; restored surplus land to tribes; permitted voluntary exchanges of restricted trust land for tribal corporation shares; and provided for the drafting of tribal constitutions and organization of tribal governments, creation of tribal corporations, and financial aid for Indian students. Indians also received preferential treatment in securing jobs with the Bureau of Indian Affairs.* Finally, in 1935 the Indian Arts and Crafts Board* was created to encourage and improve Indian-made products and protect them by a government trademark.

By 1939 Collier's "Indian New Deal" was besieged by financial cuts and congressional critics who saw the programs as impediments to assimilation.* And with the advent of World War II, attention was shifted from domestic reforms to foreign affairs. Collier realized his growing ineffectiveness and tendered his resignation in February 1945. After his resignation he taught at the City College of New York and at Knox College. John Collier died on May 8, 1968, in Talpa, New Mexico.

Suggested Reading: John Collier, *From Every Zenith: A Memoir and Some Essays on Life and Thought*, 1963; Lawrence C. Kelly, *The Assault on Assimilation: John Collier and the Origins of Indian Policy Reform*, 1983; Kenneth R. Philp, *John Collier's Crusade for Indian Reform, 1920–1954*, 1977.

RAYMOND WILSON

COLLIFLOWER v. GARLAND. See **MADELINE COLLIFLOWER v. JOHN GARLAND, SHERIFF OF COUNTY OF BLAINE, MONTANA (1965).**

COLORADO RIVER WATER CONSERVATION DISTRICT v. UNITED STATES (1976). In the *Colorado River Water Conservation District v. United States* case of 1976, the U.S. Supreme Court rendered a decision that had a major impact on Indian water rights.* Also known as the Akin case, the decision reversed the long-standing Indian immunity from state law. For decades the courts had recognized only federal jurisdiction over Indian water rights, a judicial policy that protected Indian rights but made comprehensive water planning by state authorities in the West very difficult. Non-Indian economic interests in most western states wanted to scuttle federal control and turn Indian water resources over to state jurisdiction, where white majorities could dictate policy.

The Akin case made that possible. The Court ruled that all reserved* water rights, including those of American Indians, could be adjudicated in state courts as long as the state had already developed a carefully conceived, comprehensive plan for water allocation and use. Westerners hailed the decision, but the Bureau of Indian Affairs* protested it bitterly. Eventually, however, state interest groups prevailed, especially when the Supreme Court rendered similar decisions in *Arizona et al. v. San Carlos Apache Tribe** and *Montana et al. v. Northern Cheyenne Tribe of the Northern Cheyenne Reservation* in 1983.

Suggested Reading: Lloyd Burton, *American Indian Water Rights and the Limits of the Law*, 1993; Daniel McCool, *Command of the Waters: Iron Triangles, Federal Water Development, and Indian Water*, 1987.

JAMES S. OLSON

COLUMBIA RIVER INTER-TRIBAL FISH COMMISSION. The Columbia River Inter-Tribal Fish Commission was established in 1977. Because the construction of dozens of hydroelectric dams along the Columbia River in the 1930s, 1940s, and 1950s had covered with water a number of traditional tribal salmon fishing sites, several groups of American Indians sued in the federal courts, arguing that their treaty rights to be able to fish at "usual and accustomed places" had been compromised by dam construction. A series of federal court decisions in the 1960s—*United States v. Oregon,** *Sohappy v. Smith*, and *United States v. Washington I and II*—upheld Indian fishing rights,* especially their jurisdictional control over traditional fishing sites.

In 1977 the Columbia River Inter-Tribal Fish Commission was established by the Confederated Tribes of the Umatilla Reservation in Oregon, the Confederated Tribes of the Warm Springs Reservation in Oregon, the Confederated Tribes and Bands of the Yakima Nation in Washington, and the Nez Percé in Idaho. The commission's objective was to revitalize the salmon and steelhead resources of the region. In 1980 the commission helped promote passage of the Northwest Electric Power and Conservation Act, a piece of federal legislation that recognized fish conservation as an objective equal in significance to power generation. The commission has also focused on ending water pollution, expanding the number and size of wilderness areas, and improving logging techniques. In addition, the commission lobbies at the state and federal level for Indian fishing rights.

Suggested Reading: Lloyd Burton, *American Indian Water Rights and the Limits of the Law*, 1993; Armand S. La Potin, *Native American Voluntary Organizations*, 1986; Daniel McCool, *Command of the Waters: Iron Triangles, Federal Water Development, and Indian Water*, 1987.

JAMES S. OLSON

COMMISSION ON THE RIGHTS, LIBERTIES, AND RESPONSIBILITIES OF THE AMERICAN INDIAN. During the 1950s federal Indian policy, which was committed to termination* and relocation,* inspired bitter opposition from American Indian tribes. The termination and relocation policies were simply the most recent attempt by assimilationists* to integrate Indians into the larger society. Fearing the loss of their culture and identity, most Indians protested the two policies and demanded self-determination.* In March 1957, when the controversy over termination was at its peak, the Fund for the Republic, a progressive philanthropic organization, decided to establish the Commission on the Rights, Liber-

ties, and Responsibilities of the American Indian to examine the controversy and make recommendations.

Composed of Indian and non-Indian historians, anthropologists, and
government officials, the commission spent nine years studying the plight
of American Indians before issuing its final report in 1966. Instead of
shedding new light on the challenges facing American Indians, the commission's report proved once again the cultural and political impasse that
had developed in the United States over Indian rights. The report paid
lip service to the idea of self-determination by insisting that Indian cultural pride should be preserved and that programs should not be imposed on them by outside authorities without their consent. But at the
same time the report also employed typical assimilationist rhetoric, calling on Indian people to become "self-respecting and useful American
citizen[s]" and to "participate in modern civilization," a practice certain
to bring about the loss of their cultural heritage.

Suggested Reading: William A. Brophy and Sophie D. Aberle, *The Indian,
America's Unfinished Business: Report of the Commission on the Rights, Liberties
and Responsibilities of the American Indian*, 1966.

JAMES S. OLSON

COMMITTEE OF ONE HUNDRED. The Committee of One Hundred was
established in 1923 to reform Indian policy. Failure of the allotment*
program, along with controversy over the Bursum Bill,* brought about a
coalition of Native American and white reformers. Included among the
group were such Indian leaders as Arthur C. Parker,* Charles Eastman,*
and Henry Roe Cloud; political leaders such as Bernard Baruch and William Jennings Bryan; anthropologists Clark Wissler and Alfred Koreber;
and Indian rights leaders John Collier* and Matthew K. Sniffen. Arthur
Parker chaired the group. The committee called for improvements in Indian education,* increased scholarships for Indian students, preservation
of Indian mineral rights on Indian land, and an end to prohibitions on
Indian dances and ceremonies on reservations. Although the committee's
impact was limited, it did contribute to the atmosphere of reform that
eventually helped produce the Indian New Deal* in the 1930s.

Suggested Reading: Armand S. La Potin, *Native American Voluntary Organizations*, 1986; Kenneth R. Philp, *John Collier's Crusade for Indian Reform,
1920–1954*, 1977.

JAMES S. OLSON

COMPENSATION. Just after World War II, when a reaction set in against
the Indian New Deal* and the forces of assimilation* reasserted their

control over federal Indian policy, the idea of compensation surfaced as a way of bringing about the end of federal supervision of American Indian tribes. Assimilationists had long wanted to end the special trust* relationship between Indians and the federal government and assimilate them into the larger legal, political, and economic systems of the United States. Those objectives became embodied in the termination* movement of the 1950s and 1960s. Some assimilationists also wanted to relocate American Indians away from the reservations and into cities, where they would be forced to interact with Americans from other ethnic groups and perhaps, in the process, become assimilated.

But before termination and relocation* could be fully implemented, many assimilationists believed that all outstanding claims by various tribes against the U.S. government for land seizures and treaty violations should be settled. Between 1784 and 1871 the United States had negotiated 377 separate treaties with various tribes, and the controversies surrounding those treaties and the government's failure to abide by them still evoked bitterness among Native Americans. Only after these disputes had been settled could termination and relocation really succeed. The process of settling those claims was known as the compensation program.

In 1946, Congress passed the Indian Claims Commission Act to implement compensation. The act created an Indian Claims Commission* to review all Indian grievances against the federal government. Tribes had five years to file their cases, and the Indian Claims Commission had to settle each claim within a ten-year period. Each claim went through two phases. In the title phase, a tribe had to prove it had controlled the disputed land from "time immemorial"; and during the value phase, the commission would determine the value of the land at the time it was taken from the tribe. The commission would then make a monetary award for that amount to the tribe.

The Indian Claims Commission proved to be controversial from its inception. It represented a European way of settling disputes (conversion of values into dollars), and it led to bitter inter- and intratribal rivalries. Over the millennia, most tribes had migrated over vast expanses of territory; it was not uncommon for more than one tribe to claim the same land. Once the commission decided to make an award, tribes often argued over whether the money should be awarded in a block grant to the tribe or in cash payments to each individual member of the tribe. Those disputes often pitted traditionalist full-bloods against mixed-bloods within individual tribes.

Also, the work went much more slowly than assimilationists had originally hoped. By 1951, when the five-year filing period ended, the commission had dismissed 29 of 31 claims, and by 1960 it had disqualified 88 of 105 claims. The commission had awarded only $20 million in 17 claims. By 1978, when the Indian Claims Commission ceased operating, it had awarded more than $800 million to 285 claims, out of 850 claims filed. Native American groups whose claims had been denied were often vehement in their criticism of the federal government. The hope that the Indian Claims Commission would soothe Native American anger over the past proved to be a pipe dream. Termination and relocation were implemented anyway.

Suggested Reading: James S. Olson and Raymond Wilson, *Native Americans in the Twentieth Century*, 1984; Harvey D. Rosenthal, *Their Day in Court: A History of the Indian Claims Commission*, 1990.

JAMES S. OLSON

COMPETENCY. For several centuries now in the United States, non-Indians have debated the question of competency: whether individual Indians or tribal entities are ready to function successfully in a modern commercial economy. The fundamental assumption of European Americans has been that Native Americans, as individuals or in groups, are culturally, socially, and economically "incompetent"—unable to succeed economically or avoid exploitation in modern society. For the first 250 years of U.S. history—from the seventeenth century into the nineteenth century—most non-Indians believed that the only way of dealing with Indians was to segregate them on distant reservations,* to place them on land the whites did not want in order to avoid conflict and violence between the two peoples.

But that solution never worked, primarily because white economic interests eventually wanted access to all the land, water, timber, and mineral resources in the United States. By the late nineteenth century there was no land left to designate as new reservations. Reformers decided that the only way of dealing with the so-called Indian problem was to assimilate Native Americans into the larger society.

At this point, the competency concept became a key element of American Indian policy. The question of whether individual Indians or tribal groups were "ready" and "prepared" for assimilation* dominated Indian policy debates. When Congress passed the Dawes Act* of 1887, the law required that only tribes that were ready for assimilation could undergo the allotment* process. Between 1887 and 1934 the Bureau of Indian Affairs* regularly based the allotment decision on its assessment of a tribe's "competency," or preparedness, for assimilation. The Dawes Act also prevented individual Indians from selling their allotted lands for a 25-year period. That requirement was designed to protect the land titles of individual Indians who might not be "ready" for assimilation. The Burke Act* of 1906 allowed the secretary of the Interior to certify the "competency" of individuals to sell their allotted lands before the expiration of the 25-year trust period.

During the 1950s and 1960s the idea of competency also influenced public policy debates over Indian affairs. The termination* movement (designed to end federal jurisdiction over tribes and turn them over to state and local jurisdiction) also revolved around the idea of competency. Only those tribes deemed "ready" for termination by the Bureau of Indian Affairs could be terminated. The bureau's first designees were the Menominees of Wisconsin and the Klamaths of Washington. At the same time, the relocation* program was also based on the notion of competency. Before individual Indians could be relocated off the reservations to jobs and housing in cities, they had to be deemed "competent" to succeed in non-Indian society.

For many years the entire idea of federal trusteeship—federal jurisdiction and guardianship* over tribal lands and peoples—was based on the competency notion: Indians needed special legal protection to prevent white exploitation of them. In recent decades, however, the maintenance of federal trusteeship has moved away from the idea of competency, which has too many paternalistic overtones, to that of self-determination.* Federal trusteeship, its advocates now argue, provides Native Americans with a legal and political environment conducive to social and cultural self-determination.

Suggested Reading: Russel Lawrence Barsh and James Youngblood Henderson, *The Road: Indian Tribes and Political Liberty*, 1980; Vine Deloria Jr. and Clifford M. Lytle, *American Indians, American Justice*, 1983; H. Barry Holt and Gary Forrester, *Digest of American Indian Law: Cases and Chronology*, 1990; James S. Olson and Raymond Wilson, *Native Americans in the Twentieth Century*, 1984; Stephen L. Pevar, *The Rights of Indians and Tribes: The Basic ACLU Guide to Indian and Tribal Rights*, 1992; Wilcomb E. Washburn, *Red Man's Land*, *White Man's Law*, 1971; Charles F. Wilkinson, *American Indians, Time and the Law*, 1987; John R. Wunder, *"Retained by The People": A History of American Indians and the Bill of Rights*, 1994.

                                                                JAMES S. OLSON

***CONFEDERATED TRIBES OF THE WARM SPRINGS RESERVATION OF OREGON v. UNITED STATES* (1966).** Under the terms of the Indian Claims Commission Act of 1946, Indian groups suing for compensation* for lost lands were required to prove long-term residency and control of a region before the federal government would recognize the existence of their title to the land. But the question of what constituted residency and control became a source of controversy. When the Indian Claims Commission* ruled in favor of the Confederated Tribes of the Warm Springs Reservation of Oregon, the United States appealed, arguing that the tribes were demanding compensation for far more land than they had ever "controlled." The United States was viewing residency and control in terms of villages, whereas the tribes were seeing it in terms of economic habitat. The Court of Claims in a 1966 decision found in favor of the Indians, arguing that title does not just apply to areas where a tribe might have permanently lived but also to those areas that provided economic sustenance to the tribe, even if their occupation of the land was only seasonal.

Suggested Reading: Russel Lawrence Barsh and James Youngblood Henderson, *The Road: Indian Tribes and Political Liberty*, 1980; Vine Deloria Jr. and Clifford M. Lytle, *American Indians, American Justice*, 1983; H. Barry Holt and Gary Forrester, *Digest of American Indian Law: Cases and Chronology*, 1990; Stephen L. Pevar, *The Rights of Indians and Tribes: The Basic ACLU Guide to Indian and Tribal Rights*, 1992; Wilcomb E. Washburn, *Red Man's Land, White Man's Law*, 1971; Charles F. Wilkinson, *American Indians, Time and the Law*, 1987; John R. Wunder, *"Retained by The People": A History of American Indians and the Bill of Rights*, 1994.

JAMES S. OLSON

CONQUEST THEORY. When Europeans conquered the New World in the sixteenth and seventeenth centuries, they developed a theory of conquest rooted in Christianity and their concept of civilization that sustained the conquests until the twentieth century. The most important debate about the nature of the New World's inhabitants, the Native Americans or Indians, occurred at the Spanish court during the first half of the sixteenth century.

Relying on a militant, evangelistic interpretation of Christianity, classical social and political thought, diplomatic treaty, and European ethnocentrism, conquerors and theorists alike justified their actions in the New World. Although Christianity was born as a religion of the meek and powerless, by early modern times it had become the religion of the wealthy and powerful in western Europe. Using biblical injunctions in Genesis and a series of fifteenth-century papal bulls sanctioning specific Portuguese conquests along the African coast, Spanish and Portuguese monarchs sought support in Christian theology for their territorial acquisitions. Not only were the conquests to be done in the name of Christ, but justification for them was found in God's command to "go forth and multiply," to take control of lands previously not under the control of Christian kings. Fifteenth- and sixteenth-century popes gave sanction to these conquests, the most important papal statement being the proclamation issued in 1493 dividing the non-Christian world between Spain and Portugal.

The next year, Spain and Portugal reconfirmed that division diplomatically in the Treaty of Tordesillas. In both documents European monarchies rejected the notion that native peoples had title to their lands (only if they were Christianized would they have such title). The two powers divided the non-Christian world between themselves, leaving England and France, other European maritime powers, to puzzle out how to encroach on those claims in the future. They developed the doctrine of effective settlement or colonization before they would recognize the right of either Spain or Portugal to the lands they claimed. But no European nation recognized anything more than a "right in the soil" of indigenous peoples. The only issue that stopped the European powers from dividing the whole world during the Age of Discovery was the ability of a native people to protect themselves and lands from such encroachment.

Indian peoples, possessing no immunities to Euro-Asian or African diseases,* were powerless to halt the conquests by Spaniards or, later, other European peoples. The natives died in appalling numbers during precontact, contact, and settlement eras as Old World diseases such as measles, mumps, chickenpox, and especially smallpox killed Indians by the millions. What environmental historian Alfred W. Crosby has called Europe's "biological extended family" was part of the effective means by which Europeans conquered so many Indian empires (e.g., the Aztec and Inca) in such short spaces of time.

While the conquests proceeded in the West Indies, then the Mesoamerican mainland and Spanish Main, theologians in Spain and the provinces vigorously debated the justice of what the Spanish were doing. The debate addressed the questions of the origins and nature of Indians, whether they possessed souls, and how Spaniards were to treat them. The debate turned on Spanish justification for enslaving natives. Were Indians human beings? If so, what rights did they have to their lands? Could the Spanish legitimately come among them, for any purpose? Finally, could they be conquered in the name of Christianity, or must they be left alone if they resisted conversion? These central questions were argued and debated by theologians and teachers. Included among the participants were Bartolomé de las Casas,* Juan Ginés de Sepúlveda, and Francisco de Vitoria,* all of whom were theologians in the Roman Catholic Church. Although their debate ultimately resolved generally in favor of Indians, the practical consequences were nullified by the ability of the *conquistadores* to virtually ignore royal or theological injunctions against the cruel and inhuman treatment of native peoples.

Aristotelian social and political thought endorsed the natural inequality of mankind, and this reinforced the enslavement of Indians and Africans during the sixteenth century. European ethnocentrism encouraged Europeans to regard different peoples as inferior, and European biological and military capabilities permitted that ethnocentric view of Indians to support the conquest of native lands in the Americas.

But whether Spanish, Portuguese, and later European conquests would have proceeded as rapidly and completely as they did without the attractions of immediate wealth represented by the gold, silver, gems, and plantation commodities extracted from the Americas is difficult to say. Those worldly attractions brought greedy Spaniards first, then other Europeans later, to seize for themselves as much of the New World's wealth as they could. From a practical viewpoint, those involved directly in the conquest may have cared very little for the theological, juridical, and classical debate that raged at the Spanish court from the 1510s until the 1560s. To them, that debate was more hairsplitting than anything else. Their immediate concern was the opportunity to exploit the wealth of the New World.

Suggested Reading: Alfred W. Crosby, *The Columbian Exchange: Biological and Medical Consequences of 1492*, 1972; Lewis Hanke, *The Spanish Struggle for Justice in the Conquest of America*, 1965; Luis N. Rivera, *A Violent Evangelism: The Political and Religious Conquest of the Americas*; Wilcomb Washburn, *Red Man's Land, White Man's Law*, 1971; Robert A. Williams, *The American Indian in Western Legal Thought: The Discourses of Conquest*, 1990; Silvio Zavala, *The Defense of Human Rights in Latin America*, 1980.

TIMOTHY MORGAN

CONSTITUTION. Although the U.S. Constitution said little about Indians per se, it did establish the legal groundwork for the supremacy of the federal government over state and local governments in dealing with Indian affairs. As early as the sixteenth century, in the writings of such legal scholars as Francisco de Vitoria,* Europeans recognized the sovereign status of Indian tribes in the New World and their original title to the land. In 1789, when the U.S. Constitution went into effect, Indians were not considered citizens of the United States. On the contrary, they were viewed legally as tribal citizens. Article I, Section 2, of the Constitution defined the methods of determining representation in the House of Representatives. Representation was to be based on state population; but in determining the number of representatives to which each state was entitled, non-taxed Indians (i.e., Indians living under tribal authority) could not be counted.

The issue of the supremacy of federal authority was handled in Article 1, Section 8, of the Constitution. During the years of the Articles of Confederation* (1781–1789), state governments had tried to assert their authority over Indian lands within their boundaries, as had the central government. The result was a confused, haphazard, and often contradictory set of federal and state policies. State assertions of power also constituted a threat to tribal legal sovereignty.* The framers of the Constitution were convinced that following a consistent federal policy, not thirteen different state policies, was the best way of handling Indian affairs. James Madison wrote what is today known as the Indian commerce clause: Congress enjoyed the exclusive power to "regulate commerce with foreign nations, among the several states, and with the Indian tribes." Just as states could not enter into treaties with foreign governments or pass tariffs and taxes on other states, they could not do so with Indian tribes, which the Constitution viewed as essentially independent of state authority.

Suggested Reading: Charles F. Wilkinson, *American Indians, Time and the Law*, 1987.

JAMES S. OLSON

COULTER, ROBERT. Robert Coulter focuses on international human rights issues, especially those involving indigenous peoples, and currently directs the Indian Law Resource Center in Washington, D.C. A Potawatomi, Coulter was born in Rapid City, South Dakota, on September 19, 1945. He received an undergraduate degree from Williams College in 1966 and a law degree from Columbia in 1969. Coulter wrote *Indian Law—Human Law* in 1984.

Suggested Reading: Duane Champagne, ed., *The Native North American Almanac*, 1994.

JAMES S. OLSON

COUNCIL OF ENERGY RESOURCE TRIBES. The Council of Energy Resource Tribes (CERT) was established in 1976 by the leaders of twenty-five American Indian tribes. Among the most prominent was Peter Mac-Donald,* leader of the Navajo tribe of American Indians. Located on the reservations* of various American Indian tribes are up to 40 percent of all U.S. uranium, 33 percent of U.S. coal, and 5 percent of U.S. oil and natural gas resources. CERT is composed of representatives of each of the tribes whose holdings include some of those energy resources. At the time of CERT's founding, the United States was in the midst of the economically disastrous energy crisis. After the Yom Kippur War in the Middle East in 1973, oil-producing Arab nations—upset over U.S. loyalty to Israel—imposed the oil embargo. Energy prices skyrocketed.

Most energy-rich tribes had a history of leasing out their energy resources at prices well below market levels, and the energy crisis of the 1970s exacerbated that problem. CERT was committed to maximizing tribal profits by raising prices. It has negotiated with foreign governments to improve prices and has lobbied for federal legislation to protect Indian assets. CERT has also sought federal financing for training programs so Indians can acquire the engineering and technical skills necessary for effective management of those resources. In its overall design, CERT is part of the broader self-determination* movement, because many Indian activists consider economic self-sufficiency the key to real freedom and independence.

During the late 1970s and early 1980s, CERT members lobbied vigorously for federal legislation protecting the Indian resource state. In 1982 their efforts resulted in the Indian Mineral Development Act* and the Federal Oil and Gas Royalty Management Act,* both of which contained provisions allowing for the renegotiation of royalty contracts, establishment of joint ventures between mining companies and Indian tribes, amendments to national environmental laws giving tribes clear control of resource use on their own lands, education and job training programs to develop reservation expertise, and revolving funds to improve reservation infrastructures. By the mid-1990s CERT's membership included forty-three American Indian tribes and four Canadian tribes.

Suggested Reading: Marjane Ambler, *Breaking the Iron Bonds: Indian Control of Energy Development*, 1990; Vine Deloria Jr. and Clifford Lytle, *The Nations Within: The Past and Future of American Indian Sovereignty*, 1984; Roxanne Dunbar Ortiz, *Indians of the Americas: Human Rights and Self-Determination*, 1984; Hurst Hannum, *Autonomy, Self-Determination and Sovereignty: The Accommodation of Conflicting Rights*, 1990; Phyllis Mauch Messenger, ed., *The Ethics of Collecting Cultural Property: Whose Culture? Whose Property?* 1989.

JAMES S. OLSON

COUNTY OF ONEIDA v. ONEIDA INDIAN NATION (1985). In recent years, Indian activists have frequently worked to get the federal courts to enforce agreements made in the distant past. It was not at all uncommon, for example, for treaties* in the eighteenth and nineteenth centuries to promise tribes title to their lands for "time immemorial," only to have subsequent agreements extinguish those titles. The enforceability of early treaties generated considerable legal and political controversy during the decades of the Red Power* movement. One important case in resolving this question was *County of Oneida v. Oneida Indian Nation* in 1985.

In 1795 the Oneida Nation had allegedly transferred title to 100,000 acres of tribal land to the state of New York. The state had not, however, secured the necessary federal approval for the transfer. In 1970 the Oneida Nation filed suit for restoration of the land, arguing that the title transfer had been invalid. By a 5 to 4 vote the Supreme Court declared the transfer unlawful on the grounds that the Indians had a federal right to title that enjoyed supremacy to any state and local jurisdictional claims. The Oneidas had the right to sue on a common law cause of action for unlawful possession of tribal land.

Suggested Reading: Russel Lawrence Barsh and James Youngblood Henderson, *The Road: Indian Tribes and Political Liberty*, 1980; Vine Deloria Jr. and Clifford M. Lytle, *American Indians, American Justice*, 1983; H. Barry Holt and Gary Forrester, *Digest of American Indian Law: Cases and Chronology*, 1990; Stephen L. Pevar, *The Rights of Indians and Tribes: The Basic ACLU Guide to Indian and Tribal Rights*, 1992; Wilcomb E. Washburn, *Red Man's Land*, *White Man's Law*, 1971; Charles F. Wilkinson, *American Indians, Time and the Law*, 1987; John R. Wunder, *"Retained by The People": A History of American Indians and the Bill of Rights*, 1994.

JAMES S. OLSON

CRIME OF 1908. Although the Dawes Act* of 1887 was designed to break up the tribal estate and distribute reservation* lands to individual Indians, reformers were worried that non-Indians would soon acquire the land from individual Indians through purchase and leasing arrangements. One provision of the Dawes Act imposed a 25-year trust period on individual Indian land titles, prohibiting their sale. Of course, non-Indians resented the restriction because it prevented them from gaining access to valuable Indian land. Beginning with the Dead Indian Land Act* of 1902 and the Burke Act* of 1906, Congress began lifting the restriction under certain circumstances.

In 1908, Congress passed legislation ending the restriction on the sale of allotted lands of Indians married to whites and mixed-blood Indians.

The decision, known by historians as the Crime of 1908, released more than 13 million acres of Indian land for sale to whites. The legislation also turned over control of the remaining restricted lands to local county courts, where corrupt officials frequently appointed white guardians to manage Indian land; these guardians made sure that the Indian owners did not reap the bulk of the profits. At the time, there were more than 100,000 allotments that were still restricted, and the guardians, often local attorneys, charged as much as a 50 percent annual royalty to manage the land. Fraud, embezzlement, forgery, and blackmail became common in the acquisition, management, and marketing of the restricted allotments. Millions of acres of Indian land passed into white hands because of the Crime of 1908.

Suggested Reading: David M. Holford, "The Subversion of the Indian Land Allotment System, 1887–1934," *Indian Historian* 8 (Spring 1975).

JAMES S. OLSON

CROW DOG CASE. See *EX PARTE CROW DOG.*

CROW DOG, MARY. Mary Brave Bird has brought a number of problems in American Indian life to the attention of the public. She was born on the Rosebud Sioux reservation in 1953. During the late 1960s, discouraged about social and economic problems on the reservation,* she became active in the American Indian Movement* and married Leonard Crow Dog, a Sioux medicine man. He was influential in working to revive the Ghost Dance among the Sioux. Mary Crow Dog published *Lakota Woman*, her autobiography, in 1990. The book detailed the problems of alcohol* abuse and poverty* in American Indian life. She also discussed the tension between modern feminism and traditional Indian values.

Suggested Reading: Duane Champagne, ed., *The Native North American Almanac*, 1994.

JAMES S. OLSON

CURTIS ACT OF 1898. Throughout the 1890s, Congress, leaning on the investigatory advice of the Dawes Commission, enacted legislation with a view to the destruction of Indian autonomy and the general allotment* of Indian lands in severalty as already initiated by the Dawes Act* of 1887. However, the Five Civilized Tribes (Choctaws, Chickasaws, Creeks, Seminoles, and Cherokees) of Indian Territory* had been exempt from the legislation. In violation of previous solemn agreements, the Curtis Act furthered this ominous trend and effectively undermined the remnants of independent authority still remaining to the Five Civilized Tribes of Oklahoma by bringing them under the terms of the Dawes Act. The act established the inapplicability of Indian law in federal courts and dissolved the Oklahoma Territory's tribal courts* and Indian police force. Subsequent legislation in 1902 brought about the allotment of their lands. Despite Indian resistance to these heavy-handed government measures, the Five Civilized Tribes were henceforth subject to federal jurisdiction.

Suggested Reading: Francis Paul Prucha, *The Great Father*, Vol. 2, 1984; Wilcomb Washburn, *Red Man's Land*, *White Man's Law*, 1971.

MARK BAXTER

CUSTER'S LAST STAND. The term "Custer's Last Stand" refers to what is arguably the most famous, or infamous, battle in American military history. Lt. Col. George Armstrong Custer commanded the U.S. Army's Seventh Cavalry in its battles with the Cheyenne and Sioux Indians in what was then the Dakota Territory. Custer was a fierce, dashing, impulsive, and usually successful officer. When gold was discovered in the Black Hills of South Dakota, the federal government decided to relocate the Indians onto reservations.* The relocation* was to be completed by January 31, 1876. Many of the Indians ignored the relocation order. Large numbers of them joined Sitting Bull's* encampment along the Little Bighorn River in what is today southern Montana.

Custer received orders to advance up the Rosebud River with his troops, surround Sitting Bull's encampment from the rear, and wait for the arrival of two other army units before attacking. But Custer did not want to wait. Ignoring the warnings of his own scouts, who told him that the Indians vastly outnumbered the U.S. troops, Custer attacked on June 25, 1876. It was a colossal blunder. He allowed his army to be isolated on a small hill and surrounded. Within one hour, Indian warriors under the command of Sitting Bull, Crazy Horse, Gall, and Crow King annihilated Custer and his army. The defeat became a cause célèbre in the East, where some politicians called for a military crusade to push the Indians, once and for all, onto the reservations.

In recent years Custer's last stand has become an important cultural issue in the Indian civil rights movement. The United States had established a national monument at the site of the battle on the Little Bighorn, designating it the Custer Battlefield National Monument. However, Sioux and Cheyenne activists resented the name because it gave heroic attributes to Custer, whom the Indians considered to be little more than a murderer. Under political pressure, in 1993 the federal government renamed the site the Little Bighorn National Battlefield Monument.

Suggested Reading: Evan S. Connell, *Son of the Morning Star: Custer and the Little Bighorn*, 1984.

JAMES S. OLSON

D

DAWES ACT OF 1887. An essential component of the well-meaning but ill-conceived humanitarian effort to Christianize, civilize, and assimilate the Indians into mainstream American society, the Dawes Act of 1887 made provision for the allotment* of Indian land. Pushed through Congress by reform-minded Indian rights organizations, as well as land-hungry settlers, speculators, and economic interests, the policy aimed to undermine tribal authority, eradicate tribal culture, and destroy the reservation system as a whole by breaking up the Indian tribal estate and redistributing the land in small-farm allotments to individual Indian families. In the process, tribal governments would lose their authority because they would have lost their primary economic resource. In place of these traditional sources of stability, the Dawes Act offered Native Americans individual land ownership and the legal rights, protections, and responsibilities of full citizenship.*

Named for its sponsor, Massachusetts senator Henry Dawes, the measure is also known as the General Allotment Act of 1887. It was drafted in the climate of the 1880s when white reformers were convinced that as long as Indians remained economically, socially, and politically segregated on reservations,* they would never gain the skills to compete successfully in American society. And as long as they occupied huge tracts of land that were not developed economically, whites would try to acquire their property. Violence would continue to plague Indian-white relations, as had happened so often in the previous centuries.

Initially the Dawes Act distributed land (sometimes as much as 160 acres or more) to each tribal member on the basis of gender, age, or family size. The allotted land was to be held in trust by the United States for a minimum of twenty-five years. At the conclusion of this period, a fee in patent would be issued granting Indian title holders the freedom to sell their land. However, any unallotted Indian land was automatically made available for public sale. Ideally, the profits from such sales were to be divided among the various tribes for local improvements.

As later amended, the Dawes Act, which excluded most of the tribes in the Southwest (including the Five Civilized Tribes, as well as the New York Senecas, the Nebraska Sioux, and the Osages, Miamis, Peorias, and Sacs and Foxes residing in Indian territories), reduced land allotments to a flat rate of 80 acres per affected tribal member and permitted the Indians to lease land to white mining, ranching, timber, and agricultural interests. As a result, by 1934 the land in Indian possession had dwindled to less than half of its 1887 level of some 138 million acres, with roughly 60 million acres sold under the dubious designation of surplus land, and another two-thirds of the nearly 40 million acres held in severalty sold by the Indians themselves following expiration of the 25-year trust period in 1912. Viewed in retrospect, the failure of the allotment policy condemned a considerable number of Native Americans to landless poverty and humiliation. The Dawes Act was in effect until 1934, when Congress passed the Indian Reorganization Act* and ended the allotment program.

Suggested Reading: Leonard A. Carlson, *Indians, Bureaucrats and Land: The Dawes Act and the Decline of Indian Farming*, 1981; James S. Olson and Raymond Wilson, *Native Americans in the Twentieth Century*, 1984; D. S. Otis, *The Dawes Act and the Allotment of Indian Lands*, 1973; Francis Paul Prucha, *The Great Father*, Vol. 2, 1984; Wilcomb E. Washburn, *The Assault on Indian Tribalism: The General Allotment Law (Dawes Act) of 1887*, 1975.

MARK BAXTER

DAWES SEVERALTY ACT OF 1887. See **DAWES ACT OF 1887.**

DEAD INDIAN LAND ACT OF 1902. When reformers succeeded in convincing Congress to pass the Dawes Act* of 1887 and launch the allotment* program, they were concerned that many Indians who were not willing or able to succeed as commercial farmers might quickly sell their allotted land to white farmers. They would then live for a few months or perhaps a year off the proceeds, only to end up without money or land. To prevent that scenario and protect individual title to the allotted land, Congress wrote a clause into the Dawes Act prohibiting the sale of allotted lands for twenty-five years.

But white economic interest groups and many mixed-blood Indians chafed under the restriction, and pressure mounted on Congress to ease the restriction. Whites wanted the land, and many Indians wanted their money. Many Indians also resented the paternalism inherent in the restriction. In 1902, Congress yielded to the growing political pressure and passed the Dead Indian Land Act, which waived the trust status of inherited allotments and permitted heirs to allotted land to sell their property. The Dead Indian Land Act was one in a series of federal government decisions that helped alienate millions of acres of Native American land during the 1890s and early 1900s.

Suggested Reading: James S. Olson and Raymond Wilson, *Native Americans in the Twentieth Century*, 1984; D. S. Otis, *The Dawes Act and the Allotment of Indian Lands*, 1973; Francis Paul Prucha, *The Great Father*, Vol. 2, 1984.

JAMES S. OLSON

DEER, ADA. Ada Deer, a Menominee, was appointed head of the Bureau of Indian Affairs* by President Bill Clinton in 1993. Born on August 7, 1935, in Keshena, Wisconsin, in 1957 she graduated from the University of Wisconsin at Madison and then earned a master's degree in social work at Columbia. The battle to reverse the federal government's termination* of the Menominee Indians became Deer's passion in the late 1960s. By the early 1970s she was vice-president and chief Washington lobbyist of the National Committee to Save the Menominee People and Forest, and from 1973 to 1976 she served as chair of the Menominee Restoration Committee. Deer taught at the University of Wisconsin at Madison. She became assistant secretary for Indian affairs early in 1993, and a few months later President Clinton named her head of the Bureau of Indian Affairs.

Suggested Reading: Duane Champagne, ed., *The Native North American Almanac*, 1994.

JAMES S. OLSON

DELORIA, VINE, JR. A forceful and active spokesman for the Indian community, Vine Deloria Jr., author, attorney, educator, and grandson of a Yankton Sioux chief, was born in 1933 in Martin, South Dakota. Deloria graduated from Iowa State University in 1958 and received a law degree from the Univesity of Colorado in 1970. Through his best-selling books, *Custer Died for Your Sins* (1969) and *God Is Red* (1973), Deloria presented the details of the Red Power* activism agenda to a global audience. *Custer* remains one of the most incisive polemics written concerning the relationship of the U.S. government to the Native American. Deloria is also the author of *American Indians, American Justice* with C. Lytle (1983); *The Nations Within: The Past and Future of American Indian Sovereignty* also with C. Lytle (1984); *American Indian Policy in the Twentieth Century* (1985); *Behind the Trail of Broken Treaties: An Indian Declaration of Independence* (1974); and *Red Earth, White Lies: Native Americans and the Myth of the Scientific Fact* (1995).

Deloria served as executive director of the National Congress of American Indians* from 1965 to 1967 and provided leadership in other organizations, such as the Citizens Crusade against Poverty and the Indian Rights Association.* In 1971 he and two other Indian attorneys, Franklin D. Ducheneaux and Kirke Kickingbird, founded the Institute for the Development of Indian Law. The purpose of this nonprofit legal research organization was to strengthen the rights of Indian governmental and societal institutions in order to guarantee their ability to govern themselves in an efficient and sovereign manner. Since 1991, Deloria has taught political science at the University of Colorado at Boulder.

Suggested Reading: Robert Allen Warrior, "Vine Deloria Jr.'s 'It's about Time to Be Interested in Indians Again,' " *Progressive* 54 (April 1990), 24–27.

DAVID RITCHEY

DEPARTMENT OF TAXATION AND FINANCE OF NEW YORK STATE v. MILHELM ATTEA & BROS. (1994). The question of state taxing jurisdiction over Indians and Indian reservations has been a source of considerable debate in recent years. Early in the 1990s, New York state officials sued in state courts to collect tax revenues on cigarette sales made on Indian reservations to non-Indians. The state claimed that non-Indians were avoiding paying sales taxes by purchasing their cigarettes on reservations. State officials claimed that the lost tax revenues reached more than $65 million annually. The New York Court of Appeals found in favor of the Indians, but the state appealed the decision in the federal courts. In 1994 the U.S. Supreme Court rendered its decision in *Department of Taxation and Finance of New York State v. Milhelm Attea & Bros.*, overturning the New York State Court of Appeals decision and ordering Indians to tax the sales of cigarettes to non-Indians.

Suggested Reading: Russel Lawrence Barsh and James Youngblood Henderson, *The Road: Indian Tribes and Political Liberty*, 1980; H. Barry Holt and Gary Forrester, *Digest of American Indian Law: Cases and Chronology*, 1990; Stephen L. Pevar, *The Rights of Indians and Tribes: The Basic ACLU Guide to Indian and Tribal Rights*, 1992; Wilcomb E. Washburn, *Red Man's Land, White Man's Law*, 1971; Charles F. Wilkinson, *American Indians, Time and the Law*,

1987; John R. Wunder, *"Retained by The People": A History of American Indians and the Bill of Rights*, 1994.

JAMES S. OLSON

DEPENDENCY. See TRUST RESPONSIBILITY.

DESERT LAND ACT OF 1877. In the years after the Civil War the federal government wanted to encourage settlement of the Far West, but much of the region was too arid to attract farmers, especially if they were confined to only the 160 acres allowed them under the Homestead Act* of 1862. The Desert Land Act of 1877 was designed to encourage settlement. It allowed a settler to purchase up to 640 acres of federal land for $1.25 an acre if the settler managed to irrigate the land within three years. Eventually even that incentive proved to be insufficient to attract settlers. The Carey Act* of 1894 and the Newlands Reclamation Act* of 1902 were both designed to follow up on the Desert Land Act of 1877. The impact of the Desert Land Act, along with these other measures, was to accelerate the settlement of the Southwest and the alienation of Indian land.

Suggested Reading: John T. Ganoe, "The Desert Land Act in Operation, 1877–1891," *Agricultural History* 11 (1937): 152–67.

JAMES S. OLSON

DETRIBALIZATION. A term applied to the attempt of white Americans during the nineteenth century to abolish Indian tribal customs and attachments. Governmental policy, Christian missionary efforts, and educational movements alike aimed at extermination of Indian tribal life. From the first English settlements in the early seventeenth century to the twentieth century, Christian missionary impulses sought conversion of Indians to white ways. Intent on "civilizing" Indians, whites believed that Indians had to become individuals in order to progress and prosper in the new society. The tribal identity, which subordinated individual identities, seemed certain to retard Indian assimilation.* (Many whites, however, also believed that Indians should become extinct, as they seemed to be doing during the nineteenth century.) One purpose of the reservation* movement in the nineteenth century was to prepare Indians for assimilation into white society by "individualizing" them.

The culmination of the detribalization movement occurred when Congress passed the General Allotment Act of 1887, popularly called the Dawes Act.* This legislation represented efforts of those calling themselves "Friends of the Indian," who wanted Indians brought into the mainstream of American life through allotment and the individuation it represented, and those who simply desired expropriation of Indian reservation lands for purposes such as railroad construction, cattle ranching, or, later, oil drilling. The law allotted reservation lands to individual Indians at the rate of 160 acres per head of household, 80 acres per single Indian over age 18, and 40 acres per Indian under age 18. Once a tribe's reservation lands had been so allotted, the remainder (usually well over one-half the acreage) was to be sold to whites. It was believed that allotments would force Indians to work for themselves as individual farmers, and that the sale of unallotted lands would then surround Indians with whites who would be examples of "proper" behavior.

In the early twentieth century, congressional investigations of allotment* showed how wrong the assumptions had been. Indians had not become "white" except in a few cases. In most instances the natives had been swindled of their allotments, leaving them with less land than before allotment occurred. Although restitution efforts were made through the Indian Reorganization Act* of 1934, after World War II Congress reversed itself once again and began another phase of detribalization known as termination.* Utah senator Arthur Watkins and South Dakota representative E. Y. Berry pushed for passage of House Concurrent Resolution 108* (1953). In that resolution Congress unilaterally ended treaty relations with sixty-one tribes between 1954 and 1962, stripping them of federal services and protection. Historians generally agree that termination, like allotment, did Indians great harm. The evils of termination were quickly pointed out, but it remained a covert part of federal policy during the 1960s. Studies and investigations of the results of termination revealed how terribly it had affected those terminated. The policy fell publicly into disfavor, and in 1970 President Richard M. Nixon denounced it, favoring a policy that would strengthen Indian autonomy without threatening their concept of community.

Suggested Reading: Russel Lawrence Barsh and James Youngblood Henderson, *The Road: Indian Tribes and Political Liberty*, 1980; Arrell Morgan Gibson, *The American Indian: Prehistory to the Present*, 1980; D. S. Otis, *The Dawes Act and the Allotment of Indian Land*, 1973; Wilcomb E. Washburn, *Red Man's Land, White Man's Law*, 1971; John R. Wunder, *"Retained by The People": A History of American Indians and the Bill of Rights*, 1994.

TIMOTHY MORGAN

DISCOVERY, AS A SOURCE OF TITLE. Much has been made of the statement that Columbus "discovered" America in 1492. Although the land was already inhabited by the Native Americans, from the European perspective the New World was a new discovery. And the European view was—to the Europeans, at least—the only view that mattered legally. Discovery of new lands gave the European nations certain legal rights that international convention respected. Conquest had long been accepted as a valid method of gaining sovereignty* over an area, and the discovery of new areas of the world was treated very similarly.

The European states agreed that whoever discovered an area first gained all the rights to that area against any other European nation. Natives in the area were to be negotiated with by the discovering power only, and other nations had no right to negotiate with the affected indigenous peoples. Because other European nations had no legal claim to areas previously staked out by a European nation, except by conquest, the discovering power treated the Indians as it saw fit. Indian relations were a purely domestic concern of the imperial power. Moreover, the discovering power had the free and clear title to the land of the Indians in the eyes of the European world.

The United States, in dealing with Native Americans, claimed that the discovery rights of Great Britain had been passed on to the United States after the American Revolution.* Therefore, the United States had clear title to the Indian lands in regard to any other country. Objections that the Native Americans might have original title to this land were settled either by treaty or by force. The concept of discovery was addressed by the U.S. Supreme Court in *Johnson's and Graham's Lessee v. M'Intosh* (1823).

Suggested Reading: Russel Lawrence Barsh and James Youngblood Henderson, *The Road: Indian Tribes and Political Liberty*, 1980; Monroe E. Price, *Law and the American Indian: Readings, Notes and Cases*, 1973.

DARREN PIERSON

DISEASE. The history of disease among Native Americans in the United States can be broken down into two distinct phases: the pandemic disasters that struck American Indians during their initial contact with Europeans, and the more contemporary diseases born of poverty* in Native American communities.

When Europeans first arrived in British North America in the early seventeenth century, the indigenous population stood somewhere between one and two million people. By 1776, however, the Native American population of what is today the continental United States had dropped to approximately 600,000 people. Disease, not violent confrontation with European settlers, explains most of the decline. Native Americans had no

immunities to such contagious diseases as smallpox, chickenpox, diph-
theria, influenza, measles, and mumps. When those diseases appeared in
their communities, death rates were extremely high. By 1870 the indigenous population of the United States had fallen to only 350,000, and by
1910 it was down to about 225,000 people, where it stabilized. By that
time, surviving American Indians enjoyed improved levels of immunities
to the contagious diseases that had so devastated their ancestors. After
1910 the Native American population began a long-term increase. In 1990
the U.S. Census claimed that there were just over 2 million Indians in
the United States, perhaps just what there had been in 1600.

Although the Native American population has been increasing since
1910, it is still plagued by disease rates far higher than the national average. Contemporary Native American health problems are more the consequence of poverty than of compromised immune systems. The
tuberculosis rate among Native Americans is six times the national average. Because of contaminated water supplies, Indians are seventy times
more likely than other Americans to suffer from dysentery. Their influenza and pneumonia rates are three times the national average, and they
are ten times more likely to get strep throat, eight times more likely to
get hepatitis, and three to four times more likely to catch mumps, chickenpox, and whooping cough. Because of high rates of alcoholism, Indians
are five times more likely than the average American to die of cirrhosis
of the liver. The Indian suicide rate is six times the rate of any other
ethnic group in the United States. The Native American lifespan is eight
years less than the average for European Americans.

Suggested Reading: James S. Olson and Raymond Wilson, *Native Americans
in the Twentieth Century*, 1984; John G. Todd, "Implication of Policy Management Decisions for Native Americans," *International Journal of Health Planning
and Management* 2 (1987), 259–68.

                                                                  JAMES S. OLSON

DODGE v. NAKAI (1969). The *Dodge v. Nakai* case of 1969 represented one of the first real tests of the Indian Civil Rights Act* of 1968.
Before passage of the law, Indian tribes had been immune from lawsuits
under federal common law. It was accepted at the time that the law
would not permit individual Indians to launch civil rights lawsuits against
tribal governments. But the *Dodge v. Nakai* case did just that. A non-
Indian attorney brought suit against Raymond Nakai, chairman of the
Navajo tribal council, seeking monetary damages in a dispute with the
tribal council. The tribal council felt the suit was frivolous and out of

order, because tribal sovereignty* offered it immunity. The federal district court disagreed and upheld the suit against the tribal council; it argued that since Congress had established Indian civil rights in the 1968 legislation, the federal courts automatically received a jurisdiction more compelling than that of the tribes, essentially overriding the notion of tribal sovereign immunity.

Suggested Reading: Russel Lawrence Barsh and James Youngblood Henderson, *The Road: Indian Tribes and Political Liberty*, 1980; Vine Deloria Jr. and Clifford M. Lytle, *American Indians, American Justice*, 1983; H. Barry Holt and Gary Forrester, *Digest of American Indian Law: Cases and Chronology*, 1990; Stephen L. Pevar, *The Rights of Indians and Tribes: The Basic ACLU Guide to Indian and Tribal Rights*, 1992; Wilcomb E. Washburn, *Red Man's Land*, *White Man's Law*, 1971; Charles F. Wilkinson, *American Indians, Time and the Law*, 1987; John R. Wunder, *"Retained by The People": A History of American Indians and the Bill of Rights*, 1994.

JAMES S. OLSON

DULL KNIFE. Dull Knife was the leader of the Northern Cheyenne people when they tried their desperate attempt to escape Indian Territory* in 1878. They had agreed in 1877 to leave eastern Montana and western North Dakota and relocate in Indian Territory, but Dull Knife found life there intolerable. In October 1878 he took 353 of his people and fled northward. Soldiers chased them for more than four hundred miles before capturing them. When Dull Knife still refused to move back to Indian Territory, army officials decided to cut off the group's rations. In January 1879, freezing and starving, they took flight again, with U.S. soldiers close on their heels. When the chase was over, sixty-four Northern Cheyenne had been killed.

The flight of Dull Knife and the Northern Cheyenne, like that of Chief Joseph* and the Nez Percé, captured the national imagination and led to federal policy reform. Because of Dull Knife's campaign, the federal government abandoned its policy of removing all Native Americans to Indian Territory. In 1883 the Northern Cheyenne received a reservation* in eastern Montana.

Suggested Reading: Mari Sandoz, *Cheyenne Autumn*, 1993.

JAMES S. OLSON

DURO v. REINA (1990). During the twentieth century, as the legal status of American Indian tribes evolved, the relationship between the rights of individual Indians and the powers of tribal legal institutions has been a source of continuing controversy. The case of *Duro v. Reina* was one such example. In 1990 the U.S. Supreme Court ruled that tribal courts* did not possess jurisdiction over misdemeanor crimes committed on reservations* by Indians who were not enrolled members of the tribe. In essence, the Court's order implied that the jurisdiction of tribal courts was confined only to enrolled members of the tribe. But many reservations were the homes of Indians from different tribes. On the Quinault reservation in the state of Washington, for example, 1,147 residents were enrolled Quinaults, but 300 Indians from other tribes lived there, as did 273 non-Indians. The Quinaults protested the Court's decision in *Duro v. Reina*, arguing that it weakened the tribe's capacity to maintain law and order on the reservation. In 1992, Congress effectively overturned the *Duro* decision by passing legislation giving tribal courts jurisdiction over all people living on the reservation.

Suggested Reading: Russel Lawrence Barsh and James Youngblood Henderson, *The Road: Indian Tribes and Political Liberty*, 1980; Vine Deloria Jr. and Clifford M. Lytle, *American Indians, American Justice*, 1983; H. Barry Holt and Gary Forrester, *Digest of American Indian Law: Cases and Chronology*, 1990; Stephen L. Pevar, *The Rights of Indians and Tribes: The Basic ACLU Guide to Indian and Tribal Rights*, 1992; Wilcomb E. Washburn, *Red Man's Land, White Man's Law*, 1971; Charles F. Wilkinson, *American Indians, Time and the Law*, 1987; John R. Wunder, *"Retained by The People": A History of American Indians and the Bill of Rights*, 1994.

JAMES S. OLSON

DUTCH INDIAN POLICY. The Dutch were relatively late arrivals in the New World. The United Netherlands was the leading commercial power in Europe by 1600 and had little interest in colonizing when profits could be made more easily through trade. Henry Hudson inadvertently initiated Dutch interest in the New World when he sailed up the Hudson River in 1609, searching for the elusive Northwest Passage. In the vicinity of what is modern-day Albany he traded profitably with a band of Mahican Indians. The Dutch continued to visit the Mahicans annually and in 1624 established Fort Orange at the site.

The powerful Five Nations Iroquois, who were too distant to do business with English and French traders, quickly monopolized the Dutch trade by attacking and defeating the Mahicans. The victorious Mohawks, the nearest of the Five Nations, established a brisk trade with the Dutch, supplying them with high quality fur in exchange for European goods. A few years after beginning trade with the Dutch, the Mohawks suffered a devastating attack of smallpox. The weakened Iroquois strengthened their ties with their European allies at Fort Orange. Likewise, the Dutch desire for furs led them to forgive Mohawk transgressions.

In the 1640s the Dutch began supplying the Mohawks with muskets and encouraged them to attack nearby tribes that refused to pay tribute to the Dutch. The supply of Dutch guns, powder, and lead allowed the Mohawks and the other Five Nations Iroquois to expand their dominance in the region.

Despite their apparent success dealing with the Iroquois, the population of New Netherlands remained small. The prosperity of the homeland did not encourage immigration or large financial ventures in the American wilderness. As a result, when the second Anglo-Dutch war broke out in 1665, the English had little trouble overrunning the small Dutch colony. The Dutch removal from New Netherlands forced the Iroquois to scramble for a new trading partner. Their relations with the French and English would eventually decline, but during the period of trade with the Dutch they had conquered or dispersed many of their Indian neighbors and dominated a vast area of northeastern North America.

Suggested Reading: Denys Delage, *Bitter Feast: Amerindians and Europeans in Northeastern North America, 1600–64*, 1993; Francis Jennings, *The Ambiguous Iroquois Empire*, 1984; Ian K. Steele, *Warpaths: Invasions of North America*, 1994.

JEFFREY D. CARLISLE

E

EAGLE PROTECTION ACT OF 1940. See *UNITED STATES v. DION* (1986).

EASTERN ASSOCIATION ON INDIAN AFFAIRS. The Eastern Association on Indian Affairs was established in 1922 to protest the Bursum Bill,* which proposed to recognize the land title claims of white squatters on Pueblo Indian land in New Mexico. Most of the leaders of the Eastern Association on Indian Affairs were from New York City and Boston; they included such people as Ellwood Hendrick, a Columbia University chemist, and Herbert Spinden, a prominent anthropologist. They joined with such groups as the American Indian Defense Association* and campaigned nationally against the Bursum Bill. They played a key role in the measure's demise. During the rest of the 1920s, the Eastern Association on Indian Affairs raised money to study the problems of trachoma and poverty* on Indian reservations.* In 1933 Oliver La Farge was elected president of the association, and he renamed it the National Association on Indian Affairs. In 1936 the National Association on Indian Affairs merged with the American Indian Defense Association to become the American Association on Indian Affairs.

Suggested Reading: Armand S. La Potin, *Native American Voluntary Organizations*, 1986; D'Arcy McNickle, *Indian Man: A Life of Oliver La Farge*, 1971.

JAMES S. OLSON

EASTMAN, CHARLES. Charles Eastman, a Native American writer, was born in 1858 in Redwood Falls, Minnesota, to a Santee Sioux family. He was raised traditionally by his father's family. When the family moved to South Dakota in 1874, he enrolled in school and proved to be a brilliant student. He went on to obtain a bachelor's degree at Dartmouth and a medical degree at Boston University. Eastman then returned to the Pine Ridge reservation as its first Indian physician.

Early in his career Eastman became fascinated with the dilemma facing so many Indians: how to succeed in white society without losing a sense of culture and identity. His autobiography—*Indian Boyhood* (1902)—deals with that dilemma in his own life, and he went on to write a number of novels with similar themes: *Red Hunters and the Animal People* (1904), *Old Indian Days* (1907), *Wigwam Evenings: Sioux Folktales Retold* (1909), and *The Soul of an Indian* (1911). He updated his autobiography in 1916 with *From the Deep Woods to Civilization*. In the book, Eastman criticized the individualistic, competitive, commercial nature of white society and condemned the forced assimilation* policies of the federal government. Eastman was active in the Society of American Indians* and personally believed that assimilation was inevitable, but he believed it should take place on Indian terms and at an Indian pace. Charles Eastman died in 1939.

Suggested Reading: Raymond Wilson, *Ohiyesa: Charles Eastman, Santee Sioux*, 1983.

JAMES S. OLSON

ECHOHAWK, JOHN. Executive director of the Native American Rights Fund.* A Pawnee, Echohawk was born in Albuquerque, New Mexico, on August 11, 1945. He received undergraduate and law degrees from the University of New Mexico in 1967 and 1970. After a stint with California Indian Legal Services, Echohawk joined the Native American Rights Fund and became its executive director in 1977.

Suggested Reading: Duane Champagne, ed., *The Native North American Almanac*, 1994.

JAMES S. OLSON

ECHOHAWK, WALTER. Senior attorney with the Native American Rights Fund,* Walter Echohawk specializes in issues of religious freedom,* prisoner rights,* and reburial rights. Echohawk was born on the Pawnee reservation near Pawnee, Oklahoma, on June 23, 1948. He graduated from Oklahoma State University in 1970 and then earned a law degree from the University of New Mexico in 1973. He played a leading role in the repatriation* movement of the late 1980s and early 1990s, especially the Native American Graves Protection and Repatriation Act* of 1990.

Suggested Reading: Duane Champagne, ed., *The Native North American Almanac*, 1994.

JAMES S. OLSON

ECONOMIC OPPORTUNITY ACT OF 1964. Fashioned on a bill submitted to Congress by President Lyndon B. Johnson as part of America's "war on poverty," the Economic Opportunity Act aimed to ease the plight of the nation's poor and open new avenues of opportunity through government-sponsored educational and job training programs. The measure targeted the country's disadvantaged youth and fostered the cooperation and direct participation of the poverty-stricken in a variety of locally administered community improvement projects and programs. Although the act fell well short of eliminating poverty on the reservation* and produced fewer jobs than had been projected, in 1968 alone the American Indian communities benefited from some $22 million in additional government aid. Congress allotted the sum for direct distribution by the communal leaders of various tribes who utilized the bulk of the money to finance Head Start and home improvement programs.

Suggested Reading: Vine Deloria Jr. and Clifford M. Lytle, *American Indians, American Justice*, 1983; Francis Paul Prucha, *The Great Father*, Vol. 2, 1984.

JAMES S. OLSON

EDUCATION. Ever since the first Europeans—Spanish, Portuguese, French, and English—arrived in the New World, the idea of Indian education has been synonymous with pressures to assimilate Native American peoples to Western values. Until the late nineteenth century, responsibility for educating Indians in the United States was largely the province of churches and missionary societies, which established schools for that purpose. In spite of the Establishment Clause of the First Amendment to the Constitution,* the federal government even financed those schools. Much of the impetus for establishing reservations* and reservation schools came from religious groups anxious to concentrate Indians within narrow geographic regions in order to facilitate their education. Most officials dealing with Indian affairs in the federal government during the nineteenth and early twentieth centuries shared that point of view. Religious organizations and their schoolteachers were not likely to have access to nomadic tribes occupying vast territories. The various programs to educate Native Americans all had assimilation* as their ultimate objective: to convert Indians to European religious values, to the systems of a commercial economy, and to Anglo-American legal institutions.

It was not until after the Civil War* that education to assimilate the Indians became a direct responsibility of the U.S. government. Success in assimilating the Indians, even through Christian schools, had been unsuccessful. Most Bureau of Indian Affairs* (BIA) officials believed at the time that assimilation was the only way to end the cycle of violence and land loss that had affected Native American life for the previous three centuries in the New World. Because federal law placed Indian reservations under the legal guardianship* of the federal government, the BIA ultimately became responsible for Indian education.

The question of how to educate Indian children was a source of intense debate. Richard Henry Pratt,* an army officer and founder of the Carlisle Indian Industrial School, believed in immediate assimilation by removing Indian children from the reservations and teaching them at boarding schools in the East. Distant boarding schools, Pratt was convinced, would help children sever their ties to tribal culture, become fluent in English, and acquire a classical and industrial education. Only then would they be ready for complete assimilation. Other reformers, such as John Oberly, who served as superintendent of Indian education in the Department of the Interior, believed Pratt's idea of boarding school education was impractical and expensive. Oberly called instead for creating a system of reservation day schools and boarding schools. For a time, Pratt's vision prevailed. The BIA established dozens of nonreservation boarding schools, including ones in Santa Fe (1890), Carson (1890), Phoenix (1890), Pierre (1891), and Flandreau (1893). By 1905 there were twenty-five nonreservation boarding schools enrolling 9,736 Indian students. There were also ninety-three reservation boarding schools with an enrollment of 11,402 students.

The curriculum was heavy-handed, designed to accelerate the assimilation process. Discipline was strict. Indian children were not allowed to speak tribal languages; they functioned in an English-only environment. They were also forcibly converted to Christianity and denied the right to practice their own religions. They were required to patriotically celebrate major American holidays and to learn job skills.

By the early 1900s, however, doubts about the effectiveness of the boarding schools increased. The programs were expensive, and upon graduation the Indian students showed a marked propensity for returning to the reservations and resuming their lives as Indians. Assimilation did not appear to be taking place. To deal with the expense, as well as the failures, of boarding school educations, the federal government began emphasizing vocational training in reservation day schools. After 1910 the BIA also worked at placing Indian children in neighboring public schools. By 1930 there were 21,000 Indian children in boarding schools, 5,000 in reservation schools, and 36,000 in public schools near the reservations.

During the 1930s the major changes in government education policies occured when Commissioner of Indian Affairs John Collier* ended compulsory religious instruction in government schools and provided voluntary instruction in native religions. Congress also passed the Johnson-O'Malley Act* of 1934, which allowed the BIA to contract with state and local authorities to provide public education to Indian students. What soon became obvious, however, was that Indian students in local public schools often faced racism and discrimination from non-Indian students and teachers, and that local authorities were more interested in getting the federal money than in developing special programs to assist Indian children.

The problem of racism and discrimination in public schools fueled the demand for educational self-determination* in the 1960s and 1970s. To protect their children from racism, to preserve their heritage, and to prevent arbitrary decisions by local school boards and by BIA officials, Native Americans began demanding Indian control of school boards and curricula. In 1971 the Coalition of Indian Controlled School Boards was established to promote self-determination. Its demands resulted in the Indian Education Act* of 1972. The act mandated parental and tribal participation in all federal impact-aid programs to public schools; allocated funds to encourage the establishment of community-run schools; provided funds for the development of new and bilingual curricula, including Indian history and culture; helped fund adult education projects; and established an Office of Indian Education, controlled by the National Advisory Council on Indian Education, to administer the programs. The Indian Self-Determination and Education Assistance Act of 1975 reinforced these policies. All school districts enjoying funds under the Johnson-O'Malley Act had to guarantee that those moneys would be used only for Native American students; and where Indians do not control a school board, an Indian Parents Committee must be consulted on all decisions affecting Native American children. The Tribally Controlled Schools Act of 1988 strengthened these provisions.

Suggested Reading: Michael C. Cleman, *American Indian Children at School, 1850–1930*, 1993; David H. Dejong, *Promises of the Past: A History of Indian Education in the United States*, 1993; Basil H. Johnston, *Indian School Days*,

1989; Margaret Szasz, *Education and the American Indian: The Road to Self-Determination since 1928*, 1977.

JAMES S. OLSON

EDUCATION AMENDMENTS ACT OF 1978. Enacted to ensure proper implementation of the federally sanctioned Native American educational reforms initiated by the Indian Education Act* of 1972 and the Indian Self-Determination and Education Assistance Act of 1975, the Education Amendments Act included a reform clause intended to rectify the poor coordination and apparent mismanagement of Indian education by the overtly paternal Bureau of Indian Affairs* (BIA). To assist in the formulation and application of new reform proposals, Congress appointed an Advisory Study Group on Indian Education, which identified the following problem areas: the absence of Indian representation and direct participation in determining the direction and content of Indian education, insufficient funding for various programs of both basic and special instruction, nonexistent educational standards, a dearth of qualified educators in supervisory positions, inadequate boarding facilities, and a scarcity of reliable information on the amount of school construction to be required in the future.

The congressional plan of attack called for a more equitable disbursement of federal school funding and established priorities for the construction of modern educational facilities for Native American students. Moreover, under the Federal Impacted Areas Act, Congress linked the allocation and amount of federal assistance entitlements to a specific degree of Indian input in the decision-making process. The secretary of the Interior was instructed to collaborate with the American Indian community to produce basic education standards to guide the conduct of the BIA as well as the various contract schools and dormitories. The act of 1978 also amended the Indian Education Act of 1972 by providing expanded federal assistance for special education, gifted students, and preschoolers, and by voiding many of the eligibility requirements previously tied to government funding for Indian-operated contract schools.

At the same time the education administration of the Bureau of Indian Affairs underwent an extensive renovation, as considerable authority was placed in the hands of local bureau school boards. Taken as a whole, the Education Amendments Act of 1978 ensured increased Indian participation and self-determination* in the education process, respected the rights of the student, preserved family bonds and freedom of worship, and contributed to the creation of inventive alternative programs.

Suggested Reading: Estelle Fuchs and Robert J. Havighurst, *To Live on This Earth: American Indian Education*, 1983; James S. Olson and Raymond Wilson, *Native Americans in the Twentieth Century*, 1984; Francis Paul Prucha, *The Great Father*, Vol. 2, 1984.

JAMES S. OLSON

ELEMENTARY AND SECONDARY EDUCATION ACT OF 1965. A central element of President Lyndon B. Johnson's Great Society program was the improvement of American education,* and the Elementary and Secondary Education Act of 1965 became a keystone of federal education policy. There was a widespread belief that poorly funded school systems perpetuated poverty in many areas of America. Because school funding was tied to the property tax base in most areas, a vicious cycle dominated the schools. The act therefore provided federal funds to improve school libraries, language laboratories, learning centers, and support services in poor school districts. As a result of the legislation, the funding of Indian schools—federal as well as state and local—increased dramatically.

Suggested Reading: Lyndon B. Johnson, *The Vantage Point*, 1970.

JAMES S. OLSON

***ELK v. WILKINS* (1884).** In 1881 the city council of Omaha, Nebraska, denied John Elk, an Indian, the right to vote. Elk, an English-speaking farmer living in Omaha, claimed that his Fourteenth Amendment* rights as a citizen of the United States had been violated. Omaha officials, however, claimed that because the Fourteenth Amendment specifically excluded Indians from its provisions, Elk was not a citizen of the United States, even if he had been born there, and was not entitled to vote. Elk filed suit in the federal courts, and in 1884 the Supreme Court rendered its decision in *Elk v. Wilkins*. It found in favor of the city officials, claiming that Elk had not been "born" in the United States but "born to an Indian nation" and that he had not been naturalized. As a result, he could not vote. The decision enraged Indian reformers, who feared that the inability to vote would retard their efforts to assimilate Indians. The *Elk v. Wilkins* decision played a central role in Senator Henry Dawes's decision to promote Indian citizenship* through allotment.*

Suggested Reading: Russel Lawrence Barsh and James Youngblood Henderson, *The Road: Indian Tribes and Political Liberty*, 1980; Vine Deloria Jr. and Clifford M. Lytle, *American Indians, American Justice*, 1983; Stephen L. Pevar, *The Rights of Indians and Tribes: The Basic ACLU Guide to Indian and Tribal Rights*, 1992; Wilcomb E. Washburn, *Red Man's Land, White Man's Law*, 1971; Charles F. Wilkinson, *American Indians, Time and the Law*, 1987; John R. Wun-

der, *"Retained by The People": A History of American Indians and the Bill of Rights*, 1994.

JAMES S. OLSON

EMPLOYMENT DIVISION, DEPARTMENT OF HUMAN RESOURCES OF OREGON, ET AL. v. ALFRED L. SMITH (1990). Although Congress passed the American Indian Religious Freedom Act* in 1978 to protect the First Amendment rights of Native American peoples, the diversity of their religious traditions has often posed difficult legal and constitutional questions. The issue of tribal sovereignty* as opposed to individual rights has also complicated the matter. Peyote* use has been particularly controversial. American society in general condemns the use of drugs, but the ceremonial use of peyote is central to the religious beliefs of members of the Native American Church. In *Employment Division, Department of Human Resources of Oregon, et al. v. Alfred L. Smith* in 1990, the Supreme Court heard a case involving the firing of a Native American from a state job because of his peyote use. The Supreme Court heard the case but decided to make no exceptions to existing state drug laws for Indian religious beliefs. The Court agreed that state governments could fire Indians who use peyote during religious ceremonies and could deny them unemployment benefits as well. Many Native American activists protested the decision, but with no success.

Suggested Reading: Russel Lawrence Barsh and James Youngblood Henderson, *The Road: Indian Tribes and Political Liberty*, 1980; Vine Deloria Jr. and Clifford M. Lytle, *American Indians, American Justice*, 1983; H. Barry Holt and Gary Forrester, *Digest of American Indian Law: Cases and Chronology*, 1990; Stephen L. Pevar, *The Rights of Indians and Tribes: The Basic ACLU Guide to Indian and Tribal Rights*, 1992; Wilcomb E. Washburn, *Red Man's Land, White Man's Law*, 1971; Charles F. Wilkinson, *American Indians, Time and the Law*, 1987; John R. Wunder, *"Retained by The People": A History of American Indians and the Bill of Rights*, 1994.

JAMES S. OLSON

ENDANGERED SPECIES ACT OF 1973. See *UNITED STATES v. DION* (1986).

ENVIRONMENTAL MOVEMENT. The environment has always held a central place in the relationship between Indian and non-Indian peoples in North America. Indeed, in many ways North American history is the history of environmental exploitation and conflict. Concern for protecting the North American environment became apparent near the end of the nineteenth century. Wide-scale settlement of the United States and a general decline in the resources available for exploitation caused many people to rethink the way in which natural resources were being used and allocated. By the end of the century, the realization that both renewable and nonrenewable natural resources were rapidly declining challenged the previously held myth that North America's resources were abundant beyond any possibility of exhaustion.

Perhaps the best example of the myth of superabundance was the decline in the plains buffalo. Whereas they once numbered in the tens of millions, by the last decades of the nineteenth century the plains buffalo declined in numbers so rapidly that they were virtually extinct in the United States by 1900. By 1914 the passenger pigeon, which once darkened North American skies by the millions, was also extinct. The loss of these and other species, as well as the loss of millions of acres of critical habitat these species required to survive, caused a heightened awareness of and intensified concern for North America's environment. This led directly to various and diverse attempts to more effectively manage, allocate, and protect threatened species and habitat.

The twentieth-century environmental movement was marked by a growth in the scientific management of natural resources, as well as a redefinition of what were acceptable uses of all natural resources. The environmental ideas of *preservation* and *wise use* characterized new strategies in managing natural resources. Although many environmentalists adhered to the preservationist views of the popular naturalists like John Muir, many others saw the economically motivated spirit of wise use as the direction in which environmental science and management should turn. President Theodore Roosevelt's chief forester, Gifford Pinchot, best represents the concept of wise use. Pinchot saw the economic value of wise use as the future of environmental management, and his influential concepts of wise use in forest management spread to other areas of natural resource management as well.

Neither philosophy left room for traditional Indian subsistence hunting, fishing, or gathering techniques. Although the advent of the environmental movement marked the beginning of government's attempts to preserve the natural environment, it also marked the beginning of a renewed assault on traditional Indian pursuits of subsistence hunting, fishing, and gathering. Indians were often scapegoated for the decline of fish and game populations, when indeed it was in their best interests to see that these and other endangered species were preserved for future generations. Non-Indian environmentalists likened traditional subsistence hunting and fishing activities to market hunting or fishing, activities that were often charged with decimating many wild fish and game species.

Even as they sought to protect critical habitat, more often than not environmentalists also sought to restrict the subsistence uses of fish and game populations in favor of sport hunting and fishing. At the same time, environmentalists sought to preserve forest and mineral resources to meet the economic needs of the market. Although restrictions on over-hunting and over-fishing, as well as sound management of the environment, were needed to protect declining resources, such restrictions did not take into account the subsistence needs of indigenous peoples who relied on the fur, fish, game, and forest resources for their daily survival. Indeed, many declining fish and game species received a much greater level of protection than did the Indian peoples who hunted for food, clothing, and economic stability.

The early twentieth-century environmental movement witnessed the enhanced, and much needed, protection of both flora and fauna. The origin of the national parks system is rooted in this movement. On the other hand, the movement also was an integral part of the assault on Indian culture and livelihood throughout much of the twentieth century. Ironically, the modern environmental movement has occasionally adopted the image of the Native American as a symbol of caring and concern for the environment even though Indians were often falsely blamed for destroying the very resources on which they relied. During the last three decades, a renewed concern for the environment has been visible in such symbolic festivals as the annual Earth Day, first celebrated in 1970. Indians have continued their struggle to remain close to the environment, and they continue to fight state and federal attempts to undermine their reliance on the environment for food, clothing, and a spiritual closeness to the land on which they live. Most visibly, this struggle is being played out in state and federal courts, where Indians sue to protect both the environment on which they rely as well as their right to utilize that environment for their spiritual and economic interests.

Suggested Reading: Janet Foster, *Working for Wildlife: The Beginning of Preservation in Canada*, 1978; William Leiss, *The Domination of Nature*, 1972; Roderick Nash, ed., *The American Environment: Readings in the History of Conservation*, 1968; Donald Worster, *Nature's Economy: A History of Ecological Ideas*, 1994.

ANTHONY GULIG

ESKIMOS. The Eskimos are people of Arctic Mongoloid ancestry inhabiting scattered enclaves in the coastal areas of Greenland, northeastern Siberia, and Arctic North America. The name "Eskimo" derives from the inaccurately applied descriptive term for "raw flesh eaters." Their name for themselves is Inuit or Yuit, meaning "the people." Physiological, archaeological, and linguistic evidence indicates that the Eskimos migrated across the Bering Strait to Arctic North America during a period of extreme glaciation. The Inuit share many cultural traits with people indigenous to the Siberian Arctic and were probably a later arrival to the New World than other Native American groups.

Eskimo technology was designed to meet the harsh conditions of an Arctic environment. The arrival of American commercial whalers in far northern Alaska in the middle 1800s began a process of change that dramatically transformed the traditional stability of Eskimo life. The introduction of steel and iron implements, firearms, and medicines eased some of the pressures of an aboriginal subsistence existence. However, this in turn somewhat reduced the need for kinship group sharing and cooperation and lessened the prestige of the hunter and the validity of the indigenous religion. The threat of punishment from a supernatural force for deviating from traditional Eskimo practices lost its impact.

The white whalers were followed by missionaries, teachers, doctors, and military personnel. The changes brought about by this infusion of knowledge occurred slowly, due to the fact that the newer arrivals constantly had to adapt their way of life to that of the Eskimo to survive. As is true with almost any colonizing power, America's efforts among the Eskimos were based on a set of moral assumptions and beliefs. Missionary and government officials attempted to limit the use of the traditional Inuit language, change centuries-old cultural practices, destroy the indigenous religion, and eliminate existing sexual mores and customs considered barbarous to the newcomers. Failure of the Eskimos to assimilate quickly into the economic and social mainstream was usually explained by references to the widely held belief in the inferiority of the Arctic Mongoloid stock.

The admittance of Alaska to statehood in 1959 set into motion the modern political and economic development of the Eskimos. In 1966, eight regionally based native associations that had been formed to protect native land rights combined to form the Alaska Federation of Natives* (AFN). By mid-1967, the AFN had submitted land title claims to almost 99 percent of Alaska's 375 million acres. This was followed in 1968 by major oil discoveries at Prudhoe Bay and the resultant $900 million land lease sale by the state to oil corporations. The federal government responded to these events by halting the disposal of Alaskan public lands that were subject to native claims. The Eskimos found themselves in a position of real political strength for the first time.

AFN leaders adopted an agenda on land claims that included the following elements: (1) adequate compensation must be provided for lands that were illegally taken in the past; (2) enough land must be maintained to allow Native Americans who choose to retain their traditional way of life to sustain a subsistence economy; (3) Native Americans must receive a perpetual royalty interest on land removed from Alaskan Native title; and (4) Native Americans must have self-determination* over the money and land they receive. Several years of negotiation resulted in passage of the Alaska Native Claims Settlement Act* in 1971, which settled the dispute over who owned Alaska land. This act gave the Eskimos and other Native American groups $962.5 million and 44 million acres of land upon extinguishment of native claims to the remaining territory.

In May 1973 an international congress met in France to consider the escalating threat of off-shore oil and gas development along Alaska's Arctic coast. Participants in the conference included technicians and researchers from the oil and gas companies, representatives from Canadian Inuit and other North American Indian organizations, and Greenlandic Inuit. This group expanded by November 1973 into the Arctic Peoples' Conference held in Christianborg, Denmark. Two resolutions resulted, demanding the recognition of Arctic populations as peoples and claiming direct involvement in and influence on development in Arctic areas. A lack of financial support prevented further formal discussion and activity by this group.

The Inuit Circumpolar Conference (ICC), founded in 1977, resulted from efforts to continue the work of the Arctic Peoples' Conference by Mayor Eben Hopson of Barrow, Alaska. The ICC meets every three years to provide a forum for North American and Greenlandic Inuit to discuss common problems, lobby for an Arctic Native voice in economic development, and promote environmental preservation. The ICC developed a comprehensive Arctic policy document to guide actions and policies affecting Arctic areas. The ICC has assumed the position of world leader in the promotion and sustaining of indigenous human rights. The conference maintains close ties with the United Nations Working Group on Indigenous Peoples, an organization that monitors the status of indigenous peoples worldwide. The ICC has become a vital force in the global networking of aboriginal and indigenous peoples throughout the world. Yielding to pressure, the Canadian government in 1991 agreed to the creation of a new territory known as Nunavut in the eastern Northwest Territories. Approved by referendum in 1992, Nunavut will have an area of approximately 772,500 square miles. The Inuit will exercise broad economic and political control over this area.

Suggested Reading: Ernest S. Burch, *The Eskimos*, 1988; Norman Chance, *The Inupiat and Arctic Alaska: An Ethnography of Development*, 1990; Aron Crowell, "Prehistory of Alaska's Pacific Coast," in William W. Fitzhugh and Aron Crowell, eds., *Crossroads of Continents: Cultures of Siberia and Alaska*, 1988; Vine Deloria Jr., *American Indian Policy in the Twentieth Century*, 1985; Robert F. Spencer, *The North Alaskan Eskimo: A Study in Ecology and Society*, 1976.

DAVID RITCHEY

EX PARTE CROW DOG **(1883).** An appeal to the U.S. Supreme Court in 1883 over tribal versus federal authority in the murder of an Indian by an Indian, *Ex Parte Crow Dog* reflected national interest in Indian affairs in the mid-1880s and ultimately affected the development of allotment* policy. In 1883 Crow Dog murdered Spotted Tail, a Brûlé Sioux chief known for his pro-government positions in Sioux affairs. The federal government could always count on Spotted Tail to take its part in negotiations with the Sioux. The government rewarded him well for his efforts, supplying him with a two-story house located at the agency named for him on Rosebud Creek in modern-day South Dakota. Crow Dog, a traditionalist who despised pro-government natives, killed Spotted Tail in Indian country,* and following traditional Sioux custom, the two families worked out compensation to be paid to Spotted Tail's family for the killing. Crow Dog was then considered to have made his restitution for the killing and satisfied Sioux justice.

Spotted Tail, however, was popular among whites because he had supported the government. The government ordered Crow Dog's arrest and trial for the murder of Spotted Tail. Convicted and sentenced to death, he convinced the federal marshal to let him go home to settle his affairs. He returned on the day appointed, much to the surprise of the marshal and whites generally. Because of his honorable act in returning, white opinion reversed itself and demanded his release. Such could not be done without judicial appeal. A writ of habeas corpus (to release him from custody) was filed on his behalf, and in *Ex Parte Crow Dog*, 109 U.S. 556 (1883), the Supreme Court granted the writ.

The Court held that because the killing took place in Indian country between two Indians, white judicial systems had no authority. Crow Dog had to be set free. Once again, white opinion reversed and now demanded that such a large gap in federal law be closed. Whites wanted Indian affairs ended through assimilation* and the sale of reservations.* Compensating a victim's family as a means of restitution was not what whites wanted as punishment for crimes.

Congress responded in 1885 with the Major Crimes Act,* which defined seven capital crimes committed in Indian country, no matter by what race, as punishable under white law. One year later this act was challenged in *United States v. Kagama** (1886), and the Supreme Court upheld the legislation on guardianship* theory. Indian tribes were constitutionally defined as wards of the national government, the Court said, and therefore Congress could extend its authority over Indians and the communities in which they lived, even on reservations. The Court said that Congress not only had the right but the duty to do so. The Court overlooked or ignored the fact that tribal courts* traditionally held jurisdiction over capital crimes.

Did that jurisdiction remain as concurrent jurisdiction, or was it surrendered via the Major Crimes Act? Over the years, court decisions and federal legislation have stripped tribal courts of whatever concurrent jurisdiction they had. The Major Crimes Act closed one large gap in federal legislation, trying to abolish tribal identities and individuate Indians into becoming "civilized." Shortly after Congress passed the legislation, it passed the Dawes Act,* which renewed allotment and emphasized the destruction of reservations.

Suggested Reading: Russel Lawrence Barsh and James Youngblood Henderson, *The Road: Indian Tribes and Political Liberty*, 1980; Vine Deloria Jr. and Clifford M. Lytle, *American Indians, American Justice*, 1983; Sidney L. Harring, "Crow Dog's Case: A Chapter in the Legal History of Tribal Sovereignty," *American Indian Law Review* 14 (1989), 191–239; Sidney L. Harring, *Crow Dog's Case: American Indian Sovereignty, Tribal Law, and United States Law in the Nineteenth Century*, 1994; H. Barry Holt and Gary Forrester, *Digest of American Indian Law: Cases and Chronology*, 1990; Stephen L. Pevar, *The Rights of Indians and Tribes: The Basic ACLU Guide to Indian and Tribal Rights*, 1992; Wilcomb E. Washburn, *Red Man's Land, White Man's Law*, 1971; Charles F. Wilkinson, *American Indians, Time and the Law*, 1987; John R. Wunder, *"Retained by The People": A History of American Indians and the Bill of Rights*, 1994.

TIMOTHY MORGAN

F

FEDERAL ACKNOWLEDGEMENT PROJECT. A procedure established in 1979 by the Bureau of Indian Affairs* (BIA) to regulate Indian tribes' petitions for federal acknowledgement as legal tribal entities. Federal recognition is sought by tribes because it brings certain benefits and responsibilities, such as free medical and dental care, small business loans, and college scholarships. Traditionally the BIA had handled tribal petitions for official recognition on an ad hoc, case-by-case basis. Hundreds of tribes had long been recognized by congressional statutes as legal tribal entities, but many other Indian groups did not enjoy such status and the federal benefits accompanying them. In response to a congressional clamor in the 1970s for a more systematic approach to the problem, the BIA submitted its proposal to regulate the process.

In 1979 the BIA established the Federal Acknowledgement Project, today known as the Branch of Acknowledgement and Research, to evaluate petitions for federal recognition. Each petitioning tribe had to meet seven criteria establishing a continuity from the past to the present through indisputable ethnic, cultural, and historical links to a particular geographic region. Those seven factors included the following:

1. The tribe must prove its existence as a functional entity from historical times to the present.
2. The tribe must prove that its members inhabit a specific area as a community and have done so since historical times.
3. The tribe must prove that it has maintained political authority over its members as an autonomous entity throughout history until the present.
4. The tribe must provide a tribal government document describing tribal membership requirements and tribal governing procedures.

5. The tribe must provide evidence that the tribal membership consists of people who have descended from a historical tribal entity.

6. The tribe must show that its tribal members consist of individuals who are not simultaneously members of other tribes.

7. The tribe must show that it is not expressly terminated or forbidden by federal statute from participating in the federal-Indian relationship.

At the time of the formal establishment of the Federal Acknowledgement Project, forty Indian tribes had applied to the BIA for recognition.

The process, however, proved cumbersome and controversial. Legal hassles, bureaucratic inertia, and unreasonable documentary requirements complicated and delayed the process. In addition to the forty original petitioners, another 124 petitions for recognition were soon filed. But by 1994 only ten tribes had received formal recognition: Grand Traverse Band of Ottawa and Chippewa in Minnesota (1980); the James Klallam Tribe of Washington (1981); the Tunica-Biloxi Indian Tribe of Louisiana (1981); the Death Valley Timbi-Sha Shoshone Band of California (1983); the Narragansett Indian Tribe of Rhode Island (1983); the Poarch Band of Creeks in Alabama (1984); the Wampanoag Tribal Council of Gay Head, Massachusetts (1987); the San Juan Southern Paiute Tribe of Arizona (1990); the Snoqualmie Tribe of Washington (1993); and the Mohegan Tribe of Connecticut (1994). Frustrated with the time-consuming process, a number of other tribes have secured recognition directly through congressional statute, outside the Federal Acknowledgement Project.

Suggested Reading: James S. Olson and Raymond Wilson, *Native Americans in the Twentieth Century*, 1984; Francis Paul Prucha, *The Great Father*, Vol. 2, 1984; William W. Quinn Jr., "Federal Acknowledgement of American Indian Tribes: The Historical Development of a Legal Concept," *American Journal of Legal History* 34 (October 1990), 331–64; Allogan Slagle, "Branch of Acknowledgement and Research," in Mary B. Davis, ed., *Native Americans in the Twentieth Century: An Encyclopedia*, 1994.

MARK BAXTER

FEDERAL OIL AND GAS ROYALTY MANAGEMENT ACT OF 1982.
This legislation maximizes tribal profits through the management, control, and sale of natural resources on reservation lands. Located on the reservations* of various American Indian tribes are significant amounts of uranium, coal, oil, and natural gas. Those resources became particularly important, to Indians and to non-Indians, during the energy crisis of the 1970s. After the Yom Kippur War in the Middle East in 1973, oil-

producing Arab nations, upset with U.S. loyalty to Israel, imposed an oil embargo. Supplies of oil became tight and energy prices skyrocketed, creating economic as well as national security problems. Indian natural resources gained immediately in value.

But most energy-rich tribes had been leasing out their resources at prices well below market levels, and the energy crisis of the 1970s exacerbated that problem. With oil, natural gas, and coal prices escalating rapidly, many tribes found themselves bound to low-paying, long-term royalty contracts with major energy companies. The energy companies were reaping huge profits, harvesting tribal energy resources for a pittance and then marketing them at world price levels.

Indian activists reacted with the formation of the Council of Energy Resource Tribes* (CERT) in 1976. CERT was committed to maximizing tribal profits by raising prices. During the late 1970s and early 1980s the Council of Energy Resource Tribes lobbied vigorously for federal legislation protecting the Indian resource state. In 1982 its efforts resulted in the Indian Mineral Development Act* and the Federal Oil and Gas Royalty Management Act, both of which contained provisions allowing for the renegotiation of royalty contracts, establishment of joint ventures between mining companies and Indian tribes, amendments to national environmental laws giving tribes clear control of resource use on their own lands, education and job training programs to develop reservation expertise, and revolving funds to improve reservation infrastructures. The Federal Oil and Gas Royalty Management Act also developed cooperative administrative and auditing systems between federal, state, and tribal authorities to guarantee that accurate royalty payments were made. Both laws are considered landmark events in the history of the self-determination* movement, because many Indians believe economic self-sufficiency is central to tribal sovereignty.*

Suggested Reading: Marjane Ambler, *Breaking the Iron Bonds: Indian Control of Energy Development*, 1990; Vine Deloria Jr. and Clifford Lytle, *The Nations Within: The Past and Future of American Indian Sovereignty*, 1984; Roxanne Dunbar Ortiz, *Indians of the Americas: Human Rights and Self-Determination*, 1984; Hurst Hannum, *Autonomy, Self-Determination and Sovereignty: The Accommodation of Conflicting Rights*, 1990; Phyllis Mauch Messenger, ed., *The Ethics of Collecting Cultural Property: Whose Culture? Whose Property?* 1989.

JAMES S. OLSON

FEE SIMPLE TITLE. In law, a fee simple title is one in which the title holder possesses ownership without limitations or qualifications. This includes the right of disposition, that is, the right to sell the property. In the early years after its creation, the U.S. government occasionally allotted "reservations"* of land in fee simple to individual Indians or families. Under the 1887 Dawes Act,* the federal government attempted to replace tribal ownership of reservation lands with fee simple titles for individual Indians. Indians were to receive patents (titles) to their allotments* of land after a 25-year trust period expired.

The patents were a double-edged sword. On the one hand, they gave Indians absolute title to land, which provided protection against white encroachment. The Omaha tribe requested allotments in 1882 for this very reason, trying to avoid the experience of the Poncas, who had been forcibly removed to Indian Territory.* On the other hand, the ability to sell left allotment owners vulnerable to pressure from land speculators, railroad developers, and timber companies. Vast amounts of land passed from Indians to non-Indians through the sale of fee simple lands.

The Department of the Interior developed a practice of issuing fee simple patents to allottees deemed "competent" to handle their own affairs. Between 1917 and 1920 this policy resulted in over 17,000 fee patents to Indians, and many of these title holders sold their lands. The Department of the Interior slowed down its issue of fee patents in the 1920s, moving back toward retaining Indian lands in trust* status. The Indian Reorganization Act* of 1934 prevented further allotments and extended restrictions against the sale of Indian lands indefinitely. During the termination* policy of the 1950s and 1960s, the federal government renewed its attempt to grant fee simple titles to allottees. Terminated tribes lost federal trust status over their lands. Again, Indian land loss contributed to disillusionment with federal policy, and termination was brought to an end. Currently, Indian reservations encompass a mix of fee simple lands (held by both Indians and non-Indians), individual and tribal lands held in trust, and federal lands.

Suggested Reading: Russel Lawrence Barsh and James Youngblood Henderson, *The Road: Indian Tribes and Political Liberty*, 1980; Vine Deloria Jr. and Clifford M. Lytle, *American Indians, American Justice*, 1983; H. Barry Holt and Gary Forrester, *Digest of American Indian Law: Cases and Chronology*, 1990; Stephen L. Pevar, *The Rights of Indians and Tribes: The Basic ACLU Guide to Indian and Tribal Rights*, 1992; Wilcomb E. Washburn, *Red Man's Land, White Man's Law*, 1971; Charles F. Wilkinson, *American Indians, Time and the Law*, 1987; John R. Wunder, *"Retained by The People": A History of American Indians and the Bill of Rights*, 1994.

EMILY GREENWALD

FETAL ALCOHOL SYNDROME. See **ALCOHOL.**

FIFTH AMENDMENT. The Fifth Amendment to the U.S. Constitution* was ratified and went into effect in 1791. It essentially guaranteed the rights of individual citizens against the powers of the new federal government. More specifically, the Fifth Amendment required an indictment by a grand jury before an individual could be brought to trial for a serious crime, outlawed double jeopardy (being tried twice for the same crime), guaranteed an individual equality before the law, prohibited forced self-incrimination, and required just compensation when property owners lost assets in eminent domain procedures (legal government seizure of private property for public projects). The Fourteenth Amendment, ratified in 1868, guaranteed these same individual rights against abuse by state and local governments.

A ticklish issue in constitutional history, however, has been whether or not tribal governments fell under the same legal requirements. In the *Talton v. Mayes** case of 1896, the Supreme Court decided that the Bill of Rights* applied to actions of federal and state governments, not tribal governments, because tribes are not subordinate bodies of those governments. John Talton, a Cherokee, had murdered a Cherokee Indian on the Cherokee reservation.* A five-man Cherokee grand jury indicted him for murder, and a Cherokee court convicted him. He appealed to the federal courts, arguing that his Fifth Amendment rights had been violated because a proper, six-man grand jury had not been impaneled. The Supreme Court rejected his argument. Tribal sovereignty,* the Court argued, flows from the tribe's aboriginal independence, which preceded the writing of the Constitution.

After 1924, when all American Indians had become citizens of the United States, controversy frequently erupted over whether a tribal government was bound by the Fifth and Fourteenth* Amendments. Hundreds of cases revolving around the issue made their way through the federal court system, and beginning in the early 1960s Congress began to respond to numerous complaints by individual tribal members who contended that tribal officials were abusive and tyrannical. They appealed to Congress to pass legislation that would protect them from such mistreatment. Congressional hearings convened in 1962 to investigate their complaints of misconduct, and several congressmen concluded that individual Indians needed "some guaranteed form of civil rights against the actions of their own governments."

In 1965 the case of *Madeline Colliflower v. John Garland, Sheriff of County of Blaine, Montana,** provided new impetus for civil rights legislation. Madeline Colliflower, a Gros Ventre Indian living on the Fort

Belknap reservation* in Blaine County, Montana, was arrested by Indian police* for refusing to remove her cattle from land leased by another individual on the reservation. A tribal court* convicted and sentenced her to a fine of $25 or five days in jail. She filed a writ of habeus corpus (to release her from custody) in the federal district court, claiming that her Sixth* and Fourteenth Amendment rights had been violated because the tribal court had not given her the right to legal counsel and had refused to confront her with the witnesses against her. Fort Belknap tribal officials argued that the due process clauses of the U.S. Constitution did not apply to reservation legal institutions. The federal district court, uncertain of its own jurisdiction over reservation legal institutions, declined to act on the writ and the case went to the U.S. Court of Appeals. In the end, the Court of Appeals decided that the federal district did indeed have jurisdiction over the writ. The Court of Appeals justices decided that in light of the recent history of Indian tribes, tribal courts were—at least to some degree—extensions of a federal agency, and that as such were subject to due process requirements. Individual Indians, therefore, enjoyed due process rights in tribal courts as well as in non-Indian jurisdictions.

The decision led directly to passage of the Indian Civil Rights Act* of 1968, which, in its own words, was designed to "ensure that the American Indian is afforded the broad Constitutional rights secured to other Americans . . . [in order to] protect individual Indians from arbitrary and unjust actions of tribal governments." Legislatively, it confers certain rights on all persons who are subject to the jurisdiction of a tribal government, and the act authorizes federal courts to enforce these rights. The Indian Civil Rights Act guarantees almost all the fundamental rights enumerated in the U.S. Constitution, with the exception of four. Tribal governments are not subject to the Establishment Clause (which prohibits government aid to churches) of the First Amendment, do not have to provide legal counsel (free of charge) to indigent defendants, nor do they have to provide a trial by jury in civil cases or provide grand jury indictments in criminal cases. These amendments or protections were not included because Congress surmised that they would be a potential threat to political stability within tribal governments.

The Indian Civil Rights Act has fundamentally changed the procedural aspects of the tribal judicial system. Prior to its enactment, procedural uniformity was nonexistent. Tribes would invariably employ their own methods of conflict resolution. The Indian Civil Rights Act, however, requires that all tribes adhere to certain procedural standards. In particular, federal courts mandate that tribal courts advise criminal defendants of their right to a trial by jury, write their criminal laws in clear and certain language, honor a criminal defendant's right against self-incrimination, prohibit the trial judge from also being the prosecutor, and maintain complete records of judicial proceedings.

Suggested Reading: Russel Lawrence Barsh and James Youngblood Henderson, *The Road: Indian Tribes and Political Liberty*, 1980; Vine Deloria Jr. and Clifford M. Lytle, *American Indians, American Justice*, 1983; H. Barry Holt and Gary Forrester, *Digest of American Indian Law: Cases and Chronology*, 1990; Stephen L. Pevar, *The Rights of Indians and Tribes: The Basic ACLU Guide to Indian and Tribal Rights*, 1992; Wilcomb E. Washburn, *Red Man's Land, White Man's Law*, 1971; Charles F. Wilkinson, *American Indians, Time and the Law*, 1987; John R. Wunder, *"Retained by The People": A History of American Indians and the Bill of Rights*, 1994.

JAMES S. OLSON

FIREARMS. Firearms were a cardinal element of trade between Europeans and Indians. As Europeans came to the Americas after 1500, they brought with them their Iron Age technology. Indian tribes had experienced trade with each other, and the introduction of new lines of trade goods enticed them into a relationship resulting in surrender of their Neolithic culture for the Iron Age culture of the Europeans.

Items such as pots or small boats were quite familiar to Indians who had long made clay pots or dugout canoes. Ready-made goods such as iron pots or dories, which could be bought for a few beaver pelts or deerskins, quickly replaced the traditionally made goods. Woolen blankets or shirts, greatcoats or matchcoats, trinkets, hatchets or axes—all were attractive to native hunters and trappers, but firearms were the most attractive until alcohol.* Europeans' earliest guns were poor substitutes for the bows and arrows that Indian hunters and warriors had traditionally used. The wheelocks or matchlocks were heavy, inaccurate, and extremely unreliable, but the Dutch introduced the first flintlock muskets (vast improvements over matchlocks) in the mid-seventeenth century. Soon the Iroquois warriors wanted the new weapons, and the Iroquois Confederation of the Mohawk River Valley and interior of New York became an ardent ally of the Dutch, an alliance that passed to the English when they conquered the Dutch New Netherland colony in 1664.

In the 1630s the Iroquois, using more accurate and reliable firearms, began systematic conquests of western Indians in order to absorb the fur trade* and redirect it from the French in the St. Lawrence to the Mohawk-Hudson arena. By the late seventeenth century, the competition for furs had generalized the gun trade to such an extent that most Indian peoples, despite attempted prohibitions, could acquire them.

With rifling techniques promoting increased flintlock musket accuracy, guns became integral elements of eastern Indian trade needs. By 1700, European traders used guns and alcohol as attractions in their trade with Indians. Until the end of the nineteenth century, guns remained important trade items for Indians. With the spread of guns to the Great Plains in the late eighteenth century and then the development of repeating rifles in the nineteenth century, Indian hunters could kill American bison in sufficient numbers to supply their villages and peoples with enough food to warrant the adoption of nomadic lifestyles and migration onto the Plains themselves. Eastern Indian hunters abandoned the bow and arrow by 1700, and as gun technology moved westward, so did abandonment of Neolithic culture generally.

The cultural consequences of the adoption of Iron Age technology meant overhunting of traditional game, even to extinction. It meant adoption of economic motivations rather than traditional ideas of communal and tribal sharing and status in the village. When coupled with alcohol, guns meant devastation in Indian towns and villages, especially after reservation* life began. Despair and depression coupled with guns and alcohol to produce deadly combinations in Indian life. Guns became one of the most important means by which Indians became dependent on Euroamericans in the seventeenth, eighteenth, and nineteenth centuries.

Suggested Reading: Arrell Morgan Gibson, *The American Indian: Prehistory to the Present*, 1980; Timothy Silver, *A New Face on the Countryside: Indians, Colonists, and Slaves in South Atlantic Forests, 1500–1800*, 1990.

TIMOTHY MORGAN

FIRST AMENDMENT. See **RELIGIOUS FREEDOM.**

FISHER v. DISTRICT COURT OF MONTANA **(1976).** An Indian tribe has the right to exercise civil jurisdiction within the territory it controls. This is true even if tribes have previously failed to assert these rights. Furthermore, denying access to state courts in such situations does not constitute racial discrimination and does not violate the equal protection clause of the Fourteenth Amendment.*

In *Fisher*, the state of Montana had exercised jurisdiction over the adoption* of children on Cheyenne reservations until 1935, when the tribe established a tribal court* as authorized by the Indian Reorganization Act* of 1934. Fisher argued that the tribe's assertion of authority was preempted by the state's prior exercise of jurisdiction, that the tribe had in effect surrendered its civil jurisdiction by failing to assert it prior to 1935.

The U.S. Supreme Court held that where all concerned parties were residents of the reservation,* the tribal court possessed exclusive civil jurisdiction. Furthermore, this exclusive jurisdiction did not constitute racial discrimination because "the exclusive jurisdiction of the tribal court does not derive from the race of the plaintiff but rather from the quasi-sovereign status of the North Dakota tribe under federal law." The Court emphasized that its decision was based on its recognition of the political authority of the tribe, rather than on racial preference.

The failure of the tribe to exercise jurisdiction prior to 1935 did not mean that the tribe was unable to assert its jurisdiction in the face of existing state jurisdiction. The state court's attempt to assume jurisdiction represented an infringement on the tribal powers of self-government and self-determination.*

Suggested Reading: Russel Lawrence Barsh and James Youngblood Henderson, *The Road: Indian Tribes and Political Liberty*, 1980; Vine Deloria Jr. and Clifford M. Lytle, *American Indians, American Justice*, 1983; H. Barry Holt and Gary Forrester, *Digest of American Indian Law: Cases and Chronology*, 1990; Stephen L. Pevar, *The Rights of Indians and Tribes: The Basic ACLU Guide to Indian and Tribal Rights*, 1992; Wilcomb E. Washburn, *Red Man's Land, White Man's Law*, 1971; Charles F. Wilkinson, *American Indians, Time and the Law*, 1987; John R. Wunder, *"Retained by The People": A History of American Indians and the Bill of Rights*, 1994.

CRAIG HEMMENS

"FISH-INS." See **ADAMS, HANK.**

FISHING RIGHTS. A defining feature of Native American culture is a closeness to the land and its resources. An intrinsic aspect of that relationship to the land is a historic, and in many cases contemporary, reliance on the fish inhabiting nearby lakes, rivers, streams, and oceans. When Indian tribes and bands ceded their traditional land base to the federal government, they often endeavored to retain or reserve the right to continue to harvest fish for subsistence and commercial purposes—much as they had in the years before treaties* extinguished aboriginal title to their lands.

Although the treaties identifying fishing rights were negotiated with the federal government, in more recent years state governments have often tried to restrict Indians in their subsistence and commercial fishing activities. The states have argued that since inland, as well as most ocean, fishing grounds are regulated by state authorities, Indian fishing should also be subordinate to state authority. Beginning in the late nineteenth century and continuing throughout much of the twentieth century, many state governments actively prohibited Indian commercial and subsistence fishing in spite of prior treaty provisions that specifically provided for such activity. Although they were not the only states actively interfering with Indian fishing rights, Washington and Wisconsin stood out in their efforts to prohibit Indians from fishing beyond restrictive state regulation originally intended to manage sport anglers and commercial fishing industries.

Where fishing rights were included in a treaty document or entrenched in aboriginal title by custom, Indians rarely relinquished their usufructuary right (i.e., right to use another's property as long as it is not damaged or altered) to the valuable resource at hand. In spite of this, for much of the twentieth century, state fish and wildlife agencies, as well as sport and commercial fishing interest groups, openly campaigned against Indian access to fishing grounds, complaining that Indians possessed some sort of "special" or "extra-constitutional" right. In many cases the regulating agencies or special interest groups argued against the Indian fishing rights under the guise of conservation. Lobbying groups in the Pacific Northwest, such as S/SPAWN (Steelhead and Salmon Protection Action Now), and in the Midwest such as STA (Stop Treaty Abuse) and PARR (Protect America's Rights and Resources), engaged in openly challenging the courts' upholding of fishing rights and Indians who exercised those rights. Purporting to be acting in the interest of conservation, these groups STA, PARR, and S/SPAWN claimed that Indians were overfishing an already scarce resource. In many cases conservation was a central issue, but more often than not the controversy centered on access to valuable, fragile, and dwindling inland and ocean fishing grounds. These agencies and protesters failed to recognize the fact that fishing rights, as part of the Indian's treaty negotiations, were property rights and in no way "special" or "extra-constitutional." As well, they failed or refused to recognize the importance of the aboriginal relationship between community and environment.

In the last thirty years, tribes who retained fishing rights—either by treaty or custom—have sued in federal court to have those rights recognized by state and local authorities. In federal cases such as *Puyallup Tribe v. Department of Game* in Washington, *Lac Courte*

Oreilles Band of Lake Superior Chippewa Indians v. Lester P. Voigt in Wisconsin, and *United States v. Michigan* in Michigan, the courts ruled in favor of the Indian tribes involved, stating in essence what the tribes knew all along: fishing rights identified by treaty or custom were indeed property rights. Equally important, the rights involved were reserved by the Indians during the treaty negotiation process. These reserved* rights were not granted by any state or federal government, but were retained by the tribes when they had negotiated treaties with the federal government.

Suggested Reading: Fay G. Cohen, *Treaties on Trial: The Continuing Controversy over Northwest Indian Fishing Rights*, 1986; Robert Doherty, *Disputed Waters: Native Americans and the Great Lakes Fishery*, 1990; Gary D. Meyers, ''Different Sides of the Same Coin: A Comparative View of Indian Hunting and Fishing Rights in the United States and Canada,'' *Journal of Environmental Law* 10 (1991), 67–121; Francis Paul Prucha, *American Indian Treaties: The History of a Political Anomaly*, 1994; Charles F. Wilkinson, *American Indians, Time and the Law*, 1987.

ANTHONY GULIG

FLETCHER v. PECK (1810). In January 1795, the Georgia state legislature approved the sale of 35 million acres of state land in what is today the Yazoo River Valley of Alabama and Mississippi. Four land companies, whose owners included several members of the Georgia state legislature, purchased the property for $500,000. Smelling a corrupt bargain, the next Georgia state legislature, which convened in 1796, rescinded the sale. The buyers argued that such a decision was an unconstitutional violation of contracts. The issue then entered a complicated pattern of litigation in the federal court system. In 1802, Georgia ceded all of its western land claims to the federal government, including the Yazoo property.

Eventually, the case made its way to the U.S. Supreme Court, then presided over by Chief Justice John Marshall.* He wrote the majority opinion in the case, which became known as *Fletcher v. Peck* and was decided in 1810. The Court decided that it did not have the power to investigate the motives of the legislators who originally completed the Yazoo land sale; therefore, the sale was indeed a contract within the meaning of the Constitution. As such, the act of the 1796 legislature rescinding the deal was a violation of a legitimate contract and therefore unconstitutional.

Fletcher v. Peck had an impact on Native Americans because it forced the Supreme Court to address the question of land title and sovereignty.

Did the state of Georgia really have the right to sell land which was still occupied by its original Indian inhabitants? Had the original sale been invalid because it violated Indian land titles, then the entire question was moot because the original contract had not been valid. But in describing the nature of Indian ownership, the Court concluded that Native Americans did not really hold title to the land, at least in the way that English common law defined title. Marshall wrote that a state could claim title to land within its borders without necessarily violating the right of Indians to occupy and use the land. If the state of Georgia sold the land, which it did, it would be up to the purchaser to arrive at a satisfactory arrangement with the Indians living on the land. In essence, *Fletcher v. Peck* allowed for widespread, legal seizures of Indian land, even when the occupying tribes were not willing to sell.

                                                                    JAMES S. OLSON

Suggested Reading: C. Peter Magrath, Yazoo: Law and Politics in the New Republic, 1966.

***FOOL'S CROW v. GULLETT* (1983).** One of the main concerns of Red Power* advocates over the years has been the protection of the Indian landed estate. Indians have lost their land because of economic development, or they have had its use compromised because of economic development. This has often been a critical issue to Indian religious practitioners, because for many tribes the ancestral lands possess sacred, religious significance. The *Fool's Crow v. Gullett* case of 1983 involved such a dispute. To many Plains tribes, the Bear Butte region of South Dakota holds great religious significance. When the federal government proposed building a series of viewing areas, roads, gutters, trails, and parking lots there to assist tourists, several Plains tribes protested the plan and contested it in federal courts, arguing that white tourists, by their very presence, would degrade the religious significance of the site. However, federal courts decided in favor of the government, arguing that its construction plans did not violate the First Amendment right to religious freedom.

Suggested Reading: Vine Deloria Jr., "Sacred Lands and Religious Freedom," *NARF Law Review* 16 (Spring/Summer 1991), 1–6; Christopher Vecsey, *Handbook of American Indian Religious Freedom*, 1991.

                                                                    JAMES S. OLSON

FORT BERTHOLD INDIAN DEFENSE ASSOCIATION. In 1946, representatives of Mandan, Srickaraes, and Gros Ventres peoples on the Fort Berthold reservation in North Dakota established the Fort Berthold Indian Defense Association to protest the federal government's plans to build the Garrison Dam and Reservoir Project on the Upper Missouri River. Construction of the dam threatened to flood 275,000 acres of reservation* land and to require the relocation of 1,500 Indians. Leaders of the association claimed that the Garrison Dam Act of 1946 violated their treaty* rights and would compromise their ability to raise livestock feed, a major source of reservation income. Although the Indian leaders launched a lecture and letter-writing campaign, the association failed to stop construction of the dam. Congress did compensate the Indians for loss of their land.

Suggested Reading: Armand S. La Potin, *Native American Voluntary Organizations*, 1986.

JAMES S. OLSON

FORT LARAMIE, TREATY OF (1851). In view of the inexorable advance of white settlers across the Great Plains, the United States became increasingly concerned about the potential for armed clashes with the powerful tribes in the region. In an effort to speed the process of westward expansion and forestall unnecessary bloodshed, government agents invited some 10,000 warriors representing the Teton Sioux, Cheyennes, Arapahoes, Crows, Mandans, Gros Ventres, Assiniboines, and Aricharas to attend a great council at Fort Laramie. For allowing white pioneers peaceful passage through Indian country,* the affected tribes were promised a yearly stipend of $50,000 in material goods as compensation for any damages sustained to tribal lands or any diminution of the buffalo herds. In exchange, the assembled tribes agreed to stay within the boundaries established by the federal government, to refrain from warring among themselves, and to make restitution for any violence perpetrated against whites while in lawful transit. The treaty also stipulated that the lands turned over for roads and military posts would retain Indian ownership.

Although the contracting parties pledged that the Treaty of Fort Laramie (September 17, 1851) would remain in force for a period of fifty years, the Senate refused to ratify the agreement and limited its terms to ten years without seeking prior Indian approval. Nevertheless, the United States adhered to the parameters of the treaty until 1865 and thus temporarily postponed the inevitable resort to open warfare with the Indians inhabiting the Great Plains.

Suggested Reading: Francis Paul Prucha, *The Great Father*, Vol. 1, 1984; Wilcomb Washburn, *The American Indian and the United States: A Documentary History*, Vol. 4, 1973.

MARK BAXTER

FORT LARAMIE, TREATY OF (1868). Signed at the close of the Red Cloud War, this treaty promised the Sioux perpetual possession of South Dakota's bountiful Black Hills.* As an act of good faith, the United States agreed to remove or raze various outposts and forts located in the Powder River country, the unceded portions of which were set aside as a Sioux hunting grounds. Many of the assembled chiefs agreed to take up residency on the Great Sioux Reserve situated west of the Missouri River, where the two sides agreed to preserve an everlasting peace along mutually recognized fixed boundaries designed to forestall both Indian incursions and white encroachments.

By assigning each tribal member anywhere from 80 to 320 acres of land to be apportioned according to age, gender, or marital status, misguided reformers hoped to convert the warlike Plains Indians into the white ideal of the independent farmer. Prospective Indian farmers were to receive the necessary farming implements and instruction in planting techniques for an initial period of three to four years. To encourage agricultural output, cash prizes were to be awarded to the most productive Indian farmers, and Indian tradesmen were to be given preference in government hiring. At the same time, the Sioux were required to place all of their children, aged 6 to 16, in government-operated schools. Ultimately, however, this ill-conceived, paternalistic, and idealistic attempt to civilize the Indians achieved little in the way of positive results.

In any case, the discovery of gold in the Black Hills region marked the death knell of the Fort Laramie Treaty of 1868. Clashes between the Sioux and trespassing white prospectors led to an increased U.S. military presence, which ended in General Custer's* crushing defeat at the Battle of Little Big Horn in 1876. Shortly thereafter, Congress abrogated the treaty. During the 1960s and 1970s, American Indian Movement (AIM) activists demanded that the federal government adhere to the clauses in the Fort Laramie Treaty of 1868. Finally, in 1980 the U.S. Supreme Court ruled that the Sioux should receive monetary compensation for the illegal seizure of the Black Hills in 1876.

Suggested Reading: James S. Olson and Raymond Wilson, *Native Americans in the Twentieth Century*, 1984; Francis Paul Prucha, *The Great Father*, Vol. 1, 1984.

MARK BAXTER

FORT STANWIX, TREATY OF (1784). In the wake of America's successful War of Independence (1775–1783), the recently liberated colonies engineered the Treaty of Fort Stanwix, which redrew the former frontier boundaries at the expense of the Six Nations (Mohawks, Tuscaroras, Oneidas, Onondogas, Cayugas, and Senecas) who were scattered on New England's northwest periphery. Four of the Iroquois tribes had allied themselves to the British Crown. Because the Treaty of Paris (1783) had made no provision for the future status of the Indian nations, the United States signed several similarly lopsided treaties* with the various adjacent tribes and in the process acquired large tracts of land in piecemeal fashion. Although the federal government later claimed that the cession of tribal land had been extracted from the vanquished as spoils of war, the Indians argued otherwise and objected to the divide-and-conquer tactics of the U.S. government.

The affected tribes—the Six Nations, the Hurons, Delawares, Shawnees, Ottawas, Chippewas, Potawatomis, Twightwees, Cherokees, and Wabash Confederates—gathered at a great council fire on December 17, 1786, and lodged a protest with Congress denouncing the Treaties of Fort Stanwix and Fort McIntosh (1785). While professing their desire for lasting peace, the participants in the Indian council petitioned the federal government to repeal the disputed treaties, to desist from further encroachments on Indian land, and to negotiate a new and more thoroughgoing treaty with Indian representatives popularly elected by the tribes. At the urging of Secretary of War Henry Knox, who asserted that the cession of Indian land by the dubious right of conquest* would only result in protracted frontier warfare, the United States proffered monetary compensation for earlier annexations, renegotiated the Treaties of Fort Stanwix and Fort McIntosh, and incorporated them into the Treaty of Fort Harmar (1789).

Suggested Reading: Francis Paul Prucha, *The Great Father*, Vol. 1, 1984; Wilcomb Washburn, *The American Indian and the United States: A Documentary History*, Vol. 4, 1973.

MARK BAXTER

FORT WAYNE, TREATY OF (1809). The Treaty of Fort Wayne, concluded on September 30, 1809, ceded between 2.5 and 3 million acres of Indian land to the United States. Located along the Wabash River in what is now modern-day Indiana and Illinois, plus a small tract in eastern Indiana, the lands belonged to the Delawares, Potawatomis, Miamis, and Eel Rivers. Chiefs of those tribes signed the treaty for their peoples, and William Henry Harrison, governor of the Indiana Territory, signed for the U.S. government. In return for the land cession, the Indians received compensation of about 2 cents per acre. The government gave trade goods valued at $5,200 plus increased annuities from $250 to $500 per year.

For Harrison, the treaty was the signal achievement in his career dealing with Indians in the Old Northwest Territory. The chiefs who signed the treaty were all "government chiefs," willing to deal with the U.S. government. More militant warriors, however, saw the treaty as a sign that Harrison and the government would take all their lands. Indian peoples all over the Old Northwest held councils and meetings to denounce the treaty and discuss the future. The treaty spurred militancy among many of the region's native peoples, providing Tecumseh* and his brother Tenskwatawa political ammunition to secure more native support for their then-small confederation to resist the whites' westward movement. Some historians now argue that the two followed the militants' lead rather than steering Indian opinion against whites. The treaty is regarded as an important step toward the outbreak of the War of 1812 because it created a sense of betrayal among Indians and intensified their hostility toward the U.S. government. Whites in the western states accused Great Britain of stirring up Indian resentment of the United States. It also illustrates the federal government's tactic of taking lands by surrounding Indian populations in order to later force them off their lands entirely.

Suggested Reading: Gregory Evans Dowd, *A Spirited Resistance: The North American Indian Struggle for Unity, 1745–1815*, 1992; R. David Edmunds, *The Shawnee Prophet*, 1983; Arrell Morgan Gibson, *The American Indian: Prehistory to the Present*, 1980.

TIMOTHY MORGAN

FOURTEENTH AMENDMENT. The Fourteenth Amendment to the Constitution,* which was ratified by the states and went into effect in 1868, awarded citizenship* to all persons born or naturalized in the United States, prohibited state governments from denying due process and equal protection under the law to any of its citizens, and provided for the apportionment of representation in Congress. Over the years, the federal courts generally held that the due process clause of the Fourteenth Amendment included the entire panoply of rights outlined in the first ten amendments, or Bill of Rights,* to the Constitution, thereby preventing state governments from violating the individual civil rights of any of their citizens. But the language of the Fourteenth Amendment, when referring to apportionment, specifically "excluded Indians not taxed," a phrase that essentially acknowledged that the Indian tribes and their members stood outside the legal jurisdiction of the federal government and the state governments. Individual Indians did not then enjoy civil rights because they were not citizens of the United States.

But beginning in 1871, the nature of Indian civil rights and their protection under the Fourteenth Amendment began to change. In 1871, Congress passed legislation specifically ending the federal government's policy of dealing with the Indian tribes as sovereign, domestic nations. At that point, Indians were no longer considered citizens of Indian nations, which did not legally exist, but they were not yet citizens of the United States either. In fact, the U.S. Supreme Court, in *Elk v. Wilkins** (1884), decided that the Fourteenth Amendment excluded Indians from citizenship and argued that even those Indians separating themselves from their tribes could not become U.S. citizens. But when the allotment* program began with the Dawes Act* of 1887, individual Indians received U.S. citizenship upon taking title to allotted lands. Between 1887 and 1924, a series of allotment programs and specific congressional legislation eventually extended citizenship to all Native Americans, ostensibly bringing them under the protection of the Fourteenth Amendment.

In many areas of the Southwest, however, state and local governments still made it difficult—and sometimes impossible—for Indians to enjoy Fourteenth Amendment protections. Claiming that Indians were not taxed, some states denied them the franchise (i.e., the right to vote) or claimed that because they lived on reservations* and not in the states, they were not eligible to vote. New Mexico and Arizona did not extend the franchise to Indians until 1948. In some localities, discrimination was still common, however. During the 1960s the civil rights movement produced the Voting Rights Act* of 1965, which assigned federal marshals to certain areas to make sure that Indians were allowed to vote.

During the 1960s, however, the most controversial aspect of the Fourteenth Amendment's application to Native Americans revolved around the powers of tribal governments and the rights of individual Indians. The movement for tribal self-determination* gained momentum in the 1960s, with tribal governments demanding the right to establish social, political, and economic policy on the reservations. But on many occasions certified tribal leaders behaved arbitrarily, often denying fundamental civil rights to tribal members. The question then arose as to whether the Fourteenth Amendment protected individual Indians from the actions of their own tribal governments. Congress investigated the matter and passed the Indian Civil Rights Act* of 1968. An attempt to find a compromise between the demand for tribal autonomy and the individual rights of tribal members, this act guaranteed due process and freedom of religion, speech, press, assembly, and petition to individual Indians; extended to them protections against unreasonable searches and seizures; and gave those accused of criminal acts the protection of the Fifth* and Sixth* Amendments, except for the right to legal counsel. However, the legislation did allow tribal governments to establish an official tribal religion as long as discrimination did not take place against Indian members of other religious groups. In essence, the Indian Civil Rights Act of 1968 applied most of the Fourteenth Amendment's protections to individual Indians.

Suggested Reading: Russel Lawrence Barsh and James Youngblood Henderson, *The Road: Indian Tribes and Political Liberty*, 1980; Vine Deloria Jr. and Clifford M. Lytle, *American Indians, American Justice*, 1983; H. Barry Holt and Gary Forrester, *Digest of American Indian Law: Cases and Chronology*, 1990; R. Alton Lee, "Indian Citizenship and the Fourteenth Amendment," *South Dakota History* 4 (Spring 1974); Stephen L. Pevar, *The Rights of Indians and Tribes: The Basic ACLU Guide to Indian and Tribal Rights*, 1992; Wilcomb E. Washburn, *Red Man's Land, White Man's Law*, 1971; Charles F. Wilkinson, *American Indians, Time and the Law*, 1987; John R. Wunder, *"Retained by The People": A History of American Indians and the Bill of Rights*, 1994.

JAMES S. OLSON

FRANK, BILLY, JR. Billy Frank Jr., a Nisqually Indian, has campaigned actively for Indian fishing rights* since the early 1960s. He eventually emerged as a leader in the movement to exempt Native American peoples from state fish and game regulations in the Pacific Northwest. In the 1850s, Frank argued, the United States negotiated treaties* with the tribes providing those rights, and state governments cannot abrogate them. During the 1960s Frank intentionally fished before and after state fishing seasons, which he considered acts of civil disobedience. He was arrested and jailed many times for his actions. Frank may have lost those battles, but he won the war when the Boldt Decisions* in 1974 upheld treaty fishing rights. Born in 1931 and raised in eastern Washington, today Frank is chairman of the Northwest Indian Fisheries Commission.

Suggested Reading: Duane Champagne, ed., *The Native North American Almanac*, 1994; *New York Times*, November 26, 1992.

JAMES S. OLSON

FREEDOM OF RELIGION. See RELIGIOUS FREEDOM.

FRENCH AND INDIAN WAR. By the beginning of the eighteenth century, the English and French empires in North America were on a collision course. The British colonies were poised for expansion westward into the Ohio Valley, and French fur traders were ready to move southward into the same area. Fighting began between the Virginians and the French in the Ohio Valley in 1754, and the French were generally successful in the early stages of the war.

On May 18, 1756, England declared war on France. The conflict became known as the Seven Years War in Europe and the French and Indian War in America. Soon after rising to the head of the British government in December 1756, Prime Minister William Pitt decided to drive France from the New World. Only then would England be able to achieve its mercantilistic aims of securing a permanent source of raw materials and opening new markets for its goods. The attack began in earnest in 1758. In July the English conquered Louisbourg, cutting Canada's supply line to France. Small in population and limited in resources, French Canada could not resist the English onslaught without reinforcements and supplies. The French therefore made alliances with most of the Indian tribes (the Iroquois being the notable exception), but even then the English drove the French out of their forts in the Ohio Valley and the Lake Region of New York. By 1759 the English general James Wolfe had begun the siege of Quebec. Using brilliant tactics, Wolfe attacked and defeated the French at Quebec in September 1759, breaking the back of the French empire in the New World. The French army in Canada surrendered to the English in September 1760.

Because of the conflict in Europe and elsewhere in the world, formal peace did not arrive until 1763; but in that year the Treaty of Paris* gave England title to all of Canada. Except for French Guiana, the islands of Guadeloupe and Martinique in the Caribbean, and St. Pierre and Miquelon in the North Atlantic, the French empire in the New World no longer existed.

By siding with the loser of the French and Indian War, Native Americans set themselves up for postwar vengeance from white settlers. As white settlers moved across the Appalachian Mountains in the 1760s and 1770s, they often took punitive action against the Indians and seized their lands as retribution.

Suggested Reading: W. J. Eccles, *France in America*, 1972; Howard H. Peckham, *The Colonial Wars, 1689–1762*, 1964.

JAMES S. OLSON

FRENCH INDIAN POLICY. During the colonial period, because the French empire in the New World was based on the fur trade and not on agriculture, French relations with Indian tribes were better than those of the British and the Spanish. Native Americans actively participated in the fur trade and profited from it, and the French often took the time to learn Indian languages and customs as a means of improving business. The French established a series of trading posts to enhance the fur trade, but the practice tended to widely scatter the white population, reducing Native American fears about loss of their land. They did not feel the same pressures from French settlement as they did from British settlers. By the early 1760s there were only 60,000 French settlers in North America, compared to more than one million British and Scottish settlers. Because the French did not try to promote densely populated agricultural settlements in Canada, their political relationship with the Indians was peaceful and productive. It is hardly surprising that during the colonial wars between France and Great Britain of the late seventeenth and eighteenth centuries, most Native American tribes sided with the French.

Suggested Reading: W. J. Eccles, *France in America*, 1972.

JAMES S. OLSON

FRIENDS OF THE INDIAN. See LAKE MOHONK CONFERENCES.

FUR TRADE. Trade in furs became a very important part of European colonization in the New World. It also had a decisive impact on the lives of the Indians. The high demand for furs in Europe during the seventeenth century caused a rivalry among the Dutch, English, and French and pulled the Indians into their conflicts. Once introduced to European supplies, tools, and guns, the Indians desired to increase their trade; this led to the depletion of fur-bearing animals in their vicinity and bound the Indians to their European suppliers.

The depletion of fur-bearing animals caused the Indians to search for new sources of furs, usually at the expense of neighboring tribes. European powers actually encouraged tribes to attack their rivals in attempts to monopolize the trade. Wars between Indian tribes took on a new character as a result of the demand for furs. Prior to the arrival of Europeans in the New World, the main goals of Indian-Indian warfare were plunder and—to a lesser extent—the taking of captives. With increased demands for furs, the Iroquois in particular began launching attacks to exterminate their rivals, which for the most part they accomplished.

In addition to the high cost in human lives, the fur trade had many other detrimental effects on Indian society. Hunting for fur, which was becoming increasingly rare, used up a great amount of time. Indian trappers had to travel farther from home in order to find fur-bearing animals. This led to the need for more food production in order to make the extended trips, which took time away from other hunting. European tools helped increase Indian productivity, but this increase was more than off-set by the longer time expended in hunting and trapping. Women's work-load increased as well: cleaning an increasing number of furs and planting and harvesting larger fields to increase food production added to the lot of the Indian women, who were not compensated for the extra work.

Because the Indians could not produce the items they acquired from the Europeans, they became dependent on them; the fur trade became a symbol of this dominance.

Suggested Reading: Denys Delage, *Bitter Feast: Amerindians and Europeans in Northeastern North America, 1600–64*, 1993; Paul Chrisler Phillips, *The Fur Trade*, 2 vols., 1961; Lewis O. Saum, *The Fur Trader and the Indian*, 1965.

JEFFREY D. CARLISLE

G

GALLAHAN v. HOLYFIELD (1982). *Gallahan v. Holyfield* addressed the right to religious freedom of an imprisoned Cherokee Indian. Prison authorities had insisted that Gallahan cut his hair as part of the institutional disciplinary code, but Gallahan claimed a right to keep his hair long for religious reasons. The prison system argued that its short-hair policy was necessary for security reasons: to make visual identification of the inmate easier, to prevent inmates from hiding contraband in their hair, and to prevent sanitary problems. The case went to the Supreme Court, which found in favor of Gallahan, arguing that the prison had not presented reasonable evidence for the necessity of the policy.

SUGGESTED READING: John R. Wunder, *"Retained by The People": A History of American Indians and the Bill of Rights*, 1994.

JAMES S. OLSON

GAMBLING. See **GAMING.**

GAMING. Late in the 1970s and early in the 1980s, congressional cuts in appropriations for the Bureau of Indian Affairs* and other federal agencies serving Native Americans created a financial crisis on many reservations.* Along with federal money, services on the reservations declined and so did employment. Perhaps 15 percent of the reservations had a natural resource capable of generating revenues for tribal needs, but most tribes had to begin searching for some way to replace the declining volume of federal dollars. Many of them turned to gaming operations.

The decision to raise revenue by establishing off-track betting parlors, gambling casinos, and bingo games on reservations created much controversy in most states, where commercial gambling was illegal. Native Americans justified their decision on the basis of tribal sovereignty,* claiming that state jurisdiction stopped at the reservation boundary. By 1983, 180 tribes had created bingo parlors and 20 tribes had constructed full-scale casinos. In 1987 the Supreme Court upheld the Indian notion in *California v. Cabazon Band of Mission Indians*.* Gaming operations on reservations were legal, whether or not state authorities approved.

By 1995, tribes operated 102 bingo operations and 61 casinos on the reservations. State officials complained about the wholesale multiplication of Indian gambling operations, as did nonreservation businesses, which claimed that the casinos absorbed a disproportionate share of tourist dollars. In response, Congress passed the Indian Gaming Regulatory Act* of 1988, which legalized those activities as long as (1) there was a formal tribal ordinance authorizing gambling enterprises, and (2) a legal compact had been drawn up between the tribe and the state. The law also established federal standards and regulations for gaming activities on Indian land. A National Indian Gaming Commission was established to enforce those regulations. The Indian Gaming Regulatory Act authorized tribes to file suit in federal courts against state governments that did not negotiate in good faith about opening and operating gambling casinos on reservations.

Many state governments, however, refused to engage in negotiations to establish such compacts, arguing that the Indian Gaming Regulatory Act was a violation of the Eleventh Amendment to the Constitution.* One of those suits, *Seminole Tribe v. Florida*,* reached the U.S. Supreme Court in 1996. The Court upheld a decision of the Court of Appeals for the Eleventh Circuit, which had ruled that the Seminole tribe could not file suit under the Indian Gaming Regulatory Act requiring Florida to negotiate a contract to open a casino on Seminole land. According to the justices, the section of the Indian Gaming Regulatory Act allowing the Seminoles to file suit was a violation of the Eleventh Amendment to the Constitution. Chief Justice William Rehnquist, who wrote the majority opinion, claimed that the law violated the Eleventh Amendment by bringing about an unacceptable incursion on state sovereignty.

The Supreme Court's decision created legal and political turmoil in many regions, especially in tourist areas where non-Indian businesses wanted to close down the casinos. Early in 1996, for example, the attorney general of New Mexico ordered a shutdown of all casinos that had not been founded as part of a compact with the state. More than a dozen tribes operating bingo parlors and casinos protested the decision and threatened legal action. State officials responded, however, with the argument that the Supreme Court had already ruled on the matter. A number of Indian activists promised to engage in civil disobedience protest by blocking Interstate highways 10, 25, and 40 until the attorney general lifted the order. Protests were averted, but the matter remains in litigation.

Suggested Reading: Pam Greenberg and Jody Zelio, *States and the Indian Gaming Regulatory Act*, 1992; National Indian Policy Center, *Reservation-Based Gaming*, 1993; *New York Times*, March 28, 1996; Wilcomb E. Washburn, *Red Man's Land, White Man's Law: A Study of The Past and Present Status of the American Indian*, 1971.

JAMES S. OLSON

GARMENT, LEONARD. Leonard Garment, special counsel and advisor on minority affairs to President Richard Nixon, was sympathetic to the needs of American Indian people and negotiated in their interests during three critical events: the 1969 occupation of Alcatraz Island;* the 1972 occupation of the Bureau of Indian Affairs* building in Washington, D.C.; and the 1973 occupation of Wounded Knee,* South Dakota.

Born in 1924 and having graduated from Brooklyn Law School in 1949, Garment used his position as special counsel to the president to support Indian people. He was instrumental in the drafting of President Nixon's 1970 message setting forth his American Indian policy of self-determination* without termination.* In this statement, drafted by Garment and his assistant Bradley H. Patterson Jr., Nixon told the American people, "[I]t is long past time that the Indian policies of the Federal government began to recognize and build upon the capacities and insights of the Indian people." Garment was also the central figure in three significant events that affected the American Indian people and the perception of Indian people by the American public at large:

Alcatraz Island. On November 20, 1969, eighty-nine American Indians landed on Alcatraz Island in San Francisco Bay. Identifying themselves as "Indians of All Tribes,"* this group of young urban Indian college students claimed the island by "right of discovery."* The occupiers demanded clear title to Alcatraz Island and the establishment of an American Indian University, an American Indian Cultural Center, and an American Indian Museum on Alcatraz Island. When U.S. marshals were ordered to remove the Indians from the island at gunpoint, Garment recognized the potential danger of the use of excessive force and the public relations problems the Nixon administration would face if blood was shed in an attempt to remove the Indians from the island. Garment instructed the General Services Administration (GSA) office in Washington, D.C., to call off the marshals and issued instructions that the White House would coordinate all future actions with the Indian occupiers directly with the San Francisco GSA office. Garment and his assistant, Bradley H. Patterson Jr., orchestrated the government's actions, reactions, and negotiations that took place over a nineteen-month period ending on June 11, 1971, when the few remaining occupiers were removed from the island. Garment was sympathetic to Indian issues and felt that his feelings mirrored those of President Nixon; he recognized that the Alcatraz occupation was an attempt on the part of urban Indians to focus the attention of the American people—particularly politicians in Washington, D.C.—on their needs.

Bureau of Indian Affairs. In the fall of 1972, Indian leaders from the American Indian Movement* (AIM) planned a civil rights march to Washington, D.C., that became known as the Trail of Broken Treaties.* The march was a cross-county caravan starting at three separate points on the West Coast, picking up Indian people from reservations* as it went along, arriving in Washington, D.C., just prior to the 1972 presidential election. Several hundred Indian people arrived in the capital on November 2; however, no arrangements had been made to provide housing or meals. A few Indians were housed with the assistance of the Department of the Interior. However, many had no place to stay and nothing to eat. The Indian people met at the Bureau of Indian Affairs (BIA) building on Constitution Avenue and awaited word on housing. When shelter could not be found, the Department of the Interior offered the use of the BIA building auditorium. The Indians accepted, and as BIA employees left the building at the end of the work day, some young Indians were shoved out the door by some of the guards. The Indians believed they were being shoved outside into a waiting District of Columbia riot squad. They stopped, turned around, and then seized the BIA building. They barricaded the doors, blocked the widows, upended desks, and piled metal chairs against doors to prevent forcible removal.

On November 6, 1972, a judge ordered the forcible removal of the Indians by 6:00 P.M. that day. The situation inside the BIA building worsened as tensions grew. The Indians decided to wait until 5:45 P.M. for the government to respond to their demands for reform of the BIA, increased federal appropriations for Indian education, and amnesty for the protestors; if they had not heard anything positive or seen any police withdrawal, they would set the building on fire. Leonard Garment, along with Office of Management and Budget (OMB) director Frank Carlucci, Secretary of the Interior Rogers Morton, and Commissioner of Indian Affairs Louis Bruce, agreed to negotiate with the Indian people on behalf of the president. On election morning Garment, Carlucci, and Bruce met with the Indians. A federal task force was established to review the complaints of the Indian people. It would examine many issues in Indian country.* Amnesty was promised. Negotiations were conducted under direct White House auspices with Leonard Garment in charge. A settlement was reached whereby the government would provide $66,500 in travel expenses to get the Indians home, and in return the Indian people would leave the BIA building. They left the building before a 9:00 P.M. November 8, 1972, deadline.

Wounded Knee. On the evening of February 27, 1973, some two hundred Indian people occupied the village of Wounded Knee, South Dakota, the site of the 1890 Wounded Knee massacre of 150 Lakota Indians, to protest the corrupt tribal government headed by Richard "Dicky" Wilson and numerous uninvestigated murders of Indian people on the Pine Ridge Indian reservation. The White House was immediately notified of the occupation, and Leonard Garment once again became the federal government's pointman for the negotiations. Keenly aware of the president's views and concerns for American Indian people, Garment established the initial policy against the use of violence to remove the Indian occupiers from the village. However, the Indian occupiers had various weapons with them, and the three hundred federal police aligned against them had in their possession fifteen armored personnel carriers and over one hundred M-16 rifles. Soon rifle fire was exchanged and two Indian occupiers were killed, fourteen Indian occupiers were injured, and one FBI agent was wounded.

During the occupation of Wounded Knee three hundred newspeople, including representatives from twelve foreign countries, converged on Wounded Knee. The attention of the nation was focused there. In Washington, D.C., the decision-making machinery was entirely under White House direction—specifically Leonard Garment. Despite the urgency of the situation and the involvement of the assistant attorney general, Garment's decisions carried the most weight—that of the president of the United States. The occupation of Wounded Knee lasted seventy-one days and required patience, persistence, and trying negotiations, a task at which Leonard Garment had become a master.

Suggested Reading: Leonard Garment, *Crazy Rhythm: Richard Nixon and All That Jazz*, 1997.

TROY JOHNSON

GENERAL ALLOTMENT ACT OF 1877. See DAWES ACT OF 1877.

GENERAL LEASING ACT OF 1920. This act permitted private firms to exploit the raw material resources found within the public domain. Moreover, the measure removed leasing authority from the Bureau of Indian Affairs* (BIA) and placed it under the supervision of the General Land Office. In 1922 Albert Fall, the secretary of the Interior during the corrupt administration of President Warren G. Harding, declared that executive order reservations* (which had been created by presidential decree rather than by treaty or congressional act) belonged to the public domain. According to Fall, conservation of the more than 22 million acres of land included within the executive order reservations was a temporary expedient that had outlived its usefulness. The Indians were to receive a comparatively meager amount of the new revenues gained from leasing to private oil, gas, and mining interests.

However, Fall's controversial policy encountered a phalanx of criticism from Indian rights advocates who closed ranks to condemn the procedure. In 1924, after Fall had resigned in disgrace over the Teapot Dome scandal in which he accepted kickbacks from oil companies drilling petroleum on government land, the measure was rescinded. Yet the actual status of Indian rights on executive order reservations remained in limbo. Not until passage of the Indian Oil Leasing Act* in 1927 were Indian residents of executive order reservations guaranteed a reasonable share of the income from leases. In what amounted to a victory for Native Americans, the act of 1927 returned leasing authority to the BIA, established semi-permanent boundaries to the executive order reservations, and provided for the direct taxation of business concerns operating on such lands.

Suggested Reading: James S. Olson and Raymond Wilson, *Native Americans in the Twentieth Century*, 1984; Francis Paul Prucha, *The Great Father*, Vol. 2, 1984.

JAMES S. OLSON

GEORGIA v. TASSEL (1830). The case of *Georgia v. Tassel* (1830) established the pugnacious attitude held by the state of Georgia regarding its claims to sovereignty* and presaged what historians agree are the two most important Supreme Court decisions involving Native American land claims: *Cherokee Nation v. State of Georgia** (1831) and *Worcester v. Georgia** (1832). Corn (George) Tassel, convicted of murder in Indian territory under state rather than Indian law, appealed the decision to the Supreme Court, citing original jurisdiction. A writ of error was granted by Chief Justice John Marshall* in order to bring the case before the federal courts for reconsideration. Such an order should have brought about a stay of execution, but the state legislature had passed a resolution directing the governor and all state officers to ignore any mandates from the Supreme Court pertaining to the case because such directives were perceived as interference and a gross violation of states' rights. In defiance of the writ of the Court and of the supremacy clause of the Constitution,* Tassel was hanged. Georgia had nothing to fear from the federal government in terms of retribution, as President Andrew Jackson* had made clear his position in favor of the rights of the states and his unwillingness to use federal authority to protect Indian interests.

Suggested Reading: J. C. Burke, ''The Cherokee Cases: A Study in Law, Politics, and Morality,'' *Stanford Law Review* 21 (1969), 500–531; C. G. Haines, *The Role of the Supreme Court in American Government and Politics, 1789–1835*, 1960; J. Norgren, *The Cherokee Cases: The Confrontation of Law and Politics*, 1996.

PHILIP HUCKINS

GERBER v. UNITED STATES (1993). John Gerber was arrested and convicted, under the Archaeological Resources Protection Act* of 1979, of stealing Indian relics from the property of the General Electric Company in Mount Vernon, Indiana. He had then tried to sell the relics in Owensburg, Kentucky. The American Indian Movement* had vigorously demanded his prosecution. Gerber appealed his conviction, arguing that the law did not apply to him because he had taken the relics from private property, not from federal land or an Indian reservation.* However, a federal court of appeals decided in favor of the government, upholding his conviction on the grounds that federal law applies to any artifact taken in violation of state laws and transported across state lines.

Suggested Reading: *New York Times*, July 25, 1993.

JAMES S. OLSON

GERONIMO. Geronimo, whose Indian name was Goyathlay (One Who Yawns), was born near what is today Clifton, Arizona, in 1829 among a band of Chiricahua Apaches. He was an impressive young man, and at the age of 17 he was admitted to the tribal war council. The arid deserts of the Southwest were the last regions of the United States to receive large numbers of non-Indian settlers, but by the 1880s deadly confrontations with Apaches became common. Vicious warfare resulted, with both sides being guilty of barbarous excess. In the mid-1880s, Geronimo led the Chiricahua attacks on white settlements and supply lines. He eventually surrendered to Gen. George Crook early in 1886 but then escaped, only to be forced to surrender again in September 1886. All the Chiricahua Apaches, including Geronimo, were then relocated to a military fort in St. Augustine, Florida, where many of them remained for the next twenty-eight years. Geronimo was resettled in Fort Sill, Oklahoma, in 1894. Given a tract of allotted land, he tried his hand at farming. In the late 1890s and early 1900s he traveled widely in the United States, appearing at various expositions in the American West. By the time he dictated his biography in 1906, he had become an American icon. Geronimo died in 1909.

SUGGESTED READING: Alexander B. Adams, *Geronimo: A Biography*, 1971.

JAMES S. OLSON

GHOST DANCE RELIGION. See **WOVOKA.**

GRAY [SALTER], JOHN HUNTER. Civil rights activist for the rights of minorities, John Hunter Gray was born in Flagstaff, Arizona, on February 14, 1934, of Micmac, Abenaki, and Mohawk heritage. He graduated from Arizona State University in 1958 and then earned a master's degree in sociology there in 1960. Until 1995 he used the surname Salter, after his adoptive parents.

His social and libertarian views were influenced by his ancestor, John Gray (Mohawk), and by Industrial Workers of the World (IWW) philosopher-activist Ralph Chaplain. An IWW member in the 1950s, Salter was influenced by the IWW heritage in the Mine, Mill, and Smelter Workers Union. A member of the National Rifle Association, he is now an advocate for the right of minorities to possess arms for self-defense against racist violence. His career has encompassed multiethnic organizing in the Southwest; civil rights organizing in the deep South in the 1950s and 1960s, where he served as key advisor in Jackson, Mississippi, to civil rights worker Medgar Evers and assisted Indians in eastern North Carolina; and urban multiethnic, rural, and small-town Indian community organizations from the 1970s through the present. From 1960 through

1994 he taught at Tougaloo College, Mississippi, and Coe College, Iowa; supervised the urban and regional planning graduate program at the University of Iowa; chaired the social science division at Navajo Community College; and headed the Department of Indian Studies, University of North Dakota, retiring in 1994 as professor.

After assisting the National Association for the Advancement of Colored People in Mississippi, he went to North Carolina in anti-poverty community organization. He worked in minority hiring and training for Pacific Northwest Bell in 1968; was a community organizer in the multiethnic Chicago Commons Association from 1969 to 1973; was a member of the Iowa State Indian Education Advisory Committee from 1974 to 1976; was active as one of three Indians on Iowa's State Archaeologist Committee securing legislation to protect native burial sites; worked as a volunteer at Iowa State Penitentiary organizing inmate American Indian/Chicano cultural centers from 1973 to 1976; acted as chair of the Native American Community Organizational Training Center in Chicago from 1973 to 1977; and was director of the office of human development of the Roman Catholic diocese of Rochester, New York, from 1976 to 1978. There he organized a strike of Algonquin fur traders in Ontario County.

In North Dakota, Salter's civil rights work was exclusively devoted to Indian issues: from 1982 to 1986 he chaired the Grand Forks Mayor's Committee on Police Policy, organizing civil rights campaigns for police reform. He also coordinated legal defense of Native American Church religious freedom cases in North Dakota in 1984. In 1987 and 1988 he led civil rights campaigns for Indians in Devil's Lake, North Dakota. He has chaired the Community Relations Board of Grand Forks since 1992.

Suggested Reading: John Hunter Gray, *Jackson, Mississippi: An American Chronicle of Struggle and Schism*, 1979.

                                                                                    ROY WORTMAN

GREAT LAKES INTER-TRIBAL COUNCIL. The Great Lakes Inter-Tribal Council was established in 1961 to protest the federal government's termination* policies. It represented ten Native American groups: the Wisconsin-Winnebagos, the Stockbridge-Munsee Mohicans, the Oneidas, the Forest County Potawatomis, and the Red Cliff, Bad River, Mole Lake, Lac du Flambeau, Lac Courte Oreilles, and St. Croix bands of the Ojibways. They worked at promoting tribal self-determination,* improving the educational and economic status of the reservations,* and educating the non-Indian public about Native American culture. By the 1970s and 1980s the Great Lakes Inter-Tribal Council employed more than two hundred people who administered more than forty programs for the ten tribes. Today the Council is headquartered at the Lac du Flambeau Ojibway reservation.

Suggested Reading: Armand S. La Potin, *Native American Voluntary Organizations*, 1986.

JAMES S. OLSON

GREAT SIOUX AGREEMENT OF 1889. The Great Sioux Agreement, also known as the Sioux Bill, marked the final step in the process of reducing Sioux landholdings in the Dakotas. After Congress passed the 1887 Dawes Act* and the 1889 Omnibus Bill (which created the states of North and South Dakota), it had the leverage necessary to break apart the Great Sioux reservation and open sections of it to Euroamerican settlers. Congress passed legislation, known as the Sioux Bill, calling for the cession of nine million acres and the creation of six separate Sioux reservations*: Pine Ridge, Rosebud, Standing Rock, Cheyenne River, Lower Brule, and Crow Creek. The bill also provided for the allotment* of reservation lands to individual Indians (in essence, a Lakota version of the Dawes Act, but it authorized double-sized allotments of 320 acres).

In order to implement the bill, the federal government had to secure approval of three-fourths of adult Lakota men, as specified in an 1868 treaty signed at Fort Laramie.* The commission sent to obtain the required signatures worked in the shadow of two failed attempts (1883 and 1886) to gain Lakota approval of land cessions. The legacy of those past experiences may have caused the commissioners to use pressure tactics or coerce signatures. Clearly, the Lakota people were divided on the issue. At Cheyenne River, the disagreements turned physical on two occasions. The commission gathered only three hundred Cheyenne River signatures before leaving, but government agents later added another 320 by suspicious methods. The commission similarly managed to obtain the required number of signatures at the other Sioux agencies.

The Great Sioux Agreement created the present-day Sioux reservation boundaries, but it also opened the door for further cessions after allotment took place. Some sections of the reservation were subsequently opened up to Euroamerican settlers, so the process of land loss did not end completely in 1889.

Suggested Reading: Jerome A. Green, "The Sioux Land Commission of 1889: Prelude to Wounded Knee," *South Dakota History* 1 (Winter 1970), 41–72; Herbert T. Hoover, "The Sioux Agreement of 1889 and Its Aftermath," *South Dakota History* 19 (Spring 1989), 56–94; George E. Hyde, *A Sioux Chronicle*, 1956.

EMILY GREENWALD

GREAT SIOUX UPRISING OF 1862. In Mankato, Minnesota, on the day following Christmas in 1862, a crowd of 4,000 people gathered to watch 38 Dakota Sioux being hanged for their participation in the Great Sioux Uprising of that fall. These men, who in October 1862 had raided white settlements in Minnesota and the Dakota Territory in order to discourage the arrival of more non-Indian farmers, were victims of the largest mass execution in American history, symbolizing the white justice system's treatment of the American Indian. In retrospect, the circumstances under which these men were accused, tried, and convicted were at least illegal, if not immoral.

When the uprising ended in October, Colonel Henry Hastings Sibley met with the "friendly" half of the Dakota tribe (those who had worked to secure the safety of the white captives during the uprising). A few days following their meeting, Sibley and his men decided to secure each adult male and bring him before a military commission on charges of participation in the outbreak. In a reversal of American law, the accused were considered guilty until they were able to prove their innocence. This was especially difficult because the accused were neither told of the charges against them before they were brought before the commission nor allowed legal representation; they were not permitted to call witnesses in their defense. Most of the defendants were unable to speak English but were provided with interpreters; however, the interpreters were not sworn in. The accused were charged with plunder, murder, rape, or participation in battle. If a witness could place a defendant at a battle or massacre or even had heard of the man's participation, the individual was convicted. Plundering was punishable by imprisonment; any other crime was punishable by death. At its peak, the commission heard forty cases per day and disposed of most in less than five minutes each. After trying over 400 cases, the commission sentenced 303 of the accused to death.

After reviewing the cases, President Abraham Lincoln pardoned all but 39 of the condemned men (one was pardoned later). However, the records of the trials were confused and several men who had been pardoned were hanged. The remaining members of the Dakota tribe were imprisoned until the spring of 1863; 315 died of disease and exposure while in custody. Those who had been condemned were moved to Davenport, Iowa; the remaining Dakotas and the Winnebago tribe (whose members had not participated in the war) were removed to Crow Creek reservation in Dakota Territory. The land was desolate, and it was impossible for the people to acquire adequate shelter and provisions. Three hundred more people died in the first three months on the reservation; many more followed. After three years, the federal government admitted that the movement to Crow Creek had been disastrous; government agents finally moved the survivors to a more hospitable environment in Nebraska.

Suggested Reading: Gary Clayton Anderson and Alan R. Woolworth, eds., *Through Dakota Eyes: Narrative Accounts of the Minnesota Indian War of 1862*, 1988; Charles S. Bryant, *A History of the Great Massacre by the Sioux Indians in Minnesota: Including the Personal Narratives of Many Who Escaped*, 1864; Isaac V. D. Heard, *History of the Sioux War*, 1864; David A. Nichols, *Lincoln and the Indian: Civil War Policy and Politics*, 1978.

MARA RUTTEN

GUADALUPE HIDALGO, TREATY OF. The Treaty of Guadalupe Hidalgo formally brought an end to the Mexican War in 1848. Under the terms of the treaty, Mexico ceded California and New Mexico to the United States and renounced its claims to Texas. The Rio Grande River was designated as the point of demarcation between Texas and Mexico. In return, the United States paid Mexico $15 million and assumed responsibility for the payment of outstanding claims by American nationals against the Mexican government. Mexican nationals residing within the territories annexed by the United States were granted American citizenship. Other treaty provisions pledged the United States to curb Indian raids into Mexican territory and to exact punishment against the offending tribes after the fact. Moreover, Mexican property or captives captured by Indian bandits operating from American soil were to be confiscated and returned by U.S. authorities.

The Indians had no say in the transfer of their land from the Mexican to the U.S. government. However, the United States did respect Pueblo Indian claims to some 700,000 acres of land along the Rio Grande. The Pueblos, as former Mexican citizens, were devoid of ward status and thus remained free to dispose of their land until the Supreme Court ruled otherwise in 1913. At any rate, although the Treaty of Guadalupe Hildago obligated the United States to maintain the status held by the Indians under Mexican rule, American officials were woefully ignorant of the tribes inhabiting the West and Southwest. Indeed, in future years actions by the United States encouraging railroad construction and white settlement only managed to arouse the hostility of the Apaches and Navajos who had warred with the Spaniards in Mexico in centuries past.

Suggested Reading: James S. Olson and Raymond Wilson, *Native Americans in the Twentieth Century*, 1984; Francis Paul Prucha, *The Great Father*, Vol. 1, 1984.

MARK BAXTER

GUARDIANSHIP. The term "guardianship" arose from the Supreme Court decision in *Cherokee Nation v. State of Georgia* (1831) in which the Court, under the direction of Chief Justice John Marshall,* called Indian tribes "domestic dependent nations," using the analogy of "ward" (Indian tribes) to "guardian" (federal government). Marshall, a product of his own culture, believed in individualism, self-reliance, and what historians have called the atomization of American society in the nineteenth century. The analogy suggests American individualism and the tutelage implied in such a relationship. In the decision Marshall stated that the Indians

> look to our government for protection; rely upon its kindness and its power; appeal to it for relief to their wants; and address the president as their great father. They and their country are considered by foreign nations, as well as by ourselves, as being completely under the sovereignty of the United States, that any attempt to acquire their lands, or to form a political connection with them, would be considered by all as an invasion of our territory, and an act of hostility. [30 U.S. (5 Pet.), I, 16 (1831)]

Just how correct Marshall was in his appraisal of Indian willingness to submit so totally to federal power is questionable, but upon this perception of Indian-federal structure he wrote the decision.

In the early 1830s the federal government proceeded to build a body of guardianship theory and precedent over Indian peoples. The most important example of guardianship theory as applied to Indian relations is found in reservation* development. The U.S. government continued to make reservation treaties with Indian peoples until 1871, when Congress unilaterally halted all reservation-making and began to implement termination* and allotment* policies, which would sever Indians from their relationships with the federal government.

Guardianship theory also supports federal administrative structure overseeing Indian relationships. The Constitution* gives the president and Congress shared authority over Indian affairs. The president is to direct Indian affairs in his roles as commander-in-chief, chief treaty negotiator, and principal administrator of federal affairs. Presidents have delegated Indian responsibility first through the Department of War (created in 1789), then through the Bureau of Indian Affairs* (BIA) (created in the 1820s as part of the War Department), and, finally, through shifting the BIA to the newly created Department of the Interior in 1849.

Congressional authority over Indian affairs arises from control of the nation's purse strings and control of commerce with Indian peoples.

Monies and authorizations related to monies must come from Congress; such control means that Congress often influences executive orders and administrative regulations. Over the years congressional enactments have created federal agencies to carry out one or another of the responsibilities assigned through the Constitution or the guardianship notion. Although constitutional powers enable the federal government to operate widely in terms of Indian affairs, guardianship theory makes the federal government virtually complete in its authority over Indian affairs. As political scientists Vine Deloria Jr.* and Clifford M. Lytle state in *American Indians, American Justice*: "The political influence that Congress wields over Indian affairs has been characterized as plenary, which means complete, absolute, and unqualified, and in practice this has proven to be true."

Suggested Reading: Russel Lawrence Barsh and James Youngblood Henderson, *The Road: Indian Tribes and Political Liberty*, 1980; Vine Deloria Jr. and Clifford M. Lytle, *American Indians, American Justice*, 1983; H. Barry Holt and Gary Forrester, *Digest of American Indian Law: Cases and Chronology*, 1990; Stephen L. Pevar, *The Rights of Indians and Tribes: The Basic ACLU Guide to Indian and Tribal Rights*, 1992; Wilcomb E. Washburn, *Red Man's Land, White Man's Law*, 1971; Charles F. Wilkinson, *American Indians, Time and the Law*, 1987; John R. Wunder, *"Retained by The People": A History of American Indians and the Bill of Rights*, 1994.

TIMOTHY MORGAN

H

HAILMANN, WILLIAM. Superintendent of Indian schools under President Grover Cleveland from 1894 to 1898, Hailmann greatly improved the Indian educational system. William Hailmann was born on October 20, 1836, at Glaris, Switzerland. He immigrated to the United States in 1854. After a lengthy career in school administration, he was appointed by President Grover S. Cleveland to serve as the superintendent of Indian schools. A student of the Froebelian movement (which emphasized a student-centered approach to education, activity-based learning, and the integration of community and family into the schools), Hailmann led the Indian schools toward an attitude of individual dignity, cooperation, and a balance between respect for adults and the need for children to make independent decisions.

Convinced that Indians were intellectually and morally equal to whites, Hailmann began to restructure the curriculum for Indian schools with a syllabus for language work and another for mathematics. His administration established the practice of boys, girls, and staff members eating together at small tables. Further, Hailmann encouraged the telling of tribal legends and working cooperatively.

Hailmann had several concerns about the quality of off-reservation boarding school education, staffing, sanitary conditions, and recruiting practice. He knew that there were teachers in the Indian service who had neither the qualifications nor the disposition to work with Indian children, and that unsatisfactory educational outcomes followed from these attitudes.

In addition to their treatment when they were at school, Hailmann was concerned about the way Native American children were brought to the schools. He established a policy that proscribed children from being taken to boarding schools without parental consent. The measure also made it unlawful for an Indian agent to induce a parent to send a child beyond the borders of the reservation* by threatening to withhold rations; this directly overturned previously established policy that mandated agents to withhold government rations from parents who refused to send their children away to school.

Hailmann's *Syllabus of Number Work and Suggestions to Teachers concerning Lessons in Arithmetic for the Use of Indian Schools* (1894) reflects the degree to which he believed that children should be allowed to develop through such exercises as play. Hailmann applied these ideas to older students. He saw the classroom as extending beyond the schoolhouse walls. Further, he thought that lessons should have a life that carried beyond the threshold of the classroom, and thus he hoped that teachers would combine exercises with problems.

In his annual reports Hailmann suggested a tiered system of Indian schooling, with students moving from a kindergarten program to reservation day schools, to reservation boarding schools, with some moving to off-reservation boarding schools. This represented a change, as the off-reservation boarding schools were heretofore seen as the flagship of the assimilation* process. Hailmann also felt it would be beneficial to have Indian students enroll in public schools wherever possible.

Hailmann sought to temper the means of assimilation employed by the originators of the off-reservation boarding school program. However, his tenure as superintendent of Indian schools was brief, his legacy clouded by the return to more traditional methodologies when Estelle Reel, the new superintendent, was appointed by President William McKinley.

Suggested Reading: BIA, *Report of the Superintendent of Indian Schools*, 1894; Committee of Nineteen, *Pioneers of the Kindergarten in America*, 1924; D. W. Hewes, "The First Good Years of Indian Education: 1894–1898," *American Indian Culture and Research Journal* 5 (1981), 63–82.

PHILIP HUCKINS

HARJO, CHITTO. Charismatic leader of the Creek nation, Chitto Harjo (Crazy Snake) was born in Indian Territory* in 1846. Harjo emerged as the leader of the Creek Nation in the 1890s, and he actively resisted the Curtis Act* of 1898, which applied allotment* to the Indian Territory and tried to abolish tribal governments. Conservative Creeks, led by Harjo, formed a shadow government called the "Snakes," and they were headquartered at Hickory Ground, a sacred Creek village. Harjo argued that the Creek Treaty of 1832 guaranteed forever the right of the Creek people to maintain their own government, and the Snakes refused to recognize federal authority over them. In 1903 Harjo lost the election as principal Creek chief to Pleasant Porter, who was more accommodationist in his approach to the U.S. government. For nearly a decade the Snakes continued their acts of resistance, and several times federal troops were called in to put down Snake rebellions. In 1912 Harjo was wounded in such a skirmish and subsequently died of his wounds. Without his charismatic leadership, the Snake movement disintegrated.

Suggested Reading: Duane Champagne, ed., *The Native North American Almanac*, 1994; Angie Debo, *The Road to Disappearance: A History of the Creek Indians*, 1979.

JAMES S. OLSON

HARRIS, LADONNA. Political leader and champion of the rights of Indian peoples, LaDonna Harris was born on February 15, 1931, in Temple, Oklahoma. She was raised in a conservative, traditional Comanche home, speaking only Comanche until she attended public schools. She married Fred Harris, who became the Democratic U.S. senator from Oklahoma, and soon emerged as a political leader in her own right. In 1965 Harris founded Oklahomans for Indian Opportunity, which soon became a nationally prominent Indian self-help group. Five years later she established Americans for Indian Opportunity,* a similar organization that functioned on a national level and promoted Indian self-determination.* Today, LaDonna Harris is active in the world peace movement.

Suggested Reading: Duane Champagne, ed., *The Native North American Almanac*, 1994.

JAMES S. OLSON

HARRISON v. LAVEEN (1948). Although the Snyder Act* of 1924 conferred U.S. citizenship* on all American Indians, some state governments continued to prevent Indians from exercising the franchise (i.e., the right to vote). State governments justified denial of the franchise on the grounds that (1) Indians did not pay state taxes, or (2) because reservations were not state property, Indians were not legally state residents. In 1948, however, the Supreme Court resolved the issue constitutionally. In *Harrison v. Laveen*, the Court granted Arizona Indians the right to vote in all state and local elections.

Suggested Reading: Stephen L. Pevar, *The Rights of Indians and Tribes: The Basic ACLU Guide to Indian and Tribal Rights*, 1992.

JAMES S. OLSON

HISTORIC PRESERVATION ACT OF 1966. In recent decades, Native American activists have targeted archaeological remains as one focus for the Red Power* movement. Throughout U.S. history, economic developers and scientists often plundered Indian archaeological sites and burial grounds, and Indian people could do little to protect what they considered to be sacred. But in the early 1960s, when the environmental movement* was getting under way, Indian activists joined with environmentalists and historical preservationists and convinced Congress to pass the Historic Preservation Act of 1966. The law required the federal government to develop a comprehensive, nationwide management plan to identify, protect, and rehabilitate significant historic sites in the United States. The law created the National Register of Historic Places. Once a historic site was recognized by the National Register of Historic Places, it enjoyed protection from economic developers. Subsequently, many Indian groups began registering sacred sites with the National Register.

Suggested Reading: Michael M. Ames, *Cannibal Tours and Glass Boxes: The Anthropology of Museums*, 1992; Douglas Cole, *Captured Heritage: The Scramble for Northwest Coast Artifacts*, 1985; George P. Horse Capture, *The Concept of Sacred Materials and Their Place in the World*, 1989; Phyllis Mauch Messenger, ed., *The Ethics of Collecting Cultural Property: Whose Culture? Whose Property?* 1989; H. Marcus Price, *Disputing the Dead: U.S. Law on Aboriginal Remains and Grave Goods*, 1991.

JAMES S. OLSON

HOMESTEAD ACT. The Homestead Act of 1862 was one of the most important pieces of legislation in American economic history, because it opened up millions of acres of the public domain to settlement and accelerated the economic development of the West. In the process, it dramatically increased the political pressure of white settlers demanding access to Indian tribal lands on the Great Plains and in the Southwest.

For decades, the Whig Party and then the Republican Party had progressively been promoting more generous policies for the sale of public lands in order to encourage settlement of the West and economic development. Democrats, especially Southern Democrats, often opposed such land sale policies for fear that the West would dwarf the South in population and forge strong economic links with the North; politically, this trend would threaten slavery. But when Southern Democrats left Congress with the secession movement in 1861, Republicans quickly passed the Homestead Act of 1862, which offered 160 acres of public land to any male individual over 21 years of age. If the individual lived on the land for at least six months and farmed it, he could take title to it after paying $1.25 an acre. If he lived on the land for five years and farmed it, he would receive outright title with no payment. The logic of the Homestead Act—that 160 acres of land was enough to establish a successful farm—affected the subsequent allotment* program when the Dawes Act* of 1887 authorized similar-sized farms to American Indians.

Suggested Reading: Paul Gates, *History of Public Land Development*, 1968; George M. Stephenson, *The Political History of the Public Lands from 1840 to 1862*, 1917.

JAMES S. OLSON

HOOVER COMMISSION. In the years following World War II, the pendulum of American public policy began swinging away from the New Deal's emphasis on using the federal government to solve national problems in favor of action at the state and local levels in the private sector. Republicans took over Congress in 1946, and the movement away from New Deal policies accelerated. To develop plans for the consolidation and downsizing of the federal government, Congress asked former president Herbert Hoover to preside over a special investigative commission. In terms of federal Indian policy, the trend meant the dismantling of the so-called Indian New Deal* of President Franklin D. Roosevelt and John Collier.*

In its final report, the Hoover Commission gave credence to both the termination* and relocation* policies, which eventually came to dominate federal Indian policy in the 1950s and 1960s. The commission called for the "discontinuance of all specialized Indian activity on the part of the federal government" and recommended that the Bureau of Indian Affairs* "terminate" its relationship with Indian tribes by turning over jurisdiction to state officials. To solve the numbing poverty* on the reservations,* the Hoover Commission recommended that a relocation program be implemented to drain the reservations of surplus labor by moving Indians to new homes in cities and suburbs, where they could find jobs and assimilate into the larger society. During the early 1950s the federal government acted on both recommendations and implemented the termination and relocation programs, in spite of bitter opposition from most reservation Indians.

Suggested Reading: Larry W. Burt, *Tribalism in Crisis: Federal Indian Policy, 1953–1961*, 1982; U.S. Government, *The Hoover Commission on Organization of the Executive Branch of the Government*, 1949.

JAMES S. OLSON

HOUSE CONCURRENT RESOLUTION 108. The mid-twentieth century saw increased support of the concept of termination* for Native Americans. Termination called for the ending of all special tribal relationships in the United States, with Indians becoming "normal" citizens. The program, it was argued, would finally put to rest the "Indian problem" that Congress had been dealing with since its creation. The Bureau of Indian Affairs* (BIA) created and studied plans to phase out the tribes and reservations within fifty years, but the BIA did not wish to lose its funding. In 1952 the BIA requested a funding increase of 70 percent, resulting in a dramatic congressional backlash. The backlash was in the form of House Concurrent Resolution 108 (HCR 108), passed without any objections, which advocated the complete termination of Native Americans.

HCR 108 called for the equality of the American Indian within American society. The Indian was to become a legally indistinguishable citizen of the United States. The dependency of the American Indian on the government was to stop, and all tribes within Texas, California, New York, and Florida were to be terminated immediately. Five other named tribes were also dissolved under the law.

Proponents of the law claimed that HCR 108 was giving a freedom to the Native American that had long been denied. This belief made sense if one accepted that all Indians really wanted to be like most other Americans. Tribalism and the Indian culture had to be seen as evil, or at least harmful, to justify this position. The Native Americans were not consulted about their desire to lose their special legal status. Opponents of the law argued that the Indians were still being treated as children with no regard for what they wanted. HCR 108 would open the way to the termination of millions of acres of land and the relocation of thousands of individuals.

Suggested Reading: Russell Lawrence Barsh and James Youngblood Henderson, *The Road: Indian Tribes and Political Liberty*, 1980; Wilcomb E. Washburn, *Red Man's Land, White Man's Law*, 1971; John R. Wunder, *"Retained by The People": A History of American Indians and the Bill of Rights*, 1994.

DARREN PIERSON

HOUSE RESOLUTION 698. In the years after World War II, the retreat from the Indian New Deal* of the Roosevelt administration accelerated and the pressures to assimilate* American Indians increased dramatically. Opposition to federal supervision of the Indian tribes and tribal resources increased as well, primarily because local economic interests wanted access to Indian land. Early in the 1950s the termination* movement came to represent the desires of those non-Indians who wanted to end federal supervision of Indian tribes. Senator Arthur V. Watkins of Utah and Congressman E. Y. Berry of South Dakota sponsored the termination movement in Congress. In 1952, House Resolution 698 asked Dillon Myer,* head of the Bureau of Indian Affairs* (BIA), to report on the status of the BIA and to prepare a termination program. The resolution also requested a list of BIA services that could be turned over to the states or terminated outright. House Resolution 698 was the opening salvo in what became the termination wars of the 1950s and 1960s.

Suggested Reading: Larry W. Burt, *Tribalism in Crisis: Federal Indian Policy, 1953–1961*, 1982.

JAMES S. OLSON

HOUSE RESOLUTION 6355. See **SNYDER ACT OF 1924.**

HUNTING RIGHTS. Since time immemorial, Native Americans have shaped their existence on the North American continent by hunting and gathering. These activities not only provided the food, clothing, and shelter required for survival but also cemented the Indians' relationship to the land and natural environment in which they lived. When the federal government negotiated treaties with native peoples living in the United States, the Indians often sought to retain the ability to hunt, fish, and gather as they had in the years before Europeans arrived in North America. Even though the Indians ceded title to their lands, they often succeeded in reserving the right to hunt, fish, and gather. These reserved* rights helped them remain spiritually close to the land and also provided food, clothing, and shelter as in the years before the treaties.

By the beginning of the twentieth century, many state governments were aggressively regulating hunting and fishing activities. In spite of historic treaty rights* upholding Indian access to valuable fur, fish, and game resources, state and local wildlife agencies often attempted to actively regulate Indian subsistence hunting as a sport activity—when in fact Indians hunted not for sport but to supply food and clothing to their families and community. Nonetheless, state governments were successful for much of the twentieth century in imposing regulations intended for sport hunting. The imposition of state regulations on Indian subsistence hunters beginning in the late nineteenth and early twentieth centuries went hand-in-hand with the misguided belief that Indians were largely responsible for the destruction of many species of game animals. In many cases, state wildlife regulating agencies and sport hunting organizations scapegoated Indians for the destruction of game species even though it was in the Indians' best interest to preserve these valuable species for future generations.

Not until the last few decades have Indians been successful in gaining recognition for their treaty hunting rights by state and local wildlife regulating agencies. This recognition did not come easily. Even before it was forced by federal court cases such as *New Mexico v. Mescalero Apache Tribe** (1983), Indian bands and tribes had often taken an active role in managing their own access to valuable game resources. Cases such as *New Mexico v. Mescalero Apache Tribe* recognized that Indians not only have a right of access based on reserved hunting rights but also have a responsibility as well as a vested interest in state and tribal wildlife management programs. Historic and contemporary hunting rights are not based on race, but instead are part of the political process by which Indian peoples ceded land and aboriginal title to the federal government.

Suggested Reading: Gary D. Meyers, "Different Sides of the Same Coin: A Comparative View of Indian Hunting and Fishing Rights in the United States and Canada," *Journal of Environmental Law* 10 (1991), 67–121; Francis Paul Prucha, *American Indian Treaties: The History of a Political Anomaly*, 1994; Charles F. Wilkinson, *American Indians, Time and the Law*, 1987.

ANTHONY GULIG

I

INDIAN APPROPRIATIONS ACT OF 1871. The Indian Appropriations Act of 1871, although a routine measure to fund the federal government's Indian programs, proved to be of major significance in the history of Indian civil rights and legal status. Until passage of the Indian Appropriations Act of 1871, the federal government treated the Indian tribes as sovereign nations, although they were often referred to as "domestic dependent" nations. The government dealt with them through treaties that had to be ratified by the Senate. Assimilationists,* however, were intent on incorporating Native Americans into the larger legal system. The practice of treating Indians as members of sovereign groups rather than as individual citizens was consistent with that vision. Assimilationists inserted into the Indian Appropriations Act of 1871 an amendment that ended tribal sovereignty.* Henceforth, Congress dealt directly with the tribes and the federal government administered programs through the Department of the Interior, not through negotiated, ratified treaties. The irony of the Indian Appropriations Act was the fact that it took away from tribes their status as sovereign nations without awarding U.S. citizenship* to individual Indians. Until passage of the Snyder Act* of 1924, which awarded citizenship to Native Americans, most Native Americans occupied a legal no man's land in the United States, where they were subject to the law but not protected by it.

Suggested Reading: Roxanne Dunbar Ortiz, *Indians of the Americas: Human Rights and Self-Determination*, 1984; Hurst Hannum, *Autonomy, Self-Determination and Sovereignty: The Accommodation of Conflicting Rights*, 1990.

JAMES S. OLSON

INDIAN ARTS AND CRAFTS BOARD. On August 27, 1935, President Franklin D. Roosevelt signed into law the Indian Arts and Crafts Board

Act, a component of Indian Commissioner John Collier's* "Indian New Deal"* program. The act created the Indian Arts and Crafts Board. Five commissioners appointed for four-year terms comprised the Board, which sought to improve the quality and expand the distribution of Indian arts and crafts. To improve the market for authentic Indian crafts and undermine the production of mass-produced copies, the Board established government trademarks for Indian-made products to ensure their authenticity. Those attempting to misrepresent Indian products or counterfeit government trademarks faced possible imprisonment not exceeding six months, a fine up to $2,000, or both.

Rene d'Harnoncourt, a European-born artist who helped revive Mexican arts and crafts, served ably as the Board's first general manager. One of the major challenges the Board overcame was the establishment of standards for affixing the government trademark on Indian-made products. Other successful Board activities included creating craft guilds on reservations* to help Indian artists and craftsmen and serve as marketing outlets; organizing art classes in federal schools; providing weaving, silverwork, leatherwork, and beadwork projects; exhibiting Indian-made objects at the 1939 San Francisco World's Fair; and publishing *Indian Art of the United States* (1941) in cooperation with the Museum of Modern Art in New York. Congressional cuts of appropriations to the Board and attacks on d'Harnoncourt's foreign birth crippled the Board's effectiveness. Nevertheless, the Indian Arts and Crafts Board improved the quality and marketing of Indian-made products, preserved the Indians' artistic heritage, promoted an appreciation of Indians' artistic abilities by non-Indians, and supplied needed income to many destitute Indians.

In 1990, Congress passed a new version of the Indian Arts and Crafts Act. Under the new legislation, the Indian Arts and Crafts Board received the power to bring civil and criminal suits against individuals who knowingly claimed authenticity for non-Indian manufactured arts and crafts.

Suggested Reading: James S. Olson and Raymond Wilson, *Native Americans in the Twentieth Century*, 1984; Robert Fay Schrader, *The Indian Arts and Crafts Board: An Aspect of New Deal Indian Policy*, 1983.

RAYMOND WILSON

INDIAN BILL OF RIGHTS. See INDIAN CIVIL RIGHTS ACT OF 1968.

INDIAN CHILD WELFARE ACT OF 1978. The Indian Child Welfare Act is one of the most sweeping and powerful congressional acts affecting Indians ever passed. It gives broad powers to Indian tribal governments to determine what is best for Native American children of the tribe, and it effectively limits state intrusions into this area of Indian case law. The law was passed in response to situations in which sometimes 25 to 35 percent of Indian children were separated from their families and placed in foster care or other institutions. The premise of the legislation is that tribes, as sovereign nations, have a vital interest in the placement of Indian children away from their families. As such, Indian tribal courts,* not state courts, should have jurisdiction over such placements. The act ensured that other courts would respect Indian and tribal intervention and jurisdiction in such matters. The general principle of the law is that except in very limited cases, an Indian child in need of adoption* should be placed with a member of the child's extended family, other members of the child's tribe, or other Indian families, before adoption by whites. Similar preferences are required for foster care placement.

This act effectively ended the sometimes unwarranted removal of Indian children by nontribal public and private agencies. It established a complicated but comprehensive set of rules that protected Indian and tribal preference and control over such matters. It was and remains a controversial act, for some feel that it protects the best interests of the tribe more than it protects the best interests of the child, which is the usual determinant in adoptions and placements. On the positive side, it has provided substantial sums to the tribes to improve their family courts and foster care facilities, making many nontribal placements unnecessary. In addition, this strong congressional reaffirmation of tribal sovereignty* is seen by most to be a positive development in tribal government–federal government relations and in the restoration of self-determination* to Indian peoples.

In 1996, however, the question of adoption again surfaced as a matter of public policy. For years, the National Association of Social Workers, an African-American advocacy group, had opposed interracial adoptions on the grounds that African-American children adopted by white or Hispanic parents are certain to lose their sense of cultural heritage. Native American activists had long made the same argument in opposing the adoption of Indian children by white families. In the summer of 1996, the Clinton administration proposed tax credits and funding grants to promote adoption as public policy, but it specifically denied those benefits to states that prohibited interracial adoptions. Although the Clinton administration's proposal was designed primarily to reduce the number of African-American children in foster care and increase adoption rates, it had a direct impact on American Indian adoption policies as well. One dimension of the Clinton administration's proposal centered on shifting adoption policy jurisdiction from tribal to state courts. The proposed legislation calls for transferring jurisdiction over a child from tribal to state courts when the biological parents do not maintain "significant social, cultural or political affiliation with the tribe." Because the bill does not define the meaning of the term "significant," Indian activists view it as a major threat to tribal sovereignty.

Suggested Reading: William C. Canby, *American Indian Law in a Nutshell*, 1988; *Houston Chronicle*, June 25, 1996; Linda A. Marousek, "The Indian Child Welfare Act of 1978: Provisions and Policy," *South Dakota Law Review* 25 (Winter 1980), 98–115; Gaylene J. McCartney, "The American Indian Child-Welfare Crisis: Cultural Genocide or First Amendment Preservation?" *Columbia Human Rights Law Review* 7 (Fall–Winter 1975–1976), 529–51; Charles F. Wilkinson, *American Indians, Time and the Law*, 1987.

JASON M. TETZLOFF

INDIAN CIVIL RIGHTS ACT OF 1968. In 1968, Congress passed the Indian Civil Rights Act (ICRA), also known as the Indian Bill of Rights. Because this act authorizes federal courts to intervene in intratribal disputes and expressly limits the power of tribes to regulate internal affairs, many Native Americans perceive it to be a threat to their self-determination* and have characterized it as an attempt by the federal government to preempt overall sovereignty.* Their dissent implies a genuine suspicion and skepticism, both of which have resulted in extensive criticism of this statute.

In 1896 the Supreme Court decided the *Talton v. Mayes** case, which stressed that Indian tribes possessed the inherent right to govern themselves. The decision stated that the Bill of Rights* applied to actions of federal and state governments, not tribal governments, because tribes are not subordinate bodies of those governments. Tribal sovereignty,* the Court argued, flows from their aboriginal independence, which preceded the writing of the Constitution.* Talton, a white man, had murdered a Cherokee Indian on the Cherokee reservation. A five-man Cherokee grand jury indicted him for murder, and a Cherokee court convicted him. Talton appealed to the federal courts, arguing that his Fifth Amendment* rights had been violated because a proper, six-man grand jury had not been impaneled. The Supreme Court rejected his argument, holding that the U.S. Constitution placed no limits or restrictions on the manner in which this right manifested itself. In the absence of such limitation, intratribal disputes and complaints against tribal officials had to be resolved within the tribe; the net result was a system that denied tribal members the opportunity to challenge those decisions that they felt were arbitrary and unfair. Because Indian tribes were recognized as independent nations within a nation, the U.S. Supreme Court argued that they enjoyed the same "sovereign immunity" from suit that the state and federal governments enjoy.

Beginning in the early 1960s, Congress began to respond to numerous complaints by individual tribal members who contended that tribal officials were abusive and tyrannical. They appealed to Congress to pass legislation that would protect them from such mistreatment. Congressional hearings convened in 1962 to investigate these complaints of misconduct, and several congressmen concluded that individual Indians needed "some guaranteed form of civil rights against the actions of their own governments."

According to congressional records, the ICRA was passed to "ensure that the American Indian is afforded the broad Constitutional rights secured to other Americans . . . [in order to] protect individual Indians from arbitrary and unjust actions of tribal governments." Legislatively, it confers certain rights on all persons who are subject to the jurisdiction of a tribal government, and the act authorizes federal courts to enforce these rights. The purpose and scope of the Indian Civil Rights Act is similar to that of the U.S. Constitution; however, Congress did deny certain individual rights, which it felt were inherently dangerous to the survival of tribal self-government. Consequently, the ICRA guarantees almost all the fundamental rights enumerated in the U.S. Constitution, with the exception of four. Tribal governments are not subject to the Establishment Clause of the First Amendment (prohibits government sponsorship of churches), do not have to provide legal counsel (free of charge) to indigent defendants, and do not have to provide a trial by jury in civil cases or provide grand jury indictments in criminal cases. These amendments or protections were not included because Congress surmised that they would be a potential threat to political stability within tribal governments.

The Indian Civil Rights Act has fundamentally changed the procedural aspects of the tribal judicial system. Prior to its enactment, procedural uniformity was nonexistent. Tribes would invariably employ their own methods of conflict resolution. The Indian Civil Rights Act, however, requires that all tribes adhere to certain procedural standards. In particular, federal courts mandate that tribal courts advise criminal defendants of their right to a trial by jury, write their criminal laws in clear and certain language, honor a criminal defendant's right against self-incrimination, prohibit the trial judge from also being the prosecutor, and maintain complete records of judicial proceedings. Some Native Americans have considered these changes to be a direct threat to self-determination and tribal sovereignty. The ICRA, they contend, by implication suggests that the rights of individual Indians are more important than the survival of the tribe itself. Consequently, many Native Americans have expressed continued opposition to the Indian Civil Rights Act of 1968.

Suggested Reading: Marjane Ambler, *Breaking the Iron Bonds: Indian Control of Energy Development*, 1990; Donald L. Burnett, "An Historical Analysis of the 1968 'Indian Civil Rights Act,' " *Harvard Journal of Legislation* 9 (1972); Vine Deloria Jr. and Clifford Lytle, *The Nations Within: The Past and Future of American Indian Sovereignty*, 1984; Roxanne Dunbar Ortiz, *Indians of the Americas: Human Rights and Self-Determination*, 1984; Hurst Hannum, *Autonomy, Self-Determination and Sovereignty: The Accommodation of Conflicting Rights*, 1990.

CARLOS RAINER

INDIAN CLAIMS COMMISSION. See **COMPENSATION.**

INDIAN COMMERCE CLAUSE. See **CONSTITUTION.**

INDIAN COUNTRY. The term "Indian country" is a legal definition for Native American political and legal jurisdiction. Specifically included in Indian country is all reservation* land under the jurisdiction of the U.S. government, all Indian allotments* whose original titles are still intact, and all dependent Indian communities within the borders of the United States. In 1948, with its general revision of the federal criminal code, Congress provided that precise definition of "Indian country." The 1948 code applied to cases of criminal jurisdiction; but in 1975, in *DeCoteau v. District County Court*, the Supreme Court gave the federal government jurisdiction over civil cases in Indian country as well.

Suggested Reading: Peter Matthiessen, *Indian Country*, 1984; Stephen L. Pevar, *The Rights of Indians and Tribes*, 1992; Charles F. Wilkinson, *American Indians, Time and the Law*, 1987.

JAMES S. OLSON

INDIAN COUNTRY CRIMES ACT OF 1834. In the wake of the Indian Removal Act* of 1830, Congress had to deal with the question of criminal jurisdiction over American Indians. Hundreds of thousands of Indians were being relocated from eastern reservations and settlements to more western regions and to the Indian Territory,* and a jurisdictional question arose over criminal acts committed by American Indians. In passing the Indian Country Crimes Act, Congress gave exclusive criminal jurisdiction over Indians to the federal government, except in cases of crimes committed by one Indian against another Indian or the property of another Indian. Indian tribes retained exclusive jurisdiction in those instances. However, in no case under the Indian Country Crimes Act did state governments enjoy criminal jurisdiction. Indian tribal jurisdiction in criminal cases did not change until 1885, when Congress passed the Major Crimes Act* in the wake of the *Ex Parte Crow Dog** controversy.

Suggested Reading: Stephen L. Pevar, *The Rights of Indians and Tribes: The Basic ACLU Guide to Indian and Tribal Rights*, 1992.

JAMES S. OLSON

INDIAN CRIMES ACT OF 1976. As part of a continuing campaign to guarantee the individual civil rights of American Indians against the arbitrary actions of federal, state, local, and tribal governments, Congress passed the Indian Crimes Act of 1976. The legislation guaranteed equal treatment before the law for all individuals, Indians as well as non-Indians, accused of committing crimes on all federal territories, including military installations and reservations.*

Suggested Reading: Duane Champagne, ed., *Chronology of Native North American History*, 1994.

JAMES S. OLSON

INDIAN DEFENSE LEAGUE OF AMERICA. The Indian Defense League of America was organized in 1926 by Clinton Rickard, a Tuscarora, and David Hill, a Mohawk, to protest what they considered to be U.S. violation of Jay's Treaty. Ratified in 1794 between Great Britain and the United States, Jay's Treaty guaranteed Iroquois peoples free movement across the U.S.–Canadian border. Ever since, the Iroquois have argued that such freedom of movement implied a recognized tribal sovereignty* for them. In the 1920s, both Canada and the United States passed more restrictive immigration policies that compromised free movement between Iroquois on both sides of the border. The Indian Defense League of America protested those policies and then went on to more nationalistic issues. In 1949 the League tried to secure United Nations recognition of Iroquois nationhood and was also in the forefront of the Kinzua Dam* battle. In more recent decades the Indian Defense League of America has promoted a variety of self-determination* issues.

Suggested Reading: Lawrence M. Hauptman, *The Iroquois and the New Deal*, 1981; Armand S. La Potin, *Native American Voluntary Organizations*, 1986.

JAMES S. OLSON

INDIAN EDUCATION ACT OF 1972. During the 1960s, concern about the state of Indian education* increased dramatically throughout the United States. Lyndon B. Johnson's Great Society programs had focused their attention on civil rights and anti-poverty campaigns, and Native Americans suffered from the effects of both racism and poverty.* Many Indians felt culturally alienated from public schools, had extremely high dropout rates at the middle school and high school levels, were unlikely to go on to higher education, and suffered inordinately high rates of poverty.

In 1969 the Kennedy Report* targeted Indian education as an important area for the federal government's attention, and in 1971 the Legal Defense Fund of the National Association for the Advancement of Colored People released its own report—*An Even Chance*—calling for Indian education reform. Congress implemented those reforms when it passed the Indian Education Act of 1972. The legislation mandated parental and tribal participation in all federal aid programs to public schools with Indian students; appropriated funds to assist community-run schools; allocated money to state and local education agencies, colleges, universities, and tribes to develop new Indian history, culture, and bilingual curricula; funded tribal adult education programs; provided funds for teacher training at Bureau of Indian Affairs* schools; and established an Office of Indian Education to administer the Indian Education Act. The Office of Indian Education was staffed completely by American Indians. Herschel Sahmaunt, a Kiowa and head of the National Indian Education Association,* enthusiastically praised the Indian Education Act of 1972, because it "gives Indian people in reservations, in rural settings, and in the cities control over their own education."

Suggested Reading: Estelle Fuchs and Robert J. Havighurst, *To Live on This Earth: American Indian Education*, 1973; James S. Olson and Raymond Wilson, *Native Americans in the Twentieth Century*, 1984; Margaret Connell Szasz, *Education and the American Indian: The Road to Self-Determination since 1928*, 1977.

JAMES S. OLSON

INDIAN FINANCE ACT OF 1974. During the 1970s the movement for Indian self-determination* came to dominate federal Indian policy, and the Indian Finance Act of 1974 was an important element in the movement. As a reaction to the termination* movement of the 1950s and 1960s, Congress had restored federal protection to most tribes by restoring the trust* relationship, and the desire to upgrade the reservations* economically was very strong. During the termination era, Congress had emphasized relocating Indians away from reservations rather than strengthening reservation economies, but the new political paradigm placed a high premium on reservation economic viability. The Indian Finance Act of 1974 provided new moneys for reservation economic development and individual entrepreneurship, creating a loan guarantee and insurance fund, partially subsidizing loan costs, and providing grants for new businesses. Although the Indian Finance Act did not transform reservation economies, it did provide new opportunities for many Indian entrepreneurs.

Suggested Reading: James S. Olson and Raymond Wilson, *Native Americans in the Twentieth Century*, 1984.

JAMES S. OLSON

INDIAN GAMING REGULATORY ACT OF 1988. During the second half of the twentieth century the self-determination* movement resurrected the notion of tribal sovereignty,* which had dominated government policy in the late eighteenth century and throughout much of the nineteenth century. With the termination* movement having ended by 1970, state jurisdiction over Indian tribes was weaker than ever before. To raise money and provide employment to tribal members, some tribes began developing gambling casinos on reservation land, even when state law prohibited it. By the late 1980s nearly one hundred tribes had established gaming operations. In response to complaints from state authorities and non-Indian businesses near the reservations, Congress passed the Indian Gaming Regulatory Act of 1988; the measure legalized those activities as long as there was a formal tribal ordinance authorizing gambling enterprises and as long as a legal compact had been drawn up between the tribe and the state. The law also established federal standards and regulations for gaming activities on Indian land. A National Indian Gaming Commission was established to enforce those regulations.

In 1996, however, the U.S. Supreme Court declared a portion of the Indian Gaming Regulatory Act of 1988 unconstitutional. In the case of *Seminole Tribe v. Florida*,* the Supreme Court upheld a decision of the Court of Appeals for the Eleventh Circuit. In 1994 the Court of Appeals had ruled that the Seminole tribe of Florida could not file suit under the Indian Gaming Regulatory Act requiring Florida to negotiate a contract to open a casino on Seminole land. According to the justices, the section of the Indian Gaming Regulatory Act allowing the Seminoles to file suit was a violation of the Eleventh Amendment to the Constitution.* The Indian Gaming Regulatory Act authorized tribes to file suit in federal courts against state governments that did not negotiate in good faith about opening and operating gambling casinos on reservations.* Chief Justice William Rehnquist, who wrote the majority opinion, claimed that the law violated the Eleventh Amendment by bringing about an unacceptable incursion on state sovereignty.*

Suggested Reading: Pam Greenberg and Jody Zelio, *States and the Indian Gaming Regulatory Act*, 1992; *New York Times*, March 28, 1996; National Indian Policy Center, *Reservation-Based Gaming*, 1993; Wilcomb E. Washburn, *Red Man's Land, White Man's Law: A Study of the Past and Present Status of the American Indian*, 1971.

JAMES S. OLSON

INDIAN HOMESTEAD ACT OF 1875. In the years after the Civil War,* when white settlement of the Great Plains and Far West accelerated, criticism of the amount of land held by various Indian tribes increased. Non-Indian economic interests, yearning for access to reservation natural resources, charged the Indians with inefficient land use practices. Whites could not condone the maintenance of subsistence hunting and gathering lifestyles that required so much land. Many white reformers, intent on assimilating American Indians into the larger economy and society, were also convinced that tribal land holdings actually stalled the assimilation process, leaving hundreds of thousands of American Indians in tribal settings with community-owned property. Most whites, on the other hand, believed in the fee simple* concept, in which title to land was owned by individual heads of families. They were convinced that assimilation* would not really occur until most Indians had become individual farmers working their own land.

Eventually, Congress would decide to break up tribal land holdings and to allot the acreage to individual Indians. That legislation was embodied in the Dawes Act* of 1887. The Indian Homestead Act, patterned after the Homestead Act* of 1862, was designed to promote the economic assimilation of Native Americans by encouraging some Indians to leave the reservations* and take up their own individual homesteads. Once they had lived on the land for five years and made annual improvements on it, title to the acreage passed to them. Over the long term, however, the Indian Homestead Act had little impact on Native American assimilation. The arid lands of the Far West required significant amounts of land, capital, and technology to make farming commercially viable, and 160 acres was simply not enough.

Suggested Reading: James S. Olson and Raymond Wilson, *Native Americans in the Twentieth Century*, 1984; Loring Benson Priest, *Uncle Sam's Stepchildren: The Reformation of United States Indian Policy, 1865–1887*, 1942.

JAMES S. OLSON

INDIAN HOPE ASSOCIATION. The Indian Hope Association was founded in 1877 in New York City by whites interested in reforming Indian policy. By reform, they meant assimilation.* Led by Mary C. Morgan, the association protested the treatment of the Nez Percés, the Poncas, and the Cheyennes. The Indian Hope Association became one of the moving forces behind the allotment* crusade, which resulted in the Dawes Act* of 1887. After 1887 the Indian Hope Association ceased functioning.

Suggested Reading: Armand S. La Potin, *Native American Voluntary Organizations*, 1986.

JAMES S. OLSON

INDIAN LANDS MINING ACT OF 1938. The debate over tribal sovereignty* for Indian peoples has often revolved around the issue of control of natural resources on the reservations.* Although many reservations were rich in timber, coal, oil, uranium, natural gas, and other mineral resources, non-Indian commercial interests had generally exploited them in the past. Poverty* remained a severe problem on the reservations in spite of those resources. During the Indian New Deal* era, Commissioner of Indian Affairs John Collier* worked to both restore tribal sovereignty after the half-century of allotment* and develop the reservations economically.

In 1938, at Collier's urging, the Roosevelt administration supported and Congress passed the Indian Lands Mining Act, which authorized the secretary of the Interior to negotiate long-term leases with commercial interests to develop Indian resources. The extraction industries would provide jobs for Native Americans and royalty income for the tribes. As it worked out, however, the legislation proved harmful to Native Americans. It was not at all uncommon for the secretary of the Interior to negotiate very long-term leases. Those leases were based on mineral prices as they existed in the depressed economy of the Great Depression.

As mineral price levels rose in subsequent years, many tribes found them-selves trapped in long-term, unfavorable contracts.

Suggested Reading: Marjane Ambler, *Breaking the Iron Bonds: Indian Control of Energy Development*, 1990; Vine Deloria Jr. and Clifford Lytle, *The Nations Within: The Past and Future of American Indian Sovereignty*, 1984; Roxanne Dunbar Ortiz, *Indians of the Americas: Human Rights and Self-Determination*, 1984; Hurst Hannum, *Autonomy, Self-Determination and Sovereignty: The Accommodation of Conflicting Rights*, 1990; Phyllis Mauch Messenger, ed., *The Ethics of Collecting Cultural Property: Whose Culture? Whose Property?* 1989.

JAMES S. OLSON

INDIAN MAJOR CRIMES ACT OF 1885. See **MAJOR CRIMES ACT OF 1885.**

INDIAN MINERAL DEVELOPMENT ACT OF 1982. Legislation that pro-motes tribal profits through the management, control, and sale of mineral resources on reservation lands. Reservation resources of uranium, coal, oil, and natural gas became particularly important, to Indians and non-Indians, during the energy crisis of the 1970s when oil-producing Arab nations imposed an oil embargo and energy prices skyrocketed. Re-source-rich Indian tribes should have expected a windfall of profits, but most of them had a history of leasing out their resources at prices well below market levels, and the energy crisis exacerbated that problem. With oil, natural gas, and coal prices escalating rapidly, many tribes found themselves bound to low-paying, long-term royalty contracts with major energy companies. The energy companies were reaping huge profits, har-vesting tribal energy resources for a pittance and then marketing them at world price levels.

Indian activists reacted with the formation of the Council of Energy Resource Tribes* (CERT) in 1976. CERT was committed to maximizing tribal profits by raising prices and augmenting self-determination* by giv-ing tribes more control over their own resources. During the late 1970s and early 1980s CERT lobbied vigorously for federal legislation to protect the Indian resource state. In 1982 its efforts resulted in the Indian Min-eral Development Act and the Federal Oil and Gas Royalty Management Act,* both of which allowed for the renegotiation of royalty contracts, establishment of joint ventures between mining companies and Indian tribes, amendments to national environmental laws giving tribes clear control of resource use on their own lands, education and job training programs to develop reservation expertise, and revolving funds to im-prove reservation* infrastructures. Both laws are considered landmark events in the history of the self-determination movement, because many Indians believe economic self-sufficiency is central to tribal sovereignty.*

Suggested Reading: Marjane Ambler, *Breaking the Iron Bonds: Indian Control of Energy Development*, 1990; Vine Deloria Jr. and Clifford Lytle, *The Nations Within: The Past and Future of American Indian Sovereignty*, 1984; Roxanne Dunbar Ortiz, *Indians of the Americas: Human Rights and Self-Determination*, 1984; Hurst Hannum, *Autonomy, Self-Determination and Sovereignty: The Accommodation of Conflicting Rights*, 1990; Phyllis Mauch Messenger, ed., *The Ethics of Collecting Cultural Property: Whose Culture? Whose Property?* 1989.

JAMES S. OLSON

INDIAN NATIONS AT RISK TASK FORCE. In 1990, at the direction of President George Bush, the Department of Education established the Indian Nations at Risk Task Force to address the problem of Indian education* and tribal cultural survival. Alarm had long since developed among Indian peoples about the loss of their traditional cultures; and modern society, with its mass communication systems, seemed to be accelerating the process of assimilation* even without the heavy hand of the federal government. The purpose of the Indian Nations at Risk Task Force was to identify ways in which public education systems could assist in the survival of tribal cultures.

The Task Force made its recommendation in 1991. Among its more important proposals was development of greater cooperation between federal, state, local, tribal, and private schools to generate comprehensive educational goals; to develop partnerships between schools, parents, tribes, universities, industry, and health and social service agencies to improve Indian education; to emphasize parent-based early childhood programs that are culturally and linguistically appropriate; to promote Indian languages in the public schools; and to increase the number of trained Native American educators.

Suggested Reading: Michael C. Cleman, *American Indian Children at School, 1850–1930*, 1993; David H. Dejong, *Promises of the Past: A History of Indian Education in the United States*, 1993; Basil H. Johnston, *Indian School Days*, 1989; Margaret Szasz, *Education and the American Indian: The Road to Self-Determination since 1928*, 1977.

JAMES S. OLSON

INDIAN NEW DEAL. The term "Indian New Deal" has been commonly used to describe John Collier's* tenure as head of the Bureau of Indian Affairs* (BIA) during the years of the Great Depression and World War II. By the 1920s, after more than thirty years' experience with the allotment* program created under the Dawes Act* of 1887, a number of white reformers and most tribal leaders were calling for a thorough revision in federal Indian policy. The allotment program had done little more than rob Native Americans of tens of millions of acres of land and reduce them to desperate poverty.* Secretary of the Interior Albert Fall's attempt to promote the Bursum Bill* and to destroy Indian sovereignty* on executive order reservations* created a storm of controversy in the United States, and the 1928 Meriam Report* only confirmed the suspicions of many that federal Indian policy in the late nineteenth and early twentieth centuries had been catastrophic for Indian peoples. The movement to reform federal Indian policy gained momentum.

The leading figure among the reformers was John Collier, head of the American Indian Defense Association.* In 1933 President Franklin D. Roosevelt named Collier commissioner of Indian affairs. Once an outside group demanding change in federal policy, the reformers had now captured control of the Bureau of Indian Affairs. Collier hoped to reverse the trends of the previous half-century by ending the allotment program, restoring sovereignty to tribal governments, returning to Indian tribes as much of their landed estate as possible, and attacking reservation poverty through economic development.

The so-called Indian New Deal consisted of three major pieces of legislation: the Indian Reorganization Act* of 1934, the Johnson-O'Malley Act* of 1934, and the Indian Arts and Crafts Board* Act of 1935. The Indian Reorganization Act ended allotment, restored to tribes surplus reservation lands that the Dawes Act of 1887 had created, and allowed for voluntary exchanges of restricted trust* lands for shares in tribal corporations. Congress appropriated $2 million annually to the secretary of the Interior for the acquisition of additional lands for tribes. The legislation also created a $10 million revolving credit fund to provide loans to tribal corporations. An annual appropriation of $250,000 was provided to aid Indians in organizing tribal governments. Additional appropriations of $250,000 a year established a fund to help Indian students attend colleges and vocational schools. Finally, the act relaxed civil service requirements for Indians seeking employment in the Indian Service (employment branch of the BIA). It also permitted the Bureau of Indian Affairs to give Indians preference over non-Indians in hiring policies. Indians in Alaska and Oklahoma were initially excluded from the law, but Congress made up for the oversight in 1936 with passage of the Alaska Reorganization Act* and the Oklahoma Indian Welfare Act.*

The Johnson-O'Malley Act was designed to improve Indian education* and reverse the centuries-old policy of using federal Indian schools as a front for attacking Indian cultures and promoting assimilation.* The legislation authorized the secretary of the Interior to enter into contracts with states and territories to provide monetary assistance for Indian educational, medical, agricultural, and social welfare services. Although federal funds had been provided to public schools for over forty years, this act finally compromised on a federal and state arrangement to overcome the previously complicated contracting method between individual school districts and the federal government. Collier hoped that by providing federal funds to local districts, the federal government could promote Indian education. He also hoped that the presence of federal funds would permit the Bureau of Indian Affairs to lessen the impact of racism and discrimination on Indian children by making public school curricula more culturally sensitive.

The Indian Arts and Crafts Board Act established the Indian Arts and Crafts Board. Its primary purpose was to promote reservation economic self-sufficiency by strengthening arts and crafts operations. The law established an Indian Arts and Crafts Board consisting of five commissioners serving four-year terms. The Board's goal was to improve the quality and expand the distribution of Indian arts and crafts. To improve the market for authentic Indian crafts, the Board established government trademarks for Indian-made products to ensure their authenticity. Those attempting to misrepresent Indian products or counterfeit government trademarks faced possible imprisonment not exceeding six months, a fine up to $2,000, or both. Collier hoped such trademarks would undermine the production of cheap, mass-produced copies of Indian art.

Although the Indian New Deal failed to achieve all its goals, historians and most Indian people remember it today as a beneficial program. The loss of tribal land, so steady for more than three hundred years, came to an end. Federal investment in reservation economies improved the standard of living for tens of thousands of American Indians. Decades of racism and discrimination in federal schools were thwarted as the government promoted the expression of tribal values and customs. The Indian death rate fell dramatically, and the Indian population began to increase. Fears of the extinction of Indian peoples disappeared. Vine Deloria Jr. has termed the Indian New Deal the "greatest days of Indian life in the twentieth century."

Unfortunately, the Indian New Deal came to an end almost before it really started. As the United States drifted toward world war in 1939 and 1940, Americans became less interested in reform and more interested in reasserting traditional identities. The Indian New Deal's emphasis on community rather than private property, tribal rather than individual values, and ethnic autonomy rather than assimilation and national unity seemed suspect, especially with authoritarianism enjoying a global revival. In 1937, Senator Burton K. Wheeler, author of the Indian Reorganization Act, had reversed himself and called for the assimilation of Indian peoples. The defection of some of the original supporters of the Indian Reorganization Act, the financial and bureaucratic pressures created by World War II, the growing ideological fear of radicalism, and the resignation of John Collier in 1945 cut the political props from under the Indian New Deal. After World War II the "Red Scare" only intensified suspicions of the Indian New Deal. A new drive to "reform" federal policy was under way, and it soon led to the compensation,* termination,* and relocation* programs. The Indian New Deal was dead.

Suggested Reading: Lawrence C. Kelly, *The Assault on Assimilation: John Collier and the Origins of Indian Policy Reform*, 1983; Donald L. Parman, *The Navajos and the New Deal*, 1976; Kenneth R. Philp, *John Collier's Crusade for Indian Reform, 1920–1954*, 1977; Graham D. Taylor, *The New Deal and American Indian Tribalism: The Administration of the Indian Reorganization Act, 1934–1945*, 1980.

JAMES S. OLSON

INDIAN OIL LEASING ACT OF 1927. During the presidential administration of Warren G. Harding, the federal government pursued a number of policies designed to rob Native Americans of their land and mineral resources. Albert Fall of New Mexico served as secretary of the Interior under Harding, and his sympathies lay completely with non-Indian economic interests. One of Fall's most controversial decisions involved executive order reservations.* Throughout American history, Indian reservations had been established by formal treaty arrangements between tribal governments and the executive and legislative branches of the federal government, or by simple executive orders of the president. Fall decided to declare that Indian tribes enjoyed sovereignty* only over treaty reservations. They did not possess permanent sovereignty over the lands of executive order reservations. On the contrary, he claimed, all executive order reservation land was part of the public domain and open to white settlement.

The decision generated a storm of protest in the United States. Groups such as the Indian Rights Association* and the American Indian Defense Association* protested the decision. Partly because of the political pressure and partly because of Albert Fall's resignation under the cloud of the Teapot Dome scandal (in which he had accepted kickbacks from energy companies drilling on government land), the policy was never implemented. In 1927 Congress passed the Indian Oil Lease Act, which guaranteed to Indian residents of executive order reservations a reasonable share of the income from leases. In what amounted to a victory for Native Americans, the act returned leasing authority to the Bureau of Indian Affairs,* established semipermanent boundaries to the executive order reservations, and made provision for the direct taxation of business concerns operating on such lands.

Suggested Reading: Marjane Ambler, *Breaking the Iron Bonds: Indian Control of Energy Development*, 1990; James S. Olson and Raymond Wilson, *Native Americans in the Twentieth Century*, 1984; Francis Paul Prucha, *The Great Father*, Vol. 2, 1984.

JAMES S. OLSON

INDIAN PEACE COMMISSION. See PEACE POLICY.

INDIAN POLICE. The need to enforce laws has confronted all societies, including that of Native Americans. The increasing assumption of power by the United States, and the subsequent loss of power by the Indian nations, forced the United States to try and find a way of enforcing American law on the reservations.* This need had not existed prior to or during the early nineteenth century because of the Indians' own ability to enforce law and order within the reservations. However, as the nineteenth century came to a close, the increased control over American Indians by the federal government demanded new methods of reservation law enforcement.

As early as the 1860s some Indian agents had seen a need for Indian police forces. The Pawnees had a small, uniformed police force in 1862, and other tribes gained their own police forces in the 1870s. The creation of Indian police forces allowed the federal government to execute its policies with less resistance and violence, because the issue of ethnicity was absent from the enforcement process. The successes of the early attempts at Indian police forces encouraged the federal government to push for greater adoption of the idea. The commissioner of Indian affairs in 1878 ordered all tribes to maintain police forces if it was practical to do so. The Indian police gained judicial powers in the 1880s when limited Indian courts were founded.

The Indian police forces used Native Americans for officers, but the

Indians adopted white methods of dress and appearance. These police forces played an important role for both the Indians and the federal government. The government used the police to enforce its laws and regulations without having to send the military or other forces onto the reservations. Native Americans could join the police forces and assume a familiar, albeit extremely limited, role of warrior and scout. In this way the Indian police offered Native Americans the only federally sanctioned avenue to regain limited martial self-respect. Whether or not the price was acceptable depended on one's view of the policies the Indian police had to enforce.

One important controversy revolving around Indian police was that of individual rights and tribal sovereignty.* As citizens of the United States, all American Indians are protected by the Bill of Rights.* At the same time, however, tribal governments, in the name of tribal sovereignty* and self-determination,* have been awarded criminal jurisdiction over Indians in Indian country.* The civil rights question arose when Indian police and tribal courts* did not respect constitutionally guaranteed civil rights. Advocates of complete tribal sovereignty claimed that Indian police were not bound by the Bill of Rights. The Indian Civil Rights Act* of 1968 partially resolved the controversy by imposing such obligations on Indian police. Henceforth, as a result of the legislation, Indian police had to read defendants their Fifth Amendment* rights against self-incrimination and their Sixth Amendment right to legal counsel.

Suggested Reading: Wilcomb E. Washburn, *Red Man's Land, White Man's Law*, 1971; John R. Wunder, *"Retained by The People": A History of American Indians and the Bill of Rights*, 1994.

DARREN PIERSON

INDIAN REMOVAL ACT OF 1830. In the Treaty of Paris* of 1783, Great Britain awarded to the United States all its territory between the Appalachian Mountains and the Mississippi River, south of Canada. With the American War of Independence won, tens of thousands of white settlers began pouring across the mountains into what is today Ohio, Illinois, Indiana, Kentucky, Tennessee, Alabama, and Mississippi. Not surprisingly, the arrival of so many whites precipitated a series of violent conflicts with various Native American tribes.

Prominent American leaders, such as President Thomas Jefferson,* began toying with the idea of relocating all the Indians west of the Mississippi River—where few white men, they erroneously assumed, would ever want to live. One of Jefferson's reasons for the Louisiana Purchase* of 1803 was to provide territory for Indian country.* Many assimilation-ists* were convinced that removal was the only way of ending violence against Indian peoples. Economic interests anxious to take possession of Indian land jumped at the idea as well. In 1830, Congress passed and President Andrew Jackson* signed the Indian Removal Act, which pro-vided for the relocation* of Indian tribes to reservations* west of the Mississippi, particularly in the Indian Territory* of what would later be-come the state of Oklahoma.

Most Indian peoples did not want to move; they resisted, some vio-lently and others through legal channels. The Cherokees tried the federal courts, and even though the Supreme Court found in their favor, Andrew Jackson had federal troops forcibly evict them from their Georgia lands anyway. Some tribes, like the Seminoles in Florida and the Sacs and Foxes in the Midwest, carried out guerrilla wars against federal authorities. In the end, however, under the pressures of massive white settlement, the federal government prevailed, leading to what is now known as the Trail of Tears* relocations of the 1830s and 1840s.

Suggested Reading: Arthur H. DeRosier Jr., *The Removal of the Choctaw In-dians*, 1970; John Ehle, *Trail of Tears: The Rise and Fall of the Cherokee Nation*, 1988; Grant Foreman, *Indian Removal: The Emigration of the Five Civilized Tribes of Indians*, 1932; Michael Paul Rogin, *Fathers and Children: Andrew Jack-son and the Subjugation of the American Indians*, 1975; Anthony F. Wallace, *The Long Bitter Trail: Andrew Jackson and the Indians*, 1993.

JAMES S. OLSON

INDIAN REORGANIZATION ACT OF 1934. When John Collier* be-came commissioner of Indian affairs in April 1933, he promised an "In-dian New Deal"* for Native Americans. Following the anti-Indian policies of the Warren Harding administration (1921–1923), the 1920s had breathed new life into the movement to reform Indian policy, and John Collier had been a leading figure in the campaign. For Collier, the blatant assimilationist policies of the previous half-century, particularly the allot-ment* program, had to be scrapped. He wanted to restore land and po-litical power to tribal governments. The cornerstone of this new direction in federal Indian policy was the Indian Reorganization Act of 1934. Col-lier, Assistant Commissioner of Indian Affairs William Zimmerman, and members of the Department of Interior's legal staff (particularly Nathan Margold and Felix Cohen), wrote the original draft of the Indian Reor-ganization Act. Representative Edgar Howard of Nebraska introduced the bill in the House, and Senator Burton K. Wheeler of Montana sponsored it in the Senate. The Wheeler-Howard bill was forty-eight pages long and contained four titles regarding Indian self-government, education,* lands, and a special court for Indian affairs.

Although Collier held several meetings with Indian tribes throughout the West to explain the benefits of the legislation and subsequently reported that most of the tribes embraced the bill, congressional critics and others remained unconvinced. They charged that the Wheeler-Howard bill severely retarded the process of assimilation* by segregating Indians from the dominant society and perpetuating federal guardianship* over them, promoted communism among Indians by restoring community properties, and threatened individual Indian land ownership and heirship lands. To overcome these criticisms and others, Collier accepted several major revisions of the original draft. For example, the special Indian court was eliminated and the powers of tribal self-government were reduced. After receiving congressional approval, the bill was signed into law by President Franklin D. Roosevelt on June 18, 1934.

In its amended form, the Indian Reorganization Act (sometimes called the Wheeler-Howard Act) repealed the allotment in severalty laws, restored to tribes the surplus reservation lands that the Dawes Act* of 1887 had created, and allowed for voluntary exchanges of restricted trust* lands for shares in tribal corporations. Congressional appropriations of $2 million annually to the secretary of the Interior were authorized for the acquisition of additional lands for tribes. A $10 million revolving credit fund was created to provide loans to tribal corporations, and an annual appropriation of $250,000 was provided to aid Indians in organizing tribal governments. Additional appropriations of $250,000 a year established a fund to help Indian students attend colleges and vocational schools. Finally, the act relaxed civil service requirements for Indians seeking employment in the Indian Service (employment branch of the Bureau of Indian Affairs* [BIA]). Because of various circumstances, Indians in Alaska and Oklahoma were excluded from certain provisions of the Indian Reorganization Act. In 1936 Congress addressed these matters and passed both the Alaska Reorganization Act* and the Oklahoma Indian Welfare Act,* allowing Alaskan Indians to establish tribal corporations and Oklahoma Indians to create tribal governments and corporations.

Indian tribes had the right to accept or reject the Indian reorganization through tribal referenda. Those accepting the act could hold additional elections to establish self-governments and charters of incorporation. Although the figures vary, approximately 181 tribes with a population of 129,750 accepted the act, and 77 tribes numbering 86,365, including the

Navajos, rejected it. Moreover, only 93 tribes adopted constitutions and only 73 established charters of incorporation. Of the over 100,000 Indians living in Oklahoma, only 18 tribes numbering 13,241 wrote constitutions, and 13 tribes with a population of 5,741 drew up charters of incorporation under the Oklahoma Indian Welfare Act. In Alaska, 49 villages with a total population of 10,899 established constitutions and incorporation charters under the Alaska Reorganization Act.

Although the Indian Reorganization Act did not achieve the Indian millennium that Collier desired, it ended the policy of land allotments, increased the land base of reservations,* allowed tribes to have a greater degree of control over their political and economic destinies, and promoted Indian culture. Reasons for the act's failure to achieve its objectives include the overall lack of support from Indians, members of Congress, and BIA officials; the recurring fear that the act retarded assimilation; and Collier's inability to recognize the complexities of Native American tribalism.

Suggested Reading: Lawrence C. Kelly, *The Assault on Assimilation: John Collier and the Origins of Indian Policy Reform*, 1983; Donald L. Parman, *The Navajos and the New Deal*, 1976; Kenneth R. Philp, *John Collier's Crusade for Indian Reform, 1920–1954*, 1977; Graham D. Taylor, *The New Deal and American Indian Tribalism: The Administration of the Indian Reorganization Act, 1934–1945*, 1980.

RAYMOND WILSON

INDIAN RIGHTS ASSOCIATION. The Indian Rights Association (IRA) was founded by Herbert Welsh in 1882. An interdenominational religious organization concerned about the plight of American Indians, the IRA was headquartered in Philadelphia and dedicated to the assimilationist policies prevalent at the time. Welsh headed the group until 1927, giving the organization excellent leadership and real continuity. The IRA acted as a lobbying group before Congress and committed itself to the breakup of the tribal estate, citizenship* for all Indian peoples, and legislation to bring Native Americans under the legal sovereignty* of state governments. By the 1920s, the Indian Rights Association was increasingly out-of-step as a reform organization. A new generation of reformers, led by John Collier,* opposed assimilation* and wanted to restore tribal authority and federal protection of the tribes. During the 1930s, the IRA openly opposed the Indian Reorganization Act* of 1934 and came to be seen as an anachronistic group. Its influence declined dramatically after World War II, even though it opposed termination* and tried to help the

Senecas oppose the Kinzua Dam* project. The last meeting of the Indian Rights Association was held in 1986.

Suggested Reading: William T. Hagan, *The Indian Rights Association: The Herbert Welsh Years, 1882–1904*, 1985; Francis Paul Prucha, *The Great Father: The United States Government and the American Indians*, 1984.

JAMES S. OLSON

INDIAN TERRITORY. "Indian Territory" is a term used to describe the region settled by the eastern Indian tribes who were removed from their eastern homelands in the 1830s. As white settlement advanced westward, condensing the Indian population, "Indian Territory" came to apply to Oklahoma (excluding its panhandle) alone. This region was dominated by the so-called Five Civilized Tribes: the Cherokee, Choctaw, Chickasaw, Creek, and Seminole. Although these southern tribes held title to almost all of present-day Oklahoma, they were concentrated in the eastern half of the Oklahoma region, eventually leasing the western half to the United States for the settlement of the Plains and other Indians.

As white settlers flooded across the Mississippi, the federal government attempted to convince the Five Civilized Tribes to surrender a portion of their territory or accept allotments* of individual farms for each Indian. The Indians held fast against these demands, and the level of their accomplishments convinced the government to back down. As early as the 1850s, the Five Civilized Tribes had developed a prosperous society.

Even though the Indians had nothing at stake during the American Civil War,* it had a pronounced effect on their territory. Most of the tribes chose to support the Confederacy. As a result, after the war the government used the tribes' sympathies with the South to force concessions from them. Other tribes were crowded into their territory as white settlers encroached on their former lands. Indian Territory was not exempt from this land hunger.

In 1888, Congress created the Oklahoma Territory out of the western half of Indian Territory. The Five Tribes retained control of the eastern half of the territory. Indians in the Oklahoma Territory received allotments according to the Dawes Act,* and the surplus lands were opened to white settlement. The Five Tribes resisted allotment, but neither they nor the national government could keep white settlers from invading their lands. The Five Tribes, under constant pressure, realized that a negotiated settlement would be more advantageous than a forced settlement and agreed to meet with the Dawes Commission. The tribal members became U.S. citizens in 1901, and in 1907 Indian and Oklahoma

Territories were combined and entered the Union as the state of Oklahoma. The idea of an independent Indian state was abandoned forever.

Suggested Reading: Angie Debo, *A History of the Indians of the United States*, 1970; Arrell Morgan Gibson, ed., *America's Exiles: Indian Colonization in Oklahoma*, 1976; Francis Paul Prucha, *The Great Father: The United States Government and the American Indians*, 2 vols., 1984.

JEFFREY D. CARLISLE

INDIAN TRADE AND INTERCOURSE ACTS OF THE 1790s. When George Washington, the new president in 1789, began to organize his administration, he assigned Indian affairs to Secretary of War Henry Knox of Massachusetts. Knox was one of the more sympathetic toward Indians of all U.S. administrators. He adopted the British idea that Indian land should be purchased and was exclusively theirs until purchased. He further stressed the new Constitution's* provision in Article I, Section 8, that "Congress shall have power . . . to regulate trade . . . with the Indian tribes." The result was a series of Indian Trade and Intercourse Acts in 1790, 1793, and 1796 that set the first general policy of the United States toward Indians.

Essentially, two interrelated policies to deal with peaceful Indian tribes evolved out of these three laws. The first was the adoption of the former British policy of appointing agents to live among the Indian tribes. Before 1815, the aim of these agents was twofold: to maintain annuities and gifts and to prevent foreign intrigue, especially by the British or Spanish governments; and to encourage a policy of civilization of the Indians by training them in commerical agriculture, domestic arts, and animal husbandry. As assistance in this latter area, federal funds were provided to Protestant missionary agencies that would establish schools among the Indians. Beginning with the highly successful Benjamin Hawkins, employed as Creek agent in 1796, the number of agents reached 12 by 1812 and approximately 100 (agents and assistants) by 1832.

The second policy was to establish trading posts among the Indians—federally constructed and funded, and staffed by federal employees. These were called factories; thus the policy acquired the name of the Federal Factory System. In 1796 the factory system replaced a system of licensing private traders, which the British and American governments had used since 1763. Because the private trader often disturbed harmonious relationships between Indians and whites by introducing his cheap goods, sharp trading policy, provision of alcohol, and sale of guns, the

Federal Factory System was intended as a reform. Government traders paid full price for furs, did not sell alcohol or guns, and sold other high-grade goods at cost. By 1800, posts at Coleraine in Georgia and Tellico in Tennessee had opened, and eventually twenty-eight posts were in operation before the factory system was ended in 1822.

Unfortunately, what had the potential of protecting Indian rights was quickly abused. The educational policy assumed that white culture and Christianity had full priority over and preempted Indian culture and religions. The factories could extend credit, as President Thomas Jefferson* specifically urged in order to force the purchase of Indian lands. This happened with the large Chickasaw debt at the Chickasaw Bluffs (Memphis) factory in the Jackson Purchase of 1819. With the ending of the factory system in 1822 and the adoption of the Jacksonian Indian removal policy, the effects of the Indian Trade and Intercourse Acts of 1790, 1793, and 1796 faded from use.

Suggested Reading: Francis Paul Prucha, *American Indian Policy in the Formative Years: The Indian Trade and Intercourse Acts, 1790–1834*, 1962.

FRED S. ROLATER

INDIAN TRIBAL GOVERNMENTAL TAX STATUS ACT OF 1982. See **TAXATION.**

INDIAN VETERAN CITIZENSHIP ACT OF 1919. During the late nineteenth and early twentieth centuries, when assimilation* pressures were intense concerning Indian policy, the movement to award citizenship* to Native Americans accelerated. The Dawes Act* of 1887 had provided citizenship to each Indian receiving a land allotment,* and gradually between 1887 and 1914 tens of thousands of Native Americans became citizens of the United States. Senator Homer Snyder of New York was a powerful advocate of citizenship, which he believed would integrate Native Americans into the larger body politic. In 1919 he decided that all Native Americans who had served in the military during World War I should be entitled to citizenship. The logic was simple: those who fight for their country and risk their lives should be eligible for all the rights afforded citizens. Snyder drafted the Indian Veteran Citizenship Act, and Congress passed the measure in 1919. All Indian veterans of World War I who applied for citizenship would receive it.

Suggested Reading: Arrell Morgan Gibson, *Between Two Worlds*, 1986.

JAMES S. OLSON

INDIANS OF ALL TRIBES. On November 20, 1969, a group of 89 young urban American Indian college students identifying themselves as "Indians of All Tribes" landed on Alcatraz Island* in San Francisco Bay. They claimed the island by "right of discovery"* and by the terms of the 1868 Sioux Treaty of Fort Laramie,* which they interpreted as giving Indians the right to claim unused federal property that had been Indian land previously. The occupiers demanded clear title to Alcatraz Island and the establishment of an American Indian University, an American Indian Cultural Center, and an American Indian Museum on Alcatraz Island.

The Indian group initially used the name "United Native Americans" but recognized that the name was not representative of the large number of Indian tribes who participated in the occupation. While casting about for a name, Belvia Cottier, a Lakota Indian woman who had been instrumental in the planning of a brief 1964 occupation of Alcatraz Island as well as the 1969 occupation, suggested the name "Indians of All Tribes." This name was more appropriate because Indian people from tribes from all across the United States participated in the planning and carrying out of the occupation. The name was adopted and remained unchanged until January 15, 1970, at which time the group filed legal articles of incorporation with the state of California and became a legal entity, "Indians of All Tribes, Inc." The corporation's principal office was listed as Alcatraz Island in San Francisco, California.

The specific and primary purpose of the incorporated group was to promote the welfare of all Indians on Alcatraz Island and elsewhere. The general purposes and powers were listed as: (1) to administer Alcatraz Island; (2) to promote the welfare of residents of Alcatraz Island; (3) to negotiate with the federal government for the purpose of obtaining title to Alcatraz Island and realizing other demands; (4) to establish Indian educational and cultural centers on Alcatraz Island and elsewhere; (5) to enter into and perform contracts, agreements, and other transactions of any description; and (6) to receive, own, possess, administer, and dispose of money and property of any description, individually in its own name, as trustee, or fiduciary, jointly with others or in any other manner. The corporation was organized pursuant to the California General Nonprofit Corporation Law; its Board of Directors, known as Council members, were all Indian people: Stella Leach (Colville/Sioux), Alan Miller (Seminole), Judy Scraper (Shawnee), David Leach (Colville/Sioux), Denis Turner (Luiseno), Richard Oakes (Mohawk), and Ray Spang (Northern Cheyenne).

Criteria for membership in Indians of All Tribes, Inc., was set forth in the bylaws of the organization:

> Every Indian on Alcatraz Island in San Francisco Bay is a member of the corporation if he or she (a) is registered with the coordinator's office as a resident, and (b) has lived continuously on Alcatraz for at least seven days. An Indian loses his membership if (a) he leaves Alcatraz for more than seventy-two (72) hours in any calendar week, without permission from Council; or (b) a majority of the Council votes to revoke his membership for violation of the security rules. If membership was lost by leaving Alcatraz for more than seventy-two hours, it could be regained by re-registering as a resident and living continuously on Alcatraz for at least seven (7) days.

The members of the island council established by Indians of All Tribes, Inc., changed numerous times during the nineteen-month occupation of Alcatraz Island, which ended on June 11, 1971. Provisions in the bylaws called for regular elections so that the island leadership would reflect the preferences of the Indian people on the island. Throughout much of the nineteen-month occupation, Indians of All Tribes, Inc., provided a sound framework for the diverse groups of Indian occupiers. The Council subcommittees provided for housing, security, finance, public relations, sanitation, cooking, day care, and medical care, as well as a negotiation team to meet with federal officials during the occupation. Every resident of Alcatraz Island was assigned duties in one of these areas. Indians of All Tribes, Inc., ceased to exist following the Alcatraz occupation; however, the name remains today as part of the United Indians of All Tribes Foundation in Seattle, Washington.

Suggested Reading: Troy R. Johnson, *The Occupation of Alcatraz Island: Indian Self-Determination and the Rise of Indian Activism*, 1996.

TROY JOHNSON

INSTITUTE FOR THE DEVELOPMENT OF INDIAN LAW. The Institute for the Development of Indian Law was founded in 1971 by Vine Deloria Jr.,* Franklin D. Ducheneaux, and Kirke Kickingbird. Dedicated to the implementation of tribal sovereignty* and self-determination,* the Institute provides research, publication, and legal assistance to Indian tribes. In addition to publishing such books as *Taxing Those They Found Here*; *100 Million Acres*; and *Indians and the Constitution: A Forgotten Legacy*, the Institute has played a key role in litigating Indian civil rights cases and has assisted in the formation of the Coalition of Eastern Native Americans, an organization dedicated to promoting the economic and political welfare of Atlantic Coast tribes. The Institute is headquartered in Oklahoma City.

Suggested Reading: Kirke Kickingbird, "Institute for the Development of Indian Law," in Mary B. Davis, ed., *Native Americans in the Twentieth Century*, 1994.

JAMES S. OLSON

INTERCOURSE ACT OF 1802. The Trade and Intercourse Act of 1802 is for the most part a permanent restatement of the acts of 1796 and 1799. The two prior acts having proven themselves, within limits, to be successful, President Thomas Jefferson* saw no reason to depart from his predecessors' policies. As the date of expiration of the 1799 law approached, Jefferson called Congress's attention to the fact and suggested only that some restriction be placed on the liquor traffic among the Indians, which he noted was requested by the Indians themselves.

Accordingly, Congress inserted a section authorizing the president to take any action he deemed necessary to "prevent or restrain the vending or distribution of spirituous liquors among all or any of the said Indian tribes." On March 30, 1802, the new Trade and Intercourse Act became law; it remained, with occasional amendments, the basis of U.S. Indian trade policy until it was replaced in 1834.

Suggested Reading: Francis Paul Prucha, *The Great Father: The United States Government and the American Indians*, 2 vols., 1984; Francis Paul Prucha, *American Indian Policy in the Formative Years: The Indian Trade and Intercourse Acts, 1790–1834*, 1962; Ronald Satz, *American Indian Policy in the Jacksonian Era*, 1975.

JEFFREY D. CARLISLE

INTERCOURSE ACT OF 1834. The Intercourse Act of 1834 was developed to replace the Intercourse Act* of 1802 and correct abuses that had been committed against the Indians. American settlers often encroached on Indian land, traders ignored regulations, and liquor continued to flow freely to the Indians. Therefore, the first part of the act redefined "Indian country"* as all U.S. land west of the Mississippi (excluding Missouri, Louisiana, and the Arkansas Territory) and land east of the Mississippi that was not within a state and had not had the Indian title extinguished. This definition accepted Indian removal as an accomplished fact. Any Indian living within a state or in a territory west of the Mississippi River was no longer considered to be in Indian country. In addition, as Indian title was extinguished from lands east of the Mississippi River, that land automatically ceased to be Indian country. Only legislative enactment could change the status of Indian country west of the Mississippi River. It was hoped that this definition would help create a fluid, stable boundary to replace previous poorly defined boundaries of Indian country.

The act strengthened the licensing system by giving Indian agents discretionary power in issuing licenses and by designating specific locations where trade would be carried out. In addition, licenses could be revoked if traders proved to be troublesome, and goods could be withheld to bring pressure against hostile tribes. The integrity of the Indian country was deemed better protected with more explicit restrictions and higher fines allowed for trespassers. The act also called for a prohibition on the use of alcohol in trade.

Perhaps the greatest change brought about by the 1834 act was the government's new attitude toward Indian-Indian warfare. Prior to this act the government had been reluctant to interfere in purely Indian affairs, but in 1834 it reversed its policy. The act gave the War Department the authority to use military force to end or prevent Indian wars.

Congress approved the law on June 30, 1834. Its effect on Indian tribes was pronounced. The presence of federal agents and the potential for military interference threatened tribal sovereignty.* The agents encouraged the Indians to respect specific tribal authorities by recognizing certain leaders and using them as spokesmen for entire tribes. In cases involving Indians and whites, American laws took precedence over Indian laws and violators were tried in Arkansas or Missouri courts, putting the Indians at a distinct disadvantage. Thus the law, which was designed to protect the Indians from white injustices, did little but place the Indians in closer contact with government officials and the military.

Suggested Reading: Francis Paul Prucha, *The Great Father: The United States Government and the American Indians*, 2 vols, 1984; Francis Paul Prucha, *American Indian Policy in the Formative Years: The Indian Trade and Intercourse Acts, 1790–1834*, 1962; Ronald Satz, *American Indian Policy in the Jacksonian Era*, 1975.

JEFFREY D. CARLISLE

INTERNATIONAL INDIAN TREATY COUNCIL. In June 1974, representatives of ninety-seven indigenous peoples from North America, Central America, and South America gathered at the Standing Rock Sioux reservation in South Dakota for the First International Indian Treaty Conference. Organized by the American Indian Movement,* the conference was designed to protest the exploitation of indigenous peoples and to organize an international political force to stop such exploitation in the future. The conference organized the International Indian Treaty Council (ITC) to lobby for its goals of Indian independence throughout the Western Hemisphere. Three years later, the United Nations formally recognized the ITC as a nongovernmental organization on its Economic and Social Council. As a result of that recognition, the ITC sponsored the 1977 International Non-Governmental Organizations' Conference on Indigenous Peoples of the Americas in Geneva, Switzerland. The conference called on the United Nations to declare Columbus Day—October 12—an "International Day of Solidarity and Mourning with Indigenous Peoples of the Americas." It also recommended formation of a United Nations Working Group on Indigenous Populations, which the United Nations established in 1981. Out of the working group have come a number of recommendations to promote Indian self-determination* and protect tribal landed estates.

Suggested Reading: Roxanne Dunbar Ortiz, *Indians of the Americas: Human Rights and Self-Determination*, 1984.

JAMES S. OLSON

INTOXICATION IN INDIAN COUNTRY ACT. See **ALCOHOL.**

INUIT. See **ESKIMOS.**

INUPIAT COMMUNITY OF THE ARCTIC SLOPE v. UNITED STATES **(1982).** In the case of *Inupiat Community of the Arctic Slope v. United States*, the U.S. Supreme Court rejected Eskimo claims for damages due to trespass on their lands by oil exploration teams. As oil company interest developed in the Arctic or North Slope, Congress hurried to settle all the native claims based on original land titles. The result was the Alaska Native Claims Settlement Act* (ANCSA) of 1971, supplemented in 1976, which extinguished the Eskimos' interest in the North Slope. The Court ruled that it was within the discretion of Congress to determine the extent to which original lands would or would not be protected. Thus the government was not liable for failure to protect the North Slope from trespass even before passage of ANCSA. That the Inupiats had no input in the matter was of no consequence. Congress had the power to make the act retroactive if it wished, the Court ruled. This was "a political decision not subject to judicial reexamination."

The Court did note that in compensation for their losses under ANCSA, the Inupiats had received approximately $48 million and 5 million acres of land. Although the language of the decision gives no hint that the result would have been any different, legal scholars have questioned whether the Court would have been so willing to refuse relief in this case if no compensation had been provided to the Inupiats under ANCSA. In reaching its decision, the Court relied heavily on *United States v. Atlantic Richfield* (1980) and *Tee-Hit-Ton Indians, An Identifiable Group of Alaska Indians v. United States** (1955).

Suggested Reading: 680 *Federal Reporter* 2d, 122; David H. Getches and Charles F. Wilkinson, *Cases and Materials on Federal Indian Law*, 1993; 459 *U.S. Reporter* 969.

J. JEFFERSON MACKINNON

IOWA MUTUAL INSURANCE COMPANY v. LAPLANTE (1987). See *NATIONAL FARMERS UNION INSURANCE COMPANY v. CROW TRIBE* (1985).

IRON CROW v. OGLALA SIOUX TRIBE (1956).

The question of tribal sovereignty* has been at the heart of Indian law cases for two centuries. As the number of mixed-blood and assimilated full-blood Indians in the United States increased in the late nineteenth and twentieth centuries, so did the number of cases brought by Indians against their own tribal governments. Indians disagreeing with the decision of a tribal court* or tribal council often tried to have the decision overturned by denying the tribal institution's constitutional authority. Such was the case of *Iron Crow v. Oglala Sioux Tribe* in 1956.

Thomas Iron Crow, an Oglala Sioux, had been leasing his land on the reservation to a non-Indian. The Oglala tribal council decided to tax his income from the lease. He refused to accept the decision of the Oglala tribal court, arguing that because it was of recent creation it did not possess jurisdictional authority over tribal members. A federal judge in South Dakota first heard the case and rejected the plaintiff's argument, holding that although the specific tribal court functioning in the 1950s was indeed of recent creation, the Sioux tradition of self-government was not. According to the federal district judge, "From time immemorial the members of the Oglala Sioux tribe have exercised powers of local self-government, regulating domestic problems and conducting foreign affairs including in later years the negotiation of treaties and agreements with the United States." In 1958 the Eighth Circuit Court affirmed the lower court's decision, lending even more credence to the doctrine of tribal sovereignty.

Suggested Reading: Russel Lawrence Barsh and James Youngblood Henderson, *The Road: Indian Tribes and Political Liberty*, 1980; Vine Deloria Jr. and Clifford M. Lytle, *American Indians, American Justice*, 1983; H. Barry Holt and Gary Forrester, *Digest of American Indian Law: Cases and Chronology*, 1990; R. Alton Lee, "Indian Citizenship and the Fourteenth Amendment," *South Dakota History* 4 (Spring 1974); Stephen L. Pevar, *The Rights of Indians and Tribes: The Basic ACLU Guide to Indian and Tribal Rights*, 1992; Wilcomb E. Washburn, *Red Man's Land, White Man's Law*, 1971; Charles F. Wilkinson, *American Indians, Time and the Law*, 1987; John R. Wunder, *"Retained by The People": A History of American Indians and the Bill of Rights*, 1994.

JAMES S. OLSON

J

J. GREGORY MERRION AND ROBERT L. BAYLESS, ET AL., AND AMOCO PRODUCTION COMPANY AND MARATHON OIL COMPANY v. JICARILLA APACHE INDIAN TRIBE. See *MERRION v. JICARILLA APACHE TRIBE* (1982).

JACKSON, ANDREW. Seventh president of the United States, who pursued paternalistic Indian policies and placed the nation's growth, unity, and security before Indian needs. Andrew Jackson was born on March 15, 1767, in South Carolina. His career as a soldier began during the American Revolution* and continued for many years in the U.S. Army, where Jackson earned the nickname "Old Hickory." His civil rights record is mixed. He held black slaves on his Tennessee plantation, but he also hired black soldiers while fighting the British in New Orleans. He fought the Cherokees and Creeks, ruthlessly killing many men, but adopted an orphan Creek boy as his own son.

Jackson took office as president in March 1829. He believed in "the legitimate sphere of state sovereignty" and viewed federal treaty-making policies as absurd and anachronistic. He campaigned on a policy of Indian removal, requesting from the legislature a territory where the Indians could dwell outside the boundaries of states. Jackson supported southern states' laws that extended their sovereignty* over Indian tribes who resided within state boundaries, and he offered individual Indians who wished to remain within state boundaries the option of becoming U.S. citizens and receiving individual allotments* of land.

Believing that a bloody conflict between Indians and states would ensue if the federal government did not mediate, Jackson asked Congress for "an ample district west of the Mississippi without limits of any State or Territory to be guaranteed to the Indian tribes as long they shall occupy it." Each tribe was to have distinct control over its portion of the territory. Intense partisan debate ensued between religious and humanitarian groups who sided with the Indians and those who sided with Jackson. The district ultimately became the Indian Territory.*

In 1830 Congress approved the Indian Removal Act, which authorized the president to exchange land in the public domain west of the Mississippi for Indian land in the east. It passed by a narrow margin—102 to 97. Those who were opposed to Jackson included Henry Clay and Daniel Webster, who believed the Indians held clear title to their lands.

Jackson hired a humanitarian, Thomas McKenny, to promote removal as a humane policy to the public. McKenny served as superintendent of Indian Affairs from 1816 to 1822 and as head of the Bureau of Indian Affairs* in 1824. McKenny promoted Jackson's policies, but Jackson had little use for the humanitarian; he was fired by the president after the Removal Act was passed.

Eventually, public opinion was swayed in favor of removal. The administration hired private businesses to move the Creeks, but they did so under miserable conditions. Those Creeks who refused to migrate were placed in chains. The Choctaws set out in December 1832, in frigid weather and scantily clad. The Seminoles signed an agreement under duress to migrate to the west. More than 4,000 of the 15,000 migrating Cherokees died on the "Trail of Tears"* in 1838, cruelly driven by the troops of General Winfield Scott. Jackson himself reneged on his promise to the Indians that they would enjoy self-rule in their new territory. He decided to allow the Indians to regulate their own municipal affairs, but he appointed a governor with a militia and veto power over tribal declarations of war.

Suggested Reading: Michael Paul Rogin, *Fathers and Children: Andrew Jackson and the Subjugation of the American Indians*, 1975; Ronald Satz, *American Indian Policy in the Jacksonian Era*, 1975; Anthony F. C. Wallace, *The Long and Bitter Trail: Andrew Jackson and the American Indian*, 1993.

PAULEENA M. MACDOUGALL

JACKSON, HELEN HUNT. Born in 1830, Helen Hunt Jackson became a prominent nineteenth-century reformer and critic of the U.S. government's Indian policies. In two books, several magazine articles, hundreds of letters, and a government report, Jackson exposed the American people to what she called (in her book *A Century of Dishonor*) "a shameful record of broken treaties and unfulfilled promises." She influenced many other reformers, leaving several Indian reform organizations to carry on her work following her death.

Jackson had been a decidedly apolitical poet until she was won over to the Indians' cause after hearing a speech by the Ponca* chief Standing Bear in Boston in 1879. She immediately threw all her energy into helping the Poncas, whom she believed were being unfairly uprooted from their reservation* in South Dakota. Two years later, when Jackson completed her seething exposé, *A Century of Dishonor*, she personally paid for a copy to be sent to every member of Congress. After her first book prompted government inspections of Indian Territory,* Jackson shifted her attention to the plight of former Mission Indians in Southern California, who were then almost landless. She traveled throughout California to view their living conditions and subsequently shaped the agenda of the California Women's National Indian Association. Her book *Ramona*, released in 1883, was intended as a protest novel about the Mission Indians, but ironically it found success as a romantic love story. Jackson nevertheless continued her work, keeping constant pressure on friends, publishers, other writers, and politicians to change government policies.

Jackson's incessant efforts on behalf of Native Americans caused her to ignore her own failing health; she became bedridden and died of cancer in 1885. Although her reform work had spanned only six years, she served as a catalyst for groups like the Women's National Indian Association* and the Lake Mohonk* reformers, who carried on and largely completed her work after her death. The 1891 Act for the Relief of the Mission Indians in California was drawn primarily from Jackson's government report issued while she was agent to the Mission Indians. Jackson did not live long enough to see her struggles reach fruition.

Suggested Reading: Valerie Sherer Mathes, *Helen Hunt Jackson and Her Indian Reform Policy*, 1990.

JERRY LARSON

JEFFERSON, THOMAS. Thomas Jefferson—governor of Virginia, author of the Declaration of Independence, and third president of the United States—played a central role in formulating U.S. Indian policy. During the first administration of George Washington, Jefferson served as secretary of state and, as such, played an important role in establishing Indian policy. At the time, non-Indians viewed the tribes as sovereign nations. In 1793, when President Washington asked his cabinet how to approach Indian policy, Jefferson developed what became known as the preemption* doctrine. Indians had enjoyed the natural rights accorded by God to all human beings and, therefore, sovereign title to their land. But that sovereignty* posed a problem to the Washington administration: the Indians had title to their land, but they did not possess the military strength to protect it from foreign powers—such as France, England, or Spain—that might have designs on it.

Jefferson posed preemption as a reasonable solution. The United States had the legal right to purchase the land as long as the Indian tribes wished to sell it. Preemption, Jefferson told Washington, prevents "other nations from taking possession, and so defeating our expectancy; that the Indians had the full, undivided, and independent sovereignty as long as they choose to keep it, and that this might be forever." In practice, over the course of the next century, preemption was hardly as magnanimous to the Indians as was Jefferson's theoretical proposition. Under continual pressure from white settlers moving into the western frontier, the United States repeatedly forced Native American tribes to sign treaties* selling their land to the government, which then promptly distributed it to white settlers. During his own presidency from 1801 to 1809, Jefferson became an advocate of "removal": relocating Indian tribes west of the Mississippi River as a means of protecting them from white violence and opening up new land to white settlers. Jefferson's removal policies ultimately made a mockery of his preemption ideology.

Suggested Reading: Reginald Horsman, *Expansion and American Indian Policy, 1783–1812*, 1967; Bernard W. Sheehan, *Seeds of Extinction: Jeffersonian Philanthropy and the American Indian*, 1973.

JAMES S. OLSON

JIM CROW LAWS. Jim Crow laws are usually associated with African-American history but have also been used extensively to discriminate against the Native American population in the United States. Jim Crow laws are laws or customs designed specifically to segregate or to deny a certain group political, economic, or social rights. Under Jim Crow laws and customs, Native Americans experienced discrimination in all areas. For example, Indians were routinely denied equal access to public institutions such as schools and hospitals, and they often were either segregated or denied entrance to movie theaters, restaurants, and public parks. Native Americans also experienced considerable discrimination in housing and employment.

More onerous were state and federal laws that denied Native Americans basic civil liberties and access to governmental programs. Although all

Indians received full citizenship* in 1924 and should have been able to vote after that date, many states in the North and the South actively discouraged Indians from voting by illegally requiring literacy tests or simply denying that Indians had the right to vote. States such as Wyoming, New Mexico, and Arizona denied them this right until the late 1940s. In addition, states generally controlled welfare and Social Security benefits, and states with large Indian populations often denied Indian applicants who qualified for this financial assistance. Only under considerable pressure from twentieth-century pan-Indian groups such as the Society of American Indians,* the National Congress of American Indians,* the Alaska Native Brotherhood,* and the American Indian Movement* has this systematic discrimination faded.

Suggested Reading: Christine Bolt, *American Indian Policy and American Reform*, 1987; Stephen Haycox, "William Paul, Sr., and the Alaska Voters' Literacy Act of 1925," *Alaska History* 2 (1986), 17–38; Lawrence C. Kelly, *The Navajo Indians and Federal Indian Policy, 1900–1935*, 1968; Donald L. Parman, *Indians and the American West in the Twentieth Century*, 1994; C. Vann Woodward, *The Strange Career of Jim Crow*, 1974.

JASON M. TETZLOFF

JOHNSON'S AND GRAHAM'S LESSEE v. M'INTOSH (1823). In 1823 the U.S. Supreme Court heard the case *Johnson v. M'Intosh*, which centered around the debate over who had clear title to disputed Indian lands. Both litigants were non-Indians, with the plaintiff gaining title from the Indians and the defendant's title coming from U.S. land grants. The Court had to decide who had the proper title to the disputed land.

Chief Justice John Marshall* used the concept of discovery* to explain the Court's decision. Discovery, as a source of title, states that a discovering nation has free and clear title to the new lands with respect to other European nations. The local native population had to deal with the newly arrived colonial power as best it could. Of course, if the Indians had the power to drive the colonists back into the sea, the rights of discovery would have been very short-lived.

The Court announced that the title to the lands discovered by the British had passed to the United States after the American Revolution.* This had given the United States title to all Indian lands in what had become the United States of America. Indian land rights and titles had to be settled in American courts and according to American laws. Marshall argued that discovery had been coupled with the right of conquest to ensure American sovereignty* over the Native Americans. Although the United

States often negotiated with the Indians, force had been used to control the native population by both the British and the Americans. Conquerors had no legal obligations to respect the desires of the subjugated peoples, but public opinion often forced them to do so. The United States had no duty to safeguard Indian land interests, but the country would do so because it was right, Chief Justice Marshall claimed.

The Court ruled that the defendant had title to the land in question. The right of conquest and discovery had given the United States the right to dispose of Indian lands as the government saw fit. The Native Americans shared title to all their lands with the United States and could not dispose of land without the permission of the U.S. government.

Suggested Reading: Russel Lawrence Barsh and James Youngblood Henderson, *The Road: Indian Tribes and Political Liberty*, 1980; Monroe E. Price, *Law and the American Indian: Readings, Notes and Cases*, 1973.

DARREN PIERSON

JOHNSON-O'MALLEY ACT OF 1934. On April 16, 1934, Congress passed the Johnson-O'Malley Act as part of Commissioner of Indian Affairs John Collier's* "Indian New Deal."* The act was similar to earlier proposed legislation that had failed to gain congressional approval. The Johnson-O'Malley Act authorized the secretary of the Interior to enter into contracts with states and territories to provide monetary assistance for Indian educational, medical, agricultural, and social welfare services. Although federal funds had been provided to public schools for over forty years, this act finally compromised on a federal and state arrangement to overcome the previously complicated contracting method between individual school districts and the federal government.

Collier had high expectations for the act, but several problems soon arose. The act was based on the belief that state and federal officials could work together harmoniously to help Indians. Such was not the case, however. State administrators viewed Bureau of Indian Affairs* (BIA) staff as threats to their authority and jealously guarded their independence from federal interference. BIA officials, on the other hand, tended to have a "superior-than-thou" attitude toward the state people, causing strained relations. Moreover, the BIA educators predicted correctly that the public schools would not use the federal funds properly. Indeed, in most cases the states channeled Johnson-O'Malley money, which was supposed to be earmarked for special Indian programs, into their general operating budgets.

Between 1934 and 1938 the states of California (1934), Washington

(1935), Minnesota (1937), and Arizona (1938) contracted for Johnson-O'Malley funds. All these states except Minnesota (whose extremely efficient department of education was already interested in Indian programs) encountered some of the above-mentioned difficulties. There were other problems as well. For example, racism on the part of local communities and schoolteachers, and non-Indian students' attitude toward Indian children, hampered the act's effectiveness. Moreover, some BIA officials believed that Indian students were better off in federally run schools than in public ones.

Thus the Johnson-O'Malley Act fell short, in most cases, of providing better opportunities for Indian children in public schools. Later legislation improved the act substantially, providing for tribal control over the funds and more accountability on the part of the states to have special Indian educational programs. In 1981–1982, twenty-six states with approximately 165,988 Indian students received Johnson-O'Malley funds.

Suggested Reading: Margaret Szasz, *Education and the American Indian: The Road to Self-Determination since 1928*, 1977.

RAYMOND WILSON

JOSEPH, CHIEF. Joseph, known to his family and people as Hinmah-tooyaahlatkekt, or "Thunder Coming from Water over Land," was leader of the Nez Percé people of the Washington Territory. Although the Nez Percé had never agreed to do so in treaty arrangements with the federal government, the U.S. Army ordered their relocation to a reservation* after the Battle of the Little Bighorn in 1876. During the migration in 1877, several young Nez Percé warriors exchanged fire with U.S. troops and the Nez Percé War began. Chief Joseph then led his people in flight. They tried at first to move to Wyoming, where they hoped to link up with the Crow people and live as buffalo hunters. But the Crows wanted nothing to do with the Nez Percé, so Joseph tried to take his people into Canada. Army troops defeated them 40 miles south of the Canadian border. Joseph and the Nez Percé agreed to settle on a reservation in Idaho, but General William Tecumseh Sherman arrested them as prisoners of war. Eventually they were relocated to the Indian Territory.*

Joseph worked indefatigably to right the wrong, although he realized that violence would no longer be a viable Nez Percé option. Meanwhile the plight of the Nez Percé had captured the national imagination, where sympathy for Indians and a desire for policy reform were growing in strength. In 1879 Chief Joseph traveled to Washington, D.C., where he demanded that the government live up to its original agreement and allow the Nez Percé to live in Idaho. In an interview with the *North American Review* he reiterated that demand, and national support for the Nez Percé grew even more. In 1885 the federal government allowed the Nez Percé to return, but Joseph was forced to live out his life at the Colville reservation in north central Washington. He died there in 1904.

Suggested Reading: Marian Taylor, *Chief Joseph*, 1993.

JAMES S. OLSON

Sioux Indians and white men posing at the Pine Ridge Reservation shortly after the massacre at Wounded Knee, South Dakota, in 1890. (Courtesy National Archives)

Native American children who have just been relocated from the reservation to Los Angeles in 1954 pose in front of their home. (Courtesy National Archives)

Olympia, Wash., February 5, 1965—A group of about 35 Indians marched this morning in Olympia in a protest over fishing rights on the Nisqually River. (AP/Wide World Photos)

San Francisco, November 20, 1970—John Trudell, one of the leaders of the Alcatraz Indians' seven-member board, stands beside a symbolic Indian tepee erected on the island, a one-time federal prison site, invaded by a group the previous year. In the background is the Golden Gate Bridge, a white man's engineering feat. (AP/Wide World Photos)

Plymouth, Mass., November 23, 1970—Indians climbed into the rigging of the *Mayflower II* at Plymouth and one person threw a seventeenth-century British flag into the air after pulling it from the rigging. Indians left peacefully when police were called for assistance. (AP/Wide World Photos)

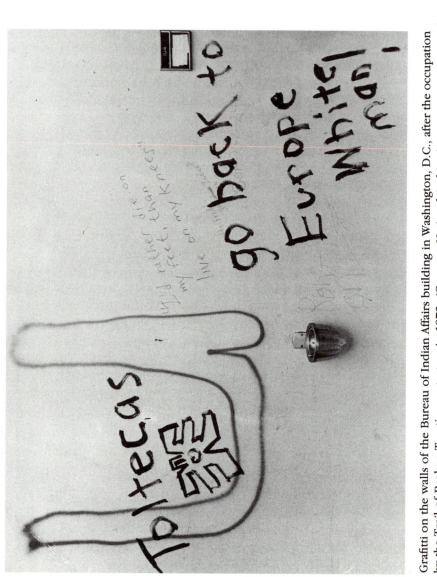

Grafitti on the walls of the Bureau of Indian Affairs building in Washington, D.C., after the occupation by the Trail of Broken Treaties protestors in 1972. (Courtesy National Archives)

Wounded Knee, S.D., March 8, 1973—One of the AIM Indians at Wounded Knee, on the Pine Ridge reservation, raises his rifle and lets out a lusty cheer after receiving the news that the government had extended the cease fire for further negotiations. (AP/Wide World Photos)

Rapid City, S.D., October 1, 1982—A marcher in a parade in support of the Dakota American Indian Movement's Yellow Thunder Camp raises his fist and a sign typical of many carried through downtown Rapid City. The rally afterward ended two days of demonstrations and marches in support of the camp's religious freedom. (AP/Wide World Photos)

Wewoka, Okla., October 29, 1982—Truman Wassana, a Seminole, carries a hand-lettered sign protesting a recent decision by the Bureau of Indian Affairs. Members from the Seminole nation gathered for a planned demonstration and march. (AP/Wide World Photos)

Big Mountain, Ariz., July 7, 1986—A few hundred Navajo Indian veterans and supporters march through the reservation in a show of solidarity against giving up their land. The deadline for relocation was July 6 and the Navajo feeling is to not give up any land to the Hopi Indians. (AP/Wide World Photos)

K

KANSAS v. COLORADO (1907). Water is a scarce and valuable resource, particularly in the arid regions of the United States. Water rights law is of particular interest to Indian tribes, as many Indian reservations* are located in western arid regions. Whereas the eastern part of the country followed the "riparian rights" doctrine, the western region followed the "prior appropriation" doctrine. Under this doctrine (which granted all landowners along a riverbank equal amounts of water), the earliest appropriator of water has a continuing right to the same amount of water, even if it is to the detriment of his neighbors downstream.

In *Kansas v. Colorado* the U.S. Supreme Court ruled that the federal government had the authority to regulate the arid lands, but that this power did not authorize Congress to prevent the prior appropriation by one state of water from a river flowing through several states. The decision, although not directly related to Indian rights, served as the basis for the developing Indian water rights law. In a later decision, *Winters v. United States** (1908), the Court held that Congress, in granting reservation land in arid regions, intended that the reservations have an adequate water supply despite the existence of a prior appropriation. This was based on Congress's power to reserve water for federal lands, which the Court had supported in *Kansas v. Colorado*.

Suggested Reading: Terry I. Anderson, *Property Rights, Constitutions and Indian Economies*, 1992; Lloyd Burton, *American Indian Water Rights and the Limits of the Law*, 1993; Charles T. DuMars, Marilyn O'Leary, and Albert E. Utton, *Pueblo Indian Water Rights: Struggle for a Precious Resource*, 1984; Daniel McCool, *Command of the Waters*, 1987.

CRAIG HEMMENS

THE KANSAS INDIANS (1866). The question of tribal sovereignty* has been at the heart of Indian law cases for two centuries. But as some Indians have assimilated into the larger society, the question arises as to when such individuals become subject to state and local jurisdiction as opposed to federal and tribal jurisdiction. In general, federal and tribal jurisdiction has prevailed in cases involving Indians in Indian country.* An important mid-nineteenth-century case outlining the supremacy of federal jurisdiction was *The Kansas Indians* in 1866. The state of Kansas had imposed a property tax on tribal lands within state boundaries. Ten tribes joined together and filed a lawsuit against the state. The Supreme Court found in favor of the Indians, arguing that tribal lands were exempt from taxation as long as there was no specific federal legislation to the contrary and as long as the tribe continued to functionally exist as a legal and social unit.

Suggested Reading: Russel Lawrence Barsh and James Youngblood Henderson, *The Road: Indian Tribes and Political Liberty*, 1980; Vine Deloria Jr. and Clifford M. Lytle, *American Indians, American Justice*, 1983; H. Barry Holt and Gary Forrester, *Digest of American Indian Law: Cases and Chronology*, 1990; Stephen L. Pevar, *The Rights of Indians and Tribes: The Basic ACLU Guide to Indian and Tribal Rights*, 1992; Wilcomb E. Washburn, *Red Man's Land, White Man's Law*, 1971; Charles F. Wilkinson, *American Indians, Time and the Law*, 1987; John R. Wunder, *"Retained by The People": A History of American Indians and the Bill of Rights*, 1994.

                                                                                    JAMES S. OLSON

KENNEDY REPORT. By the late 1960s the movement against termination* and for Indian civil rights* was gaining momentum, and a number of prominent political liberals took up the Indian cause. One of these liberals was Senator Edward (Ted) Kennedy, Democrat, from Massachusetts. Late in 1968, several months after the assassination of his brother, Senator Robert F. Kennedy of New York, Ted Kennedy inherited his brother's crusade for Indian rights. The Indian education subcommittee of the U.S. Senate had been conducting a study of Indian education, and in 1969 it published its findings as *Indian Education: A National Tragedy—A National Challenge*.

Also called the Kennedy Report, the document argued that the basic conditions of Indian education* had not changed since the 1920s. In many ways, there had been little progress since the Meriam Report* of 1928. The Kennedy Report stated that racism, poverty, discrimination, cultural oppression, absenteeism, and academic underachievement still plagued Native American education. The report condemned the termination program; called for the addition of Native American history, culture, and language to school curricula; and insisted that Indian parents and tribal leaders be intimately involved in local school decision making. Many of the recommendations of the Kennedy Report were implemented in the Indian Education Act* of 1972.

Suggested Reading: David H. DeJong, *Promises of the Past: A History of Indian Education in the United States*, 1993; Margaret Connell Szasz, *Education and the American Indian: The Road to Self-Determination since 1928*, 1977.

JAMES S. OLSON

KENNERLY v. DISTRICT COURT (1971). In the *Kennerly v. District Court* decision of 1971, the Supreme Court upheld the notion of federal and tribal supremacy over state jurisdiction in legal matters involving Indians in Indian country.* The Montana case involved the Blackfeet tribal council. A non-Indian was suing a Blackfeet Indian for nonpayment of a debt. The Blackfeet tribal council passed a resolution granting concurrent jurisdiction over the case to a Montana state court. The Montana Supreme Court first heard the case and upheld the tribal council's decision; but in 1971 the Supreme Court reversed the decision, arguing that the tribal council had not followed established statutory procedures for such transfers. The Court also decided that a tribe could not voluntarily divest itself of exclusive jurisdiction.

Suggested Reading: Russel Lawrence Barsh and James Youngblood Henderson, *The Road: Indian Tribes and Political Liberty*, 1980; Vine Deloria Jr. and Clifford M. Lytle, *American Indians, American Justice*, 1983; H. Barry Holt and Gary Forrester, *Digest of American Indian Law: Cases and Chronology*, 1990; Stephen L. Pevar, *The Rights of Indians and Tribes: The Basic ACLU Guide to Indian and Tribal Rights*, 1992; Wilcomb E. Washburn, *Red Man's Land, White Man's Law*, 1971; Charles F. Wilkinson, *American Indians, Time and the Law*, 1987; John R. Wunder, *"Retained by The People": A History of American Indians and the Bill of Rights*, 1994.

JAMES S. OLSON

KERR-MCGEE CORP. v. NAVAJO TRIBE (1985). An important victory in the Indian movement for self-determination.* During the early stages of the Red Power* movement in the 1960s, there was considerable sentiment among Indian activists that reservation* mineral resources were being unfairly exploited by white interest groups. The drive to secure tribal control over those resources became a central dimension of the self-determination movement, culminating in such interest groups as the Council of Energy Resource Tribes* (CERT). Indian activists also believed that Indian tribes should be able to tax the profits of non-Indian entities doing business on the reservation. A number of tribes sought redress in the federal courts, trying to establish tribal authority over those resources. The Navajos, in particular, resented needing the permission of the secretary of the Interior to impose value-added and property taxes.

In 1985 the Supreme Court made its decision in the *Kerr-McGee Corp. v. Navajo Tribe* case. The tribe had signed a lease contract allowing the Kerr-McGee Corporation to extract coal in return for a set royalty from the reservation. The tribe then levied a tax on the coal, which the company refused to pay, arguing that the tax had not been part of the original contract. The Supreme Court ruled in favor of the Navajos, giving them permission to levy value-added taxes and property taxes on the Kerr-McGee Corporation even if the secretary of the Interior had not approved the taxes.

Suggested Reading: Marjane Ambler, *Breaking the Iron Bonds: Indian Control of Energy Development*, 1990; Vine Deloria Jr. and Clifford Lytle, *The Nations Within: The Past and Future of American Indian Sovereignty*, 1984; Roxanne Dunbar Ortiz, *Indians of the Americas: Human Rights and Self-Determination*, 1984; Hurst Hannum, *Autonomy, Self-Determination and Sovereignty: The Accommodation of Conflicting Rights*, 1990; Phyllis Mauch Messenger, ed., *The Ethics of Collecting Cultural Property: Whose Culture? Whose Property?* 1989.

JAMES S. OLSON

KIMBALL v. CALLAHAN (1974). The case of *Kimball v. Callahan*, decided at the federal district court level in 1974, revolved around the issues of treaty rights and termination.* The Klamath people of Oregon were among the first tribes "terminated" during the crusade for assimilation* in the 1950s. By the early 1970s, when termination had been reversed by the administration of President Richard Nixon, the question of Klamath hunting rights* arose in Oregon. Oregon fish and game officials arrested Klamath Indians who were hunting without state licenses and out of season on former Klamath reservation* land. But the Indians claimed their hunting rights were protected by treaty. The case went to the federal courts, and in 1974 it was decided to honor the hunting rights of Klamath Indians who had not voluntarily agreed to termination but to deny those same rights to individual Klamaths who had voluntarily resigned their tribal memberships.

Suggested Reading: Mary Pearson, "Hunting Rights: Retention of Treaty Rights after Termination—*Kimball v. Callahan*," *American Indian Law Review* 4 (1976), 121–33.

JAMES S. OLSON

KING PHILIP'S WAR. King Philip's War was one of the most savage racial conflicts in American history. Born in 1616 near what is today War-ren, Rhode Island, King Philip, or Metacomet, became chief of the Wam-panoag tribe in 1662. By the 1660s the British North American colonies in New England were growing rapidly in population and pressing directly on Indian land. Resentful of white settlements, violations of land titles, and assaults on individual Indians, King Philip attacked a number of white settlements on July 4, 1675. Joined by other tribes, including the Narragansetts, Nipmucs, and Penobscots, the Wampanoags destroyed 20 New England towns and killed more than 3,000 people. It was only a temporary victory, however, for in the Battle of Great Swamp in Decem-ber 1675 Philip saw more than 1,000 of his warriors die. He himself was killed in 1676. By 1678 the colonial forces had cleared southern New England of Indians, opening the area to white settlers. King Philip's family was sold into slavery,* and the back of Indian resistance in New England was permanently broken.

Suggested Reading: Francis Jennings, *The Invasion of America: Indians, Co-lonialism, and the Cant of Conquest*, 1975; Douglas Leach, *Flintlock and Tom-ahawk: New England in King Philip's War*, 1958.

JAMES S. OLSON

KINZUA DAM CASE. The Treaty of Canandaigua, negotiated between the state of New York and the Seneca Indians in 1794, granted reserva-tion* land in perpetuity to the tribe. Early in the 1960s, however, the state of New York decided to build the Kinzua Dam and Allegheny Res-ervoir, which would flood significant portions of the Seneca reservation. Seneca tribal leaders vigorously protested the decision, calling it a vio-lation of the 1794 treaty and vowing to fight it vigorously in the courts. Although the case elicited some sympathy from whites, the dam seemed too important an economic development to most people, and the Sen-ecas could not stop its construction.

Supporters of the Senecas testified before Congress in 1963, claiming that to Indian people, ancestral lands had enormous cultural significance. To take away their land was to take away their culture and to violate their rights. Anthropologists such as Stanley Diamond of Syracuse University and William C. Sturtevant of the Smithsonian Institution asked Congress to compensate the Indians "financially and culturally" by allowing them to rebuild their reservation in another location in upstate New York. Eventually, New York State conceded only to financial compensation, agreeing to make a per capita payment of $3,000 to each Seneca Indian.

The Senecas were allowed to build homes on reservation land not flooded by the project.

Suggested Reading: Russel Lawrence Barsh and James Youngblood Henderson, *The Road: Indian Tribes and Political Liberty*, 1980; Vine Deloria Jr. and Clifford M. Lytle, *American Indians, American Justice*, 1983; H. Barry Holt and Gary Forrester, *Digest of American Indian Law: Cases and Chronology*, 1990; Stephen L. Pevar, *The Rights of Indians and Tribes: The Basic ACLU Guide to Indian and Tribal Rights*, 1992; Wilcomb E. Washburn, *Red Man's Land, White Man's Law*, 1971; Charles F. Wilkinson, *American Indians, Time and the Law*, 1987; John R. Wunder, *"Retained by The People": A History of American Indians and the Bill of Rights*, 1994.

JAMES S. OLSON

L

LAC COURTE OREILLES BAND OF LAKE SUPERIOR CHIPPEWA INDIANS ET AL. v. STATE OF WISCONSIN (1991). The case of *Lac Courte Oreilles Band of Lake Superior Chippewa Indians et al. v. State of Wisconsin* revolved around fishing rights* and tribal sovereignty.* Wisconsin fish and game officials had tried to impose restrictions on the length of the Chippewa spearfishing season, the number of lakes they could fish, and the size of their catches when they fished off of reservation* land. The Chippewas argued in return that treaties* with the federal government in 1837 and 1842 had granted them unrestricted fishing rights on and off their reservations. A federal district court decided in favor of the Chippewas in 1989, holding that Chippewa treaties guaranteed such fishing rights unless the state could demonstrate compelling health or ecological reasons for establishing such restrictions.

Suggested Reading: Duane Champagne, ed., *Chronology of Native North American History*, 1994.

JAMES S. OLSON

LA FLESCHE, SUSETTE. Susette La Flesche, known to her family and people as Bright Eyes, led the campaign to assist the Ponca* Indians. The daughter of Omaha chief Joseph La Flesche, she was born in 1854 on the Omaha reservation* in Nebraska. Educated in Christian missionary schools and at the University of Nebraska, she became a teacher at a school for Omaha children in the early 1870s. Later in the decade, La Flesche came to national prominence for her efforts on behalf of the Ponca Indians. The federal government had forcibly relocated the Poncas from their Nebraska reservation to Indian Territory* in 1877. The Poncas, led by their chief, Standing Bear, resisted the relocation, and in 1879 and

1880 La Flesche embarked on a national speaking tour to bring their plight to national attention. With Standing Bear, she wrote *Ploughed Under: The Story of an Indian Chief*. During the 1880s and 1890s, La Flesche traveled widely throughout the United States and Europe trying to generate financial and political support for Omaha and Ponca peoples. In the mid-1890s she became editor of a Populist political journal, the *Weekly Independent*. She died in 1903.

Suggested Reading: Duane Champagne, ed., *Chronology of Native North American History*, 1994; Duane Champagne, ed., *The Native North American Almanac*, 1994.

JAMES S. OLSON

LAKE MOHONK CONFERENCES. In 1879, President Rutherford B. Hayes named Albert Smiley to the Board of Indian Commissioners,* an advisory agency established ten years earlier by President Ulysses S. Grant to oversee his "Peace Policy."* Hayes and Smiley met in Washington, D.C., each January along with representatives from missionary agencies and various reform groups to suggest ways the government could deal with its "Indian Problem." In 1883, Smiley complained to his wife that the meetings were too hurried for careful, thoughtful contemplation of possible solutions to the various problems. She suggested he invite one hundred or so people to be their guests, and in October of that year and in the fall of each year thereafter for the rest of the century, the Lake Mohonk Conference of the Friends of the Indian was held. Mohonk House lay in splendid rusticity along the shores of Lake Mohonk in the Catskill Mountains about 100 miles upstate from New York City. The twin brothers Albert and Alfred ran the resort without liquor and with great seriousness and weekly sermons for doctors, lawyers, clergymen, and public officials and their families.

For four days each fall a distinguished group met, discussed, heard papers, and planned Indian policy. Spokesmen represented the Indian Rights Association,* the Women's National Indian Association,* the Ladies' National Indian League, the Boston Indian Citizenship Committee,* and the Board of Indian Commissioners*; there were also educators, missionaries, congressmen, and often the Commissioner of Indian Affairs himself. The sessions were usually presided over by Merrill Gates, president of Rutgers College (later, of Amherst College) and a member of the Board of Indian Commissioners, or by Clinton Fisk, founder of Fisk University. The leading theorists were theologian Lyman Abbott, editor of the *Christian Union*, and Herbert Welsh, founder of the Indian Rights Association. Also present were Mrs. Amelia Strong Quinton, a crusader for temperance and Indian policy reform, and U.S. senator Henry L. Dawes, the Massachusetts patrician.

The participants were convinced that the answer to the Indian problem lay in the answer to their 1895 platform that "Our American civilization is founded upon Christianity. A pagan people cannot be fitted for citizenship without learning the principles and acquiring something of the spirit of a Christian people." Darwinian, Christian, ethnocentric, patriotic, and individualistic in their attitudes, the Friends of the Indian agreed that it was necessary to achieve the following: (1) an end to tribalism and reservations* and the replacement of both with individual ownership of land; (2) the granting of citizenship* to all Indians; and (3) educating Indian children to provide leadership during assimilation* into white society. They also advocated reform in the Bureau of Indian Affairs.*

The greatest triumph of the Lake Mohonk reformers was passage of the General Allotment Act, or Dawes Act,* of 1887. They saw great promise in allotment and had no difficulties at first with disposing of leftover land, thereby participating in one of the greatest disasters ever visited on the American Indian. Although they often disagreed over methodology, they agreed with Captain Richard Henry Pratt,* a frequent conference participant, about the necessity of educating the potential leaders of the tribes. Change in Indian identity was one of their greatest aims. Thus the Lake Mohonk Conferences stood for reforming governmental services, providing for health and educational needs, and improving the Indians' economic condition—but at the expense of the Indians' culture, languages, and civil rights.

Suggested Reading: Henry F. Fritz, *The Movement for Indian Assimilation, 1860–1890*, 1963; Everett Arthur Gilcreast, *Richard Henry Pratt and American Indian Policy, 1877–1906*, 1967; Robert W. Mardock, *The Reformers and the American Indian*, 1971; Francis Paul Prucha, *American Indian Policy in Crisis: Christian Reformers and the Indian, 1865–1900*, 1976.

FRED S. ROLATER

LAND ACT OF 1796. In 1787 Congress passed the Northwest Ordinance,* which outlined the process of political development for the Northwest Territory. Nine years later, the Land Act of 1796 provided for the economic development of the region. The law stipulated that the public domain could be sold in tracts of 640 to 5,120 acres to the highest bidder, or for $2 per acre. The government hoped to encourage settlement as well as to provide a good revenue base. The measure proved expensive for small farmers, who felt that it only helped land speculators to make a fortune at their expense. Those small farmers demanded the sale of public lands at cheaper prices, and their political clout led to the Land Acts of 1800,* 1804, and 1832 and the Homestead Act* of 1862. For American Indians, the Land Act of 1796 accelerated settlement of the Old Northwest and eventually led to the removal policies of the 1830s.

Suggested Reading: Walter Havighurst, *Wilderness for Sale: The Story of the First Western Land Rush*, 1956.

JAMES S. OLSON

LAND ACT OF 1800. When small farmers complained that the Land Act of 1796,* which authorized the sale of public lands in parcels of 640 to 5,120 acres, was woefully inadequate, political pressure mounted in Congress for adjustments in the law. The Land Act of 1800 reduced the minimum purchase to 320 acres and extended the payment period from one to two years. The price of land remained at $2 per acre, and small farmers still complained. In 1804 Congress revised the law again, this time lowering the price to $1.64 per acre and reducing the minimum tract size to 160 acres. For American Indians, the Land Act of 1800 accelerated settlement of the Old Northwest and the Southwest and eventually led to the removal policies of the 1830s.

Suggested Reading: Walter Havighurst, *Wilderness for Sale: The Story of the First Western Land Rush*, 1956.

JAMES S. OLSON

LAND ACT OF 1804. See **LAND ACT OF 1800.**

LAND ACT OF 1820. Although the Land Acts of 1800* and 1804 had steadily reduced both the price per acre and minimum tract size of public land sales, small farmers still complained bitterly that speculators were the real beneficiaries of government land policies. Congress responded to those complaints with the Land Act of 1820, which further reduced the price per acre to $1.25 and the minimum tract size to 80 acres. An amendment in 1832 reduced the minimum tract size further to only 40 acres. Still the agitation for more liberal policies continued and resulted in the Preemption Act of 1841, which protected squatter land claims, and the Homestead Act* of 1862, which offered up to 160 acres of public land for free if the settler would live on the parcel and develop it. For American Indians, the Land Act of 1820 further accelerated settlement of the Old Northwest and the Southwest and eventually led to the removal policies of the 1830s.

Suggested Reading: Benjamin H. Hubbard, *History of Public Land Policies*, 1939.

JAMES S. OLSON

LAND ACT OF 1832. See **LAND ACT OF 1820.**

LAND MANAGEMENT, BUREAU OF. In 1812, Congress established the General Land Office within the Treasury Department to handle the public domain. Since land was the center of American life and ownership of land a basic tenet of the Jeffersonian political system, the General Land Office was a critically important agency: it saw to the management and sale of government-owned land. The establishment of the General Land Office was soon followed by a huge population movement into the trans-Mississippi West. In 1832, the General Land Office issued 40,000 separate patents to land purchasers, and that number increased to 110,000 in 1834 and 320,000 in 1836. The General Land Office could not handle all the business until Congress passed the Reorganization Act of 1836, which expanded its budget and number of personnel. The Oregon Treaty of 1846, the Treaty of Guadalupe-Hidalgo* of 1848, and the Gadsden Purchase* of 1853 all added greatly to the public domain.

After the Civil War,* in addition to its traditional responsibilities, the General Land Office received new duties involving mining laws, railroad land grants, and conservation. All involved adjudicating public and private land claims. With the close of the frontier in the late nineteenth and early twentieth centuries, the duties of the General Land Office gradually changed from conducting surveys and public land sales to conservation, land management, and resource development. The General Land Office supervised the distribution of Indian reservation* land under the Dawes Act* of 1887 and the withdrawal of land from the public domain for inclusion into national forests, which Congress authorized in 1891. During the New Deal of the 1930s the General Land Office was charged with administering the Taylor Grazing Act and the Indian Reorganization Act.* In 1946, Congress created the Bureau of Land Management, which absorbed the General Land Office. Since that time it has continued to manage land owned by the federal government.

Suggested Reading: Roy M. Robbins, *Our Landed Heritage: The Public Do-*

main, 1776–1970, 1976; Paul Wallace, *History of Public Land Law Development*, 1968.

JAMES S. OLSON

LAND ORDINANCE OF 1785. One of the great problems facing the United States after the American Revolution* was how to provide direction to the westward movement and how to logically dispose of public domain land. On May 20, 1785, Congress passed the Land Ordinance of 1785. The law provided for federal surveys of public domain land and the division of that land into rectangular segments 6 miles square. Those segments would be called townships. Each township would then be divided into 36 segments of 640 acres each, with each segment being called a lot. One of the 36 lots would be set aside for a public school. Congress debated setting aside another lot in each township to help support the church attended by the majority of the adult men in the community, but the proposal failed. Finally, the law called for selling each lot at $1 per acre, or $640. The effect of the legislation on American Indians was very real: the law promoted white settlement of Indian lands in the western territories.

Suggested Reading: Walter Havighurst, *Wilderness for Sale: The Story of the First Western Land Rush*, 1956.

JAMES S. OLSON

LAS CASAS, BARTOLOMÉ DE. Sixteenth-century advocate of Indian rights. Bartolomé de Las Casas was born on November 11, 1474, in Seville, Spain. After being educated at the cathedral academy of Seville, he joined the Spanish army and was posted to Cuba. There he became outraged at the Spaniards' treatment of the indigenous peoples of the island. Las Casas returned to Spain and took vows to the Dominican order. In 1522 he wrote *A Very Brief Recital of the Destruction of the Indies*, a graphic description of the Spaniards' cruelty and widespread violation of Indian rights. With its publication, he became the world's most well known advocate of Indian rights. His criticism led the Spanish monarchy to issue the New Laws of 1542, which ended some of the most abhorrent abuses. His 1530 treatise, *The Only Method of Attracting Men to the True Faith*, argued that Indians should not be forcibly converted but should be treated with patience and respect. His writings gave birth to what has since been known as the "Black Legend." In 1544, Las Casas became bishop of Chiapas and continued to promote Indian rights. Bartolomé de Las Casas died in Madrid, Spain, on July 18, 1566.

Suggested Reading: Henry Raup Wagner and Helen Rand Parish, *The Life and Writings of Bartolomé de Las Casas*, 1967.

JAMES S. OLSON

***LAU v. NICHOLS* (1974).** The case for bilingual education for children whose first language was not English was made in the *Lau v. Nichols* case of 1974. It began with a class action suit against the San Francisco Unified School District by Chinese students in the school system in 1970. It was argued that no special programs were available to meet the linguistic needs of these students. As a consequence, they were prevented from deriving benefit from instruction in English and were not receiving equal treatment under the law. The appeal was made on the basis of the Civil Rights Act* of 1964, which stated: "No person in the United States shall, on the ground of race, color or national origin, be excluded from participation in, or be denied the benefits of, or be subject to discrimination under any program actively receiving Federal financial assistance." The case was lost locally but won on appeal to the Supreme Court in 1974. *Lau v. Nichols* was a landmark because it was the first time in U.S. history that the language rights of non-English speakers were recognized as a civil right. In subsequent years, the federal government used the case to require public schools involved in the education of non-English-speaking children—including American Indians—to provide bilingual programs.

Suggested Reading: David H. DeJong, *Promises of the Past: A History of Indian Education in the United States*, 1993; Judy Olson, *Whole Language Alternative Approach for English Language Acquisition among Young Japanese Women*, 1991; Margaret Connell Szasz, *Education and the American Indian: The Road to Self-Determination since 1928*, 1977.

JUDITH E. OLSON

LAW OF NATIONS. When the European empires began penetrating the New World in the sixteenth century, they faced a legal dilemma over making claims of territorial sovereignty.* The first European explorers in a particular region invariably claimed the land they had "discovered" for their own king or queen, whether he or she was English, Portuguese, French, or Spanish. At the same time, however, they usually dealt with the resident Indian tribes as sovereign nations, negotiating treaties with them. In terms of international law, confusion existed about how to proclaim sovereignty over a region when Native American leaders refused to cooperate. In 1758, Emmerich Von Vattel, one of the first Europeans to write about international law, provided imperial authorities with a convenient legal rationalization. His book *Law of Nations* formally established the principle of "superior use." Since European societies, he argued, were more centralized and sophisticated than those of Native Americans, they were prepared to make better use of the land and therefore deserved sovereignty over it. As far as Vattel was concerned, "civilized men" had a higher claim to the land. His *Law of Nations*, and its "superior use" doctrine, came to dominate international law in the age of European imperialism.

Suggested Reading: Alfred W. Crosby, *The Columbian Exchange: Biological and Medical Consequences of 1492*, 1972; Lewis Hanke, *The Spanish Struggle for Justice in the Conquest of America*, 1965; Luis N. Rivera, *A Violent Evangelism: The Political and Religious Conquest of the Americas*, 1968; Emmerich Von Vattel, *Law of Nations*, 1758; Wilcomb Washburn, *Red Man's Land, White Man's Law*, 1971; Robert A. Williams, *The American Indian in Western Legal Thought: The Discourses of Conquest*, 1990; Silvio Zavala, *The Defense of Human Rights in Latin America*, 1980.

JAMES S. OLSON

LIPAN APACHE TRIBE, ETC., MESCALERO APACHE TRIBE, ETC., AND THE APACHE TRIBE OF THE MESCALERO RESERVATION, ETC. v. THE UNITED STATES (1967). In 1858 and 1859, U.S. and Texas troops attacked the Lipan and Mescalero Apaches in Texas and pushed them off their ancestral lands. Under the Indian Claims Commission Act of 1946, the Lipans and Mescaleros sued for compensation. However, the Indian Claims Commission* denied their claim, arguing that the Lipans and Mescaleros had no title to the land or right of occupancy because the Republic of Texas, before its annexation in 1845 by the United States, had never recognized such right or title. The United States, therefore, did not inherit any obligation to compensate the Indians. But the Lipans and Mescaleros appealed to the Court of Claims, and in 1967—in *Lipan Apache Tribe, etc., Mescalero Apache Tribe, etc., and the Apache Tribe of the Mescalero Reservation, etc. v. the United States*—the Court of Claims reversed the commission's decision, arguing that "Indian title based on aboriginal [original] possession does not depend upon sovereign recognitions or affirmative acceptance for its survival. Once established in fact, it endures until extinguished or abandoned." The Court of Claims also argued that the state of Texas's decision in 1846 not to recognize any Indian land titles was unconstitutional.

Suggested Reading: Russel Lawrence Barsh and James Youngblood Henderson, *The Road: Indian Tribes and Political Liberty*, 1980; Vine Deloria Jr. and

Clifford M. Lytle, *American Indians, American Justice*, 1983; H. Barry Holt and Gary Forrester, *Digest of American Indian Law: Cases and Chronology*, 1990; Stephen L. Pevar, *The Rights of Indians and Tribes: The Basic ACLU Guide to Indian and Tribal Rights*, 1992; Wilcomb E. Washburn, *Red Man's Land, White Man's Law*, 1971; Charles F. Wilkinson, *American Indians, Time and the Law*, 1987; John R. Wunder, *"Retained by The People"*: *A History of American Indians and the Bill of Rights*, 1994.

JAMES S. OLSON

LITTLEFEATHER, SACHEEN. Sacheen Littlefeather had a brief moment of fame in the history of American Indian civil rights in 1973. Marlon Brando, the actor, sympathized with the plight of American Indians, and at the Academy Awards ceremony in 1973 he decided to make a personal statement. When he received the Best Actor award for his portrayal of Vito Corleone in *The Godfather*, he had Sacheen Littlefeather accept the award on his behalf. Wearing a white buckskin dress and a leather thong headdress, she shuffled down the aisle to accept Brando's award. Claiming to be an Apache and president of the National Native American Affirmative Image Committee, she denounced the stereotyping of American Indians in film and television.

Sacheen Littlefeather was actually Maria Louise Cruz, a native of Arizona who was one-quarter Yaqui, one-quarter Apache, and half-white. She had been raised by her white grandparents in Salinas, California. In 1969 she joined Indians of All Tribes* during the occupation of Alcatraz Island* and adopted the name Sacheen Littlefeather. An aspiring actress who worked in the radio business, she had been named Miss American Vampire in 1970. Despite her dubious credentials, however, Sacheen Littlefeather's performance at the 1973 Academy Awards ceremony stimulated enormous national interest in the issue of Indian civil rights.

Suggested Reading: Peter Manso, *Brando: The Biography*, 1994.

JAMES S. OLSON

LONE WOLF v. HITCHCOCK (1903). In the case of *Lone Wolf v. Hitchcock* of 1903, Lone Wolf, a Kiowa leader, sued Ethan A. Hitchcock, secretary of the Interior, to prevent the allotment* of reservation* lands. The Medicine Lodge Treaties of 1867 had decreed that certain lands of the Comanche, Apache, and Kiowa tribes were to be held in common and could not be alloted without the approval of at least three-fourths of the adult male Indian population concerned.

The Jerome Commission (named after its leader, David Jerome) gained an agreement for the sale of excess tribal land but failed to obtain the necessary number of signatures. The government representatives and the Indian agent used fraudulent signatures in an attempt to gather the necessary number of names. The secretary of the Interior admitted to the U.S. Senate in 1899 that not enough signatures had been obtained to sell the land legally, but the Senate approved the sale anyway. Lone Wolf sued on the grounds that many of the signatures were fraudulent and that the Medicine Lodge Treaties had been violated.

The U.S. Supreme Court ruled in favor of the federal government in *Lone Wolf v. Hitchcock*, holding that the power of Congress over Indian lands was supreme. Native Americans were dependent on the United States, and the responsibility of Congress to protect the Indians could not be hindered. If an emergency arose requiring Congress to act in violation of a treaty with the Indians, necessary actions would have to be taken by Congress. Treaties* could not be allowed to limit the authority or latitude of action of the Congress, according to the Court. The Court claimed as well that the 1871 legislation ending the making of new treaties between the federal government and Indian tribes also gave Congress power to nullify previous treaties. In effect, the U.S. government was granted the right to terminate any treaty with Indians at will. This was a major constitutional blow to those who believed that Indian treaties were sacrosanct and inviolate.

Suggested Reading: Russel Lawrence Barsh and James Youngblood Henderson, *The Road: Indian Tribes and Political Liberty*, 1980; Vine Deloria Jr. and Clifford M. Lytle, *American Indians, American Justice*, 1983; Ann Laquer Estin, "*Lone Wolf v. Hitchcock*: The Long Shadow," in Sandra L. Cadwalader and Vine Deloria Jr., eds., *The Aggressions of Civilization: Federal Indian Policy since the 1880s*, 1984; H. Barry Holt and Gary Forrester, *Digest of American Indian Law: Cases and Chronology*, 1990; Stephen L. Pevar, *The Rights of Indians and Tribes: The Basic ACLU Guide to Indian and Tribal Rights*, 1992; Wilcomb E. Washburn, *Red Man's Land, White Man's Law*, 1971; Charles F. Wilkinson, *American Indians, Time and the Law*, 1987; John R. Wunder, "*Retained by The People*": *A History of American Indians and the Bill of Rights*, 1994.

DARREN PIERSON

LONG WALK (1864). As part of his plan for "subduing" Indians in New Mexico Territory, Brigadier General James H. Carleton established Fort Sumner in east-central New Mexico as a place to resettle and "civilize" Indian prisoners. He started first with the Mescalero Apaches and then turned his attention to the Navajos in the summer of 1863. The army campaign against the Navajos, led by Colonel Christopher "Kit" Carson, was one of relentless pursuit and total destruction of fields, orchards, and livestock. By February 1864, Navajos faced the decision of surrendering to the army or risking starvation, and more than 2,000 chose to turn themselves in. On March 4, 1864, they became the first wave in what became known as the Long Walk: the journey from their homelands to Fort Sumner, 400 miles away.

The Long Walk closely paralleled the Cherokee Trail of Tears* in its misery. Navajos went on foot, enduring lack of food and harsh treatment from the soldiers. Many were weakened and died of intestinal complications associated with the unfamiliar and inadequate diet the army provided. Soldiers shot those who were unable to continue and left their bodies along the trail. Stragglers were picked up by slave traders. About one in ten Navajos died on the journey. Another wave of 2,400 Navajos began the journey in April, when unexpected cold and snow made the trek even more arduous.

At Bosque Redondo, the reservation* surrounding Fort Sumner, the Navajos found themselves without sufficient food, clothing, or fuel, crowded with other Indians on land that could not possibly support their numbers. The Navajo population alone peaked around 9,000 in March 1865. They experienced forced labor, disease, and death; these conditions sparked protest against Carleton and led to his removal from Fort Sumner in 1867. The Navajos petitioned for a return to their homelands, and in 1868 they succeeded in obtaining a treaty with the United States that set aside a reservation in their original territory. They returned home in July 1868, rejoining other Navajos who had eluded the army and retreated to the far corners of Navajo land. The Navajos remember the Long Walk as a terrible moment in their history, one of extreme suffering and lack of self-determination.*

Suggested Reading: L. R. Bailey, *The Long Walk*, 1964; Ruth Roessel, *Navajo Stories of the Long Walk Period*, 1973.

EMILY GREENWALD

LONGEST WALK (1978). In 1978, to commemorate the American Indian Movement's* (AIM) "Trail of Broken Treaties"* march on Washington in 1972, Dennis Banks* sponsored another AIM demonstration. The walk commenced in San Francisco in February 1978 and moved eastward across the country. Along the way, AIM members sponsored "teach-ins" and workshops to educate the public about Indian concerns. As the journey continued across the United States, other Indians joined the march. By July 25, when they arrived at the Washington National Monument, more than 800 Indians were participating in the demonstration. They issued a manifesto demanding civil rights for American Indians, tribal sovereignty,* and the return of alienated lands.

Suggested Reading: Ward Churchill and Jim Vander Wall, *Agents of Repression: The FBI's Secret Wars against the Black Panther Party and the American Indian Movement*, 1988; Rex Weyler, *Blood of the Land: The Government and Corporate War against the American Indian Movement*, 1982.

JAMES S. OLSON

LORD DUNMORE'S WAR. The conflict known as Lord Dunmore's War involved the Indians living in the Ohio River Valley and militia forces led in part by Virginia's last royal governor, John Murray, fourth earl of Dunmore. Dunmore and Virginia speculators hoped to wrest control of the Ohio River basin from not only the Indians residing in the area but also from the rival colony, Pennsylvania. Dunmore hoped to effect this claim in 1773 by creating a new governmental district called West Augusta centered around Fort Pitt.

The flood of settlers into the Ohio River Valley inevitably caused tensions between the Indians (mainly Shawnee) and the Virginians. The senior magistrate of the region, Dr. John Connolly, alarmed the frontier settlers with rumors of impending Shawnee attacks. Virginians actually began the hostilities, however, when Daniel Greathouse and Michael Cresap independently attacked two parties of Indians in April 1774. The Indians retaliated with a "mourning war," limiting the number of colonial victims to the number of Indians slain in the attacks by Cresap and Greathouse.

The hostilities might have stopped there but for the continued belligerent stance of Connolly. Dunmore, worried by the rumors of a large-scale Indian war in the making, gathered forces to carry the war to the Shawnee. Upon his arrival at Pittsburg, Dunmore was upset to find that Connolly had exaggerated the danger of the situation; but rather than attempt a peaceful solution, Dunmore decided to continue his campaign. Part of his plan depended on isolating the Shawnee from other Indian tribes. Dunmore met with representatives of the Delaware, Iroquois, and Wyandot and convinced them to remain neutral. The three tribes had no desire to enter into a full-scale border war, so they readily agreed.

With the Shawnee effectively isolated, Dunmore's army marched down the Ohio River in several columns. The Shawnee chose to attack the most vulnerable portion of Dunmore's army at Point Pleasant. In a day-long battle the Indians, under the command of Cornstalk, battered the colonial force led by Colonel Andrew Lewis. The Indians eventually withdrew, unable to overrun Lewis's camp. They regrouped to meet Dunmore's advance; but when they could find no favorable opportunity to attack, they sent an emissary to Dunmore at Camp Charlotte to request peace negotiations.

According to the Treaty of Camp Charlotte, the Shawnee agreed to return all their captives and stolen horses and to remain north of the Ohio River, thus surrendering Kentucky to the Virginians. Despite their defeat, the Shawnee actually lost little beyond their battle casualties as a result of the war. They had never desired a full-scale war and would most likely have negotiated a similar peace with Dunmore without hostilities. They soon began hunting south of the Ohio River again, despite the terms of the treaty, and their relations with neighboring tribes remained unchanged. Dunmore's War did, however, foreshadow an increasingly militant future for the Indians in the valley as the Americans began expanding more aggressively into that region after the American Revolution.*

Suggested Reading: Irene Brand, "Dunmore's War," *West Virginia History*, 40 (1979), 28–46; Michael N. McConnell, *A Country Between: The Upper Ohio Valley and Its Peoples, 1724–1774*, 1976.

JEFFREY D. CARLISLE

LOUISIANA PURCHASE. By virtue of its extensive exploration of the land west of the Mississippi River, France claimed the region, known as Louisiana, until 1762. In the secret Treaty of Fontainebleau, France then transferred title to Spain. Thereafter, during the 1790s, the United States negotiated Pinckney's Treaty with Spain, securing the right of access and deposit at New Orleans, a matter crucial to the United States for the development of the West. In the secret Treaty of San Ildefonso of 1800, France secured the retrocession of the territory from Spain, although France did not take possession of it. When President Thomas Jefferson* first learned of the retrocession, he wrote to the U.S. minister to France, Robert R. Livingston, expressing his grave concern over the future of access to the Mississippi if France took control. Congress appropriated $2 million to be offered to France for purchase of New Orleans. If the purchase of New Orleans was refused by the French, then a treaty guaranteeing access was to be attempted. If that too failed, Jefferson clearly implied that the United States would have little choice but "to marry ourselves to the British fleet and nation," to secure Louisiana for the "common purposes of the united British and American nations."

Hoping to drive a wedge between the United States and Great Britain,

Napoleon Bonaparte offered the entire territory to the United States for the sum of 60 million francs. Convinced that the opportunity should not be neglected for lack of authority, the American negotiators agreed to the terms. A treaty and two conventions, dated April 30, 1803, were signed early in May. The treaty ceded the Louisiana Territory to the United States, provided for the citizenship* of and guaranteed the rights of the people in the territory, upheld Spanish and Indian treaty* rights in the area, guaranteed most-favored-nation status to Spain and France in New Orleans, and provided for U.S. assumption of French debts owed to citizens of the United States. Jefferson had some constitutional doubts about the treaty, but because the Constitution* did not specifically delegate to the federal government the power to purchase territory, he decided to support the purchase, which the Senate approved on October 20, 1803.

For the modest sum of $15 million, the United States acquired about 828,000 square miles of land between the Mississippi River and the Rocky Mountains, although the exact boundaries were not determined. The Louisiana Purchase doubled the size of the nation and solved forever the problems of access to and control of the Mississippi River. However, it only created problems for the Plains Indians. Had the region remained the property of France, economic development and settlement would have been retarded. Under U.S. control, the Louisiana Territory became a new beacon for land-hungry settlers.

Suggested Reading: William Macdonald, *Select Documents Illustrative of the History of the United States*, 1920; Thomas G. Paterson et al., *American Foreign Policy*, 1983.

JOSEPH M. ROWE JR.

***LYNG v. NORTHWEST INDIAN CEMETERY PROTECTIVE ASSOCIA-TION* (1988).** One of the main concerns of Red Power* advocates over the years has been protection of the Indian landed estate. Indians have lost their land because of economic development, or its use has been compromised because of economic development. This has often been a critical issue to Indian religious practitioners, because for so many tribes the ancestral lands possess sacred and religious significance. *Lyng v. Northwest Indian Cemetery Protective Association* addressed one such issue. The U.S. Forest Service wanted to construct a road in northern California through the Six Rivers National Forest to improve access to timber cutters and people interested in recreational activities. In response the Yurok, Tolowa, and Karuk peoples protested the decision, arguing that the road—and the increased traffic it would bring—would constitute a violation of burial sites in the area and, therefore, a violation of their religious freedom.

Both federal district and appellate courts ruled in favor of the Indians. But when the case was appealed to the Supreme Court in 1988, the justices decided in favor of the government. Specifically, the justices ruled that for a violation of religious freedom to have occurred, the Indians would have to prove that the federal government had intentionally set out to violate their religious freedom or had coerced individual Indians to behave contrary to their own beliefs. The Court also decided that the American Indian Religious Freedom Act* of 1978 had no jurisdiction in this case. Eventually the Forest Service designated the region a wilderness area, preserving its sacred sites from further development.

Suggested Reading: Michael M. Ames, *Cannibal Tours and Glass Boxes: The Anthropology of Museums*, 1992; Douglas Cole, *Captured Heritage: The Scramble for Northwest Coast Artifacts*, 1985; Vine Deloria Jr., "Sacred Lands and Religious Freedom," *NARF Law Review* 16 (Spring/Summer 1991), 1–6; George P. Horse Capture, *The Concept of Sacred Materials and Their Place in the World*, 1989; Stephen McAndrew, "*Lyng v. Northwest Indian Cemetery Protective Association*," in H. Marcus Price, ed., *Disputing the Dead: U.S. Law on Aboriginal Remains and Grave Goods*, 1991; Phyllis Mauch Messenger, ed., *The Ethics of Collecting Cultural Property: Whose Culture? Whose Property?* 1989.

JAMES S. OLSON

M

MacDONALD, PETER. Champion of Navajo sovereignty,* Peter Mac-Donald was born in Teec Nos Pos, Arizona, in 1928, with the Bureau of Indian Affairs* (BIA) arbitrarily assigning the date as December 16. During World War II, MacDonald served in the Marine Corps as a member of the Navajo Code Talkers. In 1957 he graduated from the University of Oklahoma with a bachelor's degree in electrical engineering. After six years of working for the Hughes Aircraft Company in California, Mac-Donald returned to Arizona to be closer to his family and to the Navajo people. Becoming involved with tribal government, he was elected to the Tribal Council in 1963.

Concerned about stronger efforts at self-determination,* in 1965 Mac-Donald helped create the Office of Navajo Economic Opportunity (ONEO). It administered projects such as Head Start, home improvement, and training in construction skills. As executive director of ONEO, MacDonald became a threat to the BIA and to various tribal rivals as well as to outside companies, all wanting to maintain the status quo.

In 1971 MacDonald became tribal council chairman, a position he held for many years: 1971–1982 and 1987–1989. His major goals were to provide opportunities for his people to grow in self-esteem, to protect the Navajo Nation's resources (i.e., coal, uranium, and water), and to improve educational offerings for Navajo children. He spent much time contesting the BIA, the state, and big businesses, which had controlled the reservation politically and economically for decades. As chairman of the Council of Energy Resource Tribes* (CERT), a consortium of over twenty tribes that was established in 1975, MacDonald fought for fair market value against old leases that had defrauded his people of millions of dollars. Calling CERT "the Native American OPEC," MacDonald led in renegotiating contracts and negotiating joint-venture agreements.

MacDonald stood firm against FBI attempts to interfere with the tribal police as well as periodic FBI attempts to discredit him personally. More troublesome by far, however, was the 1972 congressional bill that proposed the shifting of some 1.8 million acres of joint-use land to the Hopi Indians, thereby dislocating thousands of Navajo. MacDonald fought the bill unsuccessfully at both state and federal levels.

In 1989, foes on and off the reservation accused MacDonald of accepting bribes in connection with the purchase of Big Boquillas Ranch, land that he hoped would provide more economic opportunities for the tribe. In 1990 he was convicted and sentenced to six years in jail. MacDonald and his supporters have raised funds to appeal his conviction. He was recently released from custody.

Suggested Reading: Marjane Ambler, *Breaking the Iron Bonds: Indian Control of Energy Development*, 1990; R. David Edmunds, ed., *American Indian Leaders*, 1983; R. David Edmunds, Peter MacDonald, and Ted Schwarz, *The Last Warrior: Peter MacDonald and the Navajo Nation*, 1993; Philip Reno, *Mother Earth, Father Sky, and Economic Development: Navajo Resources and Their Use*, 1981.

S. CAROL BERG

MADELINE COLLIFLOWER v. JOHN GARLAND, SHERIFF OF COUNTY OF BLAINE, MONTANA (1965). The *Madeline Colliflower* case proved to be of enormous significance in bringing about congressional passage of the Indian Civil Rights Act* of 1968. One of the most difficult civil rights issues involving American Indians in the twentieth century has been the question of individual civil rights versus tribal sovereignty* and the right to tribal self-determination.* Madeline Colliflower, a Gros Ventre Indian living on the Fort Belknap reservation in Blaine County, Montana, was arrested by Indian police* on a warrant issued by the Court of Indian Offenses of the Fort Belknap jurisdiction of the U.S. Indian Service. She was charged with refusing to remove her cattle from land leased by another individual on the reservation.* A tribal court* found her guilty and sentenced her to a fine of $25 or five days in jail.

She accepted the jail sentence and then immediately filed a writ of habeas corpus (a request for release from custody) in the federal district court, claiming that her Fifth* and Fourteenth* Amendment civil rights as a U.S. citizen had been violated because the tribal court had not given her the right to legal counsel and had refused to identify the witnesses against her. The tribal court argued that the due process clauses of the U.S. Constitution* did not apply to reservation legal institutions. The federal district court, uncertain of its own jurisdiction over reservation legal institutions, declined to act on the writ and the case went to the Court of Appeals. In the end, the Court of Appeals decided that the federal district did indeed have jurisdiction over the writ. The Court of Appeals justices decided that in light of the recent history of Indian tribes, tribal courts were—at least to some extent—extensions of a federal agency and that, as such, were subject to due process requirements. Individual Indians, therefore, enjoyed due process rights in tribal courts as well as in non-Indian jurisdictions.

Suggested Reading: Russel Lawrence Barsh and James Youngblood Henderson, *The Road: Indian Tribes and Political Liberty*, 1980; Vine Deloria Jr. and Clifford M. Lytle, *American Indians, American Justice*, 1983; H. Barry Holt and Gary Forrester, *Digest of American Indian Law: Cases and Chronology*, 1990; Stephen L. Pevar, *The Rights of Indians and Tribes: The Basic ACLU Guide to Indian and Tribal Rights*, 1992; Wilcomb E. Washburn, *Red Man's Land, White Man's Law: A Study of the Past and Present Status of the American Indian*, 1971; Charles F. Wilkinson, *American Indians, Time and the Law*, 1987; John R. Wunder, *"Retained by The People": A History of American Indians and the Bill of Rights*, 1994.

JAMES S. OLSON

MAINE INDIAN CLAIMS SETTLEMENT ACT OF 1980. The Maine Indian Claims Settlement Act of 1980 was the largest Indian victory of its kind in the history of the United States. The act provided $81.5 million for the federal government to buy 300,000 acres of land within the state of Maine on behalf of the Passamaquoddy and Penobscot tribes. The tribes lived (both then and now) in three villages on lands reserved for them by the state of Maine: Indian Island (near Old Town), Indian Township (near Perry) and Peter Dana Point (near Princeton).

In a long and complicated process that began in 1957, Passamaquoddy governor John Stevens hired attorney Don Gellers to prepare a lawsuit against the state of Maine. The suit requested that the state restore 6,000 acres of land alienated from the Passamaquoddy reservation in violation of a 1794 treaty that the tribe had signed with the state of Massachusetts. In 1971 the attorney Tom Tureen took over the case, and with the Native American Rights Fund* as co-counsel he built a case on the idea that the

Indian Non-Intercourse Act of 1790 should apply to the eastern tribes—a fact that Maine and Massachusetts disputed.

Tureen based his case on precedents set in *George Lee v. Virginia* (1882) and *Oneida Indian Nation v. The County of Oneida* in New York State (1974). In the 1976 case of *Passamaquoddy v. Morton*, the judges ruled that the Non-Intercourse Act applied to the Passamaquoddies and that the act established a trust* relationship between the United States and the tribe.

In an effort to settle the dispute, President Jimmy Carter established a White House work group in October 1977. It subsequently recommended that Congress appropriate funds to provide Maine Indians with 300,000 acres of land and a $25 million trust fund. In return, the tribes would extinguish all claims against the state of Maine and individual landowners.

However, Maine was concerned about the issue of state sovereignty* over Indian people. Federally recognized tribes retained original sovereignty over their internal tribal affairs, except as limited by federal government. Nevertheless, Maine had practiced jurisdiction over Indian tribes for 160 years. Two court cases resolved the dilemma. In *Bottomly v. Maine Tribes*, the Court dismissed a case in which a lawyer sought 4 percent of the settlement on the grounds that the Maine tribes possess the same kind of sovereign immunity to civil suit that federally recognized Indian tribes in the West enjoy. In *State v. Dana*, the Court found that the state lacked jurisdiction over an offense committed on Passamaquoddy lands. The Assimilative Crimes Act of 1948* gave such jurisdiction to the federal government. These court cases led the state of Maine to negotiate a compromise.

The Maine Implementing Act, passed by both houses in the state legislature on April 3, 1980, and ratified by both tribes, provided that the state would curtail its power over Indian affairs. In return, the Indians agreed to pay state income tax, send serious criminals to state courts, and follow basic regulatory laws, including environmental laws, on the reservation.*

Once the jurisdiction question was settled, the two parties were able to agree on a settlement of the Indian claim against the state. On June 12, Senators William Cohen and George Mitchell introduced the Maine Indian Claims Settlement Act before the Senate. President Carter signed the act into law on October 10, 1980. Many Indians viewed the settlement act as a sellout. They wanted all federal protections possible, including complete sovereignty with foreign nation status. The United States would not grant nation status, but the federal government did permit some compensation* through the law for lands lost in past dealings with the United States.

Suggested Reading: Paul Brodeur, *Restitution: The Land Claims of the Mashpee, Passamaquoddy, and Penobscot Indians of New England*, 1985.

PAULEENA M. MACDOUGALL

MAJOR CRIMES ACT OF 1885. The Major Crimes Act of 1885 was an important step in defining the sovereign political powers of tribal governments and the jurisdiction of the states and the U.S. government. The law was a direct outgrowth of congressional displeasure over the Supreme Court's controversial ruling in the *Ex Parte Crow Dog** case of 1883. Crow Dog had murdered Spotted Tail of the Brûlé Sioux nation. To make amends, Crow Dog followed established Sioux custom and compensated Spotted Tail's relatives with a cash payment of $50, eight horses, and a blanket. The tribal government considered the case closed. But local non-Indian authorities thought Crow Dog should be punished to the full extent of federal law. Federal authorities arrested Crow Dog, and he was convicted of first-degree murder and sentenced to death. The case was appealed to the U.S. Supreme Court, and in its 1883 decision in *Ex Parte Crow Dog* the Court reaffirmed tribal jurisdiction over crimes committed by one Indian against another Indian in Indian country.* Under a writ of habeas corpus (a request for release from custody), the Court ordered the release of Crow Dog.

In its decision, the Court defined the Indian tribes as semi-independent nations who were exempt from federal laws because of treaty* rights. Only if Congress specifically rewrote the criminal code could Indians become subject to federal jurisdiction. In the Major Crimes Act of 1885, Congress did just that. Congress usurped the tribal government's powers of trial and sentencing for crimes perpetrated on the reservation* and claimed criminal jurisdiction over major felonies committed against Indians and non-Indians alike. Thus the tribal leadership's customary authority to lawfully punish fellow tribal members was severely restricted.

Suggested Reading: Vine Deloria Jr. and Clifford M. Lytle, *American Indians, American Justice*, 1983; Sidney L. Harring, *Crow Dog's Case: American Indian Sovereignty, Tribal Law, and United States Law in the Nineteenth Century*, 1994; Wilcomb Washburn, *The American Indian and the United States: A Documentary History*, Vol. 3, 1973; John R. Wunder, *"Retained by The People": A History of American Indians and the Bill of Rights*, 1994.

MARK BAXTER

MANIFEST DESTINY. First coined in 1845 by John L. O'Sullivan, editor of *The United States Magazine and Democratic Review*, "Manifest Destiny" became a diplomatic and popular catchword in the late 1840s and 1850s to justify U.S. expansion across the North American continent. It referred to an idea held by many Americans that God intended the United States to reach from the Atlantic to the Pacific, and that Great Britain and Mexico should surrender their territorial possessions in North America to fulfill that destiny. "Manifest Destiny" played an important role in providing political support for the annexation of Texas in 1845, the acquisition of the Oregon Territory in 1846, and the Mexican War (1846–1848), in which the United states eventually seized much of the American Southwest. It was also used, implicitly and explicitly, during the nineteenth century to justify the conquest of the Great Plains, the Pacific Northwest, the Southwest, the Great Basin, and California and the alienation of Native American land there.

Suggested Reading: Albert K. Weinberg, *Manifest Destiny*, 1935.

JAMES S. OLSON

MARSHALL, JOHN. John Marshall (1755–1835) was third chief justice of the U.S. Supreme Court, his tenure on the Court lasting from 1801 to 1835. Born in Virginia, Marshall reached adulthood during the era of the American Revolution* and made his contributions as chief justice during the Court's formative years. His decisions ranged over many constitutional questions and influenced many areas of American life and politics; but in Indian rights he made important, definitive statements, particularly during the years of Indian removal in the 1830s.

Marshall tried to secure unanimity on the Court, but he could not always do so. Its decisions in the area of Indian rights reflect that inability. Three key Indian rights decisions mark Marshall's tenure on the Court: *Johnson's and Graham's Lessee v. M'Intosh* (1823), *Cherokee Nation v. State of Georgia** (1831), and *Worcester v. Georgia** (1832). Each decision dealt with important questions left unresolved after the U.S. separation from Great Britain in 1783. In these decisions the Marshall Court defined rights of territoriality, relationships between Indian tribes and the U.S. government, and relationships between Indian tribes and state governments.

In the *M'Intosh* decision, the Court resolved the question of territorial possession and the theory under which it worked. That decision continued the long-practiced European tradition of claiming lands by right of discovery* as long as they were unoccupied by Christian peoples. (When the Spanish conquered the Americas in the 1500s, Spanish theologians argued before the Spanish Court the legality and morality of Spanish intrusion into the Americas. The decision eventually reached was that Europeans had the right to intrude peacefully into Indian lands, but that Indians retained rights of occupation of those lands.) Marshall adopted that theory but amended it with his own thinking. In *M'Intosh*, he asserted that U.S. title to lands claimed in North America descended directly from English, French, and Spanish titles based on right of prior discovery and settlement. But the United States obtained only the exclusive right to extinguish Indian title to lands. The U.S. title to the lands, then, depended on extinguishing Indian rights in the soil. Indian rights, Marshall asserted, were not extinguished by European discovery, but merely "impaired." The consequences of this decision were to diminish Indians' vested rights in their lands in exchange for a recognition of some sort of political sovereignty, undefined legally or constitutionally by that decision.

The other two important decisions, *Cherokee Nation* and *Worcester*, resolved the question of sovereignty,* at least from the U.S. perspective, although Indian peoples may have had other opinions. The two cases arose over removal of all Indian peoples from east of the Mississippi River to the region known as Indian Territory* or into the Great Plains generally. In *M'Intosh*, Marshall had left open the question of the relationship between Indian tribes and the U.S. government. In *Cherokee Nation*, he resolved that question. The state of Georgia had in the late 1820s enacted a series of laws extending its authority over the Cherokee Nation's reservation* in the northwestern corner of the state. State officials used violence to force Cherokee leaders to submit to their authority.

The Cherokees resorted to American law to challenge the issue. In 1830 the Cherokees brought suit directly in the U.S. Supreme Court demanding that as a foreign power their rights be protected by the federal government from state encroachment. For a number of reasons, the Supreme Court denied the writ the Cherokees sought. Marshall stated that the Court did not have jurisdiction, because the Constitution* gives the Court original jurisdiction in only two types of cases. The Cherokees had sued under one of those types: the right of a foreign government to sue a state government for infringement of its rights or powers. Marshall denied that the Cherokee Nation was a foreign power even though British colonial policy had operated as if Indian peoples of eastern North America were separate, foreign powers. The United States, as an infant nation after 1783, had continued that tradition, behaving as if Indian nations were foreign powers to be dealt with formally through diplomatic treaties. The Constitution made no clear statement about this question, so the Court had the opportunity at this time to resolve the issue. Relying on his own nationalism and the *M'Intosh* decision, which suggested a different relationship, Marshall declared the Cherokee Nation—and, by extension, all other Indian nations—to be "domestic dependent nations," choosing the analogy of "a ward to his guardian" to describe the relationship between Indian nations and the U.S. government—a relationship on which most future federal government responsibilities for Indian affairs rested. Because the Cherokees were not in the Court's eyes a foreign power, they could not sue under the original jurisdiction clause describing the Supreme Court's powers in the Constitution.

The *Worcester* decision, however, did support the Cherokees; but the decision arose from Marshall's sense of nationalism and his concept of the power of the federal government, not from his perception of rights or justice inherent in the Indians' position. In *Worcester*, the Court upheld a challenge to Georgia's authority. The Reverend Samuel Worcester and several other missionaries had gone by Cherokee invitation onto the Cherokee reservation, ignoring Georgia's prohibition of any whites entering the reservation without express permission from state authorities. The missionaries were arrested, tried, and sentenced to four years' hard labor. They appealed in late 1831 to the Supreme Court, which rendered its decision in early 1832. The Court held that Georgia had no right to interfere with what were purely the domestic affairs of the Cherokees. Because the Constitution seemed to say that all relations between Indians and whites rested in the hands of the federal government, Georgia had no right to interfere with Cherokee policy. The Court struck down the state's conviction of Worcester and the other missionaries; but the president of the United States, Andrew Jackson,* a strong believer in the removal of Indians, refused to execute the Court's decision. Thus it became meaningless. However, the decision extended to all laws over the Cherokee Nation that Georgia had passed, finding them unconstitutional. By 1835 the U.S. government had forcibly removed the Cherokees to Indian Territory,* although a small portion of the population found refuge on a farm in western North Carolina where they remain today, forming the Eastern Cherokee reservation.

These two cases form the foundation for federal government–Indian relationships. As such, they are quite important to the civil, political, legal, and constitutional rights of all Indians today. Each party, Indians and government, today continues to use the often contradictory ideas in the decisions to suit its own purposes.

Suggested Reading: Leonard Balke, *John Marshall: A Life in Law*, 1981; Arrell Morgan Gibson, *The American Indian: Prehistory to the Present*, 1980; Francis N. Stites, *John Marshall: Defender of the Constitution*, 1981; G. Edward White, *The Marshall Court and Cultural Change*, 1991.

TIMOTHY MORGAN

MARTINEZ v. SANTA CLARA PUEBLO (1978). In this 1978 decision, the Supreme Court reaffirmed that only tribes possess the authority to define their own membership. Tribal culture or tradition, not federal law, is the legal basis for tribal membership.

In this case, the Santa Clara Pueblo tribe was sued in federal court by a female member of the tribe who had married a nontribal member. The tribe, following tradition and tribal ordinance, had refused to accept the children of this union as members of the tribe. But the tribe *did* accept children of men who had married outside the tribe, and on this point of discrimination Julia Martinez sued the tribe for seemingly violating the equal protection clause of the Indian Civil Rights Act* (ICRA) of 1968. However, the Supreme Court ruled that granting the rights and privileges of tribal membership is the sole right of the tribe, and that the ICRA did not apply in this case.

There are several implications of this case. It did dramatically reaffirm the concept of tribal sovereignty* and the tribe's basic right to decide who could be a member. This means that federal standards for blood quantum (percent of Indian blood in an individual) as a determinant for membership were moot, for only the tribe can set these standards. It also defined the limits of the ICRA. Although the ICRA does offer some of the same protections as the U.S. Constitution* and Bill of Rights,* it does not offer the same or all of these protections, nor can the courts or federal government impose these standards on a sovereign tribe.

Suggested Reading: William C. Canby Jr., *American Indian Law in a Nutshell*, 1988; "Equal Protection under the Indian Civil Rights Act: *Martinez v. Santa Clara Pueblo*," *Harvard Law Review* 90 (January 1977), 627–36; Sharon O'Brian, *American Indian Tribal Governments*, 1989; Charles F. Wilkinson, *American Indians, Time and the Law*, 1987.

JASON M. TETZLOFF

MARTINEZ v. SOUTHERN UTE TRIBE (1955). One source of conflict and civil rights controversy among Indians in the twentieth century has involved the question of determining tribal membership. Because tribal membership gave individuals access to a variety of federal economic entitlements, the issue often became a major source of agitation. Early in the 1950s the Southern Ute tribe denied membership to Ellen Martinez, and she sued in the federal district court, arguing that the tribe had violated her civil rights in denying her membership. The federal district and later the circuit court found for the Southern Utes, arguing that the U.S. Constitution* does not create a right to tribal membership and that authority to determine membership rests exclusively with the tribal government. The decision encouraged traditional, full-blood Indians who did not want to give access to tribal benefits to mixed-blood peoples; it also marked a step on the road to tribal self-determination,* which culminated in the 1970s and 1980s.

Suggested Reading: William C. Canby Jr., *American Indian Law in a Nutshell*, 1988; Sharon O'Brian, *American Indian Tribal Governments*, 1989; Charles F. Wilkinson, *American Indians, Time and the Law*, 1987.

JAMES S. OLSON

MAYFLOWER II. On Thanksgiving Day, 1970, members of the American Indian Movement* (AIM), led by Russell Means* and Dennis Banks,* seized control of the *Mayflower II* (the replica of the original ship that carried the Pilgrims to America) as it lay at anchor off Plymouth, Massachusetts. Means used the ship as a stage to air Native American grievances, and AIM members painted Plymouth Rock red for the occasion. AIM co-founder Dennis Banks declared Thanksgiving Day a national day of mourning to commemorate the taking of Indian lands by colonists. The seizure of the ship was the first AIM attempt to focus attention on Indian issues to a national audience. Previous AIM efforts primarily provided protection for urban Indians against police and governmental harassment. Other countercelebrations followed as Means's talent for staging public demonstrations emerged.

Suggested Reading: Henry Dennis, ed., *The American Indian, 1492–1976: A Chronology and Fact Book*, 1977; Russell Means, *Where White Men Fear to Tread: The Autobiography of Russell Means*, 1995; Churchill Ward and Jim Vander Wall, *Agents of Repression: The FBI's Secret Wars against the Black Panther Party and the American Indian Movement*, 1988.

JAMES S. OLSON

McBRATNEY v. UNITED STATES (1882). The *McBratney v. United States* case involved the question of state versus federal jurisdiction in a criminal case. A non-Indian, John McBratney, had murdered Thomas

Case, a non-Indian, on the Ute reservation in Colorado. The defendant appealed his conviction on the grounds that the federal government held no jurisdiction in the matter. Although the Indian Country Crimes Act* indicated that federal jurisdiction should prevail, the Supreme Court found otherwise, giving the state of Colorado jurisdiction in the case. The Supreme Court agreed with McBratney and ruled that—in the absence of any definite exceptions or exemptions prescribed by Congress, the Colorado territorial act, the statehood act, or treaty with the Utes— the state of Colorado, by its admission to the Union, had acquired jurisdiction over all criminal cases involving non-Indian citizens in Indian country.* The Court continues to argue today that state laws take precedence over federal and tribal law with regard to events in Indian country that do not involve Indians directly and that have no effect on legitimate tribal concerns. Otherwise, federal and tribal jurisdiction prevails.

Suggested Reading: Vine Deloria Jr. and Clifford M. Lytle, *American Indians, American Justice*, 1983; H. Barry Holt and Gary Forrester, *Digest of American Indian Law: Cases and Chronology*, 1990; Stephen L. Pevar, *The Rights of Indians and Tribes: The Basic ACLU Guide to Indian and Tribal Rights*, 1992; Wilcomb E. Washburn, *Red Man's Land, White Man's Law: A Study of the Past and Present Status of the American Indian*, 1971; Charles F. Wilkinson, *American Indians, Time and the Law*, 1987; John R. Wunder, *"Retained by The People": A History of American Indians and the Bill of Rights*, 1994.

DARREN PIERSON

McCLANAHAN v. ARIZONA STATE TAX COMMISSION **(1973).** During the course of the last century, the Supreme Court has developed two overriding principles regarding the power of state and local governments to tax Indian tribes. First, no state can impose taxes on a tribe for enterprises carried out exclusively on its reservation.* Second, Indian commercial activity taking place off the reservation is subject to state taxation. In *McClanahan v. Arizona State Tax Commission*, the state of Arizona attempted to tax McClanahan's income even though McClanahan lived and worked on the Navajo reservation. The U.S. Supreme Court held that no state could tax income that Indians earn on a reservation, because such a tax interfered with the tribe's right to self-government and because federal law preempted state action. Because the Court's opinion was based on federal preemption doctrine rather than principles of tribal sovereignty,* it appeared that the Court was moving away from the concept of tribal sovereignty, referred to in *McClanahan* as a "platonic notion" and "only a backdrop" to federal preemption.

Suggested Reading: Russel Lawrence Barsh and James Youngblood Henderson, *The Road: Indian Tribes and Political Liberty*, 1980; Vine Deloria Jr. and Clifford M. Lytle, *American Indians, American Justice*, 1983; H. Barry Holt and Gary Forrester, *Digest of American Indian Law: Cases and Chronology*, 1990; Stephen L. Pevar, *The Rights of Indians and Tribes: The Basic ACLU Guide to Indian and Tribal Rights*, 1992; Wilcomb E. Washburn, *Red Man's Land, White Man's Law: A Study of the Past and Present Status of the American Indian*, 1971; Charles F. Wilkinson, *American Indians, Time and the Law*, 1987; John R. Wunder, *"Retained by The People": A History of American Indians and the Bill of Rights*, 1994.

JAMES S. OLSON

McKAY v. CAMPBELL (1870). By the late nineteenth century, as tribe after tribe was conquered and placed on reservations,* the questions of Indian citizenship* and tribal sovereignty* became even more vexing than they had been during the previous century. Historically the U.S. government had dealt with the Indians as sovereign nations and then as "domestic dependent nations," and in *McKay v. Campbell* the Supreme Court ruled that any Indian born within "tribal allegiance" had not been born within the United States and was therefore not a citizen of the United States. Indian tribes, the Court reasoned, are "distinct and independent political communities, retaining the right to self-government." The irony was that the assimilation* movement was just gaining momentum, and in 1871 Congress passed legislation ending the federal government's policy of making treaties with the Indian nations.

Suggested Reading: Russel Lawrence Barsh and James Youngblood Henderson, *The Road: Indian Tribes and Political Liberty*, 1980; Vine Deloria Jr. and Clifford M. Lytle, *American Indians, American Justice*, 1983; H. Barry Holt and Gary Forrester, *Digest of American Indian Law: Cases and Chronology*, 1990; Stephen L. Pevar, *The Rights of Indians and Tribes: The Basic ACLU Guide to Indian and Tribal Rights*, 1992; Wilcomb E. Washburn, *Red Man's Land, White Man's Law: A Study of the Past and Present Status of the American Indian*, 1971; Charles F. Wilkinson, *American Indians, Time and the Law*, 1987; John R. Wunder, *"Retained by The People": A History of American Indians and the Bill of Rights*, 1994.

JAMES S. OLSON

MEANS, RUSSELL. A powerful advocate of pan-Indianism* and the rights of indigenous peoples, Russell Means was a founder of the American Indian Movement* (AIM). Means was born in 1940 in Porcupine, South Dakota, on the Pine Ridge reservation to mixed Irish, Oglala Sioux, and Yankton Sioux parents. The family moved to Oakland, California, when Means was a child, and he was raised there. Means tried his hand at accounting, rodeo riding, and dance instructing before returning to South Dakota and taking a job in the tribal offices of the Rosebud Agency. Means then moved to Cleveland, Ohio, where he became director of the Cleveland Indian Center.

Means came to national attention in February 1972 when local thugs in Gordon, Nebraska, beat up and killed Raymond Yellow Thunder. Means organized a 200-car caravan of AIM supporters who traversed Nebraska to protest the killing and the unwillingness of local authorities to punish the perpetrators. The protest led to the firing of the police chief in Gordon. Less than a year later, when a local businessman killed Wesley Bad Bull Heart near Custer, South Dakota, a riot erupted. The FBI assigned sixty-five marshals to the Pine Ridge reservation to protect local property, enforce security, and maintain surveillance to find possible "radicals." On February 28, 1973, to protest the FBI's presence, Means led an AIM demonstration to Wounded Knee,* South Dakota, where he claimed the establishment of a sovereign nation and demanded recognition. FBI agents and federal marshals soon surrounded the group and set in motion a long-term siege. When it was over, two Indians were dead and a federal marshal was permanently paralyzed. Along with Dennis Banks,* Means was tried in federal court, but the judge threw out the indictments on grounds of misconduct by federal prosecutors.

One year later, in February 1974, Means narrowly lost the election for tribal chief to Richard Wilson. In retaliation, Wilson harassed those Sioux who supported AIM and tried to expel them from the reservation.* Means resisted the expulsion and was shot by a Bureau of Indian Affairs* official. Between 1973 and 1980 Means continued his protests, serving a year in a South Dakota prison for assault. In 1981 he laid claim to 800 acres of U.S. Forest Service land in the Black Hills,* a claim that is still being litigated. He left AIM in 1988. More recently, Means has found a home in Hollywood. In 1992 he played Chingachgook in *Last of the Mohicans*, and in 1995 he had a voice role as one of the Indians in the Disney film *Pocahontas*.

Suggested Reading: Russell Means, *Where White Men Fear to Tread: The Autobiography of Russell Means*, 1995.

JAMES S. OLSON

***MENOMINEE TRIBE OF INDIANS v. UNITED STATES* (1968).** This 1968 U.S. Supreme Court case affirmed the hunting* and fishing* rights of terminated Indian tribes (tribes no longer subject to federal guardianship). It is closely associated with two 1963 Wisconsin cases, *State v.*

Sanapaw and *State v. Basina*, in which three enrolled Menominee Indians were found guilty of violating state game laws. In both cases the Wisconsin Supreme Court decided that terminated Indian tribes were subject to state laws. Consequently, the Menominee tribe brought suit in the Court of Claims to receive compensation* for lost hunting and fishing rights.

The Menominee reservation was established in Wisconsin by the Treaty of Wolf River of 1854. This treaty set aside a tract of land for the Menominees "for a home, to be held as Indian lands are held." However, one hundred years later Congress decided to terminate the Menominee tribe. At the same time Congress also enacted Public Law 280,* which gave certain states, including Wisconsin, jurisdiction over "Indian country"* within the state. The law included a proviso that prevented states from denying Indians any hunting, fishing, or trapping rights they had been granted by treaty.

On April 30, 1961, the Menominee Termination Act of 1954 went into effect. In 1962, Wisconsin interpreted the Termination Act to mean the Menominees were subject to state hunting and fishing regulations. However, on May 27, 1968, the U.S. Supreme Court decided otherwise.

Justice Douglas stated in the opinion that the Court had considered Public Law 280 and the Termination Act jointly when deciding the case. The Treaty of Wolf River had created a reservation for the Menominees so that they could preserve their way of life, which included hunting and fishing. Public Law 280 prohibited states from depriving Indians of hunting and fishing rights that had been granted by treaty. The Court refused "to construe the Termination Act as a backhanded way of abrogating the hunting and fishing rights of the Indians." Affirming the Court of Claims decision, the Supreme Court concluded that the Menominees retained their hunting and fishing rights; therefore, they did not need compensation for the loss of those rights.

Suggested Reading: Russel Lawrence Barsh and James Youngblood Henderson, *The Road: Indian Tribes and Political Liberty*, 1980; Vine Deloria Jr. and Clifford M. Lytle, *American Indians, American Justice*, 1983; H. Barry Holt and Gary Forrester, *Digest of American Indian Law: Cases and Chronology*, 1990; Stephen L. Pevar, *The Rights of Indians and Tribes: The Basic ACLU Guide to Indian and Tribal Rights*, 1992; Wilcomb E. Washburn, *Red Man's Land, White Man's Law: A Study of the Past and Present Status of the American Indian*, 1971; Charles F. Wilkinson, *American Indians, Time and the Law*, 1987; John R. Wunder, *"Retained by The People": A History of American Indians and the Bill of Rights*, 1994.

JENNIFER BERTOLET

MERIAM REPORT. During the 1920s increasing numbers of non-Indians became concerned about the long-term effects of the allotment* policy, by which reservation* lands were broken up and redistributed in small parcels to individual members of the tribe, who then held title to those parcels. Groups such as the American Indian Defense Association* and the Committee of One Hundred* demanded a comprehensive reform of federal Indian policy. In 1926, Commissioner of Indian Affairs Hubert Work called for a special investigation, and John D. Rockefeller Jr. agreed to finance it. The Institute for Government Research, later known as the Brookings Institution, accepted the contract, and one of its social scientists—Lewis B. Meriam—headed the study. Meriam assembled a staff of specialists in anthropology, education, economics, law, public health, and Indian affairs, and for two years they conducted a careful investigation of the state of Native America. Seven months were spent on an extended field trip to ninety reservations and Indian installations throughout the country. Published as *The Problem of Indian Administration* in 1928, their work became known as the Meriam Report.

The report was a scathing indictment of the allotment policy. After forty years of allotment, the report argued, Native Americans were worse off, not better off. Indian mortality rates were the highest in the nation, and infant mortality rates were 191 per 1,000 as compared to 71 per 1,000 among non-Indians. Measles, pneumonia, trachoma, and tuberculosis were at epidemic levels among many Indian tribes, and large numbers of Native Americans suffered from malnutrition. Hospitals and schools on the reservations were underfunded and understaffed. The Meriam Report called for an increase in congressional appropriations for Native American health and educational needs, recruitment of more qualified Bureau of Indian Affairs* personnel through higher salaries, establishment of follow-up programs and placement programs for Indian students, establishment of programs to train tribal leaders in political and business affairs, severe restrictions on the allotment program, and establishment of a loan fund to promote tribal businesses. The Meriam Report characterized the assimilation*-by-allotment policy of the previous forty years as a dismal failure. The report was a major event in the reform of Indian policy that reached fruition during the New Deal of the 1930s.

Suggested Reading: Lewis Meriam, *The Problem of Indian Administration*, 1928.

JAMES S. OLSON

***MERRION v. JICARILLA APACHE TRIBE* (1982).** In 1953 the Jicarilla Apache tribe negotiated a number of oil and natural gas leases with mineral development companies. The leases paid royalties to the tribe. At the time, however, the tribal constitution made no provision for taxing authority. In 1969 the Jicarilla Apaches revised their tribal constitution, giving the tribal council taxing powers. Six years later, in 1975, the tribal council imposed a severance tax on the mineral companies. The companies went to federal court, claiming that the tribe was not entitled to royalty payments as well as tax payments. In deciding the *Merrion v. Jicarilla Apache Tribe* case, the Supreme Court found in favor of the tribal council, arguing that the tribe had the right to receive royalties as a property owner and tax payments as a sovereign political entity. "Sovereign power," the Court decided, "even when unexercised, is an enduring presence that governs all contracts subject to the sovereign's jurisdiction, and will remain intact unless surrendered in unmistakable terms."

Suggested Reading: Russel Lawrence Barsh and James Youngblood Henderson, *The Road: Indian Tribes and Political Liberty*, 1980; Vine Deloria Jr. and Clifford M. Lytle, *American Indians, American Justice*, 1983; H. Barry Holt and Gary Forrester, *Digest of American Indian Law: Cases and Chronology*, 1990; Stephen L. Pevar, *The Rights of Indians and Tribes: The Basic ACLU Guide to Indian and Tribal Rights*, 1992; Wilcomb E. Washburn, *Red Man's Land, White Man's Law: A Study of the Past and Present Status of the American Indian*, 1971; Charles F. Wilkinson, *American Indians, Time and the Law*, 1987; John R. Wunder, *"Retained by The People": A History of American Indians and the Bill of Rights*, 1994.

JAMES S. OLSON

MESCALERO APACHE TRIBE v. JONES, COMMISSIONER, BOARD OF REVENUE OF NEW MEXICO (1973).

There are two principles the Supreme Court has enunciated involving state taxation of Indian tribes. The first is that no state may tax a tribe for activities conducted entirely on its reservation.* The second is that Indian activity that occurs off the reservation may be taxed. These principles were made clear in the companion cases of *McClanahan v. Arizona State Tax Commission** and *Mescalero Apache Tribe v. Jones*.

The Supreme Court has used both tribal sovereignty* and federal pre-emption* as justification for invalidating state attempts to regulate activities on Indian reservations. *Mescalero* and *McClanahan* relied on federal pre-emption principles to invalidate state taxation attempts.

In *Mescalero*, the state of New Mexico attempted to tax the receipts from a ski resort operated by the Mesalero Apache tribe on land outside the boundaries of the tribe's reservation. The state also attempted to tax personal property the tribe purchased out of state and installed at the resort.

The Supreme Court upheld the tax on the receipts of the ski resort but not the tax on the purchase of ski equipment used at the resort. The Court distinguished *McClanahan*, which prohibited a state tax on income earned on the reservation, by saying that "tribal activities conducted outside the reservation present different considerations. . . . Absent express federal law to the contrary, Indians going beyond reservation boundaries have generally been held subject to nondiscriminatory state laws otherwise applicable to all citizens of the state." Furthermore, the Indian Reorganization Act* of 1934 did not render the off-reservation ski resort a "federal instrumentality" that was constitutionally immune from state taxes. This decision and the decision in *McClanahan* demonstrated the strong territorial component of tribal sovereignty.*

Suggested Reading: Russel Lawrence Barsh and James Youngblood Henderson, *The Road: Indian Tribes and Political Liberty*, 1980; Vine Deloria Jr. and Clifford M. Lytle, *American Indians, American Justice*, 1983; H. Barry Holt and Gary Forrester, *Digest of American Indian Law: Cases and Chronology*, 1990; Stephen L. Pevar, *The Rights of Indians and Tribes: The Basic ACLU Guide to Indian and Tribal Rights*, 1992; Wilcomb E. Washburn, *Red Man's Land, White Man's Law: A Study of the Past and Present Status of the American Indian*, 1971; Charles F. Wilkinson, *American Indians, Time and the Law*, 1987; John R. Wunder, *"Retained by The People": A History of American Indians and the Bill of Rights*, 1994.

CRAIG HEMMENS

METLAKATLA INDIAN COMMUNITY v. EGAN (1961). This fishing rights* case involved the state of Alaska and the Metlakatla Indians. Argued before the Supreme Court in December 1961, *Metlakatla* was a companion case to *Organized Village of Kake v. Egan.**

In 1887 approximately eight hundred Metlakatla Indians left British Columbia and settled in Alaska. Four years later, in an attempt to protect these Indians from expulsion or exploitation, Senator Manderson of Nebraska proposed the creation of a Metlakatla reservation. On March 3, 1891, Congress passed a bill creating the Metlakatla reservation on the Annette Islands. The legislation also placed the Metlakatlans under the supervision of the secretary of the Interior.

In 1915 the secretary of the Interior established a fish cannery on the Annette Islands to provide financial security for the reservation.* Additionally, to ensure an adequate fish supply for the cannery, the secretary authorized the Metlakatlans to obtain salmon trap permits. A year later President Woodrow Wilson furthered the cause by issuing a presidential proclamation that made waters within 3,000 feet of the Annette Islands part of the Metlakatla reservation. Wilson stipulated that the Metlakatlans use the waters "under the general fisheries laws and regulations of the United States as administered by the Secretary of Commerce."

In 1956, as Alaska moved closer to statehood, Alaskans voted in favor of Ordinance Number Three of the Alaska Constitution, which outlawed the use of fish traps. In 1959, after Alaska became a state, state officers warned the Metlakatlans that they would enforce the fish trap law. When several Metlakatlans failed to comply with the law, they were arrested. The Metlakatlans claimed exemption from the state law because their use of fish traps had been authorized by the secretary of the Interior. Conversely, Alaska claimed that the wording of the 1916 presidential proclamation had forced the Metlakatlans to comply with state laws after Alaska became a state.

On March 5, 1962, the Supreme Court decided the *Metlakatla* case. In the opinion, Justice Felix Frankfurter stated that the Court believed the secretary of the Interior did have the right to authorize the use of fish traps, but it found the reasons he cited to be erroneous. The secretary believed that the White Act and the Alaska Statehood Act enabled him to authorize the use of fish traps. The White Act allowed the secretary to regulate the number of salmon taken from a particular area. Section 4 of the Alaska Statehood Act turned over control of Indian property, including fishing rights, to the United States. The Court decided the Metlakatlans were subject to the fish trap law but could be granted special privileges under the 1891 bill that had created the reservation. Therefore the Supreme Court sent the case back to the Alaska Supreme Court, to be tried after the secretary of the Interior determined whether or not the granting of special privileges to the Metlakatlans was essential. They eventually received those privileges.

Suggested Reading: Russel Lawrence Barsh and James Youngblood Henderson, *The Road: Indian Tribes and Political Liberty*, 1980; Vine Deloria Jr. and Clifford M. Lytle, *American Indians, American Justice*, 1983; H. Barry Holt and Gary Forrester, *Digest of American Indian Law: Cases and Chronology*, 1990; Stephen L. Pevar, *The Rights of Indians and Tribes: The Basic ACLU Guide to Indian and Tribal Rights*, 1992; Wilcomb E. Washburn, *Red Man's Land, White Man's Law: A Study of the Past and Present Status of the American Indian*, 1971; Charles F. Wilkinson, *American Indians, Time and the Law*, 1987; John R. Wunder, *"Retained by The People": A History of American Indians and the Bill of Rights*, 1994.

JENNIFER BERTOLET

MINERAL RIGHTS. Management of the mineral resources on Indian lands has been a source of considerable controversy in the twentieth century. Because of the trust* relationship between the federal government and the Indian tribes, the secretary of the Interior has exercised enormous power over Indian mineral rights. Timber, water, uranium, oil, natural gas, and coal resources have all been subject to the control of federal officials. The era of leasing Indian land began in 1891 when Congress passed a general leasing act authorizing tribes to lease out their lands for grazing or mining purposes. During the years of the Indian New Deal,* new regulations required tribal approval before the government negotiated leases, but government officials were perfunctory at best in seeking approval. In 1938 Congress passed the Indian Lands Mining Act,* which empowered the secretary of the Interior to negotiate long-term leases with commercial interests to develop Indian resources. The omnibus Tribal Leasing Act* of 1938 required that tribal leases be awarded on the basis of competitive bidding and that successful bidders post performance bonds; but in most cases royalty arrangements favored the non-Indian companies rather than the tribes.

During the 1960s and 1970s, Indian activists began protesting what they considered to be the exploitation of their resources. The energy crisis of the 1970s, which dramatically increased oil and natural gas prices, exacerbated the issue because many tribes were locked into low-yielding, long-term contracts. In 1974 a number of tribal leaders formed the Native American Natural Resources Development Federation to protect resources, and in 1975 twenty-five tribes formed the Council of Energy Resource Tribes* (CERT). CERT's goal was to protect tribal resources, renegotiate unsatisfactory long-term leases, and allow tribes, not the department of the Interior, to control their own resources. CERT's lobbying resulted in the Surface Mining Control and Reclamation Act of 1977 and then the Indian Mineral Development Act of 1982,* which permitted tribes to develop their own resources and negotiate their own contracts.

Suggested Reading: Marjane Ambler, *Breaking the Iron Bonds: Indian Control of Energy Development*, 1990; James S. Olson and Raymond Wilson, *Native Americans in the Twentieth Century*, 1984; Philip Reno, *Mother Earth, Father Sky, and Economic Development: Navajo Resources and Their Use*, 1981.

JAMES S. OLSON

MISSISSIPPI BAND OF CHOCTAW INDIANS v. HOLYFIELD ET AL.

(1989). The case of *Mississippi Band of Choctaw Indians v. Holyfield et al.* was a culminating event in the history of Indian activism and Indian child welfare. Throughout the 1970s Indian activists had protested Bureau of Indian Affairs* policies regarding adoption,* and their efforts resulted in the Indian Child Welfare Act* of 1978, which made the adoption of Indian children by non-Indian families much more difficult. The legislation gave Indian tribes exclusive jurisdiction over Indian children living on the reservations,* transferred child custody proceedings from state to tribal courts,* permitted tribal governments to intervene in child custody disputes, and required state social service agencies to comply with tribal wishes in the custody placement of all Indian children.

Mississippi Band grew out of the Indian Child Welfare Act. The case revolved around two Choctaw Indian children who had been born off the reservation in 1985 to unmarried parents who were members of the Mississippi Choctaw tribe. Both parents signed consent forms allowing Mississippi social services to place the children with a non-Indian family. The final adoption decree was issued in January 1986. In March 1986 the Mississippi Choctaw band filed for vacation (i.e., voiding) of the adoption decree, arguing that under the Indian Child Welfare Act of 1978 the tribe, not the state government, had exclusive jurisdiction over the children.

For three years the case wound its way through the federal judicial system, but in 1989 the Supreme Court rendered a verdict. The Court upheld the Choctaw claim, arguing that even when parents had voluntarily terminated their parental rights, the tribe retained an interest in, and the right to retain, Indian children. More specifically, the Court claimed that "Congress enacted the Indian Child Welfare Act because of concerns going beyond the wishes of individual parents, finding that the removal of Indian children from their cultural setting seriously impacts on long-term tribal survival and has a damaging social and psychological impact on many individual Indian children."

Suggested Reading: William Byler, *The Destruction of Indian Families*, 1977; Linda A. Marousek, "The Indian Child Welfare Act of 1978: Provisions and Policy," *South Dakota Law Review* 25 (Winter 1980), 98–115; Gaylene J. McCartney, "The American Indian Child-Welfare Crisis: Cultural Genocide or First Amendment Preservation?" *Columbia Human Rights Law Review* 7 (Fall–Winter 1975–1976), 529–51; Robert Ryan, *The American Indian Family: Strengths and Stresses*, 1980.

JAMES S. OLSON

MISSOURI, KANSAS AND TEXAS RAILWAY COMPANY v. ROBERTS

(1894). For more than two centuries, the federal government has usually taken a very paternalistic approach to American Indians, assuming that Native Americans are essentially incapable of governing their own affairs in a modern commercial society. The Indian self-determination* movement of the 1970s, 1980s, and 1990s was a reaction to that paternalism. The depth of federal paternalism was especially exposed in the 1894 case of *Missouri, Kansas and Texas Railway Company v. Roberts*. Congress had granted right-of-ways across the Osage reservation to the Missouri, Kansas, and Texas Railway Company. Osage leaders protested the decision and filed suit in the federal courts, arguing that Congress could not make such a decision without tribal permission. The Supreme Court found in favor of the railroad, claiming that the "United States will be governed by such considerations of justice as will control a Christian people in their treatment of an ignorant and dependent race."

Suggested Reading: Russel Lawrence Barsh and James Youngblood Henderson, *The Road: Indian Tribes and Political Liberty*, 1980; H. Barry Holt and Gary Forrester, *Digest of American Indian Law: Cases and Chronology*, 1990; Stephen L. Pevar, *The Rights of Indians and Tribes: The Basic ACLU Guide to Indian and Tribal Rights*, 1992; Charles F. Wilkinson, *American Indians, Time and the Law*, 1987; John R. Wunder, *"Retained by The People": A History of American Indians and the Bill of Rights*, 1994.

JAMES S. OLSON

MOE v. CONFEDERATED SALISH & KOOTENAI TRIBES (1976). This case is one of the only two cases in which the Supreme Court has permitted state incursion into reservation affairs. In this case the Supreme Court allowed the state of Montana to tax non-Indians within the Flathead Indian reservation and required tribal members operating retail stores to collect state excise taxes from non-Indian customers. This collection was seen as a minimal burden that would not interfere with tribal self-government.

The *Moe* case involved an Indian tribal member who operated a smoke shop on reservation land leased from the tribe; he was charged with failure to collect a state tax on cigarettes sold to reservation residents and nonresidents.

The U.S. Supreme Court said that the supremacy clause of the federal Constitution* preempted state attempts to tax the sale of personal property within the reservation, but that the state could require an Indian retailer to tax sales to non-Indians. In a prior case, *McClanahan v. Arizona State Tax Commission*,* the Supreme Court had held that absent express congressional authority, states may not tax real or personal property located on an Indian reservation* and owned by tribal members. In *Moe* the Court struck down the tax on sales to reservation Indians but allowed an exception to the general rule of nontaxation when it permitted the state to tax sales to non-Indians.

Suggested Reading: Russel Lawrence Barsh, "The Omen: *Three Affiliated Tribes v. Moe* and the Future of Tribal Self-Government," *American Indian Law Review* 5 (1977), 1–73.

CRAIG HEMMENS

MOHAWK BLOCKADE (1968). Under Jay's Treaty, which the United States and Great Britain signed in 1794, the Mohawk Indians of upstate New York had long enjoyed the right to cross the boundary between the United States and Canada in order to visit relatives among the Canadian Mohawks. The St. Lawrence River constituted the boundary, and the Cornwall Bridge across the river was the most frequently used crossing point. During the 1950s and 1960s, however, Canadian authorities began casually, and then systematically, inhibiting the movement of Mohawks back and forth across the border—which the Indians considered a violation of solemn treaty rights.* In 1968, to protest Canada's regulation of their movement, a number of Mohawk activists intentionally blockaded the bridge, disrupting traffic flow and creating one of the earliest acts of insurgency in the modern Red Power* movement. Several Mohawks were arrested, but neither New York nor Canadian authorities were able to prosecute them since only the U.S. government had jurisdiction. Mohawk and Canadian officials eventually negotiated a settlement that preserved Mohawk rights. In the wake of the incident the Mohawks began publishing *Akwesasne Notes*, a journal that soon became the most widely recognized voice of Indian militancy.

Suggested Reading: Alvin M. Josephy Jr., *Red Power: The American Indians' Fight for Freedom*, 1971.

JAMES S. OLSON

MONTANA v. BLACKFEET TRIBES (1985). Conflicts between state, federal, and tribal governments concerning jurisdiction over Indian reservations* have long characterized Native American legal history. Indian tribes have cited the concept of tribal sovereignty* to defend themselves against regulation from both state and federal governments. Usually, however, it is state regulatory authority that Indian tribes have most wanted to avoid, especially after the termination* fiascos of the 1950s and 1960s. The federal case of *Montana v. Blackfeet Tribes* involved one of those jurisdictional disputes. The state of Montana claimed the right to impose taxes on tribal income derived from reservation oil and natural gas royalties, just as non-Indian royalties were taxed. The Blackfeet tribe, however, insisted that it was not subject to such taxation and sued in the federal courts. The Native American Rights Fund* handled the case, and in 1985 the Supreme Court sided with the tribe, denying state jurisdiction over reservation resources. The Blackfeet considered the case an important victory for tribal sovereignty.

Suggested Reading: Russel Lawrence Barsh and James Youngblood Henderson, *The Road: Indian Tribes and Political Liberty*, 1980; Vine Deloria Jr. and Clifford M. Lytle, *American Indians, American Justice*, 1983; H. Barry Holt and Gary Forrester, *Digest of American Indian Law: Cases and Chronology*, 1990; Stephen L. Pevar, *The Rights of Indians and Tribes: The Basic ACLU Guide to Indian and Tribal Rights*, 1992; Wilcomb E. Washburn, *Red Man's Land, White Man's Law: A Study of the Past and Present Status of the American Indian*, 1971; Charles F. Wilkinson, *American Indians, Time and the Law*, 1987; John R. Wunder, *"Retained by The People": A History of American Indians and the Bill of Rights*, 1994.

JAMES S. OLSON

MONTANA v. UNITED STATES **(1981).** This case that dealt a severe blow to the jurisdiction of tribal governments in the United States. According to the "equal footing" doctrine, states acquire title to the banks and beds of navigable waters within their borders. States that entered the Union after 1791 could stand on an equal footing with the original states; none of their lands were subject to prior grants by the federal government. This doctrine was first enunciated in an 1842 Supreme Court decision.

Although the Constitution* gave the federal government authority to regulate interstate commerce in navigable waters, this grant of authority did not exclude state regulation. Thus Congress may not convey title to lands that the states possess under the equal footing doctrine. Left unanswered by this doctrine was whether Congress could convey title to riverbeds and banks when reservations* were created in an area prior to that state's entry into the Union. This was at issue in the case of *Montana v. United States*.

Under an 1851 treaty, the Crow tribe was granted land for a reservation.* Subsequently this area was included in the territory of Montana, which became a state. The Crow Tribe claimed that it had received clear title to the banks and bed of the Bighorn River before Montana became a state, so the equal footing doctrine did not apply. It also argued that the tribe had exclusive jurisdiction within its reservation to regulate hunting and fishing by non-Indians.

The U.S. Supreme Court disagreed, however, finding that "the mere fact that the bed of a navigable water lies within the boundaries described in the treaty does not make the riverbed part of the conveyed land, especially when there is no express reference to the riverbed." Instead, there is a "strong presumption" that Congress "holds such lands in trust for future states, to be granted to such states when they enter the Union." In *Montana*, the trust* relationship that exists between Indian tribes and the U.S. government clashed with the trust relationship between the individual states and the federal government, and the Indians lost.

The Supreme Court refused to grant the tribe exclusive jurisdiction over the activities of nontribal members on the reservation. The Court said that "the inherent sovereign powers of an Indian tribe do not extend to the activities of non-members." The only exceptions were to regulate consensual commercial dealings and to regulate conduct by nonmembers that "threatens or has some direct effect on the political integrity, the economic security, or the health or welfare of the tribe."

The result in *Montana* is that tribes may not regulate the navigable waterways on their reservations—only the states may do so. And the tribes may not regulate the conduct of nontribal members on reservation land unless their conduct is a threat to the reservation.

Suggested Reading: Russel Lawrence Barsh and James Youngblood Henderson, *The Road: Indian Tribes and Political Liberty*, 1980; Vine Deloria Jr. and Clifford M. Lytle, *American Indians, American Justice*, 1983; H. Barry Holt and Gary Forrester, *Digest of American Indian Law: Cases and Chronology*, 1990; Stephen L. Pevar, *The Rights of Indians and Tribes: The Basic ACLU Guide to Indian and Tribal Rights*, 1992; Wilcomb E. Washburn, *Red Man's Land, White Man's Law: A Study of the Past and Present Status of the American Indian*, 1971; Charles F. Wilkinson, *American Indians, Time and the Law*, 1987; John R. Wunder, *"Retained by The People": A History of American Indians and the Bill of Rights*, 1994.

CRAIG HEMMENS

MONTOYA v. BOLACK (1962). Although the Snyder Act* of 1924 conferred U.S. citizenship* on all American Indians, some state governments continued to prevent Indians from exercising the franchise (i.e., the right to vote). State governments justified denial of the franchise on the grounds that Indians did not pay state taxes, or that because reservations were not state property the Indians were not legally state residents. In 1948, however, the Supreme Court resolved the issue constitutionally. In *Harrison v. Laveen*, the Court granted Arizona Indians the right to vote in all state and local elections. The state of New Mexico, however, continued to throw up legal roadblocks to Indian voting. In its 1962 decision in *Montoya v. Bolack*, the Supreme Court ordered New Mexico to cease those attempts and allow all of its Indians to vote in national, state, and local elections. When Joe Montoya narrowly lost the election for lieutenant governor of New Mexico he wanted to legally throw out votes from the Navajo reservation, which he claimed was federal, not state territory.

Suggested Reading: Stephen L. Pevar, *The Rights of Indians and Tribes: The Basic ACLU Guide to Indian and Tribal Rights*, 1992.

                                                                    JAMES S. OLSON

MORRILL ACT OF 1862. Also known as the College Land Grant Act of 1862, the Morrill Act of 1862 (sponsored in Congress by Congressman Justin S. Morrill of Vermont) was designed to make substantial improvements in higher education and agricultural research throughout the United States. The law assigned to each state approximately 30,000 acres of public land for each senator and representative that the state had. The land would be set aside to build colleges dedicated to the "agriculture and mechanic arts." In the South, a series of separate land grant colleges were built for blacks and whites. The law was amended in 1890 to provide an additional annual stipend of $25,000 from the federal government to each land grant college. Since then, the land grant colleges have become leading institutions in the world in higher education research.

In conjunction with the Homestead Act* of 1862, the Morrill Act had an important long-term effect on American Indians in the Great Plains and in the Far West. The two laws provided land to non-Indian settlers, and the agricultural research coming out of the land grant colleges generated new, more profitable farming technologies. Abundant land and profitable farming techniques made western lands more attractive and brought an onslought of white settlers. In the process, the Indian landed estate was brought under increased pressure. The long-term result was the loss of millions of acres.

Suggested Reading: William Belmont Parker, *Life and Public Service of Justin S. Morrill*, 1928.

                                                                    JAMES S. OLSON

MORTON v. MANCARI (1974). In *Morton v. Mancari*, the U.S. Supreme Court held that Congress could give preference to Native Americans in hiring. The Court determined that federal statutes were not race-based but instead were the result of a "special relationship" between the U.S. government and the Indians. The "special relationship" actually developed out of the government's belief that Indians were inferior to white Americans and in need of extra protection. This paternalistic attitude held sway throughout much of the twentieth century.

Section 12 of the Indian Reorganization Act* of 1934 authorizes employment preference for Indians for Bureau of Indian Affairs* (BIA) positions. Non-Indian employees claimed racial discrimination based on the

Equal Employment Act of 1972, which required equal treatment in federal employment.

Whether a person is considered an "Indian" depends not on skin color but on the existence of a "special relationship" between the person and the U.S. government, based on the trust* obligation of the federal government. The Court in *Morton* ruled that the employee hiring preference for Indians was not a racial preference outlawed by the Fourteenth Amendment. Instead, the hiring preference served merely to extend special employment rights to Indians "as members of quasi-sovereign tribal entities whose lives and activities are governed by the BIA in a unique fashion." The Supreme Court justified its decision by arguing that the statute in question could be "tied rationally to the fulfillment of Congress's unique obligation toward the Indians." According to the Court, the relationship between the federal government and the Indians is based on political rather than racial grounds, and hiring preferences based on such grounds are not prohibited by the equal protection clause.

Suggested Reading: Russel Lawrence Barsh and James Youngblood Henderson, *The Road: Indian Tribes and Political Liberty*, 1980; Vine Deloria Jr. and Clifford M. Lytle, *American Indians, American Justice*, 1983; H. Barry Holt and Gary Forrester, *Digest of American Indian Law: Cases and Chronology*, 1990; Stephen L. Pevar, *The Rights of Indians and Tribes: The Basic ACLU Guide to Indian and Tribal Rights*, 1992; Wilcomb E. Washburn, *Red Man's Land, White Man's Law: A Study of the Past and Present Status of the American Indian*, 1971; Charles F. Wilkinson, *American Indians, Time and the Law*, 1987; John R. Wunder, *"Retained by The People": A History of American Indians and the Bill of Rights*, 1994.

CRAIG HEMMENS

MUSEUMS. See **REPATRIATION.**

MUSKRAT ET AL. v. UNITED STATES (1907). By a congressional act of March 3, 1901, all Cherokees were made U.S. citizens, and by an act of July 1, 1902, all lands and funds of the Cherokee Nation were to be distributed to living Cherokees on September 1, 1902. No provision was made as to what should be done with any surplus since some Indians refused allotments. In 1906, by which time more Cherokees had been born, there was a surplus of both lands and funds still in federal hands. Congressional acts of 1906 made children born after September 1, 1902, eligible for land and funds from the surplus. This was done at the request of and with the consent of the Cherokee Nation.

During the first decade of this century, the Dawes Commission was charged with making allotments* of land for the Five Civilized Tribes, which included the Cherokees. Claimants dissatisfied with the allotment process lobbied Congress and succeeded in gaining congressional approval to take their cases to the Supreme Court at government expense. Muskrat, a Cherokee, did not like the parcel of land he received. In *Muskrat et al. v. United States*, a federal district court ruled that the acts of 1902 and 1906 were constitutional and the allotments valid. This decision was reversed by the Supreme Court, which held that the courts lacked jurisdiction because the attempt to cause the courts to rule on the validity of an act of Congress did not fit the definitions of a "case" or "controversy" under the Constitution.* The Supreme Court viewed the appeal as an attempt to get the Court to give an advisory opinion where no actual controversy in need of resolution had occurred. There have been no similar attempts by Congress and its constituents of this nature.

Suggested Reading: 44 *Court of Claims Reporter* 173; 219 *U.S. Reports* 346; Vine Deloria Jr. and Clifford M. Lytle, *American Indians, American Justice*, 1983.

J. JEFFERSON MACKINNON

MYER, DILLON. Commissioner of Indian affairs (1950–1953) and architect of the termination* policy, Dillon S. Myer was born on September 4, 1891, in Hebron, Ohio. After receiving his bachelor's degree from Ohio State University in 1914, Myer began his career in public service. From 1914 until 1942 he held a variety of field and administrative posts, mainly for the Department of Agriculture. In 1942 Myer was appointed head of the War Relocation Agency (WRA), the agency responsible for the internment of Japanese Americans during World War II. In 1950 he was chosen commissioner of Indian affairs.

Although he was an efficient administrator, Myer had never worked for the Bureau of Indian Affairs* (BIA) and knew little about Native Americans or the problems they faced. He surrounded himself with others who had worked for the WRA, and he ignored BIA officials or Indians who might have been resources. While he was commissioner he pursued a goal of reducing federal support of the Indians, and he pushed for several policy changes. He began the relocation* program, which strongly encouraged Indians to leave the reservation* to live in the cities, where they would not need or be eligible for any federal support. Myer also encouraged efforts to extend state jurisdiction over Indian civil and criminal law, and he authorized the transfer of Indian service hospitals and other Indian service responsibilities to state and local agencies. In 1952 he began to organize efforts to even further reduce federal support of the tribes when he proposed that the federal government completely terminate its trusteeship responsibility to the tribes.

Myer's so-called termination policy called for identifying which tribes were ready for such a move. It took into consideration the extent of the tribe's acculturation, economic resources, and willingness to end federal aid, and the state's willingness to assume responsibility. This policy was ready for implementation when Myer resigned in March 1953. Although the policy was applied to only a few tribes, its effects were devastating. Terminated tribes such as the Menominee of Wisconsin and the Klamath of Oregon saw their self-sufficiency and their land base decline. They also realized that the states were not willing or able to help. Terminated tribes were able to restore their tribal status only after protracted struggles.

Suggested Reading: Donald L. Fixico, *Termination and Relocation: Federal Indian Policy, 1945–60*, 1986; Robert M. Kvasnicka and Herman J. Viola, eds., *The Commissioners of Indian Affairs, 1824–77*, 1979; Donald L. Parman, *Indians and the American West in the Twentieth Century*, 1994.

JASON M. TETZLOFF

N

NADER, RALPH. Born in 1934, today Ralph Nader is a well-known and controversial consumer advocate. In 1956, as editorial manager of the Harvard Law School's *Harvard Record*, he transformed the image of the tranquil student newspaper into a vehicle for reform with an issue-length article in which he praised Native American culture. Calling the condition of the Indians America's "greatest challenge," Nader attacked the idea of Native Americans being savages and instead labeled them "the authors of the concept of federalism." Acknowledged as an excellent piece of propaganda by reformers and critics alike, Nader's article emotionally presented a series of usually neglected facts in order to force the reader to reassess the Indian situation. The article drew so much attention that Harvard's governing board eventually allowed several hundred copies to be sold through a Colorado Indian reform organization. Nader became editor-in-chief of the *Harvard Record* in 1957 and continued to contribute provocative articles, although none were to have the impact of his Indian piece.

Suggested Reading: Charles McCarry, *Citizen Nader*, 1972.

JERRY LARSON

NATIONAL AMERICAN INDIAN COURT JUDGES ASSOCIATION. Established in 1970 as an institutional product of Arrow,* Inc., the National American Indian Court Judges Association (NAICJA) was designed to improve legal services on reservations.* NAICJA officials conduct ongoing continuing education programs for tribal judges, training them in federal, state, and constitutional law. During the past quarter-century, more than four hundred Native American tribal judges have completed NAICJA training programs.

Suggested Reading: Armand S. La Potin. *Native American Voluntary Organizations*, 1986.

JAMES S. OLSON

NATIONAL CONGRESS OF AMERICAN INDIANS. The National Congress of American Indians (NCAI) is a nonpartisan political action organization founded in 1944. New Deal policies that encouraged tribal self-determination* and self-government also encouraged Native Americans from around the country to work together in a national organization to further these goals. Indian leaders such as D'Arcy McNickle, Ruth Muskrat Bronson, and Louis Bruce, along with others who received training and leadership opportunities in Commissioner of Indian Affairs John Collier's* administration, provided the initial direction of the organization.

The NCAI worked hard at convincing white leaders that the goals of cultural and tribal preservation and the full expression of the rights of U.S. citizenship* were not incompatible. With these goals in mind the NCAI worked to pressure states such as New Mexico and Arizona, which until 1948 still prohibited Indians from voting,* to conform to the laws of the land. The organization also successfully supported the establishment of the Indian Claims Commission* and lobbied hard against the federal policy of termination.* Although it was unsuccessful in blocking some efforts at termination, the NCAI's strong and generally united Indian voice did prevent wide-scale implementation of the policy. It also played a key role in President Richard Nixon's 1970 decision to end termination.

From its zenith in the 1950s, the NCAI faced new challenges in the 1960s and 1970s. More aggressive and more radical pan-Indian* groups such as the National Indian Youth Council* (NIYC) and the American Indian Movement* (AIM) appealed to a new generation of Indians, many of them well-educated urban Indians who saw the NCAI as out of touch with the majority of Indians. AIM and the NCAI were often in direct opposition to the National Congress of American Indians, as was the case when AIM members occupied Wounded Knee* in 1973. AIM's more radical methods and demands further distanced these two groups. The NCAI's support of expanded federal recognition of previously nonrecognized tribes also was opposed by recognized tribes who feared diminished federal support.

The 1970s and 1980s saw the NCAI's position as the dominant Indian voice further decline as the focus of Indian policy shifted to judicial actions. Although the NCAI was well suited for political advocacy, other groups, especially the Native American Rights Fund* (NARF), were better prepared for judicial advocacy and support. NARF's legal expertise was needed for the complicated litigations over treaty rights* that often dominated judicial calendars in the 1980s.

Despite declines from the 1950s, the NCAI still plays a valuable role in Indian affairs. It is the largest Indian advocacy and lobbying group and, as such, still wields considerable weight. It is also the longest lived; thus its opinions are still sought and respected as a source of the Indian voice in federal policy decisions.

Suggested Reading: Hazel Hertzberg, *The Search for an American Indian Identity: Modern Pan-Indian Movements*, 1971; Dorothy R. Parker, *Singing an Indian Song: A Biography of D'Arcy McNickle*, 1992.

JASON M. TETZLOFF

NATIONAL COUNCIL OF AMERICAN INDIANS. As Red Progressivism* developed during the first two decades of the twentieth century, the National Council of American Indians was a response to the declining numbers and living conditions of the Indians. Led by the 10 percent of Indians who had been educated in white ways and had become successful in integrated society, its principal emphasis called for better adjustment by the Indians to the general American lifestyle. Among its more prominent leaders were Henry Roe Cloud, Dr. Charles Eastman,* Dr. Carlos Montezuma, Arthur C. Parker,* Thomas L. Sloan, and Gertrude Bonnin.

United at first under the banner of the Society of American Indians,* Red Progressive groups split into a number of contending factions by the early 1920s. Among several new organizations that appeared was the National Council of American Indians, founded in 1926 with Gertrude Bonnin as president. The council was at first better financed than most Indian civil rights organizations because it was aligned with and supported by the General Federation of Women's Clubs, an organization of mostly Euro-American and African-American businesswomen and wealthy wives. The council's slogan was "Help the Indians Help Themselves in Protecting Their Rights and Properties." Its first major emphasis was promoting participation in politics—especially voting*—as a reaction to the passage of the Snyder Act* of 1924, which awarded citizenship* to all American Indians. Not surprising, Bonnin's organization was most successful in her native South Dakota and in Oklahoma, because of her exposure of graft and corruption there by the state's lawyers, judges, bureaucrats, and politicians. A more controversial stance urged the banning of peyote* and the Native American Church.

The greatest contribution of the National Council came in 1934. In January, Franklin Roosevelt's commissioner of Indian affairs, John Collier,* called a meeting with representatives of several organizations in Washington, D.C., to discuss methods of improving the conditions of the American Indian. After being involved in that meeting, the council strongly supported passage of the Indian Reorganization Act* in 1934 and the Indian New Deal* that followed. Its influence can be best seen in the act's requirement that tribal offices be filled by majority rule elections. Although majority rule fits with the general concept of American democracy and the ideas of the Red Progressives and the Women's Clubs, it was controversial in the vast majority of tribes, which had traditionally depended on consensus choice of leadership. In fact, this requirement prompted more opposition among the Indians to the Indian Reorganization Act than any other stipulation in the bill.

With the coming of World War II, the death of Bonnin, and the declining interest among the Women's Clubs, the National Council faded from existence. However, it had contributed greatly to Indian civil rights through its emphasis on voting and political participation. Although controversy would continue about majority rule in tribal elections, eventually that would be seen by most as a major step forward in the acquisition of Native American civil rights.

Suggested Reading: Armand S. La Potin, *Native American Voluntary Organizations*, 1986.

FRED S. ROLATER

NATIONAL FARMERS UNION INSURANCE COMPANY v. CROW TRIBE (1985).

The question of tribal sovereignty* and the jurisdictional reach of tribal courts* has long been a source of legal controversy in the United States—between federal, state, and local officials; between Indian and non-Indian individuals and various government agencies; and between private corporations and individuals making claims against them. In 1985 the Supreme Court heard the case of *National Farmers Union Insurance Company v. Crow Tribe* after a Crow Indian filed a personal injury claim against the National Farmers Union Insurance Company and the Crow tribal courts upheld the judgment. The insurance company, anxious to retry the case in a non-Indian tribunal, appealed to the federal courts, arguing that the tribal court had no jurisdiction in the case. In its 1985 decision the Supreme Court disagreed with the company, upholding the jurisdiction of tribal courts and refusing to allow other federal courts to assume jurisdiction over similar cases. Two years later the Court took the same position in the *Iowa Mutual Insurance Company v. La-Plante* case.

Suggested Reading: Stephen L. Pevar, *The Rights of Indians and Tribes*, 1992.

JAMES S. OLSON

NATIONAL INDIAN DEFENSE ASSOCIATION. The National Indian Defense Association was founded in 1885 by Theodore A. Bland. In 1881, Helen Hunt Jackson's* revealing exposé of the plight of American Indians—*A Century of Dishonor*—had inspired many white reformers to work toward better treatment of the country's indigenous peoples. Thus during the late 1880s the National Indian Defense Association lobbied for the allotment* program as a means of promoting assimilation* and ending violence against American Indians.

Suggested Reading: Armand S. La Potin, *Native American Voluntary Organizations*, 1986.

JAMES S. OLSON

NATIONAL INDIAN EDUCATION ASSOCIATION. The National Indian Education Association was first organized in Minneapolis, Minnesota, in 1970 by groups of Native Americans and Alaskan natives who wanted more resources directed into Indian education* and Indian control of curricula. Since then, the National Indian Education Association has held an annual conference and published a bimonthly newsletter, *Indian Education*, to promote its objectives. Its board of directors is composed of Indians who work today to improve communication between educators, lobby at all levels of government, and provide technical and administrative training to individuals working in the field of Indian education.

Suggested Reading: Armand S. La Potin, *Native American Voluntary Organizations*, 1986.

JAMES S. OLSON

NATIONAL INDIAN GAMING COMMISSION. See **INDIAN GAMING REGULATORY ACT OF 1988.**

NATIONAL INDIAN YOUTH COUNCIL. The National Indian Youth Council (NIYC) was established in the wake of the Conference on American Indians in Chicago in 1961. A group of University of Chicago social scientists had organized the conference with the intention of producing a comprehensive Indian policy proposal for the John F. Kennedy administration, but many younger Indians found the themes of the conference too conservative. They managed to insert into the proceedings a statement that repudiated "paternalism, even when benevolent" and insisted on the "inherent right of self-government" for Indian peoples. With encouragement from some of the elder Indians at the conference, the young radicals—led by Clyde Warrior, Shirley Hill Witt, and Mel Thom—reconvened in Gallup, New Mexico, where they drafted a constitution for the National Indian Youth Council, an organization committed to service and Indian advocacy. They established a headquarters for the group in Albuquerque, New Mexico.

During the 1960s the NIYC concentrated its efforts on protest and civil disobedience, particularly over hunting and fishing rights.* It was especially active in the Pacific Northwest, staging "fish-ins" against Washington state fish and game officials trying to abrogate treaty* rights. In 1964 it held a large protest march at the state capitol in Olympia. NIYC members also supported the civil rights drives of other American minorities. In the 1970s their focus shifted to environmental issues, and they actively opposed development projects that threatened traditional Indian habitats. As a result of its environmental activism, the NIYC has also emphasized voter registration drives and human rights issues. It has become more committed to promoting Native American participation in the political process. The NIYC has sponsored a number of voter behavior polls among Native Americans, and it has filed several lawsuits against state and local practices that make Indian participation in politics cumbersome and difficult. During the 1980s and 1990s, that campaign became more focused as the Indian Voting Project.

Suggested Reading: Marcus E. Jacobsen, *Rise Up, Make Haste. Our People Need Us! The National Indian Youth Council and the Origins of the Red Power Movement*, 1981.

JAMES S. OLSON

NATIONAL LEAGUE FOR JUSTICE TO AMERICAN INDIANS. In 1933, Marion Campbell established the National League for Justice to American Indians (NLJAI). Headquartered in Los Angeles, the NLJAI was committed to the abolition of the Bureau of Indian Affairs,* which, Campbell fervently believed, slowed the assimilation* of American Indians by maintaining separate Indian schools and controlling the use of reservation* resources. Indian affairs, the NLJAI argued, should be turned over to the states for administration. In this sense the NLJAI was a forerunner of the termination* movement. During the 1930s the National League for Justice to American Indians contended unsuccessfully with the Indian New

Deal* of John Collier.* By the time of World War II,* the NLJAI was all but defunct.

Suggested Reading: Armand S. La Potin, *Native American Voluntary Organizations*, 1986.

JAMES S. OLSON

NATIONAL MUSEUM OF THE AMERICAN INDIAN ACT OF 1989. In the 1980s, as the Red Power* movement continued to evolve, concern about the remains of human beings and sacred artifacts in American museums increased among many Indian peoples. Since the eighteenth century, excavation of Native American mounds and burial sites has been an ongoing scientific practice, and from its inception in 1846 the Smithsonian Museum has collected and stored those remains. So did a great variety of state, local, and private museums, as well as historical societies. Most of the skeletons were collected in the nineteenth century when racist notions were powerful. Non-Indian anthropologists, archaeologists, and physicians wanted to study the skeletal remains to determine differences between whites and Indians as a way of proving that Indian peoples were inferior. Red Power activists viewed the continued storage of the skeletons as an intolerable racist legacy.

Indian activists demanded the repatriation* of the bodies and reinternment in tribal burial grounds. Because the Smithsonian was one of the greatest offenders—in the mid-1980s it possessed more than 18,500 skeletal remains—it became the target of Indian protest. Congress responded to the political pressure by passing the National Museum of the American Indian Act in 1989. The measure established a separate Museum of the American Indian within the Smithsonian and ordered the Smithsonian to develop a systematic policy for the repatriation of its collection of Indian remains. Since then, the Smithsonian has repatriated hundreds of skeletal remains and various cultural and sacred objects.

Suggested Reading: Michael M. Ames, *Cannibal Tours and Glass Boxes: The Anthropology of Museums*, 1992; Douglas Cole, *Captured Heritage: The Scramble for Northwest Coast Artifacts*, 1985; George P. Horse Capture, *The Concept of Sacred Materials and Their Place in the World*, 1989; Phyllis Mauch Messenger, ed., *The Ethics of Collecting Cultural Property: Whose Culture? Whose Property?* 1989; H. Marcus Price, ed., *Disputing the Dead: U.S. Law on Aboriginal Remains and Grave Goods*, 1991.

JAMES S. OLSON

NATIONAL TRIBAL CHAIRMEN'S ASSOCIATION. During the late 1960s, when the reaction against the termination* program and the drive for self-determination* began to reach their peaks, a number of tribal chairmen began discussing the establishment of a tribal chairmen's association to act as liaison between tribes and the Bureau of Indian Affairs,* to lobby for self-determination and protection of the Indian landed estate, and to provide a pan-Indian* organization as a way of augmenting Native American political power. The National Tribal Chairmen's Association, representing more than one hundred tribes, was formed in 1971 and remains today extremely active in national Indian affairs.

Suggested Reading: Armand S. La Potin, *Native American Voluntary Organizations*, 1986.

JAMES S. OLSON

NATIVE AMERICAN CHURCH. See **PEYOTE.**

NATIVE AMERICAN CHURCH v. NAVAJO TRIBAL COUNCIL (1959). A ruling that federal courts do not have jurisdiction over tribal rulings, this case was brought when the Navajo tribal council objected to the presence and activities of the Native American Church on the Navajo reservation. The Native American Church combined Christian and traditional Native American religious beliefs and practices. The use of peyote,* a hallucinogenic drug derived from cactus, was a central part of the religious ceremony of the Native American Church. The Navajo tribal council prohibited the use, sale, or possession of peyote on the reservation* while also outlawing the Native American Church from practicing there.

The Native American Church claimed that its right to use peyote and practice its religion without prosecution was protected by the First Amendment to the Constitution.* But the Tenth Circuit Court of Appeals disagreed, holding that the First Amendment did indeed protect the right to freedom of religion but that the protection only applied to acts of Congress. Moreover, it held, the Fourteenth Amendment* extended those same restrictions to actions by the states. The Navajo tribal council, although created under congressional action, was not restricted by either the First or Fourteenth Amendments. The court ruled that Indian tribes occupied a level of their own between the states and the federal government and had unique legal standings. As such, federal courts did not have jurisdiction over tribal rulings.

Suggested Reading: Monroe E. Price, *Law and the American Indian: Readings, Notes and Cases*, 1973; John R. Wunder, *"Retained by The People": A History of American Indians and the Bill of Rights*, 1994.

JAMES S. OLSON

NATIVE AMERICAN GRAVES PROTECTION AND REPATRIATION ACT OF 1990. Since the eighteenth century, excavation of Native American mounds and burial sites has been an ongoing scientific practice. The remains of human beings and sacred artifacts have been collected and stored in the Smithsonian Museum; in a variety of state, local, and private museums; and at historical societies and universities. By the mid-1980s, anthropologists and museologists estimated that the remains of more than 600,000 Native Americans were being stored in the United States. Red Power* activists viewed the continued storage of the skeletons as an intolerable racist legacy. Indian activists demanded the repatriation* of the bodies and reinternment in tribal burial grounds.

In 1989 Congress passed the National Museum of the American Indian Act,* which mandated establishment of a separate museum of American Indians within the Smithsonian Institution and required the Smithsonian to develop a comprehensive plan to repatriate the more than 18,500 skeletal remains of Native Americans it possessed. In 1990 Congress followed up that legislation with the Native American Graves Protection and Repatriation Act. Focusing on human skeletal remains housed in federal agencies or any other institutions receiving federal funds, the law required each institution to inventory its collection of human skeletal remains and to make a concerted attempt to identify their cultural affiliation. Each institution must then notify the responsible tribes or organizations and transfer the remains if so requested. Museums had until November 16, 1995, to inventory all their holdings; by May 1, 1996, they were required to notify Indian groups of those holdings. Museums may seek extensions in developing the descriptions of their holdings, and federal budget cuts to the Bureau of Indian Affairs* and museums around the country have guaranteed that such extensions will occur. But eventually the museums must work out arrangements for the return of artifacts and skeletons to Native American groups requesting them.

Suggested Reading: Michael M. Ames, *Cannibal Tours and Glass Boxes: The Anthropology of Museums*, 1992; Douglas Cole, *Captured Heritage: The Scramble for Northwest Coast Artifacts*, 1985; George P. Horse Capture, *The Concept of Sacred Materials and Their Place in the World*, 1989; Phyllis Mauch Messenger, ed., *The Ethics of Collecting Cultural Property: Whose Culture? Whose Property?* 1989; H. Marcus Price, *Disputing the Dead: U.S. Law on Aboriginal Remains and Grave Goods*, 1991; Larry J. Zimmerman, "Sharing Control of the Past," *Archaeology* 47 (November/December 1994), 65–68.

JAMES S. OLSON

NATIVE AMERICAN LANGUAGES ACT OF 1990. Throughout much of U.S. history the federal government had promoted an assimilation* campaign with regard to American Indians. One of the primary objectives was to wipe out Indian languages and convert Indians to speaking English. By the 1980s, in the new multicultural environment affecting American politics and education, Congress passed the Native American Languages Act of 1990 to promote the preservation of those languages. The legislation authorized a federal grant to provide funding for the preservation and teaching of Native American languages throughout the United States.

Suggested Reading: Duane Champagne, ed., *Chronology of Native North American History*, 1994.

JAMES S. OLSON

NATIVE AMERICAN RIGHTS FUND. During the 1960s it became increasingly clear that the legal challenges facing Native Americans differed considerably from those facing other oppressed minority groups in the United States. Lawyers dealing with Indian civil rights cases had to be familiar with thousands of treaties, administrative rulings, state and federal legislative acts, state and federal court decisions, and tribal government actions. To provide legal assistance to American Indians, the Ford Foundation in 1970 commissioned the California Indian Legal Services to develop a program, and the Native American Rights Fund (NARF) emerged from that effort. In 1971 the Native American Rights Fund formally separated from California Indian Legal Services and established its headquarters in Boulder, Colorado. A year later, with financial assistance from the Carnegie Foundation, the Native American Rights Fund established the National Indian Law Library.

The Native American Rights Fund has developed a fivefold mission during the past quarter-century. First, it is committed to the preservation of tribal existence in both legal and cultural terms. Second, NARF works to preserve and augment the natural resource base of reservations* so that Indian tribes can remain, or become, economically viable entities. Third, NARF accepts the promotion of Indian civil rights as a major responsibility. Fourth, NARF serves as a watchdog group to make sure that governments at all levels properly enforce and administer laws relating to Indians. Finally, NARF works to develop Indian law. Over the years it has worked to help restore the Indian land base, secure federal recognition for unrecognized tribes, and guarantee tribal hunting* and fishing* rights. Today, the Native Amerian Rights Fund is perhaps the most powerful voice in the field of Indian law.

Suggested Reading: Armand S. La Potin, *Native American Voluntary Organ-*

izations, 1986; "NARF Celebrates Its 20th Anniversary," *NARF Legal Review* 15 (Summer 1990), 1–4.

JAMES S. OLSON

NAVAJO-HOPI LONG-RANGE REHABILITATION ACT OF 1950. The Navajo-Hopi Long-Range Rehabilitation Act was passed by Congress in 1950 to correct deficiencies in the infrastructure on these two reservations.* Decades of neglect and chronic underfunding by the Bureau of Indian Affairs,* along with high levels of unemployment and poverty,* made these two reservations among the poorest areas in America. Brutal winter storms in 1948 and 1949 badly damaged crops and livestock and further diminished the two tribes' ability to be self-sufficient. The natural disaster brought national attention to their problems.

The act authorized $88,570,000 to be expended over ten years on infrastructure improvements such as school, hospital, and road construction. This money was also to be spent on soil and water conservation and agricultural irrigation projects. Congress hoped the projects would someday help the tribes become economically self-sufficient. The act also authorized a stronger and more independent tribal government, especially for the Navajo tribe, and extended Social Security benefits to the two tribes for the first time. The impact of the act on these reservations can be seen today by viewing the host of new buildings and roads. The act's provisions concerning tribal government also have greatly benefited the Navajo, making it one of the largest and most powerful tribal governments in the United States.

Suggested Reading: Emily Benedek, *The Wind Won't Know Me: A History of the Navajo-Hopi Land Dispute*, 1992; Lawrence C. Kelly, *The Navajo Indians and Federal Indian Policy, 1900–1935*, 1968; Donald L. Parman, *Indians and the American West in the Twentieth Century*, 1994.

JASON M. TETZLOFF

NEVADA v. UNITED STATES (1983). The case *Nevada v. United States* revolved around the question of water rights.* The Pyramid Lake Paiutes argued that as a consequence of President Ulysses S. Grant's 1874 executive order establishing the reservation,* the tribe enjoyed reserved fishing rights* on the Truckee River. In 1944, however, a legal adjudication had recognized only minimal water rights for the Pyramid Lake Paiutes, and those rights could be used only for irrigation purposes. The Supreme Court determined that recognizing complete reserved rights on the Truckee for the Pyramid Lake Paiutes might deprive thousands of non-Indian farmers in northwestern Nevada of irrigation rights they had enjoyed for three generations. The Court let the 1944 agreement stand.

Suggested Reading: Russel Lawrence Barsh and James Youngblood Henderson, *The Road: Indian Tribes and Political Liberty*, 1980; Vine Deloria Jr. and Clifford M. Lytle, *American Indians, American Justice*, 1983; H. Barry Holt and Gary Forrester, *Digest of American Indian Law: Cases and Chronology*, 1990; Stephen L. Pevar, *The Rights of Indians and Tribes: The Basic ACLU Guide to Indian and Tribal Rights*, 1992; Wilcomb E. Washburn, *Red Man's Land, White Man's Law: A Study of the Past and Present Status of the American Indian*, 1971; Charles F. Wilkinson, *American Indians, Time and the Law*, 1987; John R. Wunder, *"Retained by The People": A History of American Indians and the Bill of Rights*, 1994.

JAMES S. OLSON

NEW JERSEY v. WILSON (1812). The *New Jersey v. Wilson* case was decided in 1812. The state of New Jersey had acquired land title from the Delaware Indians and given the tribe new lands to live on. Additionally, New Jersey had granted tax-free status to the new lands, freeing the Indians from any tax liabilities arising from the land sale. The transaction appeared to satisfy both groups. New Jersey cleared up disputed land titles, and the Delaware Indians received new lands. The problem arose years later when the tribe moved west and sold the land to non-Indians such as John Wilson.

Although the sale of the land was approved by the New Jersey legislature, the state decided to impose taxes on the land. The state argued that the previous tax exemptions had been granted to the Delaware Indians to compensate them for giving up their claims to the disputed areas, and that such exemptions ceased to be necessary once the Delawares disposed of the land. The right of the state to implement the tax was taken to court.

The U.S. Supreme Court ruled that New Jersey could not implement the tax on the land because the state and the Delaware Indians had signed a contract concerning the land. New Jersey, the Court stated, had given the land the tax exemptions, not the Indians. As such, the tax-free status remained with the land regardless of who owned or possessed the land.

Suggested Reading: Russel Lawrence Barsh and James Youngblood Henderson, *The Road: Indian Tribes and Political Liberty*, 1980; Vine Deloria Jr. and Clifford M. Lytle, *American Indians, American Justice*, 1983; H. Barry Holt and Gary Forrester, *Digest of American Indian Law: Cases and Chronology*, 1990; Stephen L. Pevar, *The Rights of Indians and Tribes: The Basic ACLU Guide to Indian and Tribal Rights*, 1992; Wilcomb E. Washburn, *Red Man's Land, White Man's Law: A Study of the Past and Present Status of the American Indian*, 1971;

Charles F. Wilkinson, *American Indians, Time and the Law*, 1987; John R. Wunder, *"Retained by The People": A History of American Indians and the Bill of Rights*, 1994.

JAMES S. OLSON

NEW MEXICO v. MESCALERO APACHE TRIBE (1983). The degree to which federally recognized Indian reservations* are subject to state jurisdiction has long been a controversial question in Indian affairs. The case of *New Mexico v. Mescalero Apache Tribe* in 1983 dealt with exactly that question. The Mescalero Apaches wanted to regulate the hunting and fishing of non-Indians on Mescalero reservation land. The state government of New Mexico argued that state fish and game laws applied to non-Indians fishing and hunting on Mescalero land. The Mescaleros, in return, denied that the state of New Mexico had any jurisdiction on their land. New Mexico sued the tribe in federal court, and the case wound its way to the Supreme Court, which handed down its decision in 1983. The Court agreed with the Mescaleros, giving them the sovereign* right to regulate hunting and fishing on reservation land and denying that right to the state government. The Court claimed that the Mescaleros enjoyed such jurisdiction because they had invested large sums of tribal moneys into development of the reservation fish and game resources.

Suggested Reading: Russel Lawrence Barsh and James Youngblood Henderson, *The Road: Indian Tribes and Political Liberty*, 1980; Vine Deloria Jr. and Clifford M. Lytle, *American Indians, American Justice*, 1983; H. Barry Holt and Gary Forrester, *Digest of American Indian Law: Cases and Chronology*, 1990; Stephen L. Pevar, *The Rights of Indians and Tribes: The Basic ACLU Guide to Indian and Tribal Rights*, 1992; Wilcomb E. Washburn, *Red Man's Land, White Man's Law: A Study of the Past and Present Status of the American Indian*, 1971; Charles F. Wilkinson, *American Indians, Time and the Law*, 1987; John R. Wunder, *"Retained by The People": A History of American Indians and the Bill of Rights*, 1994.

JAMES S. OLSON

NEWLANDS RECLAMATION ACT OF 1902. By the early 1900s the progressive movement was gaining momentum, and one of its most popular dimensions was the demand for conservation of natural resources. By far the most precious natural resource of the United States was its land; and people, especially in the western states, wanted to develop it as a renewable resource. The Desert Land Act* of 1877 and the Carey Act* of 1894 had been designed to do this, and in 1902 Congressman Francis G. Newlands of Nevada sponsored a new piece of legislation that became law on June 17, 1902. The Newlands Reclamation Act of 1902 provided for the development of land and irrigation resources by directing the federal government, through a new agency called the Reclamation Service (later, the Bureau of Reclamation) to construct irrigation projects in sixteen states. Financing was to come from the sale of public lands in parcels of up to 160 acres (later, 320 acres) and a subsequent ten-year assessment for use of the developed water. Because the Newlands Act provided new irrigation projects in the Far West, land that had long been relatively unattractive to white farmers suddenly gained in commercial potential. Inevitably, economic development of the Far West led to the loss of Indian land.

Suggested Reading: Roy E. Huffman, *Irrigation Development and Public Water Policy*, 1953.

JAMES S. OLSON

NEZ PERCÉ WAR. See **JOSEPH, CHIEF.**

NORTHWEST ELECTRIC POWER AND CONSERVATION ACT OF 1980. During the 1950s, 1960s, and 1970s the federal government, state governments, and private corporations had seen to the construction of dozens of hydroelectric dams along the Columbia River. These dams covered over dozens of traditional salmon fishing sites and made salmon migration upriver to spawn more difficult. Indian activists sued, and during the 1960s several Supreme Court decisions upheld the Indians' fishing rights.* Late in the 1970s the Columbia Inter-Tribal Fish Commission began lobbying the federal government to pass legislation protecting Indian fishing rights in future federal power development plans. In 1980 Congress passed the Northwest Electric Power and Conservation Act, which recognized fish conservation as an objective equal in significance to power generation.

Suggested Reading: Lloyd Burton, *American Indian Water Rights and the Limits of the Law*, 1993; Armand S. La Potin, *Native American Voluntary Organizations*, 1986; Daniel McCool, *Command of the Waters: Iron Triangles, Federal Water Development, and Indian Water*, 1987.

JAMES S. OLSON

NORTHWEST INDIAN FISHERIES COMMISSION. The Northwest Indian Fisheries Commission (NIFC) was founded in 1975 by western Washington tribes to help co-manage the region's on- and off-reservation fisheries. This right to co-manage the fishing resource was confirmed by the so-called Boldt Decisions,* which allocated, on the basis of treaty* provisions, at least one-half of the available catch to the Indians of the region.

Being made up of representatives from twenty-eight tribes and Indian communities, the commission performs a variety of functions. It helps negotiate allowable catch limits with the various state, federal, and international organizations that regulate the fishing industry. It coordinates resource management efforts by its members and provides them with scientific and technical expertise. This is an important task, as many of the commission's members cannot afford such technical staff with their limited tribal budgets. The NIFC works closely with other Indian organizations in the region, such as the Columbia River Inter-Tribal Fish Committee, to provide a strong Indian voice for the preservation and careful management of fish stocks—especially salmon—in the Pacific Northwest.

The NIFC faces continuing challenges as fish stocks diminish at a time when there is increased national and international fishing pressure. In addition, non-Indian sport and commercial fishermen are demanding a greater share of the catch. They are increasing their protest efforts against what many see as the special rights of the Washington Indian tribes. To combat this, the commission has increased its educational efforts to prevent a non-Indian backlash against court-ordered and court-affirmed treaty rights.

SUGGESTED READING: Daniel L. Boxberger, *To Fish in Common: The Ethnohistory of Lummi Indian Salmon Fishing*, 1989; Armand S. La Potin, *Native American Voluntary Organizations*, 1986; Robert H. Ruby and John A. Brown, *A Guide to the Indian Tribes of the Pacific Northwest*, 1992.

JASON M. TETZLOFF

NORTHWEST ORDINANCE OF 1787. The Northwest Ordinance of 1787 reasserted congressional authority over Indian affairs. It was a measured response to repeated efforts of private citizens and the states of Georgia and North Carolina to circumvent the rights of their Creek and Cherokee neighbors by bogus treaty-making and unprovoked attacks. The ordinance provided for the preservation of Indian liberties, the acquisition of Indian land by just and legal methods, and respect for Indian property rights, promising "perfect good faith toward the Indian." But the measure, which purported to protect the Indian from the white man's continued encroachments, operated more in the realm of the ideal than in reality. For the most part, the congressional measure was ignored by land-hungry settlers and virtually cast aside by future administrations.

Suggested Reading: Francis Paul Prucha, *The Great Father*, Vol. 1, 1984; Wilcomb E. Washburn, *Red Man's Land, White Man's Law*, 1971.

MARK BAXTER

O

OAKES, RICHARD. Richard Oakes, a Mohawk Indian, is best known for his leadership during the American Indian occupation of Alcatraz Island* in 1969–1971. Born on the St. Regis Indian reservation in New York, Oakes attended Salmon River Central School until he was 16 years old and quit during the eleventh grade because he felt the U.S. school system failed to offer anything relevant to his Indian culture and heritage. Oakes then began a brief career in the ironwork industry, working both on and off the reservation. Before moving to California, he attended Adirondack Community College in Glen Falls, New York, and Syracuse University. While traveling cross-country to San Francisco, Oakes visited several Indian reservations* and became aware of their political and economic situations.

Oakes worked at several jobs in San Francisco until he had an opportunity to enroll at San Francisco State College in February 1969 under the government's new economic opportunity program. During this time he met and married Annie Marufo, a Kashia Pomo Indian from northern California, and adopted her five children.

Oakes was a leader in the November 1969 occupation of Alcatraz Island, an event that became the catalyst for the emerging Indian activism that continued into the 1970s. The occupation of Alcatraz Island was an attempt by Indian college students and urban Indian people to attract national attention to the failure of U.S. government policy toward American Indians. The press and many of the Indian occupiers recognized Oakes as the "Indian leader" on Alcatraz, even though Oakes never claimed that position. He left Alcatraz in January 1970 following the death of his stepdaughter Yvonne, who died from a head injury after falling down a stairwell in a vacant building on the island. After leaving Alcatraz

Island, Oakes remained active in Indian social issues and was instrumental in the Pomo and Pit River Indian movements to regain ancestral lands in northern California. Oakes participated in the planning of additional occupations of federal property in northern California and at key places around the country.

On September 21, 1972, Oakes was shot and killed by Michael Morgan, a YMCA camp employee in Sonoma County, California. Oakes had gone to the camp to locate an Indian youth who was staying with the Oakes family. The camp employee was charged with involuntary manslaughter, but charges were later dropped on the grounds that Oakes had come "menacingly toward" him. Oakes was buried on his wife's reservation with traditional religious rites. His murder unified the various Indian protest groups and gave impetus to the Trail of Broken Treaties* march, which was planned on the Rosebud Indian reservation and scheduled to arrive in Washington, D.C., in time for the 1972 presidential campaign.

Suggested Reading: Troy R. Johnson, *The Occupation of Alcatraz Island: Indian Self-Determination and the Rise of Indian Activism*, 1996; *New York Times*, September 22, 1972.

TROY JOHNSON

OFF-RESERVATION BOARDING SCHOOLS. In 1879 the federal government began an off-reservation boarding school program to bring Native Americans into the majority through education.* The program focused on rejecting tribal language and customs and completely immersing students in mainstream culture.

Army Lieutenant Richard Henry Pratt,* the founding superintendent of the first off-reservation boarding school (the Carlisle Indian School in Carlisle, Pennsylvania), saw instruction in the English language and vocational training as the keys to this conversion. Pratt recruited students from all tribes and all regions of the country. Upon arrival at the school, students were stripped of their tribal dress, boys were given haircuts, and all were issued uniforms. Communication in tribal languages was forbidden, and transgressors were punished. Pratt also employed a program called the "outing" that placed boarding school students in the homes of area farmers and craftsmen in order to help them refine their language and vocational skills. In addition, Pratt encouraged students to adopt Christianity.

Over the next twenty years, dozens of off-reservation boarding schools dotted the nation's landscape. Although all schools aspired to the Carlisle model, not all succeeded at fulfilling their educational mission. Often schools were overcrowded and inadequately staffed. Sanitary conditions were generally poor. Despite this uneven performance the program continued until the 1920s, at which time the Meriam Report* concluded that it was inefficient and ineffective.

Suggested Reading: S. Hyler, *One House, One Voice, One Heart: Native American Education at the Santa Fe Indian School*, 1990; F. P. Prucha, ed., *Americanizing the American Indian: Writings by the "Friends of the Indian" 1880–1900*, 1973.

PHILIP HUCKINS

OGLALA SIOUX CIVIL RIGHTS ORGANIZATION. In 1973, during the peak of the Red Power* movement and the confrontations at Wounded Knee,* Gladys Bissonette and Ellen Moves Camp established the Oglala Sioux Civil Rights Organization at the Pine Ridge reservation in South Dakota. Because of the violence being committed against the Oglala people at Wounded Knee, the organization proposed armed self-defense for the Indians. In more recent years, the organization has concentrated on nonviolent forms of political action to achieve civil rights.

Suggested Reading: Duane Champagne, ed., *Chronology of Native North American History*, 1994.

JAMES S. OLSON

OKLAHOMA INDIAN WELFARE ACT OF 1936. The Indian Reorganization Act* of 1934 launched the so-called Indian New Deal,* but members of the Oklahoma congressional delegation opposed the measure to such an extent that they managed to exclude most Oklahoma tribes from its provisions. They believed the Indian Reorganization Act would retard the assimilation* of Native Americans. The measure also threatened to exempt reservation mineral deposits from state taxation and prevent Indians on individual allotments* from selling their land. However, Commissioner of Indian Affairs John Collier* was committed to the legislation and wanted to see it apply to the Indians of Oklahoma as well. In 1934, in the company of Senator Elmer Thomas of Oklahoma, Collier toured the Oklahoma reservations,* soliciting local opinion about the merits of the Indian Reorganization Act. Tribal leaders of the Five Civilized Tribes spoke highly of the legislation, particularly the provisions for new tribal governments and tribal corporations. But many mixed-blood Indians living on individual allotments hated the communal provisions of the law and opposed it.

Senator Thomas came away from the tour convinced that at least some measures of the law should be applied to Oklahoma. Collier drafted the legislation; and Thomas, along with Congressman Will Rogers of Oklahoma, sponsored it. When it finally emerged from controversial legislative hearings, the bill did apply some of the provisions of the Indian Reorganization Act to Oklahoma. It provided for the communal ownership of land, the establishment of tribal constitutions and corporations, and the right of ten or more Native Americans to establish local cooperatives and obtain loan money from a $2 million revolving credit fund. But it also allowed the state of Oklahoma to tax reservation oil and gas production. With passage of the Oklahoma Indian Welfare Act in 1936, the Oklahoma tribes became part of the Indian New Deal.

Suggested Reading: Peter M. Wright, "John Collier and the Oklahoma Indian Welfare Act of 1936," *Chronicles of Oklahoma* 50 (Autumn 1972).

JAMES S. OLSON

OKLAHOMA TAX COMMISSION v. CITIZEN BAND POTAWATOMI INDIAN TRIBE (1991). The legal relationship between sovereign* Indian tribes and state authority has long been a controversial one in American Indian history. Nothing has stimulated that controversy more than questions over the taxing power of state governments. *Oklahoma Tax Commission v. Citizen Band Potawatomi Indian Tribe* revolved around that question. The Citizen Band Potawatomis of Oklahoma denied the right of the Oklahoma Tax Commission to collect state taxes for cigarettes sold on the reservation.* Oklahoma taxing authorities demanded payment of sales taxes for cigarettes sold to non-Indians. The case made its way to the U.S. Supreme Court, which rendered a decision in 1991. It ruled that the Potawatomis were subject to the taxes on cigarettes sold to non-Indians, thereby upholding the claims of Oklahoma tax officials. But at the same time, the Court claimed that the sovereign constitutional status of the Potawatomi tribe prevented state officials from filing lawsuits to collect the taxes. In other words, Oklahoma officials had a right to the tax revenue but did not enjoy the ability to enforce the right. The taxes remain unpaid.

Suggested Reading: Russel Lawrence Barsh and James Youngblood Henderson, *The Road: Indian Tribes and Political Liberty*, 1980; Vine Deloria Jr. and Clifford M. Lytle, *American Indians, American Justice*, 1983; H. Barry Holt and Gary Forrester, *Digest of American Indian Law: Cases and Chronology*, 1990; Stephen L. Pevar, *The Rights of Indians and Tribes: The Basic ACLU Guide to Indian and Tribal Rights*, 1992; Wilcomb E. Washburn, *Red Man's Land, White Man's Law: A Study of the Past and Present Status of the American Indian*, 1971; Charles F. Wilkinson, *American Indians, Time and the Law*, 1987; John R. Wun-

der, *"Retained by The People": A History of American Indians and the Bill of Rights*, 1994.

JAMES S. OLSON

OKLAHOMA TAX COMMISSION v. MUSCOGEE (CREEK) NATION

(1988) In the mid-1980s, the Creek nation launched a commercial bingo operation on tribal trust lands in Tulsa, Oklahoma. The state of Oklahoma tried to impose a sales tax on the proceeds from the bingo operation, but the Creeks argued that they were exempt from state and local taxation because the bingo business had been located on tribal trust property. The case went all the way to the U.S. Supreme Court, which ruled in favor of the Creeks on July 8, 1988.

SUGGESTED READING: John R. Wunder, *"Retained by The People": A History of American Indians and the Bill of Rights*, 1994.

JAMES S. OLSON

OLIPHANT v. SUQUAMISH INDIAN TRIBE (1978).

In 1973 non-Indian visitors to Washington's Port Madison reservation were arrested for misdemeanor criminal violations of the tribal code. The Indian courts claimed jurisdiction over the matter and found the defendants guilty as charged. After hearing the case on appeal, the Supreme Court ruled that the Suquamish tribe possessed no such criminal jurisdiction and had exceeded its authority by prosecuting non-Indians. The Court held that in view of the dependent status of the various sovereign* tribes, such powers could only be derived through congressional consent. No such consent was forthcoming. Although the convictions were overturned, the scope of tribal jurisdiction remained subject to further clarification.

Suggested Reading: Vine Deloria Jr. and Clifford M. Lytle, *American Indians, American Justice*, 1983; H. Barry Holt and Gary Forrester, *Digest of American Indian Law: Cases and Chronology*, 1990.

MARK BAXTER

ORGANIZED VILLAGE OF KAKE v. EGAN (1962).

This U.S. Supreme Court case revoked the exclusive fishing rights* of two groups of Tlingit Indians in Alaska. Decided on March 5, 1962, *Organized Village of Kake v. Egan* was a companion case to *Metlakatla Indian Community v. Egan.**

The Organized Village of Kake and the Angoon Community Association were chartered under the Indian Reorganization Act* of 1934. Both groups of Tlingit Indians lived on Alaskan islands, and both relied on salmon fishing for their livelihood. Consequently, the federal government purchased a fish cannery for Angoon in 1948 and one for Kake in 1950. Simultaneously, Kake and Angoon were granted permits by the Army Corps of Engineers to operate fish traps and by the U.S. Forest Service to anchor the traps in Tongass National Forest.

In 1956, to protect their depleting salmon supply, Alaskans voted in favor of an ordinance to outlaw the use of fish traps. In 1959, after the Tlingits ignored the law, state officials seized one Kake trap and arrested the president of the Kake Village Council and the foreman of the fish trap crew. The Tlingits, believing their fishing rights had been violated, took their case to court.

In the Supreme Court, the appellants argued that the White Act and Alaska Statehood Act authorized the secretary of the Interior to override the fish trap law. The White Act allowed the secretary to limit fishing times, places, and methods to conserve fish. Section 4 of the Statehood Act gave the United States control of all property held by Alaskan Indians. This property included fishing rights, so Kake and Angoon argued that Alaska could not enforce the fish trap law on the Tlingits. Furthermore, Kake and Angoon believed that by passing the Statehood Act, Congress had clearly stated that it wanted Indians to be allowed to fish in the way they had before statehood.

In the opinion delivered by Justice Felix Frankfurter, the Supreme Court declared that the Statehood Act neither granted nor revoked those fishing rights. Determining that Congress had neither granted the right to use fish traps nor authorized the secretary of the Interior to do so, the court upheld the decision by the Supreme Court of Alaska. Because the Indians of Kake and Angoon did not live on the reservation, they were required to obey the state fish trap law.

Suggested Reading: Russel Lawrence Barsh and James Youngblood Henderson, *The Road: Indian Tribes and Political Liberty*, 1980; Vine Deloria Jr. and Clifford M. Lytle, *American Indians, American Justice*, 1983; H. Barry Holt and Gary Forrester, *Digest of American Indian Law: Cases and Chronology*, 1990; Stephen L. Pevar, *The Rights of Indians and Tribes: The Basic ACLU Guide to Indian and Tribal Rights*, 1992; Wilcomb E. Washburn, *Red Man's Land, White Man's Law: A Study of the Past and Present Status of the American Indian*, 1971; Charles F. Wilkinson, *American Indians, Time and the Law*, 1987; John R. Wunder, *"Retained by The People": A History of American Indians and the Bill of Rights*, 1994.

JENNIFER BERTOLET

OSAGE GUARDIANSHIP ACT OF 1925. In 1925, during the heyday of the Indian reform movement when groups like the American Indian

Defense Association* were campaigning for an end to the exploitation of Indian resources, Congress passed the Osage Guardianship Act. The discovery of oil on Osage land in Oklahoma had created an environment perfect for the abuse of Indian rights by non-Indians. District court judges in Oklahoma assumed the right to appoint guardians to manage the property and royalties of Osage minors, and the guardians often stole from the Indians by charging exorbitant fees for the legal guardianship* service or actually defrauding the royalty accounts. The legislation required federal Indian agents to approve the appointment of all guardians. The law also awarded to the Osage federal trust* protection for all mineral rights on reservation* and individual Osage land.

Suggested Reading: W. David Baird, *The Osage People*, 1972; John J. Mathews, *The Osage: Children of the Middle Waters*, 1961.

JAMES S. OLSON

P

PAN-INDIANISM. "Pan-Indianism" is a term referring to an attempt by some Indians and non-Indians over the years to de-emphasize particular tribal identities among Native Americans and to create a more generic "Indian" identity in the United States. Since the seventeenth century, Pan-Indianism has evolved through several stages. First, some tribes attempted to band together in military and political alliances to resist the onslaught of European civilization. In 1763, for example, Chief Pontiac* of the Ottawas forged an alliance to resist the great increase in white settlers after the end of the French and Indian War.* Tecumseh,* a Shawnee leader, made a similar attempt during the early 1800s. However, because of the power of narrow tribal ethnic identities, Native Americans were unable to sustain their political and military alliances long enough to succeed in blocking the white advance.

In the late nineteenth and early twentieth centuries, the focus of pan-Indianism shifted away from Native American leaders to white reformers. In hopes of stopping the violence against American Indians that was so common during the Indian Wars of the 1800s, white reformers decided that the assimilation* of Native Americans into the larger society was imperative. They felt that once Indians shared European social, economic, religious, and political models, there would be no need for violence against them. The preliminary step in giving Indians a generic "American" identity was (in the minds of groups such as Friends of the Indian and the Indian Rights Association*) to end parochial tribal identities. Government policy, they argued, should be designed to undermine specific tribal identities. During the next half-century the allotment* program, federal education* policies, and the citizenship* campaigns all worked to weaken tribal ethnic identities.

A similar process was at work among many Indians themselves, although for different reasons. The peyote* cult, for example, spread throughout the Southwest in the late nineteenth and early twentieth centuries, eventually resulting in the formation of the Native American Church, a pan-Indian organization. The first national pan-Indian organization—the Society of American Indians*—was established in 1911 by Arthur C. Parker* (Seneca), Charles Eastman* (Santee Dakota), and Carlos Montezuma (Apache). They too believed in assimilation but were convinced that it must come from Native American, not white, impetus. Other pan-Indian groups soon appeared as well, including the All Indian Pueblo Council* in 1919, the Grand Council Fire of American Indians, the Indian Association of America in 1932, and the Indian Confederation of America* in 1933. In the wake of the Indian Reorganization Act* of 1934, which led to federal support for pan-Indian groups, other organizations appeared, including the National Congress of American Indians* in 1944, the National Indian Education Association* and Native American Rights Fund* in 1970, and the National Tribal Chairman's Association in 1971.

During the late 1940s, 1950s, and early 1960s, white assimilationists once again had the upper hand in American Indian policy, and their commitment to wiping out tribal identities in order to promote an assimilationist agenda led to the termination* and relocation* programs. The termination program eventually "terminated" (i.e., ended federal protection and supervision of) 109 tribes and turned them over to state jurisdiction. The relocation program moved tens of thousands of Americans off the reservations to "intertribalize" them (i.e., place them in residential settings where Indians from all tribes lived or among whites, African Americans, and Hispanics).

From the 1960s into the 1990s, the Red Power* movement has added another dimension to pan-Indianism. The National Indian Youth Council,* organized in 1961, was the first of the pan-Indian Red Power groups. Indian activists believed—just as Pontiac and Tecumseh had centuries before—that only in unity could Native Americans hold their own in U.S. society. Narrow tribal identities and intertribal conflict would render Indians politically unable to protect their own interests. The most prominent of the pan-Indian activist organizations in recent decades are Indians of All Tribes,* the American Indian Movement,* Women of All Red Nations,* and the International Indian Treaty Council.*

Suggested Reading: Stephen Cornell, *The Return of the Native: American*

Indian Political Resurgence, 1988; Hazel W. Hertzberg, *The Search for an American Indian Identity: Modern Pan-Indian Movements*, 1971.

JAMES S. OLSON

PARIS, TREATY OF (1783). In order to reduce violence between whites and Indians on the western fringe of the British North American empire and to maintain better control of its colonies, Great Britain passed the Proclamation of 1763, prohibiting white settlers from crossing the Appalachian Mountains and taking up farms in the West. The measure enraged many colonial Americans, but it did slow the westward movement and reduce frontier violence. But in the Treaty of Paris of 1783, which ended the American War of Independence, Great Britain ceded to the United States all its territory between the Appalachian Mountains and the Mississippi River. American settlers were soon pouring by the tens of thousands into the region, reigniting violence with Native Americans and ultimately leading to the Indian Removal Act* of 1830 and the loss of most tribal land east of the Mississippi.

Suggested Reading: Wilbur R. Jacobs, *Dispossessing the American Indian: Indians and Whites on the Colonial Frontier*, 1972; Francis Paul Prucha, *American Indian Policy in the Formative Years*, 1962.

JAMES S. OLSON

PARKER, ARTHUR CASWELL. Arthur Caswell Parker was an advocate of pan-Indian* reform. Born on April 5, 1881, on the Cattaraugus reservation in upstate New York, he was a member of a prominent Seneca family and could count among his ancestors Brigadier General Ely S. Parker, whom President Ulysses S. Grant appointed commissioner of Indian affairs in 1869. Parker began his education on the Seneca reservation and then attended and graduated from high school in White Plains, New York. He attended but did not graduate from Dickinson Seminary in Williamsport, Pennsylvania.

Parker then moved to New York City and worked as a journalist for a short time. He soon became interested in anthropology. With encouragement and tutoring by other noted anthropologists, such as Alanson B. Skinner and Frederick Q. Putnam, he began his career in 1904 as an ethnologist with the New York State Library in Albany. In 1906 he was appointed archaeologist of the New York State Museum, a post he held until 1925. Then he became director of the Rochester (New York) Municipal Museum. Parker published numerous scholarly works, including fourteen books and almost three hundred other works, most of which deal with Native American topics.

Parker was best known for the important role he played in Indian affairs. He was president of the pan-Indian reform organization the Society of American Indians,* in 1914 and 1915, and he was the long-term editor of its journal, *American Indian Magazine/Quarterly Journal of the Society of American Indians*. Parker was later secretary of the New York Indian Commission. In this role he was very active in pushing for and enforcing Indian compliance with the selective service* of World War I, making him an unpopular figure on many New York reservations.* Parker played a significant part in the founding of the National Congress of American Indians* in the 1940s, continuing his long-standing and most important role as an advocate of pan-Indian reform efforts. He continued writing and commenting on Indian affairs until his death in 1955.

Suggested Reading: Hazel Hertzberg, *The Search for an American Indian Identity: Modern Pan-Indian Movements*, 1971.

JASON M. TETZLOFF

PARKER, QUANAH. Quanah Parker (1845?–1911) was a Comanche Indian who played an important role in the transition of the southern Plains Indians from life on the plains to life on the reservation.* Quanah was the son of Cynthia Ann Parker, a captive white woman, and Peta Nocona, a Comanche chief. He was raised as a Comanche warrior and fought with his tribe in the Red River War of 1874–1875. At the conclusion of that conflict many of the Comanche, including Quanah, agreed to settle on a reservation in what is now the state of Oklahoma.

Quanah soon emerged as a leader among the Comanche, Kiowa, and Kiowa-Apache on the reservation. One of his first activities was to negotiate the lease of a large section of reservation land to cattle ranchers. Quanah built a ranch house, purchased cattle, and took up ranching with a portion of his lease payment. Thus Quanah accepted many white customs, but he also remained an advocate for his people and in certain areas refused to conform to the government's demands. For example, he had six wives at one time, retained his two braids, and served privately as the principal advocate for peyote* on the reservation. On the other hand, he was a strong critic of the Ghost Dance movement (a pan-Indian religious movement of the 1880s and 1890s that predicted the destruction of all whites and the advent of an Indian millennium) and discouraged his followers from participation.

Quanah played a major role in the struggle against allotment* in severalty. Perhaps better than any other Indian, he understood that allotments would cost the Indians almost half of their reservation lands. Yet he also knew the uselessness of blind opposition. Therefore he used a delaying tactic and attempted to receive the best deal possible. He constantly badgered agents who attempted to convince the Indians of the benefits of accepting individual plots and accepting payment for the excess land. He demanded to know what price the government offered for the land on a per acre basis so that he could compare it to other land sales. Realizing that he could not defeat the plan, Parker worked to delay the plan's ratification for almost eight years. Following the division of reservation lands among individuals, he lost most of his financial base but remained a leading figure among the reservation Indians until his death in 1911.

Suggested Reading: William T. Hagan, *Quanah Parker, Comanche Chief*, 1993.

JEFFREY D. CARLISLE

PAUL, WILLIAM LEWIS, SR. William Lewis Paul, a Tlingit Indian, spent his life working to protect Tlingit and Haida land claims. Born in southeast Alaska in 1885, he attended the Carlisle Boarding School in Pennsylvania and then earned a law degree. Soon thereafter, Paul became active in the Alaskan Native Brotherhood.* By the 1920s he was a leader of the Alaskan Native Brotherhood, editing the *Alaskan Fisherman*, a newspaper devoted to Native American fishing rights.* He also criticized the tendency of non-Indians to overfish commercially, which threatened salmon stocks in the Pacific Northwest. On the civil rights front, Paul led boycotts of businesses that segregated American Indians and helped win the right to vote* for American Indians in Alaskan territorial elections. He organized Native American workers in the cannery industry and campaigned to win the right of Indian children to attend public schools. Between 1929 and 1965, on behalf of the Alaska Federation of Natives,* Paul shepherded the land claim case of the Tlingit and Haida Indians. In 1912 the United States had seized their land in the Alaskan panhandle to establish the Tongass National Forest. In 1965 the case concluded with a $7.5 million judgment in favor of the Indians. William Lewis Paul died in 1977.

Suggested Reading: Duane Champagne, ed., *The Native North American Almanac*, 1994.

JAMES S. OLSON

PEACE POLICY. Military actions such as the massacre at Sand Creek in November 1864 (in which peaceful Cheyenne and Arapaho Indians were brutally slaughtered and mutilated by Colonel Chivington of the First Colorado Cavalry) mobilized citizens in the United States to seek a humanitarian Indian policy. A new evangelical reform movement calling for better treatment of Indian people swept the country. The core of the policy was an active partnership between the federal government and Christian churches. In 1867, Congress passed the Peace Commission Act and President Andrew Johnson appointed the Indian Peace Commission to study the problem and make recommendations. Its report was released in 1868, and the so-called Peace Policy of the Grant administration emerged from it.

The Peace Policy included the following provisions. The government would place all Indians on reservations,* both to protect them from frontier settlers and to teach them agriculture and other civilized pursuits. The military would punish Indians who resisted. They would learn that they must obey the government and remain on their reservations and not pursue their former native habits and practices. The federal government vowed that supplies furnished to the Indians would be of high quality and reasonably priced. Christian organizations would aid the federal government in educating the Indians with humanity and kindness. They would provide agents who were competent, honest, moral, and religious. They would also provide churches and schools that would convince Indians of the benefits of civilization.

But at the same time, settlers rapidly moved into new territory in the West and clashed with western tribes. Unexpectedly, numerous Indian wars took place after the Peace Policy was implemented, and the military crushed resisting tribes. Thus punishment overrode the other principles of the policy. The nation's Christian humanitarianism barely succeeded in preventing the transfer of the Indian Department to the War Department between 1865 and 1880. Moreover, renewed interest in the removal of tribes to reservations in Indian Territory* created additional strife for Indian people.

Ely S. Parker, Indian commissioner under President Grant, called for Indians to be removed to new reservations placed close together in Indian Territory. Seeking total assimilation,* Parker stated, "When upon the reservation they should be given land in severalty . . . tribal relations should be discouraged."

Finally, in 1884, reformers refused to support any policy of removal of Indians from their homelands. They also refused to support any kind of reservation system. Instead, they urged that Indians be provided home-steads within their traditional territory. The division of Indian lands into severalty and the reduction of reservation territory ended the period of the Peace Policy.

Suggested Reading: Norman J. Bender, *New Hope for the Indians: The Grant Peace Policy and the Navajos in the 1870s,* 1989; Loring Benson Priest, *Uncle Sam's Stepchildren: The Reformation of United States Indian Policy, 1865–1887,* 1942.

PAULEENA M. MACDOUGALL

PELTIER, LEONARD. Leonard Peltier was a leader of the American In-dian Movement.* He was born in Grand Forks, North Dakota, in 1944 to Ojibway parents. When he was a child the family moved frequently, since Peltier's father worked as a lumberjack, truck driver, and miner. When his parents divorced, Peltier was raised in the Wahpeton Indian School, a boarding school in North Dakota. In 1970 he became active in the American Indian Movement (AIM) and soon was one of its leaders. He traveled widely with Dennis Banks,* promoting AIM's agenda in the early 1970s. Peltier was a leader of AIM's Trail of Broken Treaties* caravan to Washington, D.C., in 1972. Early in 1973, Peltier went out to the Pine Ridge Reservation in South Dakota to assist AIM in winning elections to tribal leadership positions. The struggle for power between existing Sioux leaders and AIM activists turned bloody. Between March 1972 and June 1975, more than two dozen AIM members or supporters were murdered at Pine Ridge. Agents from the Federal Bureau of Investigation (FBI) de-scended on the reservation to investigate the crimes, or, in the minds of many AIM leaders, to make sure that the existing tribal leadership re-mained in place. On June 11, 1975, Peltier was involved in a shoot-out that left two FBI agents and one AIM activist dead. Peltier was arrested, convicted of the two FBI murders, and sentenced to two life terms in a federal penitentiary. A number of Indian activists have taken up Peltier's cause, considering him a political prisoner in the United States, but as of early 1997 he was still incarcerated.

Suggested Reading: Duane Champagne, ed., *Chronology of Native North American History,* 1994.

JAMES S. OLSON

PENN, WILLIAM. Founder of Pennsylvania and an unusually honest and fair negotiator of land sales from the Delaware Indians, William Penn (1644–1718) was born and raised in an influential, politically powerful family in England. His father, Admiral William Penn, held high positions under the early Stuarts and supported the monarchic cause during the

English civil wars. The son departed from the Anglican faith in his early manhood and became a member of the Society of Friends, or Quakers. He preached Quaker principles and often found himself in trouble with English law because of his dissenting ideas. His refusal to take oaths, to remove his hat to social superiors, and to show traditional forms of respect to English institutions resulted in his imprisonment.

When his father died in 1670, William Penn approached the Crown about converting a debt King Charles II owed his father into a massive land grant in North America. In 1681 the contract was completed and Penn was able to take up the colony in the name of his fellow Quakers; it came to be called Pennsylvania. He arrived with the earliest settlers in order to plan and lay out the colony. In order to do so, however, he had to secure complete title to the lands he wished to open first to settlement.

Penn insisted that all lands on which his colonists would settle had to be purchased through formal treaty* with its Delaware Indian owners. Although Europeans believed that Indians possessed only a right in the soil (Charles II thought of the mid-Atlantic lands as his royal domain from which he could freely give), Penn believed that they owned the lands. To that end his agents or he himself negotiated directly with Lenni Lenape (Delaware) leaders, whose people possessed the lands the Quakers wanted. Purchase prices were worked out and promptly paid.

Penn insisted that his successors follow his policy and negotiate fairly and honestly with the Delawares. He wrote to the leaders of the Delaware Indians on October 18, 1681: "I have great love and regard toward you, and I desire to win and gain your love and friendship by a kind, just, and peaceable life." He instructed his agents to deal fairly with the natives, telling them to "be tender of offending the Indians . . . that they may see we have their good in our eye." Penn's dealings with the Indians were exemplified in the 1682 treaty in which the Delawares surrendered significant amounts of land but only for a fair and just price. Scholars question whether Penn's policies toward the Delawares were carried on until the end of Quaker domination of the Pennsylvania government in 1756, during the French and Indian War.* His successors did not necessarily follow his lead in dealing fairly with the Delaware Indians.

Suggested Reading: Mary Maples Dunn, *William Penn: Politics and Conscience*, 1967; Hans Fantel, *William Penn: Apostle of Dissent*, 1974; Catherine Owen Peare, *William Penn: A Biography*, 1957.

TIMOTHY MORGAN

PEOPLE v. WOODY (1964). The *People v. Woody* case revolved around the issue of religious freedom.* On April 28, 1962, John Woody and a group of Navajos met near Needles, California, and participated in a peyote* ceremony. Local police discovered the meeting, arrested them, and charged them with possession of a controlled substance. They were convicted of the drug charge in a San Bernardino County court. Woody appealed the decision, and the California Supreme Court found in his favor, arguing that the state could not apply the statute outlawing the use of peyote as a religious sacrament (not unlike the bread and wine used in Christian sacramental services). Native American activists hailed the decision as a victory for Indian self-determination* and civil rights.

Suggested Reading: James S. Olson and Raymond Wilson, *Native Americans in the Twentieth Century*, 1984.

JAMES S. OLSON

PETERSON, HELEN. Helen Peterson was an activist who promoted the needs of indigenous peoples. Born a Cheyenne in South Dakota in 1915, she was raised among the Oglala Sioux and absorbed much of their culture. She was educated at Colorado State College and decided to pursue a career in human relations, particularly minority group relations. During the late 1940s she became director of the Rocky Mountain Council on Inter-American Affairs and in 1953 became executive director of the National Congress of American Indians.* In the mid-1960s she returned to Colorado to head the Denver Commission on Community Relations and the Organization on American Development.

Suggested Reading: Duane Champagne, ed., *The Native North American Almanac*, 1994.

JAMES S. OLSON

PEYOTE. For thousands of years a number of Mexican tribes had used peyote, a stimulant drug derived from the mescal plant, in religious ceremonies. The drug provided users with hallucinogenic dreams and an improved sense of self-worth. In the mid-nineteenth century the peyote cult made its way from Mexico to the Mescalero Apaches, who passed it on to the Kiowas, Caddos, and Comanches. Among the reservation Indians of the Indian Territory,* whose traditional lifestyles had been recently disrupted, peyote found a ready audience. Quanah Parker* of the Comanches became a leading figure in the peyote cult in the late 1870s and 1880s. By that time, peyotism had spread to the Cheyennes, Shawnees, and Arapahos; and by the early 1890s to the Pawnees, Delawares, Osages, and Winnebagos. Between 1900 and 1920, peyotism won converts among large numbers of Omahas, Utes, Crows, Menominees, Iowas, Sioux, and Shoshones.

In carefully controlled religious settings, peyote devotees took small amounts of the drug, enough to induce a trance-like state-of-mind. Peyote adherents believed that once within such a trance, they enjoyed an enhanced ability to understand the universe and themselves. With the advance of European civilization out to the Great Plains and the southwest in the late 1800s, many Indians found in peyote a personal way of dealing with the loss of their land and culture.

The spread of the peyote cult posed a threat to many Indians as well as non-Indians. Many whites found the practice bizarre and certain to retard the assimilation* of American Indians. In 1898 the territorial legislature of Oklahoma outlawed the practice, and by 1923 fourteen states had passed similar legislation. The Bureau of Indian Affairs* lobbied Congress for prohibitory legislation, and border agents intercepted the shipment of peyote across national and state lines. Many Native Americans, especially traditionalists, also opposed the spread of peyote, which had pan-Indian* connotations and tended to displace traditional tribal religious ceremonies. In 1940, for example, the Navajo tribal council outlawed the possession and use of peyote on the reservation.* The Taos Pueblos, White Mountain Apaches, and several South Dakota Sioux tribes followed suit.

But the peyote cult eventually evolved into a religion of its own. An ethical code known as the "Peyote Road" developed in the religion, emphasizing brotherly love, honesty, marital fidelity, hard work, economic self-reliance, trustworthiness, family responsibility, and alcohol avoidance. In 1918, to deal with increasingly hostile state and local legislation, peyotists formally organized themselves. Under the leadership of Mack Haag (Cheyenne), Charles Dailey (Oto), George Pipestem (Oto), Frank Eagle (Ponca), and others, the Native American Church was formed as a loose umbrella organization of peyote groups throughout the country. The Native American Church promoted the use of peyote as a religious experience and claimed the constitutional right to do so. By the 1950s, more than eighty Native American tribes practiced some form of the peyote religion.

Over the years, disputes concerning the use of peyote have been a continuing source of controversy among various Indian groups and between Indians and non-Indians. Several court cases have illustrated the complexity of peyote use as a civil rights issue. In 1940, for example, the Navajo tribal council imposed a $100 fine and a 9-month jail sentence for any Navajo found importing, selling, or using peyote on the reservation. When Navajo tribal police, without search or arrest warrants, raided a peyote ceremony in 1947, the Native American Church sued the tribe, claiming violations of First and Fourteenth Amendment* rights. In 1949 the Tenth Circuit Court decided *Native American Church v. Navajo Tribal Council*,* upholding the tribe's right to outlaw peyote. But in 1964 the California Supreme Court came to a different conclusion. In 1962, John Woody and a group of Navajos near Needles, California, were arrested by local police during a peyote ceremony and charged with possession of a controlled substance. They were convicted in a local court but appealed to the state supreme court. In *People v. Woody** (1964), the court held that the state could not constitutionally apply the statute prohibiting consumption of peyote when the drug was being used as a sacrament similar to the bread and wine used in many Christian churches. Since enactment of the American Indian Religious Freedom Act* in 1978, the practice of the peyote religion has generally been protected by law. Some experts today place Native American Church membership at more than 200,000 people.

Suggested Reading: David F. Aberle, *The Peyote Religion among the Navajo*, 1966; Edward F. Anderson, *Peyote: The Divine Cactus*, 1980; Weston LaBarre, *The Peyote Culture*, 1975; Sydney J. Slotkin, *The Peyote Religion: A Study in Indian-White Relations*, 1956; Omer C. Stewart, *Peyote Religion: A History*, 1987.

JAMES S. OLSON

PIPELINES ACT OF 1904. Advocates of Indian tribal sovereignty* have long argued that individual tribes possess the sovereign power to govern their own internal affairs. During the assimilation* crusade of the late nineteenth and early twentieth centuries, reformers wanted to destroy the notion of sovereignty as a means of incorporating individual American Indians into the larger legal system. The Pipelines Act of 1904 contributed to lessening tribal sovereignty.

The discovery of large, easily recoverable petroleum reserves in Oklahoma Territory presented economic interest groups with a dilemma. The most efficient way of moving petroleum was through the construction of pipelines, but some of those pipelines would have to cross reservation lands in Indian Territory. Although some tribes refused to permit such construction, Congress forced them to do so when it passed the Pipelines Act of 1904. The legislation granted right-of-way to oil companies to construct pipelines on reservation land. As such, the legislation was a serious blow to tribal sovereignty.

Suggested Reading: Marjane Ambler, *Breaking the Iron Bonds: Indian Control of Energy Development*, 1990; Vine Deloria Jr. and Clifford Lytle, *The Nations*

Within: The Past and Future of American Indian Sovereignty, 1984; Roxanne Dunbar Ortiz, *Indians of the Americas: Human Rights and Self-Determination*, 1984.

JAMES S. OLSON

PIPER v. BIG PINE SCHOOL DISTRICT (1924). In 1920, Congress directed the Department of the Interior to make sure that all Indian children were enrolled in federal or state school systems. However, many local school districts resented the directive. In spite of the congressional order, the school district in Big Pine, California, denied admission to the public schools to Alice Piper, an Indian. Piper's family asked for a court order forcing the school district to admit her, and the California Supreme Court agreed, arguing that Piper's Fourteenth Amendment* rights to equal protection had been violated. A number of cases in other states—such as *Crawford v. School District No. 7* in Oregon in 1913, and *Grant v. Michaels* in Montana in 1933—ended similarly, with school districts being ordered to admit Indian children.

Suggested Reading: H. Barry Holt and Gary Forrester, *Digest of American Indian Law: Cases and Chronology*, 1990; Stephen L. Pevar, *The Rights of Indians and Tribes: The Basic ACLU Guide to Indian and Tribal Rights*, 1992; Charles F. Wilkinson, *American Indians, Time and the Law*, 1987; John R. Wunder, *"Retained by The People": A History of American Indians and the Bill of Rights*, 1994.

JAMES S. OLSON

POLICE BRUTALITY. During the nineteenth century, as the federal government assumed more and more authority over the Indians, the question of law enforcement became increasingly central to maintaining community stability. Native Americans, conditioned to functioning legally within an atmosphere of tribal authority, now found themselves facing white agents of the federal government. The cultural gap between law enforcement officials and community members was enormous, and the Indians frequently resisted the white agents. To deal with the problem, the federal government began developing Indian police* forces. The Pawnees had a small, uniformed police force in 1862, and other tribes gained forces in the 1870s. The creation of Indian police forces allowed the federal government to execute its policies with less resistance and violence. The successes of the early attempts at Indian police forces encouraged the federal government to push for greater adoption of the idea. In 1878 the commissioner of Indian affairs ordered all tribes to maintain police forces if practical. The Indian police gained judicial powers in the 1880s when limited Indian courts were founded.

After World War II, when large numbers of Native Americans left the reservations* and moved to American cities, the issue of police brutality became an increasing concern. Like newly arrived African Americans and Hispanics, Indians found themselves facing an urban police force that was white and ignorant of their cultural traditions. Police often used more force than necessary in dealing with Indian suspects, and the Indians themselves were less inclined to respond appropriately to white law enforcement officials than they had been to Indian police on the reservation. By the 1960s, Indian activists and Red Power* advocates had identified police brutality as one of the major difficulties of urban life for Native Americans.

When the American Indian Movement* (AIM) first emerged in the fall of 1968, its leaders attacked the systematic violence and false arrests perpetrated against American Indians by the police of Minneapolis, Minnesota. AIM established patrols to monitor police activities in Minneapolis—a "police the police" program. Squads of AIM members would follow patrol cars and police on the beat in order to provide witnesses of police activities. AIM attorneys also began filing lawsuits in Minneapolis courts, charging individual police officials with verbal abuse of Indians. The results were dramatic. During the first year of the AIM program, unprosecuted arrests of Native Americans declined by more than 50 percent in the city. Other AIM chapters established similar patrols in most cities where large communities of American Indians existed. Since then, most urban Indian advocacy groups have kept the issue of police brutality high on their civil rights agendas.

Suggested Reading: Donald E. Green and Thomas V. Tonnesen, eds., *American Indians: Social Justice and Public Policy*, 1991; Alan L. Sorkin, *The Urban American Indian*, 1978; Wilcomb E. Washburn, *Red Man's Land, White Man's Law*, 1971; John R. Wunder, *"Retained by The People": A History of American Indians and the Bill of Rights*, 1994.

JAMES S. OLSON

PONCA CONTROVERSY. See *STANDING BEAR v. CROOK* (1879).

PONTIAC'S REBELLION. Pontiac was an Ottawa chief who formed a coalition of Ottawas, Shawnees, Delawares, Miamis, and Kickapoos to resist the advance of white settlement into the trans-Appalachian West after the French and Indian War.* The tribes attacked English settlements and captured several forts. The English responded by passing the Proc-lamation of 1763, which prohibited further non-Indian settlement in the region. Between 1763 and 1765 the Shawnees, Delawares, Miamis, and Kickapoos reached separate peace treaties with the English. Pontiac and the Ottawas were the last to sign the peace treaty. Although the Procla-mation of 1763 brought some peace to the frontier region, it exacerbated tensions between the English and the American colonists, who viewed the prohibition of westward migration as a violation of their rights.

Suggested Reading: Francis Jennings, *Empire of Fortune: Crowns, Colonies, and Tribes in the Seven Years War in America*, 1988.

JAMES S. OLSON

POPE REBELLION. Following several decades of Spanish assaults on their way of life, the Pueblo Indians of New Mexico staged a major re-bellion on August 10, 1680. Causes of Pueblo discontent that led to the rebellion included Spanish exploitation of the Pueblo Indians as laborers, the church/state rivalry, smallpox and other epidemics, droughts, Indians raiding towns, and the zealous attempts of Franciscans to stamp out Pueblo religious practices. One of the key leaders was Pope, a Tewa In-dian medicine man from the village of San Juan. Wanting all the Pueblos to rebel in unison, Pope devised a plan whereby messengers would de-liver knotted cords to the Pueblos. Each day one knot was to be untied until none remained, signaling the day of the attack. However, Spanish authorities learned of the scheme, which forced Pope and others to launch their attack a day earlier than planned. The Pueblo Indians went on a rampage throughout New Mexico, killing Spanish men, women, and children and destroying all vestiges of Spanish authority. Spanish survi-vors fled to Santa Fe, which was put under siege. The Indians cut off the city's water supply, finally forcing Governor Antonio de Otermin to evac-uate Santa Fe on August 21 and head south to El Paso. The Indians had killed over 400 Spaniards, including 21 priests.

The Pueblo Indians held New Mexico for twelve years, defeating Span-ish forces sent to reconquer the province. The reconquest was finally achieved by General Diego de Vargas during the period 1692–1694. In 1696 the Pueblo Indians again staged a short-lived revolt that lasted about four months and caused the deaths of twenty-one colonists and five priests. But Spanish and Pueblo relations eventually improved. For ex-ample, the encomienda system (a method of exploiting Indians on land grants) ended, and Spanish missionaries toned down their vigorous at-tacks on the Pueblo religion.

Suggested Reading: John Francis Bannon, *The Spanish Borderlands Frontier 1513–1821*, 1970; Charles W. Hackett and Charmion C. Shelby, eds., *Revolt of the Pueblo Indians of New Mexico and Otermin's Attempted Reconquest, 1680–1682*, 2 vols., 1942; Andrew L. Knaut, *The Pueblo Revolt of 1680: Conquest and Resistance in Seventeenth Century New Mexico*, 1995.

RAYMOND WILSON

POVERTY. The question of Indian poverty has bedeviled American Indian policy for more than two centuries and has had a continuing impact on Indian civil rights issues. When the technologically advanced Europeans arrived in the New World, they immediately judged Native American society—and the Native American economy—as inferior to European models. Because of their close relationship to the land and generally subsistent economies, American Indians were considered "poor" by the European colonists. The colonists had little respect for the standard of living generated by foraging and hunting economies. They had more respect for the Indian economies that revolved around agriculture, but the community property arrangements of most tribes seemed counterproductive to most Europeans. European colonists believed that free enterprise capitalism and private property was the economic system most likely to generate individual profit.

The European bias against Indian economic life helped bring about the loss of Indian land. European settlers over the course of several centuries believed that Indians did not use the environment to its fullest potential, that they "wasted" resources by not maximizing their economic use. Taking the land away from Indians seemed a reasonable step to most whites, because land that had not been employed "productively" could be put to better use. In the 1890s, for example, the Santee Sioux of Minnesota controlled more than 980,000 acres of timber land. There were less than 2,000 members of the tribe, and white settlers did not think that so much land should be controlled by so few people, especially when those people did not "work" the land. In fact, the creation of reservations* during the seventeenth, eighteenth, and nineteenth centuries was usually justified on the grounds that land was more likely to achieve its fullest economic potential under white use than under Indian control.

In the late nineteenth and twentieth centuries, reformers have usually cited Indian poverty as the rationale for changing U.S. Indian policy. Because whites regularly identified Indian culture as the source of Indian poverty, reform programs zealously engaged in cultural imperialism over the years, trying to destroy Indian languages, religions, and social structures in order to prepare them for success in a modern commercial economy. The allotment* program, for example, was promoted as a means of breaking up reservation land and redistributing it to individual Indian families, who would then work the land as farmers and ranchers and profit from it. The idea of off-reservation boarding schools* rested on the notion that Native American culture had to be elminated from the intellectual background of an Indian child before he or she could be trained for success in a modern economy. During the 1920s, the Meriam Report* indicted the allotment program as the cause of continuing Indian poverty and led to passage of the Indian Reorganization Act* of 1934 as a means of addressing the problem. During the 1950s, the persistence of reservation poverty was used by white policymakers to justify the relocation* program, which moved tens of thousands of Native Americans to cities as a way of assimilating them.

In the 1960s, reservation poverty became a major national issue, and President Lyndon B. Johnson addressed it in his Great Society's "War on Poverty." But even then, many of the government's programs were misguided. Instead of working to attract modern industrial operations to reservations, where trained Indian workers could make good money and still enjoy the cultural infrastructure of their tribe, the federal government's job training programs were designed to train young Indian men and women for jobs that would take them away from the reservations and into major cities. Because many Indians had no interest in leaving the reservations, the training programs never achieved their desired effect.

In the 1970s, 1980s, and 1990s, Indian poverty has continued to be used as an indictment of federal policy, and reformers today hope that the idea of self-determination* can address the problem while at the same time preserving Indian culture. Modern Indian activists insist that prosperity and cultural survival must be able to co-exist peacefully and even enhance one another. Whether that goal can become a reality remains to be seen.

Suggested Reading: Vine Deloria Jr. and Clifford M. Lytle, *American Indians, American Justice*, 1983; Arrell Morgan Gibson, *The American Indian: Prehistory to the Present*, 1980; Wilbur R. Jacobs, *Dispossessing the American Indian: Indians and Whites on the Colonial Frontier*, 1972; James S. Olson and Raymond Wilson, *Native Americans in the Twentieth Century*, 1984; Francis Paul Prucha, *American Indian Policy in the Formative Years: The Indian Trade and Intercourse Acts, 1790–1834*, 1962.

JAMES S. OLSON

PRATT, RICHARD HENRY. Richard Henry Pratt is considered the father of the federal government's off-reservation boarding school* system, begun in 1879, and its most ardent advocate. Pratt was born on December 6, 1840, at Rushford, New York. As a young army lieutenant, he was given the responsibility of removing Native American prisoners to Fort Marion in St. Augustine, Florida, and overseeing their detention there. While in charge of these prisoners, Pratt came to question the efficacy of keeping prisoners in chains. He felt that they would return to their savage ways if they were not exposed to a more civilized regimen. To that end Pratt removed their shackles, put them in uniforms, gave them responsibility for themselves, and began to teach them the rudiments of written and spoken English.

When those prisoners were released, Pratt suggested they might like to continue their education,* and as many of them did, he took them to the Hampton Institute in Virginia to be educated and vocationally trained alongside recently emancipated slaves. Pratt's efforts met with great success. The commandant of the institute, General Samuel Armstrong, offered him the opportunity to open his own section of the school where Indians could be trained as farmers and industrial workers. However, Pratt sensed the alienation blacks felt at the hands of whites and wanted his students to be immersed in majority culture.

Pratt appealed to the secretary of the Interior Department and the secretary of the War Department for permission to open his own school in an area where his charges might enjoy the opportunity to mix freely with members of the community. He sought and received the authorization and funding to open a school in Carlisle, Pennsylvania, which came to be known as the Carlisle Indian Industrial School. He immediately set off to secure students from tribes all over the country, believing that his students could only be assimilated if they were taken away from the influence of family and culture.

The primary tools of indoctrination were instruction in written and spoken English and training in an industrial trade, such as blacksmithing or wagonmaking. In addition, Pratt initiated a plan known as the "outing," whereby Carlisle students were sent to the homes of local farmers and tradespeople to perfect their craft and their communication skills.

Pratt was not satisfied with only one school. He traveled throughout the country extolling his program. Although he was relieved of duty as Carlisle's superintendent in 1904, Pratt continued to be the program's most zealous defender. He died on March 16, 1924.

Suggested Reading: Everett Arthur Gilcreast, *Richard Henry Pratt and Amer-*

ican Indian Policy, 1877–1906, 1967; R. H. Pratt, *Battlefield and Classroom: Four Decades with the American Indian, 1867–1904,* 1964.

PHILIP HUCKINS

PREEMPTION DOCTRINE. As interpreted by the Supreme Court, the supremacy clause of the Constitution* specifies that federal laws and treaties take precedence over state laws. During the 1940s and 1950s, this became known as preemption. It applies to Native Americans because the federal government has sole authority over Indian affairs. Therefore, tribal lands and peoples fall under federal rather than state jurisdiction. There is less clarity in the matter of federal preemption of tribal law. Although the federal government has claimed areas in which federal courts can exercise jurisdiction, such as with "major crimes," this does not necessarily preempt tribal jurisdiction but rather creates concurrent federal and tribal jurisdiction.

Suggested Reading: Felix S. Cohen, *Handbook of Federal Indian Law,* 1982.

EMILY GREENWALD

PRISONER RIGHTS. Because of poverty,* discrimination, and high rates of alcohol* abuse, the number of American Indians currently serving in federal and state penitentiaries is more than twice their percentage of the U.S. population. The largest numbers of Indian inmates can be found in Alaska, Montana, Nebraska, North Dakota, Oklahoma, South Dakota, Minnesota, and Wyoming. Most Indian inmates have been incarcerated for offenses either directly or indirectly related to substance abuse. In prison it is common for Indian inmates to coalesce according to ethnic group, and the leaders of those groups tend to be the inmates with the strongest sense of cultural identity. Those individuals usually work to raise the ethnic consciousness of other members of the group. Most prisons with significant numbers of Native American inmates allow such groups to function formally and informally. In the Utah penitentiary, for example, the group is known as the Many Feathers Club. In the Nebraska state prison, the group is known as the Native American Spiritual and Cultural Awareness Group.

Although Indian inmates, like most non-Indian inmates in recent years, have been concerned about civil rights issues, they have focused especially on questions involving religious freedom.* During the 1960s and 1970s, a series of lawsuits were filed by Indian inmates against state and federal correctional officials, demanding the right to practice tribal religions inside prison walls and to receive visits by prominent Native American religious leaders. Nebraska became the first state prison system to permit the use of sweat lodges, and by the early 1990s sweat lodges existed in the correctional facilities of twenty-one states. Other lawsuits have charged state officials with improper handling of sacred objects, such as the Sacred Pipe, and improper use of such plants as sage, sweetgrass, and cedar, which are burned in a number of religious ceremonies. Also, no state prison permits the use of peyote* by members of the Native American Church. Today, states with large Indian populations routinely provide sensitivity training sessions for correctional personnel, sponsor special feasts and holiday celebrations, and allow lower custody inmates to go on furloughs to attend special religious events.

The complexity of the issue is revealed by a 1995 decision in the Massachusetts Superior Court. Indian prisoners in the state prison there are members of the Native American Spiritual Awareness Council, which meets weekly to promote and raise the spiritual consciousness and Indian identity of its members. In the case of *Trapp et al. v. DuBois et al.*, the prisoners charged the prison administration with systematic violation of their First Amendment right to freedom of religion because the administrators would only let Indians whose tribes enjoyed federal recognition to participate in the program, and they regularly confiscated such religious articles as pipes, drums, and headbands, labeling them contraband. In its 1995 decision, the Massachusetts Superior Court issued an order allowing the use of these sacred items and permitting any Indian to participate in the Native American Spiritual Awareness Council if he or she secured the approval of "an outside spiritual advisor or sachem [leader]."

Suggested Reading: Elizabeth S. Grobsmith, "The Impact of Litigation on the Religious Revitalization of Native American Inmates in the Nebraska Department of Corrections," *Plains Anthropologist* 34 (1989), 135–47; Art Solomon, *The Indian in the White Man's Prison: A Story of Genocide*, 1993; Charles F. Wilkinson, *American Indians, Time and the Law*, 1987; John R. Wunder, *"Retained by The People": A History of American Indians and the Bill of Rights*, 1994.

JAMES S. OLSON

PUBLIC LAW 277 (1953). The question of alcohol* abuse by Indians has long troubled many non-Indians, who often nurtured vicious stereotypes about Indians' alcohol consumption. Many states prohibited the sale of alcoholic beverages to Indians, a law that smacked of discrimination to many people. During World War II, Indian soldiers purchased alcohol around the world, and when they returned to the United States the prohibition seemed particularly irritating to veterans. In 1946 the

Bureau of Indian Affairs* sponsored legislation permitting the sale or gift of alcohol to Indians outside reservations.* The bill, however, maintained the prohibition against alcohol consumption or possession on reservations. The bill never passed, but in 1953 the Eisenhower administration sponsored Public Law 277. That bill was passed in Congress on August 15, 1953. Public Law 277 lifted the restriction against selling alcohol to Indians off the reservations and allowed tribal governments to decide if alcohol could be sold on the reservations.

Suggested Reading: Wilcomb E. Washburn, *Red Man's Land, White Man's Law*, 1971.

JAMES S. OLSON

PUBLIC LAW 280 (1953). Almost since the founding of the United States, a great debate has raged over the relationship between Indian nations and reservations* and the states. Disputes have been common as to when state laws could and should be applied on the reservations. The U.S. Congress tried to resolve this problem in 1953 with the termination* program.

Public Law 280 required certain states, and allowed others on an optional basis, where large Indian populations were opposed to assume legal jurisdictions in the Indian reservations. The states would be allowed to have jurisdiction over criminal actions taking place on the reservations, but only with laws that would apply to the entire state. States were not permitted to pass special laws for the Indian reservations alone or to regulate taxation or water rights.

Public Law 280 had no provision for Native American consent for granting the states jurisdiction over reservation criminal law enforcement. President Dwight D. Eisenhower complained of this even as he signed the bill into law. Although the western states had demanded the passage of Public Law 280, the federal government granted them no funds to pay for the necessary law enforcement expenses. The reservations were given whatever law enforcement each state chose to provide, sometimes with little or no protection being offered to the Indians.

The law also made it difficult for the states to try and remove the sovereignty* of the Indian tribes altogether. The nature of Public Law 280, requiring the state laws to have general application, would force the state to affect all self-governing groups (such as counties, cities, and towns) equally.

The reaction to Public Law 280 was not favorable within the Indian community. Native Americans worried about discrimination from state officials, and the states worried about how to pay for the newly required law enforcement services. Several of the optional states declined to assume jurisdiction over Indian country.*

Suggested Reading: Russel Lawrence Barsh and James Youngblood Henderson, *The Road: Indian Tribes and Political Liberty*, 1980; James S. Olson and Raymond Wilson, *Native Americans in the Twentieth Century*, 1984; Frederick J. Stefon, "The Irony of Termination: 1943–1958," *Indian Historian* 11 (Summer 1978), 1–13; John R. Wunder, *"Retained by The People": A History of American Indians and the Bill of Rights*, 1994.

JAMES S. OLSON

PUBLIC LAW 291 (1952). Under the leadership of Dillon S. Myer* in the early 1950s, the Bureau of Indian Affairs* (BIA) moved ahead with its plans to terminate federal responsibility over Indian tribes in favor of state control. Early in 1952, House Resolution 698 asked Myer to report on the status of the BIA and to draw up a list of its services that could be ended outright or transferred to the states. Most Indians opposed both ideas, worrying about the loss of federal funding and becoming subject to local political authority, where white majorities would have significantly more power. Myer told Congress that one federal service that could be transferred to the states was health care, particularly the BIA hospitals serving Indian communities. In April 1952 Congress acted on Myer's suggestion and passed Public Law 291, which transferred BIA hospitals to state jurisdiction. Public Law 291 was one of the earliest steps in the termination* movement.

Suggested Reading: James S. Olson and Raymond Wilson, *Native Americans in the Twentieth Century*, 1984; Frederick J. Stefon, "The Irony of Termination: 1943–1958," *Indian Historian* 11 (Summer 1978), 1–13.

JAMES S. OLSON

PUBLIC LAW 568 (1954). A follow-up to Public Law 291. During the 1950s the Bureau of Indian Affairs* (BIA) enthusiastically promoted the termination* program, ending federal responsibility over Indian tribes in favor of state control. Early in 1952, House Resolution 698 asked Dillon S. Myer,* commissioner of the Bureau of Indian Affairs, to report on the status of the BIA and to draw up a list of its services that could be ended outright or transferred to the states. Myer soon reported that health care could be transferred. In April 1952 Congress passed Public Law 291, which transferred BIA hospitals to state jurisdiction. Congress followed up on Public Law 291 with Public Law 568, passed on August 5, 1954. Public Law 568 transferred the entire Indian health program from the

Bureau of Indian Affairs to the U.S. Public Health Service. The transfer involved 3,600 employees and more than $40 million in property.

Suggested Reading: James S. Olson and Raymond Wilson, *Native Americans in the Twentieth Century*, 1984; Frederick J. Stefon, "The Irony of Termination: 1943–1958," *Indian Historian* 11 (Summer 1978), 1–13.

JAMES S. OLSON

PUBLIC LAW 647 (1987). In 1987 Congress passed Public Law 647, which awarded tax-exempt status to Indian fishing rights.* Treaty-related fishing rights for Native Americans were free of federal, state, and local taxes. The legislation was in response to an attempt by the Internal Revenue Service to impose federal taxes on Indian fishing activities.

Suggested Reading: Duane Champagne, ed., *The Native North American Almanac*, 1994.

JAMES S. OLSON

PURITAN INDIAN POLICY. Initially, relations between the Puritans of Massachusetts and local Indian tribes in the 1620s and early 1630s were friendly. Indian leaders like Squanto, Samoset, and Massasoit extended assistance to the Pilgrims who founded the Plymouth colony; for their part, Puritans viewed the Indians as "savages ripe for conversion." But Puritan ethnocentrism and the European hunger for land soon set in motion the cycle of encroachment, ethnic conflict, and war that would characterize the relationship between European settlers and Indians in American history. The Pilgrims and the Puritans were Calvinists who believed in the predestined will of God. They were certain that God had elected them to salvation and to establish a model community to be emulated by the rest of the world. They expected Native Americans to conform to that vision. When Indians refused to cooperate, the Puritans were quick to see Indian activities as conspiracies with the devil. When smallpox epidemics devastated New England Indians in 1633 and 1634, many Puritans celebrated the holocaust as the will of God.

There were some exceptions. John Eliot, a Puritan missionary, translated the Bible into several local Indian languages and established several "praying" towns—essentially reservations of Christianized Indians. Roger Williams,* who was expelled from Boston to Rhode Island in 1635 for heresy and his Indian policy views, denounced Puritan Indian policy and argued that Indians had legal title to all of their land. In 1638, New Haven established a 1,200-acre reservation* for the Quinnipiac tribe, and Massachusetts set aside 8,000 acres for the Nonantums. By 1675, thousands of Native Americans were living on government-sponsored reservations in New England. On those reservations, Puritan missionaries worked diligently to convert the Indians to Christianity.

Cordial relations came to an end in 1675 with the outbreak of King Philip's War.* Tired of the constant European pressure to take Indian land, King Philip of the Wampanoags established a military coalition with several other tribes and rose up in rebellion, killing more than six hundred white settlers and burning dozens of towns. The attack brought about a bitter reprisal from white settlers, who ultimately all but eliminated, by death or exile, the Native American communities in New England.

Suggested Reading: Francis Jennings, *The Invasion of America: Indians, Colonialism, and the Cant of Conquest*, 1975; Charles M. Segal and David C. Stineback, *Puritans, Indians, and Manifest Destiny*, 1977.

JAMES S. OLSON

PUYALLUP I. See *PUYALLUP TRIBE v. DEPARTMENT OF GAME*.

PUYALLUP II. See *PUYALLUP TRIBE v. DEPARTMENT OF GAME*.

PUYALLUP III. See *PUYALLUP TRIBE v. DEPARTMENT OF GAME*.

PUYALLUP TRIBE v. DEPARTMENT OF GAME. The Supreme Court case *Puyallup Tribe v. Department of Game* is one of a series of fishing rights* cases involving the Indian tribes of the Puget Sound region in the Pacific Northwest. Washington State, following legal precedents established in the 1942 Supreme Court case *Tulee v. Washington*,* sued the Puyallup Indians for repeatedly violating state fishing regulations. In *Tulee*, the Court had ruled that even though tribes might have reserved treaty rights allowing them to fish off the reservation, the state had the right to regulate this activity. The Puyallup tribe, on the other hand, contended that such regulation of their fishing effectively denied them their treaty* rights.

In the initial *Puyallup* case in 1968, the court decided in Washington State's favor, ruling that the state did have the right to regulate off-reservation fishing. Both sides claimed victory, though, for the Court also ruled that these regulations must not discriminate against the Indians and must be necessary for conservation. Because state regulations in this case were directed only at Indians, they were considered discriminatory;

and because non-Indian fishing was not prohibited, it was clear that the regulations were not necessary for conservation. The Court's vagueness necessitated further review, resulting in two other cases known as *Puyallup II* and *Puyallup III*.

In *Puyallup II* (*Puyallup Tribe, Inc. v. Department of Game* [414 U.S. 165, 1973]), the Court clarified its views toward the state's efforts to limit only Indian fishing. It ruled in 1973 that there was discrimination, because whereas all Indian net fishing was effectively banned, hook-and-line fishing, the primary non-Indian method of fishing, was not equally regulated. In *Puyallup II* the Court reaffirmed the state's right to regulate off-reservation fishing but was much stronger in ruling that the state must not be discriminatory in that regulation.

In *Puyallup III* (*Puyallup Tribe, Inc. v. Department of Game* [433 U.S. 165, 1977]) the issues were slightly different, for the Puyallup tribe had won a separate ruling that found that the Puyallup reservation had not been extinguished, or dissolved. Now the Puyallup case, after more than a decade, became a case about state regulation of on-reservation fishing. The Court stood by its earlier decision that the state had the right to regulate fishing on and off the reservation for conservation, but the Court predicted accurately that other cases—such as *United States v. Washington* (1979), then being appealed in federal district court—would change the rights of both parties.

Suggested Reading: Fay G. Cohen, *Treaties on Trial: The Continuing Controversy over Northwest Indian Fishing Rights*, 1986; David H. Getches and Charles F. Wilkinson, *Cases and Materials in Federal Indian Law*, 1993; Donald L. Parman, *Indians and the American West in the Twentieth Century*, 1994; Charles F. Wilkinson, *American Indians, Time and the Law*, 1987.

JASON M. TETZLOFF

PYRAMID LAKE. Pyramid Lake in western Nevada was the location of a celebrated land claim case involving the Paiute Indians. The lake was part of the traditional Paiute homeland, and a treaty negotiated with the federal government in 1859 had guaranteed their title to the lake. In 1969, however, the state of California, as part of a comprehensive water management plan, negotiated an agreement with the state of Nevada to divert the Truckee River. The engineering scheme would have destroyed Pyramid Lake. The Paiutes took the case to the federal courts, and in 1972 and 1973 they won decisions requiring the stabilization of Pyramid Lake at a level in which traditional Paiute fishing needs could be fulfilled.

The case encouraged other Native Americans to fight to protect their landed estate.

Suggested Reading: James S. Olson and Raymond Wilson, *Native Americans in the Twentieth Century*, 1984.

JAMES S. OLSON

Q

QUAKER POLICY. Quakers, led by William Penn's* example, sought to deal fairly and honestly with Delaware River Valley Indians, the Lenni Lenape. Quakers purchased lands from local natives for prices arrived at in mutually accepted negotiations. Quakers recognized Indian ownership of land and respected the need to purchase it from them. The first such treaty, made in 1682, represented Quaker policy during the next eighty years. That treaty has been celebrated in Romantic era art in the form of the painting "Peaceable Kingdoms" by Edward Hicks and other romanticized versions of Penn meeting with the Indians.

The Quakers, or Society of Friends (an offshoot of the English Protestant Reformation), was established during the great ferment of the English civil wars. Led by George Fox, the Society attracted many followers during the mid-seventeenth century. William Penn joined the Quakers as a young man and brought wealth and connections to the group. Through his connections he was able to deflect the full wrath of English religious persecution from falling on the Quakers. But he was not able to protect them completely, hence the decision to establish the Pennsylvania colony as a haven for the Quakers.

Quakers rejected the prevalent European notion that Christianity gave Christians the rights to any lands in the world possessed by non-Christians. That doctrine of general land possession was used to displace Indians in settlements in the Americas during the sixteenth and seventeenth centuries. Penn insisted that Indians owned the lands along the Delaware River and that he had to secure permission from the Delawares and purchase the lands from them. Years later, after Penn surrendered control of the colony in 1701, non-Quakers and even some Quakers undermined the well-intentioned policy through fraud and deception—

even outright force—and expelled Indians from their lands. The most famous example was the Walking Purchase fraud in 1737 in which one of Penn's own sons, Thomas, defrauded the Minisink band of Delawares and some Shawnees of their lands. Such swindles occurred more and more often after 1701 as Quaker control of Pennsylvania politics began to falter, then collapse.

Suggested Reading: Arrell Morgan Gibson, *The American Indian: Prehistory to the Present*, 1980; Francis Jennings, "Brother Miquon: Good Lord!" in Richard S. Dunn and Mary Maples Dunn, eds., *The World of William Penn*, 1986; Jean R. Soderlund, ed., *William Penn and the Founding of Pennsylvania, 1680–1684: A Documentary History*, 1983.

TIMOTHY MORGAN

QUICK BEAR v. LEUPP **(1908).** During the nineteenth century, federal Indian policy allowed various Christian denominations to establish missions on Indian reservations* and to provide schools there. Indian children were required to attend those schools, which were funded by the federal government. The Roman Catholic Church was given educational responsibility for the Rosebud Sioux reservation in South Dakota. But Reuben Quick Bear, a Sioux Protestant on the reservation, claimed that federal funding for Catholic schools was a violation of separation of church and state—essentially an establishment of religion. He sued in the federal courts. The case of *Quick Bear v. Leupp* wound its way through the federal judicial sysem, and the Supreme Court rendered a decision in 1908. The Court rejected Quick Bear's claim that a federal establishment of religion had occurred, virtually ignoring his First Amendment argument. Instead, the Court argued that to cut off funding to the Rosebud Sioux reservation schools would constitute a Fifth Amendment* violation of the rights of Roman Catholics to freely exercise their religion.

Suggested Reading: Russel Lawrence Barsh and James Youngblood Henderson, *The Road: Indian Tribes and Political Liberty*, 1980; H. Barry Holt and Gary Forrester, *Digest of American Indian Law: Cases and Chronology*, 1990; Stephen L. Pevar, *The Rights of Indians and Tribes: The Basic ACLU Guide to Indian and Tribal Rights*, 1992; Charles F. Wilkinson, *American Indians, Time and the Law*, 1987; John R. Wunder, *"Retained by The People": A History of American Indians and the Bill of Rights*, 1994.

JAMES S. OLSON

R

RECLAMATION ACT OF 1902. See **NEWLANDS RECLAMATION ACT OF 1902.**

RECOGNITION. See **FEDERAL ACKNOWLEDGEMENT PROJECT.**

RED POWER. The term "Red Power" has been used to describe the Indian civil rights movement of the 1960s and 1970s, particularly the demands of Native American activists for equality, self-determination,* and the restoration of the landed estate and traditional hunting, fishing, and movement privileges. Some historians target the American Indian Chicago Conference* of 1961 as the real beginning of the modern Red Power movement, when a younger, more urban generation of Indian leaders challenged older, more traditional tribal leaders in the National Congress of American Indians* for control of the Indian rights movement. Young men like Clyde Warrior (Ponca), Melvin Thom (Paiute), and Herbert Blatchford (Navajo) left the Chicago meeting unhappy about the slow pace of change. They reconvened in Gallup, New Mexico, and formed the National Indian Youth Council,* which demanded an end to racism, ethnocentrism, and paternalism in American Indian policy and greater influence of Native Americans in the decision-making process of the Bureau of Indian Affairs.*

By the mid-1960s, Indian activists were inspired and galvanized into action by the "Black Power" movement among African Americans. Between 1964 and 1966, activists staged "fish-ins" to proclaim Indian independence from state fish and game laws. Such groups as the Indian Land Rights Association, the Alaska Federation of Natives,* and the American Indian Civil Rights Council demanded the restoration of tribal lands, denouncing the idea of monetary compensation for the loss of the Indian estate. The Pan-Indian* movement, led by people like Lehman Brightman and his United Native Americans,* worked to overcome tribal differences and construct a united, powerful Indian political constituency in the United States. In 1969, a pan-Indian group known as Indians of All Tribes* occupied Alcatraz Island* in San Francisco Bay, demanding its return to native peoples. Groups such as the American Indian Movement,* in addition to insisting on the restoration of tribal lands, demanded complete Indian control over the Bureau of Indian Affairs. In 1972, activists Hank Adams* of the "fish-ins" and Dennis Banks* of the American Indian Movement organized the "Trail of Broken Treaties"* caravan and traveled to Washington, D.C., to demand the complete revival of tribal sovereignty* by repeal of the 1871 ban on future treaties, restoration of treaty-making status to individual tribes, provision of full government services to unrecognized eastern tribes, review of all past treaty violations, restitution for those violations, and elimination of all state court jurisdiction over American Indians. They also invaded and trashed the offices of the Bureau of Indian Affairs in Washington, D.C., to dramatize their demands.

By the early 1970s, however, the Red Power movement had increasingly developed into a campaign for self-determination. Although self-determination meant different things to different people, several controlling principles emerged during the debate over its merits. First, self-determination revolved around Indian control of the government agencies dealing most directly with them. The idea of having non-Indians administering Indian health, educational, and economic programs was unacceptable to self-determinationists. Second, self-determination called for an end to assimilationist* pressures and a restoration of tribal values and culture. Allotment,* citizenship,* compensation,* termination,* and relocation* had all aimed at the annihilation of tribal cultures, and self-determinationists wanted to prevent the future re-emergence of such programs. Third, self-determinationists insisted on maintaining the trust* status of the tribes with the federal government.

Although many non-Indians saw self-determination and the continuance of the trust status as contradictory (a combination of paternalism and independence), self-determinationists were convinced that Indians needed the trust status to protect them from non-Indian majorities at the state and local levels. Finally, self-determinationists hoped to bring about the economic development of reservation* resources so that Indians could enjoy improved standards of living without compromising their cultural integrity or tribal unity. Many of the demands of self-determinationists were achieved when Congress passed the Indian Education Act* of 1972, the Indian Finance Act* of 1974, the Indian Self-Determination and Education Assistance Act of 1975, and the Indian Child Welfare Act* of 1978.

Suggested Reading: Steven Cornell, *The Return of the Native: American Indian Political Resurgence*, 1988; Laurence M. Hauptman, *The Iroquois Struggle for Survival: World War II to Red Power*, 1986; Alvin M. Josephy Jr., *Red Power: The American Indians' Fight for Freedom*, 1971; James S. Olson and Raymond Wilson, *Native Americans in the Twentieth Century*, 1984.

JAMES S. OLSON

RED PROGRESSIVISM. By the last decades of the nineteenth century, most Americans were convinced that federal Indian policy was a failure. Although the most violent confrontations between Indian and non-Indian peoples had become a thing of the past after 1890, the Indians themselves still suffered from poverty,* disease,* and racism. Their population decline continued unabated. By 1900 the number of Native Americans in the United States stood at only 250,000 people, down from as many as 2 million in 1600 and 350,000 in 1865. Late-nineteenth-century reformers—in the guise of such groups as the National Indian Defense Association,* Friends of the Indian, and the Indian Rights Association*—set out to solve the "Indian problem" by bringing about the assimilation* of Indian peoples. Their crusade resulted in the Dawes Act* of 1887 and the allotment* program, which only produced more poverty and loss of Indian land.

The Red Progressive movement was an initial reaction to the work of this generation of "Indian reformers." During the period of the progressive movement in the early 1900s, a number of Americans—Indians and non-Indians—sought to change federal policy once again.

The Four Mother Society, founded by Eufaula Harjo and Redbird Smith,* demanded that Congress permit the preservation of tribal customs, guarantee communal ownership of tribal property, and remove all restrictions on allotments so that Indians could sell or develop their land. In 1911 such prominent Indians as Charles Eastman* (Santee Sioux), Carlos Montezuma (Yavapai), and Thomas Sloan (Omaha) founded the Society of American Indians.* The Society was dedicated to improving the power and welfare of Indian peoples on their own terms. In the 1920s, as a reaction to the conservative policies of the Warren G. Harding administration, such groups as the National Council of American Indians,* the American Indian Defense Association,* and the All Indian Pueblo Council* attacked the allotment program and other government policies that had reduced so many Indians to landless poverty. The complaints of these Red Progressives eventually led to the Indian New Deal* of the 1930s.

Suggested Reading: Robert Lewis Mardock, *The Reformers and the American Indian*, 1971; James S. Olson and Raymond Wilson, *Native Americans in the Twentieth Century*, 1984; Raymond Wilson, *Ohiyesa: Charles Eastman, Santee Sioux*, 1983.

JAMES S. OLSON

RELIGIOUS FREEDOM. The issue of the Indian right to freedom of religion under the First and Fourteenth* Amendments to the Constitution* has been a vexing one in the history of Indian law. The First Amendment states that "Congress shall pass no law respecting the establishment of religion or prohibiting the free exercise thereof," and the Fourteenth Amendment, according to decades of constitutional interpretation, applies that same prohibition to state and local governments. The so-called establishment clause refers to the separation of church and state, whereas the free exercise clause guarantees individual freedom of worship. Ever since ratification of the First Amendment in 1791, however, Indians have complained, in a variety of different situations, that federal, state, and local governments have violated their civil right to religious freedom. Literally hundreds of state and federal court cases have revolved around that problem.

One broad area of concern was the land. For most American Indian tribes, their homeland possessed religious significance and constituted a sacred geography. Each tribe believed that the Great Spirit who created the world had started with their particular homeland. For the Lakota Sioux people, for example, the first act of the Great Spirit was the creation of the Black Hills* of South Dakota. For the Seminoles, it was the Everglades of Florida. The Taos Indians of New Mexico looked to Blue Lake* for the origins of the universe. When federal and state governments and white settlers promoted policies that led to the loss of Indian land, or its defilement, Indians believed such programs constituted a violation of their religious rights. Whites had a difficult time understanding such a point of view, because they tended to view land in commercial, not religious, terms.

Since the years of the Red Power,* sovereignty,* and self-determination* movements, Indian advocates have demanded restoration and protection of their land as a religious right. In 1969, for example, Hopi and Navajo traditionalists organized the Black Mesa Defense Fund* to stop strip mining on land they believed was sacred. The Taos Indians of New Mexico refused for years to accept a cash payment for the loss of their sacred Blue Lake, and instead fought a battle in the courts and on Capitol Hill for restoration of the lake and surrounding land. They succeeded in 1970 when President Richard Nixon ordered the return of the land. The Sioux Indians of South Dakota have similarly refused to accept cash payments for the Black Hills, which they consider so sacred and central to their tribal religion that to accept money would constitute a sacrilege.

Of course, Indians have not always been this successful in protecting sacred lands, as illustrated by the *Lyng v. Northwest Indian Cemetery Protective Association** case of 1988. The U.S. Forest Service wanted to construct a road through the Six Rivers National Forest in northern California to improve access for timber cutters and people interested in recreational activities. The Yurok, Tolowa, and Karuk peoples protested the decision, arguing that the road—and the increased traffic it would bring—would constitute a violation of burial sites in the area and, therefore, a violation of their religious freedom. They appealed in the federal courts, but in 1988 the Supreme Court decided in favor of the government, ruling that for a violation of religious freedom to have occurred, Indians would have to prove that the purpose of the federal government's road construction plan was to violate tribal religious values.

Closely related to the idea of sacred geography in the minds of most Native Americans is the issue of sacred artifacts and human skeletal remains. Indian activists charged that over the centuries white economic developers and social scientists have been cavalier in their treatment of Indian burial sites, sacred objects, and human remains, either destroying them or storing them away in museums. Red Power advocates early in the 1980s began calling for the return of sacred objects and human remains from federal, state, and local museums and historical societies. Their initial success came in 1989 when the Nebraska legislature passed the Unmarked Human Burial Sites and Skeletal Remains Protection Act,* which established legal protection of unmarked burial sites and ordered the repatriation* of human remains and special burial artifacts held in state-supported agencies. Other states passed similar legislation, and at the federal level Congress passed the National Museum of the American Indian Act* of 1989 and the Native American Graves Protection and Repatriation Act* of 1990.

Indian activists have also complained that federal and state government policies over the years often constituted a violation of the establishment clause of the First Amendment. During the nineteenth century the federal government, and many state governments, turned over Indian education* to Christian religious organizations. The federal government provided monetary payments to Roman Catholic, Methodist, Congregational, Baptist, and Presbyterian churches to staff Indian schools. The curriculum in those schools was always a variety of Christianity, and Indian children were prohibited from practicing their own tribal traditions and ceremonies. The Bureau of Indian Affairs* often banned particular religious ceremonies from the reservations, even if the ceremonies were central to tribal religion. It was not until the Indian New Deal* of the 1930s that the federal government abandoned most of its blatantly ethnocentric policies.

Indian activists have also argued that government policies often constituted a direct violation of the free exercise clause of the First Amendment. The *United States v. Dion*＊ case of 1986 is a good example. The Eagle Protection Act of 1942, as amended in 1962, and the Endangered Species Act of 1973 prohibit the hunting of eagles in the United States. Dwight Dion, a Yankton Sioux, was arrested and convicted for killing four bald eagles. He sued, arguing that eagle hunting is central to the religion of the Sioux people and that therefore his conviction was a violation of First Amendment rights. The Supreme Court, however, sustained the conviction, arguing that the threat of species extinction superseded Dion's First Amendment right.

Peyote* possession has been a constant source of conflict. The *People v. Woody*＊ case revolved around peyote. John Woody and a group of Navajos met near Needles, California, in 1962 and participated in a peyote ceremony. Local police discovered the meeting, arrested them, and charged them with possession of a controlled substance. They were convicted of the drug charge in a San Bernardino County court. Woody appealed the decision, and the California Supreme Court found in his favor, arguing that the state could not apply the statute outlawing the use of peyote as a religious sacrament (not unlike the bread and wine used in Christian sacramental services). Native American activists hailed the decision as a victory for Indian self-determination and civil rights.

Government policies, however, have hardly been consistent, as illustrated in *Employment Division, Department of Human Resources of Oregon, et al. v. Alfred L. Smith*＊ in 1990. Here, the Supreme Court heard a case involving the firing of a Native American from a state job because of his peyote use. The Supreme Court heard the case but decided to make no exceptions to existing state drug laws for Indian religious beliefs. The Court agreed that state governments could fire Indians who used peyote during religious ceremonies and could deny them unemployment benefits as well. Many Native American activists protested the decision and turned to Congress for redress. Congress responded in 1993 with the Religious Freedom Restoration Act,* which overturned the *Employment Division* decision. Until *Employment Division*, state and federal governments had to show a "compelling state interest" before they could implement measures that violated religious freedom. In *Employment Division* the Supreme Court had relaxed that ruling, but the new law restored the more restrictive meaning.

Yet the issue of religious freedom has not been confined to relationships among Indians, Indian tribes, and federal and state governments. In some cases individual Indians have charged their own tribal governments with violations of their religious freedom. The First and Fourteenth Amendments specifically prohibit federal, state, and local governments from violating the U.S. Constitution, but whether those same prohibitions apply to tribal governments has been a source of considerable controversy. In these debates, the rights of individual Indians have collided with legal notions of tribal sovereignty.

One of the best examples is the *Native American Church v. Navajo Tribal Council** case of 1949. The Navajo tribal council voted to ban peyote use on the reservation, believing peyotism was a threat to traditional Navajo religious beliefs and ceremonies. The Native American Church claimed that its right to use peyote and practice its religion without prosecution was protected by the First Amendment to the Constitution. The Tenth Circuit Court of Appeals disagreed. The First Amendment did indeed protect the right to freedom of religion, it held, but the protection only applied to acts of Congress. The Fourteenth Amendment only extended those same restrictions to actions by the states. The Navajo tribal council, although created under congressional action, was not restricted by either the First or the Fourteenth Amendments. The court ruled that Indian tribes occupied a level of their own between the states and the federal government and had a unique legal standing. As such, federal courts did not have jurisdiction over tribal rulings.

Another example is *Toledo et al. v. Pueblo de Jemez et al.** of 1954. Six residents of the Jemez Pueblo in New Mexico, who were practicing Protestants, charged tribal officials of the Jemez Pueblo with religious discrimination. The tribal leaders, who were Roman Catholics, claimed that Catholicism was the official tribal religion and refused to allow the Protestants to construct a chapel on the reservation, to bury their dead in the tribal cemetery, to hold church services in their homes, or to allow Protestant missionaries to visit the reservation. The Protestants filed a lawsuit against the tribal leaders, asserting violation of their right to freedom of religion. However, the federal district court in New Mexico decided against the Protestants in 1954, refusing to hear the case and essentially upholding the power of the tribal leaders.

Native American Church v. Navajo Tribal Council and *Toledo v. Jemez*, and many similar cases, led to demands for some type of resolution between the First and Fourteenth Amendment–guaranteed civil rights of individual Indians and the sovereignty of tribal governments. Two pieces of federal legislation have addressed the problem. In the Indian Civil Rights Act* of 1968, Congress authorized federal courts to intervene in intratribal disputes and limit the power of tribes to regulate internal affairs whenever the decisions of tribal governments constitute a threat to individual rights. Ten years later Congress passed the American Indian Religious Freedom Act,* which prescribed that Native Americans should come under the free exercise clause of the First Amendment to the Constitution, even when the offending party is a tribal government.

Suggested Reading: Michael M. Ames, *Cannibal Tours and Glass Boxes: The Anthropology of Museums*, 1992; Russel Lawrence Barsh and James Youngblood Henderson, *The Road: Indian Tribes and Political Liberty*, 1980; Douglas Cole, *Captured Heritage: The Scramble for Northwest Coast Artifacts*, 1985; Vine Deloria Jr., "Sacred Lands and Religious Freedom," *NARF Law Review* 16 (Spring/Summer 1991), 1–6; Vine Deloria Jr. and Clifford M. Lytle, *American Indians, American Justice*, 1983; H. Barry Holt and Gary Forrester, *Digest of American Indian Law: Cases and Chronology*, 1990; George P. Horse Capture, *The Concept of Sacred Materials and Their Place in the World*, 1989; Stephen McAndrew, "*Lyng v. Northwest Indian Cemetery Protective Association*," in H. Marcus Price, ed. *Disputing the Dead: U.S. Law on Aboriginal Remains and Grave Goods*, 1991; Phyllis Mauch Messenger, ed., *The Ethics of Collecting Cultural Property: Whose Culture? Whose Property?* 1989; Stephen L. Pevar, *The Rights of Indians and Tribes: The Basic ACLU Guide to Indian and Tribal Rights*, 1992; Wilcomb E. Washburn, *Red Man's Land, White Man's Law*, 1971; Charles F. Wilkinson, *American Indians, Time and the Law*, 1987; John R. Wunder, *"Retained by The People": A History of American Indians and the Bill of Rights*, 1994.

JAMES S. OLSON

RELIGIOUS FREEDOM RESTORATION ACT OF 1993. In 1986 the Oregon Department of Human Resources fired Alfred L. Smith, one of its employees, when it was discovered that he was a peyote* user and a

member of the Native American Church. Smith sued for violation of his
First Amendment right to the free exercise of his religious beliefs, but in
1990 the Supreme Court sided with the state of Oregon and let the firing
stand, agreeing that state governments could fire Indians who use peyote
during religious ceremonies and could deny them unemployment benefits as well. The case was known as *Employment Division, Department
of Human Resources of Oregon et al. v. Alfred L. Smith.**

Until the *Employment Division* case, federal and state governments
were required by constitutional law to prove a "compelling state interest"
before implementing any measure that restricted individual religious freedom. *Employment Division* changed that. Subsequent to the ruling, governments could impose restrictions as long as they were not exclusively
aimed at religious groups. Laws against peyote use, for example, applied
to everyone, not just to Native Americans. Religious groups could no
longer claim a First Amendment exemption to routine legislation, administrative decisions, or court decisions. Many Native American activists protested the *Employment Division* decision and turned to Congress for
redress. They were hardly alone in their protests. Religious and civil libertarian groups throughout the country—including the National Association of Evangelicals, the Unification Church, the Mormon Church, the
Southern Baptist Convention, the National Council of Churches, the
American Civil Liberties Union, the National Conference of Catholic Bish-
ops, and the American Jewish Congress—joined Native American activists
in protesting the legislation. In 1993 Congress passed the Religious Freedom Restoration Act,* which restored the "compelling state interest" rule
to government measures restricting religious freedom.

Suggested Reading: *New York Times*, November 17, 1993.

JAMES S. OLSON

RELOCATION. After World War II, assimilationists* once again came
into control of U.S. Indian policy, and they were convinced that the continued existence of reservations* as homes to hundreds of thousands of
American Indians would only serve to perpetuate poverty* and cultural
alienation. One solution, the reformers believed, was to move Indians off
the reservations and into larger cities, where they would work in industrial jobs and send their children to public schools. In 1947 Congress
appropriated money for a Labor Recruitment and Welfare Program on
the Navajo and Hopi reservations to train people for work in Denver, Los
Angeles, Phoenix, and Salt Lake City. The Hoover Commission* soon

called for an ambitious relocation program to drain surplus labor off the reservations.

In 1949 the Bureau of Indian Affairs* established urban job bureaus for Native Americans. After the terrible blizzards of 1949–1950 Congress passed the Navajo-Hopi Long-Range Rehabilitation Act* of 1950, which provided funds to relocate thousands of Indians to cities where they could find jobs. By 1952 the Bureau of Indian Affairs was providing job training, moving expenses, housing location assistance, and a thirty-day subsistence allowance to Indians willing to leave the reservations and relocate to the cities. By 1960 more than 35,000 Indians had been relocated to Denver, Phoenix, Albuquerque, San Francisco, Dallas, Los Angeles, Oklahoma City, Tulsa, and Chicago.

The program did not live up to the expectations of its promoters. First, few reservation Indians trusted the government enough to willingly participate in the program, and most Indians felt comfortable on the reservations. City life had little appeal to most of them. Urban life, with its materialism, anonymity, and emphasis on individual aggrandizement, proved to be a cultural shock to most relocated Indians. Also, most relocated Indians experienced a new kind of poverty in the cities. On the reservations they were accustomed to free medical care and subsidized rent and utility bills, but in the cities they found themselves without that safety net, trying to make a living with low-paying, unskilled, and often seasonal employment. More than 10,000 Indians who relocated under the program eventually returned to the reservations.

Suggested Reading: Joan Ablon, "American Indian Relocation: Problems of Dependency and Management in the City," *Phylon* 26 (Winter 1965); Larry W. Burt, *Tribalism in Crisis: Federal Indian Policy, 1953–1961*, 1982; Elaine M. Neils, *Reservation to City: Indian Migration and Federal Relocation*, 1971.

JAMES S. OLSON

REPATRIATION. During the 1970s and 1980s, Red Power* advocates complained bitterly that over the years federal, state, and local agencies, as well as private museums, had badly abused Indian cultural artifacts and the remains of dead Indians. Most experts believe the remains of as many as 600,000 Native Americans are stored in the vaults of university, museum, historical society, and private collections in the United States. Indian activists began to demand the repatriation of those artifacts and remains—their removal from storage and return to the tribes who had sovereignty* over them. Many anthropologists and geneticists protested repatriation, arguing that the remains were important to scientific research; but Indian activists were adamant, claiming that storage of such remains was racist and anachronistic, a holdover from an earlier time when whites wanted to study Indian skeletons to prove their inferiority.

In 1989, Red Power activists experienced their first legislative success when the Nebraska legislature passed the Unmarked Human Burial Sites and Skeletal Remains Protection Act,* which established legal protection of unmarked burial sites and ordered the repatriation of human remains and special burial artifacts held by state-supported agencies. Many other states soon followed suit. At the federal level, Congress passed the National Museum of the American Indian Act* of 1989, which established a special museum for American Indians and ordered the Smithsonian Institution to begin a repatriation process. A Repatriation Review Committee was established at the federal level to monitor the process. Congress then passed the Native American Graves Protection and Repatriation Act* to protect all Native American burial sites on federal property and to implement repatriation policies in all federal agencies and all public and private bodies receiving federal support.

Suggested Reading: Michael M. Ames, *Cannibal Tours and Glass Boxes: The Anthropology of Museums*, 1992; Douglas Cole, *Captured Heritage: The Scramble for Northwest Coast Artifacts*, 1985; George P. Horse Capture, *The Concept of Sacred Materials and Their Place in the World*, 1989; Phyllis Mauch Messenger, ed., *The Ethics of Collecting Cultural Property: Whose Culture? Whose Property?* 1989; H. Marcus Price, ed., *Disputing the Dead: U.S. Law on Aboriginal Remains and Grave Goods*, 1991.

JAMES S. OLSON

REPEAL OF TERMINATION ACT. Although the demise of the termination* movement began during the first presidential administration of Richard M. Nixon, Congress never formally ended the program legislatively. Individual tribes had had specific termination orders repealed, but there had never been a blanket repeal. On April 28, 1988, however, Congress repaired the oversight by passing Public Law 100–297, the Repeal of Termination Act. It specifically repealed House Concurrent Resolution 108* passed on August 1, 1953. It also prohibited the Bureau of Indian Affairs* from terminating, consolidating, or transferring its schools to other jurisdictions without tribal consent.

SUGGESTED READING: John R. Wunder, *"Retained by The People": A History of American Indians and the Bill of Rights*, 1994.

JAMES S. OLSON

RESERVATION. Ever since the seventeenth century in colonial America, the "reservation" concept has been central to public Indian policy. At its most fundamental level, a reservation is a well-defined body of public land set aside for the exclusive use of an Indian tribe or tribes. Between 1776 and 1871 in the United States, reservations were legally viewed as the land of a sovereign nation. Since 1871, when the United States ended the sovereign* status of the Indian tribes, the reservations have been legally defined as tribal property enjoying the special trust* protection of the federal government. By virtue of that trust protection the reservations have been exempt from the police powers, taxing authority, and political jurisdiction of surrounding state and local governments. That exempt status has been a source of continuing controversy between reservation Indians and state and local authorities.

Reservations were created whenever the competition for land between Indians and non-Indians became intense and violent. Over the centuries, a pattern repeated itself many times. As white settlers encroached on Indian land and Indians tried to defend their property, violence escalated. To stabilize the situation, government officials promised Indians that if they agreed to vacate their existing homeland and take up new lands farther west, they would be guaranteed title to the "reserved lands" forever. In 1644, for example, the government of colonial Virginia pushed the Powhatan Indians north of the York River, reserving that land for them and promising them exclusive use of it forever. Within a few years, however, white settlers were pouring across the York River and once again putting pressure on Powhatan land, and the cycle of ethnic conflict and warfare repeated itself. Similar promises were made to other Indian tribes hundreds of times in American history. The so-called Indian reservations at first constituted land in which whites had no interest, but time, technology, resource discovery, white population growth, and the westward movement soon rendered those reservations attractive to white settlers—and the cycle repeated itself. Some tribes were moved again and again to new reservations, always with the promise that this time they would be left alone on their land.

By the late nineteenth century, many reformers had decided that the continued existence of the reservations was perpetuating the alienation of Indians and whites and preventing the assimilation* of Native Americans into the larger society. The allotment* program, best represented by the Dawes Act* of 1887, proposed to break up the reservations into small parcels of land, which would then be distributed in fee simple title* to individual Indian heads of families. Excess land not given to individual Indians would be distributed to whites. The allotment program existed for almost a half-century, and in the process nearly 100 million acres of reservation land were redistributed. It was not until the so-called Indian New Deal* of the 1930s that the allotment program was discontinued.

After World War II, however, new threats were posed to the reservation system. Federal government officials, anxious to promote assimilation, once again decided to take aim at reservations. They were convinced that reservation Indians were less likely to assimilate into the larger society than nonreservation Indians. The relocation* program of the 1950s and 1960s encouraged Indians to leave the reservation and resettle in such larger cities as Los Angeles, Dallas, Phoenix, Salt Lake City, Seattle, and Denver, where they would work in industrial jobs and their children would attend public schools with non-Indian children. Tens of thousands of reservation Indians participated in the program. At the same time the federal government promoted the termination* program, which was designed to end the special legal status of the reservations and subject Indians and their reservation lands to state and local jurisdiction. Indian leaders vociferously resisted termination, but it was not until the early 1970s that the program came to an end. Since then, no serious threat to the survival of the reservations has come from white interest groups. Today, more than 750,000 Native Americans live on nearly three hundred federal reservations and dozens of state reservations.

Suggested Reading: Robert A. Trennert Jr., *Alternative to Extinction: Federal Indian Policy and the Beginnings of the Reservation System, 1846–1851*, 1975; U.S. Department of Commerce, *Federal and State Indian Reservations: An EDA Handbook*, 1971.

JAMES S. OLSON

RESERVED RIGHTS DOCTRINE. The "reserved rights doctrine" involves the issue of Indian water rights.* American water law evolved in the seventeenth and eighteenth centuries in the moist climate of the eastern states, where rainfall was abundant. What became known as appropriative water rights awarded the priority or senior water rights to the first user on the watershed to put the water to "beneficial use." Beneficial use included domestic use, irrigation, and livestock support. Water was abundant enough in the East to allow for appropriative rights, because downstream users still had plenty of water to meet their needs.

It was a different story in the water-scarce states of the West. Appropriative rights there were often detrimental to Indian water rights. Large-scale irrigation upstream often consumed all the available water, leaving downstream Indian tribes with insufficient water resources to meet their needs. In 1908 the Supreme Court heard the *Winters v. United States** case and established the principle of "reserved rights" to compete with the notion of appropriative rights. The Supreme Court ruled that Indian tribes had a "reserved right" to all their water needs. Although most statutes creating reservations* did not mention water rights, such water rights were, in the Court's opinion, implied because the land would have little value without water. In all cases, the Court ordered, sufficient water had to be able to reach the reservation to fill tribal economic needs. The formal name for the right was the "implied reservation of water" doctrine.

Suggested Reading: Lloyd Burton, *American Indian Water Rights and the Limits of the Law*, 1993; William C. Canby Jr., *American Indian Law in a Nutshell*, 1988; William L. Kahrl, *Water and Power: The Conflict Over Los Angeles' Water Supply in the Owens Valley*, 1982; Donald L. Parman, *Indians and the American West in the Twentieth Century*, 1994; Charles F. Wilkinson, *American Indians, Time and the Law*, 1987.

JAMES S. OLSON

ROSEBUD SIOUX TRIBE v. KNEIP (1977). In recent years Indian activists have frequently worked to get the federal courts to enforce agreements made in the distant past. It was not at all uncommon, for example, for treaties* in the eighteenth and nineteenth centuries to promise tribes title to their lands for "time immemorial," only to have subsequent agreements extinguish those titles. The enforceability of ancient treaties generated considerable legal and political controversy during the decades of the Red Power* movement. An important case in establishing legal guidelines for determining enforceability was *Rosebud Sioux Tribe v. Kneip* in 1977. The case involved the external boundaries of the Rosebud Sioux reservation in South Dakota. The initial reservation* boundaries had been established by treaty, but in 1904, 1907, and 1910 specific acts of Congress opened much of the reservation to white homesteaders. By the 1970s, the population of four counties in South Dakota that had once been part of the reservation was overwhelmingly non-Indian.

The Rosebud Sioux tribal council sued in the federal courts, claiming that the transfer of reservation land titles to non-Indians living in those four counties was invalid. However, the Supreme Court ruled in favor of the non-Indian landowners, arguing that specific congressional legislation had essentially disestablished reservation title to those lands and that "the longstanding assumption of jurisdiction by the State over an area that is over 90 percent non-Indian, both in population and land use, not only demonstrates the parties' understanding of the meaning of the Act, but has created justifiable expectations which should not be upset by so strained a reading of the Acts of Congress as petitioner urges."

Suggested Reading: Russel Lawrence Barsh and James Youngblood Henderson, *The Road: Indian Tribes and Political Liberty*, 1980; Vine Deloria Jr. and Clifford M. Lytle, *American Indians, American Justice*, 1983; H. Barry Holt and Gary Forrester, *Digest of American Indian Law: Cases and Chronology*, 1990; Stephen L. Pevar, *The Rights of Indians and Tribes: The Basic ACLU Guide to Indian and Tribal Rights*, 1992; Wilcomb E. Washburn, *Red Man's Land, White Man's Law: A Study of the Past and Present Status of the American Indian*, 1971; Charles F. Wilkinson, *American Indians, Time and the Law*, 1987; John R. Wunder, *"Retained by The People": A History of American Indians and the Bill of Rights*, 1994.

JAMES S. OLSON

S

SALTER, JOHN. See **GRAY, JOHN HUNTER.**

SAND CREEK MASSACRE. During the 1860s, major confrontations between non-Indian settlers and Indians became more and more common in the Great Plains. Perhaps the worst episode of racist genocide occurred in eastern Colorado, where Cheyennes and Arapahoes resisted attempts at relocation* to reservations.* Many Coloradans agreed with militia officer John M. Chivington, who also happened to be a Methodist minister, that all Indians were "vermin deserving of extermination." In November 1864, Chivington decided to practice what he preached. He led a militia attack against a Cheyenne village at Sand Creek. Chief Black Kettle* headed the village. In an orgy of violence, with Black Kettle and others waving white flags of surrender, Chivington's men slaughtered 450 Cheyenne men, women, and children. Only a few escaped.

The Sand Creek Massacre precipitated an enormous political controversy in the United States. Large numbers of people sided with the Indians, and political pressure mounted for a more humane approach to Indian affairs. In 1867 Congress launched a special investigation of the Sand Creek Massacre, and what resulted was establishment of the Indian Peace Commission, a federal agency designed to engage in peaceful negotiations with the Indian tribes.

Suggested Reading: Duane P. Schultz, *Month of the Freezing Moon: The Sand Creek Massacre*, 1990.

JAMES S. OLSON

SELECTIVE SERVICE. During the twentieth century, when many Indian leaders have worked to preserve the notion of tribal political sovereignty,* the existence of the Selective Service posed a dilemma. The federal government's policy of drafting young men into the military service of the United States seemed, for many Native Americans, to challenge tribal sovereignty. They believed that if, indeed, an Indian tribe was a sovereign nation, its members should be immune from coerced military service on behalf of another nation. But federal law never recognized the immunity of Indian men from draft laws, and Selective Service laws during World War I, World War II, the Korean War, and the Vietnam War brought tens of thousands of American Indians into the military. To preserve their own sense of sovereignty, a number of tribal councils passed resolutions subjecting their tribal members to selective service laws. During World War I, the Iroquois went so far as to declare war on Germany in order to protect their sense of sovereignty.

The question of whether or not American Indians are subject to the Selective Service Act was decided in the 1944 case of *Green v. United States*. Warren Green, an Onondaga, protested the Selective Service Act in federal court, arguing that because the Onondagas are a sovereign and independent nation, he was not subject to the laws of the United States. The Supreme Court decided otherwise, reasoning that members of the Iroquois Confederacy (to which the Onondagas belong) are citizens of the United States and subject to its laws.

Suggested Reading: James S. Olson and Raymond Wilson, *Native Americans in the Twentieth Century*, 1984; Gary C. Stein, "The Indian Citizenship Act of 1924," *New Mexico Historical Review* 47 (July 1972).

JAMES S. OLSON

SELF-DETERMINATION. During the nineteenth century a general disregard and disrespect for tribal independence and tribal governance characterized the political leadership in Washington, D.C. The history of federal agencies dealing with Native Americans indicates that early in this period all pertinent branches of the federal government were involved: the president, the state and war departments, Congress, and the courts. Most executive activities related to Native Americans were gradually concentrated in the Bureau of Indian Affairs* (BIA). During the twentieth century, because of the paternalistic, assimilationist posture of the BIA, Native Americans had suffered through the compensation,* termination,* and relocation* programs, all of which had only served to further disempower them.

The bankruptcy of federal Indian policy became abundantly clear in the 1960s. Investigations into reservation living conditions uncovered serious problems and inconsistences. Disturbingly low levels of education, health, and income characterized Native American life. Some of the problems directly involved the government administration of Indian affairs. The termination and relocation programs of the late 1940s and 1950s had weakened reservation economies and placed tens of thousands of Indians in alien, urban settings. Public school districts trying to educate Native American children were staffed by non-Indian teachers and administrators woefully unprepared to provide the curricula and environment necessary for Indian educational achievement. BIA services on reservations were often subcontracted out to non-Indian business firms, which siphoned off high percentages of resources and often administered programs in racist, condescending ways.

Late in the 1960s, Indian activists began to demand that Native Americans assume control of the federal government's Indian policies and programs. The occupation of Alcatraz Island* in 1969 by Indians of All Tribes* marked a key focus of the Red Power* movement. The clarion call of Native American activism in the 1970s was "self-determination"— the right of Indians to shape federal policies and to administer directly the government programs affecting their lives. Congress responded to their demands in 1975 with the Indian Self-Determination and Education Assistance Act.

The introductory section of the legislation stated clearly the intention of Congress in passing the Indian Self-Determination and Education Assistance Act:

> The Congress hereby recognizes the obligation of the United States to respond to the strong expression of the Indian people for self-determination by assuring maximum Indian participation in the direction of educational as well as other Federal services to Indian communities so as to render such services more responsive to the needs and desires of those communities.
>
> The Congress declares its commitment to the maintenance of the Federal Government's unique and continuing relationship with and responsibility to the Indian people through the establishment of a meaningful Indian self-determination policy which will permit an orderly transition from Federal domination of programs for and services to Indians to effective and meaningful participation by the Indian people in the planning, conduct, and administration of those programs and services.

In particular, the act established a new relationship between federal agencies and tribal authorities. By permitting tribal governments to negotiate and contract directly with the BIA and the Department of Health, Education, and Welfare for social welfare services, the act restored tribalism in an important legal sense and gave Native Americans a greater measure of control over federal programs. Tribal governments could set goals, priorities, and administrative procedures for social and educational programs, and tribal governments could restructure and even reject those programs when they concluded that tribal needs were not being met. The act also permitted the federal government to make direct cash grants to tribal governments for training programs in financial management, administrative control, and personnel supervision; for the acquisition of any land needed to fulfill social services programs; and for the construction and operation of health facilities. Tribal leaders were to be in direct control of the programs. Finally, the Indian Self-Determination and Education Assistance Act made a number of changes in education programs. All school districts enjoying contracts under the Johnson-O'Malley Act* of 1934 were required to guarantee that funds received for Native American students were to be used only for Native American students; and, where Native Americans did not control school boards, an Indian Parents Committee had to be established and consulted on all decisions affecting Native American children.

Suggested Reading: American Indian Policy Review Commission, *Final Report*, 1977; Roxanne Dunbar Ortiz, *Indians of the Americas: Human Rights and Self-Determination*, 1984; Jack D. Forbes, *Native Americans and Nixon: Presidential Politics and Minority Self-Determination, 1969–1972*, 1981; William T. Hagan, "Tribalism Rejuvenated: The Native American since the Era of Termination," *Western Historical Quarterly* 12 (January 1981), 5–16; Hurst Hannum, *Autonomy, Self-Determination and Sovereignty: The Accommodation of Conflicting Rights*, 1990; Indian Self-Determination and Education Assistance Act, January 4, 1975, 25 USC 450; Sharon O'Brien, *American Indian Tribal Governments*, 1989; Kenneth R. Philp, ed., *Indian Self-Rule: First-Hand Accounts of Indian-White Relations from Roosevelt to Reagan*, 1986; Theodore W. Taylor, *American Indian Policy*, 1983.

DAVID RITCHEY

SEMINOLE TRIBE v. FLORIDA (1996). In the case of *Seminole Tribe v. Florida* in 1996, the Supreme Court upheld a decision of the Court of Appeals for the Eleventh Circuit. In 1994 the Court of Appeals had ruled that the Seminole tribe of Florida could not file suit under the Indian Gaming Regulatory Act* requiring Florida to negotiate a contract to open a casino on Seminole land. According to the justices, the section of the Indian Gaming Regulatory Act allowing the Seminoles to file suit was a violation of the Eleventh Amendment to the Constitution.* The Indian Gaming Regulatory Act authorized tribes to file suit in federal courts against state governments that did not negotiate in good faith about opening and operating gambling casinos on reservations.* Chief Justice William Rehnquist, who wrote the majority opinion, claimed that the law violated the Eleventh Amendment by bringing about an unacceptable incursion on state sovereignty.*

Suggested Reading: *New York Times*, March 28, 1996.

JAMES S. OLSON

SEMINOLE TRIBE OF FLORIDA v. BUTTERWORTH (1981). The *Seminole Tribe of Florida v. Butterworth* case was an important development in the process of defining tribal sovereignty.* State authorities opposed the opening of bingo parlors on Seminole land in Florida, but the tribe appealed in the federal courts. In its 1981 decision on the case, the Supreme Court ordered that tribal sovereignty guaranteed the Seminole right to engage in gaming enterprises, because state statutes did not already contain an outright ban on all gambling in Florida. In the absence of such a statute, the Seminoles could proceed. The decision led to a boom in Indian bingo parlors around the country.

Suggested Reading: Duane Champagne, ed., *Chronology of Native North American History*, 1994.

JAMES S. OLSON

SENECA NATION OF INDIANS v. UNITED STATES (1965). As part of its claim against the U.S. government in this case, the Seneca Nation demanded, before the Indian Claims Commission, compensation* for land lost before the ratification of the federal Constitution.* The Senecas argued that they had been defrauded by the colony of New York during the colonial period and that the U.S. government was responsible for compensation. For its part, the U.S. government was not willing to assume liability for the actions of colonial governments functioning under British sovereignty* or during the period of the Articles of Confederation.* The Court of Claims, in its 1965 decision in *Seneca Nation of Indians v. United States*, agreed with the government. The Indian Claims Commission Act of 1946, the court argued, did not cover the pre-1789 claims. Before that time, the Articles of Confederation had not assumed any fiduciary responsibility for Indian lands.

Suggested Reading: Russel Lawrence Barsh and James Youngblood Henderson, *The Road: Indian Tribes and Political Liberty*, 1980; Vine Deloria Jr. and

Clifford M. Lytle, *American Indians, American Justice*, 1983; H. Barry Holt and Gary Forrester, *Digest of American Indian Law: Cases and Chronology*, 1990; Stephen L. Pevar, *The Rights of Indians and Tribes: The Basic ACLU Guide to Indian and Tribal Rights*, 1992; Wilcomb E. Washburn, *Red Man's Land, White Man's Law: A Study of the Past and Present Status of the American Indian*, 1971; Charles F. Wilkinson, *American Indians, Time and the Law*, 1987; John R. Wunder, *"Retained by The People": A History of American Indians and the Bill of Rights*, 1994.

JAMES S. OLSON

***SEQUOYAH v. TENNESSEE VALLEY AUTHORITY* (1980).** One of the main concerns of Red Power* advocates over the years has been the protection of the Indian landed estate. Indians have lost their lands because of economic development, or its use has been compromised because of economic development. This has often been a critical issue to Indian religious practitioners because for many tribes the ancestral lands possess sacred, religious significance. The *Sequoyah v. Tennessee Valley Authority* case of 1980 involved such a dispute. As part of its ongoing program to develop flood control, hydroelectric power, and irrigation systems, the Tennessee Valley Authority (TVA) proposed in the 1970s to permanently flood lands the Cherokees, a subgroup of the Sequoyah, considered sacred. They tried to block TVA development plans, arguing that the project would deny their First Amendment freedom of religion rights by taking away from them land they considered central to their religious beliefs. Federal courts, however, decided in favor of the Tennessee Valley Authority.

Suggested Reading: Vine Deloria Jr., "Sacred Lands and Religious Freedom," *NARF Law Review* 16 (Spring/Summer 1991), 1–6; Howard Stambor, "Manifest Destiny and American Indian Religious Freedom: *Sequoyah, Badoni*, and the Drowned Gods," *American Indian Law Review* 10 (1982), 59–89; Christopher Vecsey, *Handbook of American Indian Religious Freedom*, 1991.

JAMES S. OLSON

SITTING BULL. Sitting Bull, or Tatanka Yotanka, was a religious and political leader of the Hunkpapa Sioux. During his lifetime (ca. 1834–1890) he established his status within his tribe by conducting military exploits against other tribes and by fostering the general perception among the Sioux that he had considerable spiritual connections and power. He was the leader of the Strong Hearts, a tribal warrior society, and he was one of the principal chiefs of the Lakota. As such, he guided the Hunkpapa from the 1850s until his death in 1890. He signed the Treaty of Fort Laramie* of 1868 and was one of the leaders of Indian protests when the treaty was repeatedly broken by goldseekers in the Black Hills* region.

Sitting Bull was considered the spiritual leader of the battle of the Little Bighorn in 1876, when George Armstrong Custer and his forces were annihilated by an Indian coalition. Although he did not take part in the battle, government troops considered him a key symbol of the Indian resistance. Sitting Bull and a small band of Hunkpapa Sioux escaped to Canada, but the near-starvation of his people caused him to finally surrender in 1881. He was allowed to return to the Standing Rock reservation in 1883. He toured with "Buffalo Bill" Cody's Wild West Show for one year and then returned to the reservation,* where he was an active and outspoken leader of the Indian opposition to further land cessions.

Indian agency officials ordered his arrest in 1890. At the time, large numbers of Sioux were converting to the Ghost Dance religion, which predicted the destruction of all whites. U.S. Army officials worried about a Sioux uprising, which they thought Sitting Bull might lead. A struggle broke out during the arrest, and Sitting Bull and twelve others were killed. However, Sitting Bull's death did not end his influence. He became a martyr to other Indians who protested federal government policies, and a symbol of government oppression. Sitting Bull's death furthered tensions that led to the battle of Wounded Knee* in December 1890.

Suggested Reading: Robert M. Utley, *The Lance and the Shield: The Life and Times of Sitting Bull*, 1993; Stanley Vestal, *Sitting Bull: Champion of the Sioux*, 1957; James S. Welch, *Killing Custer*, 1994.

JASON M. TETZLOFF

SIXTH AMENDMENT. The Sixth Amendment to the U.S. Constitution* was ratified and went into effect in 1791. It essentially guaranteed the rights of individual citizens against the powers of the new federal government. More specifically, it guaranteed all U.S. citizens the rights to a speedy and public trial, to a jury trial, to be fully informed of all criminal charges being brought against them, to be confronted with the witnesses against them, to be able to compel the testimony of witnesses in their favor, and to have the assistance of legal counsel for their defense, even if they cannot afford it. The Fourteenth Amendment,* ratified in 1868, guaranteed these same individual rights against abuse by state and local governments.

A controversial issue in constitutional history, however, has been whether or not Indian tribal governments fell under the same legal requirements. In the *Talton v. Mayes** case of 1896, the Supreme Court decided that the Bill of Rights* applied to the actions of federal and state governments, not tribal governments, because tribes are not subordinate bodies of those governments. Moreover, after 1924, when all American Indians had become citizens of the United States, controversy frequently erupted over whether a tribal government was bound by the Fifth* and Fourteenth Amendments. Hundreds of cases revolving around the issue made their way through the federal court system, and beginning in the early 1960s, Congress heard numerous complaints by individual tribal members who contended that tribal officials themselves were abusive and tyrannical. Congressional hearings were convened in 1962 to investigate these complaints of misconduct, and several congressmen concluded that individual Indians needed "some guaranteed form of civil rights against the actions of their own governments."

In 1965 the case of *Madeline Colliflower v. John Garland, Sheriff of County of Blaine, Montana,** provided new impetus for civil rights legislation. Colliflower, a Gros Ventre Indian living on the Fort Belknap reservation in Blaine County, Montana, was arrested by Indian police* for refusing to remove her cattle from land leased by another individual on the reservation. After being convicted by a tribal court, she claimed in federal district court that her Sixth and Fourteenth Amendment rights had been violated because the tribal court had not given her the right to legal counsel and had refused to confront her with the witnesses against her. Because the federal district court was uncertain of its jurisdiction over reservation legal institutions, the case went to the Court of Appeals. Ultimately the Court of Appeals decided that the federal district did indeed have jurisdiction, holding that tribal courts were extensions of a federal agency and that, as such, they were subject to due process requirements. Individual Indians, therefore, enjoyed due process rights in tribal courts as well as in non-Indian jurisdictions.

The decision led directly to passage of the Indian Civil Rights Act* of 1968, which was designed to "ensure that the American Indian is afforded the broad Constitutional rights secured to other Americans . . . [in order to] protect individual Indians from arbitrary and unjust actions of tribal governments." Legislatively, it confers certain rights on all persons who are subject to the jurisdiction of a tribal government, and it authorizes federal courts to enforce these rights.

The Indian Civil Rights Act has fundamentally changed the procedural aspects of the tribal judicial system. Prior to its enactment, procedural uniformity was nonexistent: tribes would invariably employ their own methods of conflict resolution. However, the Indian Civil Rights Act requires that all tribes adhere to certain procedural standards. Tribal courts must advise criminal defendants of their right to a trial by jury, write their criminal laws in clear and certain language, honor a criminal defendant's right against self-incrimination, prohibit the trial judge from also being the prosecutor, and maintain complete records of judicial proceedings.

Suggested Reading: Russel Lawrence Barsh and James Youngblood Henderson, *The Road: Indian Tribes and Political Liberty*, 1980; Vine Deloria Jr. and Clifford M. Lytle, *American Indians, American Justice*, 1983; H. Barry Holt and Gary Forrester, *Digest of American Indian Law: Cases and Chronology*, 1990; Stephen L. Pevar, *The Rights of Indians and Tribes: The Basic ACLU Guide to Indian and Tribal Rights*, 1992; Wilcomb E. Washburn, *Red Man's Land, White Man's Law*, 1971; Charles F. Wilkinson, *American Indians, Time and the Law*, 1987; John R. Wunder, *"Retained by The People": A History of American Indians and the Bill of Rights*, 1994.

JAMES S. OLSON

SKEEM v. UNITED STATES (1921). A significant decision in terms of Indian water rights.* On May 2, 1921, the United States brought suit on behalf of Indians of the Fort Hall reservation in Idaho to protect their rights to the waters of a creek for irrigation purposes. These Indians had taken up parcels of land under the terms of the Fort Bridger Treaty of 1869, and the remainder of the tribal lands in this southern area of the reservation* not taken up by Indians had been ceded to the U.S. government by the treaties* of 1889 and 1898. The government had subsequently made the lands available to homesteaders and real estate, mining, quarrying, and timber interests. Article 8 of the treaty of 1898 provided that "water from the streams on that portion of the reservation now sold which is necessary for irrigating on land actually cultivated and in use shall be reserved for Indians now using the same, so long as said Indians remain where they now live."

The appellants argued that the Indians were entitled to only the amount of water they had been using for irrigation purposes at the time the treaty was ratified. The District Court ruled and the Circuit Court affirmed that because this was not a grant *to* the Indians but a grant *by* the Indians to the United States, any ambiguity in the language of the treaty ought to be construed in favor of the Indians. The Indians kept their water rights. The court noted that the purpose of the treaties was to entice the Indians to give up their nomadic ways and till the soil, and that the treaties should be construed so as to make it possible for the Indians to eventually cultivate the whole of their lands. Thus three main principles are affirmed by this case: (1) all rights not specifically granted by a treaty granting Indian lands to the U.S. government are reserved to the Indians; (2) treaty provisions respecting lands occupied and culti-vated by Indians where the purpose of the government was to induce the Indians to relinquish their nomadic habits and till the soil should be liberally construed in favor of the Indian occupants; and (3) where am-biguity exists in a treaty granting Indian lands to the U.S. government, the treaty's language should not be interpreted to the prejudice of the Indians. *Skeem* also established that Indian water rights may be leased to non-Indians along with the lease of the actual land.

Suggested Reading: 273 *Federal Reporter* 2d, 93; David H. Getches and Charles F. Wilkinson, *Cases and Materials on Federal Indian Law*, 1993.

J. JEFFERSON MACKINNON

SLAVERY. Slavery was practiced by some North American Indian tribes, particularly the Pacific Northwest peoples, in the context of lifetime ser-vitude. However, many of their "slaves" were captives from another tribe who worked as servants to a family or individual but then were ultimately taken into the village or tribe as adoptees or by marriage.

The practice of slavery in North America, however, received powerful impetus with the encroachment of Europeans starting with the Spanish in the Southeast in the late sixteenth century. One attraction to North America for the Spanish and, later, European immigrants was enslave-ment of coastal and Piedmont Indian peoples. They could be sold in the West Indies or made to work on plantations and mines in the colonial South. Europeans enslaved Indians from New England to South Carolina, although only the South Carolinians were most consistent about perpet-uating the institution. The Spanish enslaved Indian peoples in Florida, many of whom (such as the Timucua) became extinct in part due to the enslavement. New England Puritans enslaved Pequots and other Indians resisting their expansionism during the seventeenth century; they sold the slaves in the West Indies. Chesapeake settlers also enslaved Indian peoples during the seventeenth century, either selling them in the West Indies or working them on tobacco plantations in the Chesapeake area.

North and South Carolinians sold Indians as slaves, especially those on whom they made war during the seventeenth and early eighteenth cen-turies. It is estimated that Carolinians sent some 12,000 Indian slaves to the West Indies by 1720. At the same time, historians calculate that Indian slaves numbered about 17 percent of the total Carolina slave force by 1720.

Indians as well enslaved Africans and other Indians. Some southern

Indians had sizeable slave populations before and after removal to Indian Territory* in the nineteenth century. Indians and escaped African slaves lived in mixed communities in what was Spanish Florida before 1819. They raided across the international border to bring African and Indian slaves (whom they then freed) to their communities, until they became part of the United States in 1819.

But enslavement of Indians was never as extensive as enslavement of Africans because Indians (1) died so readily from Eurasian and African diseases, (2) could easily melt into the environment, and (3) did not possess the agricultural skills that Africans had.

Suggested Reading: Arrell Morgan Gibson, *The American Indian: Prehistory to the Present*, 1980; Winthrop D. Jordan, *White over Black: American Attitudes toward the Negro, 1550–1812*, 1969; Timothy Silver, *A New Face on the Countryside: Indians, Colonists, and Slaves in South Atlantic Forests, 1500–1800*, 1990.

TIMOTHY MORGAN

SMITH, REDBIRD. A champion of Indian legal and political rights, Redbird Smith, a Cherokee, was born outside Fort Smith, Arkansas, in 1850. When the Curtis Act* of 1898 brought allotment* to the Five Civilized Tribes, including the Cherokee, Smith led the resistance movement against the law. He helped revive the Cherokee Keetoowah Society to proclaim Indian sovereignty,* protect tribal government and Cherokee lands, and preserve Cherokee religion and culture. The removal of the Cherokees to Indian Territory* first prompted Smith's campaign. He refused to recognize the right of the U.S. government to break up the tribal estate and distribute the land among individual Indians. Employing nonviolent tactics of civil disobedience, he tried to disrupt the distribution process. Federal authorities arrested him in 1902. Although allotment continued, Smith emerged as an important activist among other Cherokees. In 1908 he was elected principal chief. Four years later he founded the Four Mothers Society to promote Cherokee legal and political rights. Redbird Smith died in 1918.

Suggested Reading: Duane Champagne, ed., *Chronology of Native North American History*, 1994; Duane Champagne, ed., *The Native North American Almanac*, 1994.

JAMES S. OLSON

SNYDER ACT OF 1924. The Snyder Act of 1924 was the culmination of the campaign for American Indian citizenship.* In January 1924, Congressman Homer P. Snyder of New York introduced House Resolution

6355 into the House of Representatives. Snyder's law authorized the secretary of the Interior to grant U.S. citizenship to all Native Americans requesting it if they were "individually prepared" for such a responsibility. The House passed the measure. The Senate then approved a bill awarding immediate citizenship to all Native Americans. When the two bills went to a conference committee, the legislation that emerged guaranteed "that all noncitizen Indians born within the territorial limits of the United States be . . . declared to be citizens of the United States: Provided, that the granting of such citizenship shall not in any manner impair or otherwise affect the right of any Indian to tribal or other property." When the bill passed both houses of Congress, President Calvin Coolidge signed it into law.

Suggested Reading: Gary C. Stein, "The Indian Citizenship Act of 1924," *New Mexico Historical Review* 47 (July 1972).

JAMES S. OLSON

SOCIETY OF AMERICAN INDIANS. The Society of American Indians (SAI) was originally organized by Ohio State University sociologist Fayette A. McKenzie in 1911. This national Native American reform organization held its first meeting in October 1911 in Columbus, Ohio, and until its demise in the 1920s was a strong pan-Indian* voice in American Indian affairs. It provided a training ground and forum for a generation of Native American leaders and actively influenced the Bureau of Indian Affairs* and government Indian policy for more than a decade.

The SAI offered a two-tiered membership structure. Membership was offered to Indians, and associate membership was offered to non-Indians who wished to join to support the organization's mostly assimilationist* goals. Most of the Indian membership at first came from the Midwest and upstate New York, reflecting the fact that the annual October conferences were generally held east of the vast Indian reservations* of the West. The Indian officers of the SAI not only promoted assimilationist goals but were the very models of assimilated Indians, although this changed over the life of the SAI. Most officers of the society had attended off-reservation boarding schools* such as the Carlisle Indian Industrial School, but there were many who had attended and were graduated from colleges and universities, and some had earned professional degrees.

To publicize its goals and to help educate whites and Indians of the benefits of assimilation, the SAI held annual conferences and published a quarterly magazine, the *American Indian Magazine/Quarterly Journal of the Society of American Indians*.

Despite strong leadership from Native American leaders such as Henry Roe Cloud, Arthur C. Parker,* Charles Eastman,* Carlos Montezuma, Gertrude Bonnin,* Marie Baldwin, and others, the society foundered during World War I. Deep divisions occurred as the leadership struggled with two different points of view: the traditionalist faction, which favored the support of tribalism, and the progressive faction, which favored rapid assimilation. Key long-term members left the organization, and more radical individuals, who sometimes strayed from original SAI goals, took over the organization. Support and membership lagged, and the SAI held its last annual meeting in 1923.

Suggested Reading: Hazel Hertzberg, *The Search for an American Indian Identity: Modern Pan-Indian Movements*, 1971.

JASON M. TETZLOFF

SOVEREIGNTY. The question of whether or not the Indian tribes are sovereign nations has been at issue in American Indian policy for several centuries. In 1789, when the Constitution* went into effect, the U.S. government decided to approach Indian tribes just as the English had done—by treating them as independent nations and negotiating treaties* with them. From 1789 to 1849 the secretary of War was responsible for negotiating those treaties through the Office of Indian Affairs. In 1849 the Office of Indian affairs was transferred from the Department of War to the Department of the Interior. Between 1789 and 1871 a total of 370 formal, written treaties were negotiated between the United States and various Indian tribes. As far as the United States was concerned, these treaties were no different legally from other treaties negotiated with sovereign nations.

But they were different, because the federal government had also assumed a sense of responsibility for the Indian tribes. In the decision *Cherokee Nation v. State of Georgia** (1831), the Supreme Court under John Marshall's* direction called Indian tribes "domestic dependent nations," using the analogy of ward (Indian tribes) to guardian (federal government). In the decision, Chief Justice Marshall wrote that the Indians

> look to our government for protection; rely upon its kindness and its power; appeal to it for relief to their wants; and address the president as their great father. They and their country are considered by foreign nations, as well as by ourselves, as being completely under the sovereignty of the United States, that any attempt to acquire their lands, or to form a political connection with them, would be considered by all as an invasion of our territory, and an act of hostility.

Moreover, in the decision *Johnson's and Graham's Lessee v. M'Intosh** (1823), the Supreme Court had formally denied the right of Indian tribes to sell their land to whomover they wished. After the Cherokee decisions in the early 1830s, the federal government proceeded to build a body of guardianship* theory and precedent over Indian peoples.

In 1871 Congress passed legislation ending the practice of treating Indian tribes as sovereign nations and making treaties with them. Thereafter Congress dealt with them as domestic dependent nations, economic organizations, and political interest groups, legislating for them as it did for other entities in American society. Throughout the late nineteenth and early twentieth centuries, the federal government engaged in a long-term assault on the notion of Indian tribal sovereignty. The allotment* program, embodied in the Dawes Act* of 1887, eliminated tribal authority over the Indian landed estate and conferred land titles on individual Indians. For all intents and purposes, the federal government no longer recognized the political authority of the tribal governments of allotted Indian groups. The citizenship* crusade had similar motives. After 1871, Indians were no longer considered citizens of tribal nations, so the United States officially and gradually awarded them U.S. citizenship and subjected them to the rights and responsibilities of such a legal status. Between 1887 and 1924 all American Indians were awarded citizenship. The citizenship campaign's ultimate objective was to assimilate* individual American Indians into the larger American legal system.

The Indian New Deal* era from 1933 to 1945 temporarily postponed the assimilationist campaign. Under John Collier's* direction and the legislative hubris of the Indian Reorganization Act* of 1934, the Bureau of Indian Affairs* ended the allotment program and restored tribal authority. But when World War II ended, the assimilationist forces once again had the upper hand, and the termination* program worked to end federal guardianship over Indian groups and reservations* and turn them over to the legal authority of state and local governments. Against the overwhelming resistance of Indian peoples, the termination program was the backbone of federal Indian policy until the Richard Nixon administration (1969–1974).

By that time the winds of change were sweeping the country, and the termination movement lost its momentum. The civil rights* movement made the nation more aware of the needs of minority groups in the United States, and for Native Americans the demand for respect and fairness took on an anti-assimilationist perspective. While African Americans were demanding equality and integration, which many Native Americans viewed as synonymous with assimilation, Red Power* advocates began demanding the restoration of Indian sovereignty and self-determination.* Most Indians viewed the pre-1871 treaties as sacred, inviolate agreements between the U.S. government and the tribes, guaranteeing to Indians their lands "for perpetuity" and protecting their rights on those lands from white exploitation. The more radical elements of the Red Power crusade, such as members of the American Indian Movement,* insisted on the return of all confiscated lands and the restoration of complete tribal sovereignty and of the treaty-making relationship between tribal governments and the federal government.

That radical perspective did not prevail, but the simultaneous end of the termination program (which restored the guardianship* status) and the rise of Indian activism produced the self-determination movement. If Indians could not enjoy complete tribal sovereignty, they did demand instead control over tribal mineral resource development and educa-tion,* restoration of as much land as possible, protection of treaty-recognized fishing* and hunting* rights, and the right to manage their own social service programs. In the wake of the occupation of Alcatraz Island,* the Trail of Broken Treaties,* and the incidents at Wounded Knee* in the late 1960s and early 1970s, Congress passed the Indian Self-Determination and Education Assistance Act in 1975. Self-determination has today replaced sovereignty as the primary focus of mainstream Indian activists.

Suggested Reading: Marjane Ambler, *Breaking the Iron Bonds: Indian Control of Energy Development*, 1990; Vine Deloria Jr. and Clifford Lytle, *The Nations Within: The Past and Future of American Indian Sovereignty*, 1984; Roxanne Dunbar Ortiz, *Indians of the Americas: Human Rights and Self-Determination*, 1984; Hurst Hannum, *Autonomy, Self-Determination and Sovereignty: The Ac-commodation of Conflicting Rights*, 1990; Sidney L. Harring, *Crow Dog's Case: American Indian Sovereignty, Tribal Law, and United States Law in the Nine-teenth Century*, 1994; Phyllis Mauch Messenger, ed., *The Ethics of Collecting Cul-tural Property: Whose Culture? Whose Property?* 1989.

JAMES S. OLSON

SPANISH INDIAN POLICY. Spanish Indian policy can be divided into two phases: the encomienda and the mission/presidio system. When the Spanish first arrived in the New World, as rewards for their services many received encomiendas: native villages from which they exacted tribute and the labor of the native inhabitants. In return the Spaniard, or *enco-mendero*, oversaw the conversion of the natives to Christianity and man-aged their well-being and safety. In general, however, the Indians were overworked, often separated from their families, physically abused, and kept in a perpetual state of serfdom.

The abuses of the encomienda system contributed to the great loss of life among the Indians. The Spanish Crown attempted to curtail these abuses with the New Laws of 1542–1543, which called for the release of unjustly enslaved Indians and a gradual end to the encomienda system. Despite opposition to this law by New World Spaniards, the encomienda quickly declined in importance.

As the frontier of New Spain began to push northward from Mexico, missionaries led the way. Owing to a lack of Spanish immigrants, Indians were seen as potential citizens, but first they had to be "civilized." This was the duty of the missionaries. They advanced beyond the frontier, set up missions among the "pagan" Indians, and began to instruct them in the virtues of Christianity, the Spanish language, and agriculture. Approximately ten years after beginning their work, the frontier was expected to reach the frontier clergy, their missions would be secularized, and the Indians would become productive citizens. The frontier clergy would then proceed ahead of the frontier and repeat the process again.

Unfortunately, this process almost never worked. Indians were loathe to take up farming; and when they gathered in the crowded conditions at the missions, disease beset them. In addition, soldiers stationed nearby in presidios (fortified military posts) were an additional source of friction. The military and the clergy often accused each other of abusing the Indians in the region. As a result, missions seldom won many converts and the Indians avoided settling permanently in the missions, although they could be tempted to stay temporarily if supplied with gifts.

Spanish Indian policy resulted in large-scale destruction of Indian civilizations despite the fact that it was benevolent in its intentions. The high death rates caused other Europeans, and even some Spaniards, to complain of the brutality of Spanish policy. In reality, however, the Spanish had no intention of exterminating the Indians (except in rare instances where the Indians proved to be extremely hostile) but sought instead to convert them into tax-paying servants of the Crown.

Suggested Reading: Michael C. Meyer and William L. Sherman, *The Course of Mexican History*, 1979; David J. Weber, *The Spanish Frontier in North America*, 1992.

JEFFREY D. CARLISLE

SQUIRE v. CAPOEMAN (1956). The *Squire v. Capoeman* case involved the issue of taxing Indian income. The Internal Revenue Service had attempted to tax the income of an Indian who sold timber cut from his trust allotment.* The Indian taxpayer claimed that the Dawes Act* of 1887 made income from allotted property tax exempt, because the intent of the original legislation was to help Indians become economically self-sufficient. The Supreme Court found in favor of the Indian in 1956, arguing that the purpose of the Dawes Act would be frustrated if the federal government turned around and taxed what it had already given to an Indian.

Suggested Reading: Stephen L. Pevar, *The Rights of Indians and Tribes: The Basic ACLU Guide to Indian and Tribal Rights*, 1992.

                                                                    JAMES S. OLSON

STANDING BEAR v. CROOK (1879). The Ponca controversy, which occurred soon after the flight of Chief Joseph* and the Nez Percé in 1877, greatly stimulated the movement to reform American Indian policy. In 1868 the federal government awarded 96,000 acres of Ponca land in the Dakota Territory to the Sioux peoples. When the Sioux began occupying the region in 1877, the Bureau of Indian Affairs* (BIA) decided to relocate the Poncas to Indian Territory* in order to prevent violent confrontations between the two Indian peoples. The Poncas opposed the movement, but by July 1877 most of them had arrived at their new reservation.* It was worse than they had expected. Stifling heat, poverty, hunger, and malaria made their lives miserable. Early in 1879 Standing Bear, a Ponca chief, left the Indian Territory with thirty other Poncas and began traveling back to the Dakota Territory.

Standing Bear ignored BIA directives to return to the Indian Territory and continued his journey northward. The standoff soon became a national controversy. A number of prominent Americans—Mary Morgan of the Indian Hope Association,* Senator Henry Dawes of Massachusetts, Senator Algernon Paddock of Nebraska, abolitionist Wendell Phillips, Lydia Child of the American Missionary Association, and the Reform League—all came to Standing Bear's defense, demanding fair treatment of the Poncas. They filed suit on Standing Bear's behalf, and a federal district judge ruled in *Standing Bear v. Crook* that "an Indian is a 'person' within the meaning of the laws of the United States." Implying that Indians had the same rights to personal freedom and legal protection as other Americans, *Standing Bear v. Crook* was the first federal court case in U.S. history to recognize the individual civil rights* of Indians. The mounting political pressure became too much for the BIA, and in 1881 it returned the confiscated land to the Poncas.

Suggested Reading: Robert M. Murdock, *The Reformers and the American Indian*, 1971; Francis Paul Prucha, *American Indian Policy in Crisis: Christian Reformers and the Indian, 1865–1890*, 1976.

                                                                    JAMES S. OLSON

STEREOTYPING. Throughout the nineteenth century and during much of the twentieth century, American Indians have been unfavorably stereotyped in novels, films, radio, and television. Indians especially resented the standard image of bloodthirsty savages standing in the way of civilization. Like other American ethnic leaders who have battled against unfavorable stereotypes, Indian activists believe that the continued existence of unchallenged stereotypes prevents majority groups from ever dealing with minorities, Indians included, on terms of fairness and equality.

In 1911 a group of Ojibway Indians went to Washington, D.C., where they staged the first protest against such stereotyping. They specifically condemned the 1911 film *The Curse of the Red Man*, which depicts an Indian who succumbs to alcoholism, and called on Congress to pass regulations prohibiting such portrayals in the future. Similar protests occurred during the next fifty years, but they received little attention in the media. It was not until the 1960s and 1970s that white society became more conscious of the media stereotyping of Indians. In 1966, Indian actor Jay Silverheels formed two groups—the Indian Actors Guild and the Indian Actors Workshop—to promote more diverse, realistic images of American Indians and to encourage the employment of Indian actors to play Indian roles in movies and television.

Perhaps the most dramatic episode in the protest movement against the stereotyping of American Indians occurred at the 1973 Academy Awards in Los Angeles. Marlon Brando, who sympathized with American Indians, decided to make a personal statement. When he received the Best Actor award for *The Godfather*, he had Sacheen Littlefeather* accept the award on his behalf. Claiming to be an Apache and president of the National Native American Affirmative Image Committee, she denounced the stereotyping of American Indians in film and television.

Indian activists have also protested the use of Indian mascots for college and professional athletic teams. Groups such as the National Indian Youth Council* and the American Indian Movement* have demanded the abandonment of such stereotypical symbols. In 1969 Dartmouth College (which had initially been established in 1769 to educate Indians) dropped the use of an Indian mascot in its athletic teams, and in 1972 Stanford University did the same. Other colleges and universities followed suit.

Professional teams have not been so responsive. In the 1990s, Native American activists protested the mascots and team names of the Washington Redksins and the Atlanta Braves. They even demanded that Atlanta Brave fans cease the "tomahawk chop" employed to inspire the team to victory. Both teams, as well as the fans, refused to cooperate.

Suggested Reading: Gretchen M. Bataille and Charles L. P. Silet, eds., *The Pretend Indians: Images of Native Americans in the Movies*, 1980; John E. O'Connor, *The Hollywood Indian: Stereotypes of Native Americans in Film*, 1980.

JAMES S. OLSON

STOCK-RAISING HOMESTEAD ACT OF 1916. After passage of the Homestead Act* of 1862, it became clear that 160 acres of land (the amount of public land, or homestead, offered to any male over 21 years of age) would not be enough to provide for successful dry farming and grazing operations. Westerners began clamoring to expand the maximum number of acres available under the Homestead Act of 1862. In 1909 Congress passed the Enlarged Homestead Act, which allowed for 320-acre homesteads in Colorado, Montana, Nevada, Oregon, Utah, Wyoming, Washington, and Arizona. Of that 320 acres, only 80 acres had to be farmed. The law also specifically made timber and mineral lands off-limits to homesteaders. But some westerners claimed that even 320 acres was inadequate, and in 1916 Congress passed the Stock-Raising Homestead Act, which increased the maximum acreage to 640—as long as the land had no irrigation potential and was to be used for grazing and forage. Like other federal legislation encouraging settlement and economic development of the arid lands of the Far West, the Stock-Raising Homestead Act of 1916 helped bring about the loss of Native American land.

Suggested Reading: Marshall Harris, *Origins of the Land Tenure System in the United States*, 1953.

JAMES S. OLSON

SURVIVAL OF AMERICAN INDIANS ASSOCIATION. The Survival of American Indians Association was established in 1964. Its founders consisted largely of Nisqually and Puyallup Indians concerned about preserving Native American fishing rights* in western Washington. Its original leader was Hank Adams.* Today the association has a membership of five hundred people and continues to be an advocate for Indian rights.

Suggested Reading: Armand S. La Potin, *Native American Voluntary Organizations*, 1986.

JAMES S. OLSON

SWIFT v. LEACH (1920). This 1920 North Dakota Supreme Court case affirmed the right of trust patent Indians (those who had received land and title to it through prior legislation) to vote in elections. In November 1918 the residents of Sioux County, North Dakota, voted on whether or not to move the county seat from Fort Yates to Selfridge. A total of 872 people voted, 273 of whom were trust patent Indians. Martin Swift, believing trust patent Indians did not have the right to vote, brought his case before a North Dakota state court.

As background to this case, it is important to understand the legislation related to the trust patent issue. In 1887, with the passage of the Dawes Act,* Indian tribal lands had been divided and distributed to individual members. The Indians were issued patents for the land, which was to be held in trust by the federal government for 25 years. Nineteen years later, the Burke Act* amended the Dawes Act by removing the 25-year trust patent requirement. Henceforth, all Indians who were judged competent to manage their own affairs could have their trust patents converted to fee patents. This change required the signature of the secretary of the Interior, and it removed restrictions on the sale and taxation of the land.

In March 1920 a North Dakota trial judge decided that trust patent Indians did have the right to vote. Martin Swift immediately filed an appeal with the North Dakota Supreme Court. He claimed the nature of the relationship between trust patent Indians and the federal government prevented the Indians from being civilized. He also claimed the Indians could not sever their tribal relationship without the consent of the federal government, and in no place had the government issued its consent for trust patent Indians.

In May 1920 the North Dakota Supreme Court upheld the decision of the lower court. According to Judge Bronson, testimony had proven that trust patent Indians had severed their tribal relationships. As a result, they were given the right to vote by the North Dakota Constitution. The judge further stated that by placing trust patent Indians and their land under the supervision of the federal government, the Dawes and Burke Acts were not meant to deny those same Indians their state rights.

Suggested Reading: Russel Lawrence Barsh and James Youngblood Henderson, *The Road: Indian Tribes and Political Liberty*, 1980; Vine Deloria Jr. and Clifford M. Lytle, *American Indians, American Justice*, 1983; H. Barry Holt and

Gary Forrester, *Digest of American Indian Law: Cases and Chronology*, 1990; Stephen L. Pevar, *The Rights of Indians and Tribes: The Basic ACLU Guide to Indian and Tribal Rights*, 1992; Wilcomb E. Washburn, *Red Man's Land, White Man's Law: A Study of the Past and Present Status of the American Indian*, 1971; Charles F. Wilkinson, *American Indians, Time and the Law*, 1987; John R. Wunder, *"Retained by The People": A History of American Indians and the Bill of Rights*, 1994.

JENNIFER BERTOLET

T

TALTON v. MAYES (1896). The question of tribal sovereignty* and individual rights has been a controversial one since the late nineteenth century. For nearly a century, until 1871 the U.S. government treated Indian tribes as sovereign nations, dealing with them through the State Department and denying them any citizenship* rights. The question of whether individual Indians enjoy civil rights vis-à-vis their own tribal governments has also been controversial, for if the tribes truly were sovereign, the U.S. Constitution*—and more particularly the Bill of Rights*—would not protect them against abuses by tribal government.

In the *Talton v. Mayes* case of 1896 the Supreme Court decided that the Bill of Rights applied to actions of federal and state governments, not tribal governments, because tribes are not subordinate bodies of those governments. Bob Talton, a Cherokee, murdered another Cherokee on the Cherokee reservation.* A five-man Cherokee grand jury indicted him for murder, and a Cherokee court convicted him. He appealed to the federal courts, arguing that his Fifth Amendment* rights had been violated because a proper, six-man grand jury had not been impaneled. The Supreme Court rejected his argument. Tribal sovereignty, the Court argued, flows from its original independence, which preceded the writing of the Constitution. The Court ruled that Indian courts did come under federal regulation but that they were not bound by all the Fifth Amendment clauses. As a result of the decision, Indians in Indian country* could be denied their Fifth Amendment protections against illegal indictment, double jeopardy (being tried twice for the same crime), and self-incrimination. At the time of the decision there was little protest from individual Indians, but in the twentieth century the issue of tribal sovereignty and individual rights would continue to generate controversy.

Suggested Reading: Russel Lawrence Barsh and James Youngblood Henderson, *The Road: Indian Tribes and Political Liberty*, 1980; Vine Deloria Jr. and Clifford M. Lytle, *American Indians, American Justice*, 1983; H. Barry Holt and Gary Forrester, *Digest of American Indian Law: Cases and Chronology*, 1990; Stephen L. Pevar, *The Rights of Indians and Tribes: The Basic ACLU Guide to Indian and Tribal Rights*, 1992; Wilcomb E. Washburn, *Red Man's Land, White Man's Law: A Study of the Past and Present Status of the American Indian*, 1971; Charles F. Wilkinson, *American Indians, Time and the Law*, 1987; John R. Wunder, *"Retained by The People": A History of American Indians and the Bill of Rights*, 1994.

JAMES S. OLSON

TANANA-YUKON DENA' NENA' HENASH. Established in June 1962, Tanana-Yukon Dena' Nena' Henash ("Our Land Speaks") was a group of Athabascan chiefs from central Alaska. An early leader was Charles Ryan, one of the Metlakatla people. They first met to protest Alaskan state restrictions on their traditional hunting rights.* The Statehood Act of 1958 had supposedly guaranteed those rights, but the law also permitted state authorities to open up 102 million acres of Athabascan land to public domain access. The Athabascan chiefs campaigned to make sure that land near their villages was not designated as part of that public domain, and that they retained all hunting, fishing,* and mineral* rights there. The organization also demanded improved federal health care programs, escrow accounts for Indian oil and gas revenues, and economic training for young people. Most of their demands were achieved in the Alaska Native Claims Settlement Act* of 1971.

Suggested Reading: Robert D. Arnold, *Alaska Native Land Claims*, 1978; David S. Case, *Alaska Natives and American Laws*, 1984; Armand S. La Potin, *Native American Voluntary Organizations*, 1986.

JAMES S. OLSON

TASK FORCE ON AMERICAN INDIAN RELIGIOUS FREEDOM. In 1978, after Congress had passed the American Indian Religious Freedom Act,* President Jimmy Carter directed the establishment of the Task Force on American Indian Religious Freedom to evaluate federal government policies in regard to the treatment of the religious rights and cultural heritage of American Indians. Its recommendations were issued in 1979. They called for increased awareness and, if necessary, congressional legislation to protect Indian burial sites and to address the care of sacred artifacts and human skeletal remains in government museums. The task force also raised the issue of returning those artifacts and remains to Indian tribes requesting them. The findings of the Task Force on American Indian Religious Freedom eventually helped lead to the Archaeological Resources Protection Act* of 1979, the National Museum of the American Indian Act* of 1989, and the Native American Graves Protection and Repatriation Act* of 1990.

Suggested Reading: Michael M. Ames, *Cannibal Tours and Glass Boxes: The Anthropology of Museums*, 1992; Douglas Cole, *Captured Heritage: The Scramble for Northwest Coast Artifacts*, 1985; George P. Horse Capture, *The Concept of Sacred Materials and Their Place in the World*, 1989; Phyllis Mauch Messenger, ed., *The Ethics of Collecting Cultural Property: Whose Culture? Whose Property?* 1989; H. Marcus Price, ed., *Disputing the Dead: U.S. Law on Aboriginal Remains and Grave Goods*, 1991.

JAMES S. OLSON

TAXATION. Over the years, a series of congressional laws and federal court cases have defined the nature of and the extent to which Indians are subject to state and federal taxation, and the extent to which legal tribal entities possess taxing authority. In essence, Indian tribes are not considered to be taxable entities, although individual members of a tribe are taxable in the absence of specific legal or treaty exemption. However, individual tribal members are exempt from federal taxation on personal income derived from land held in trust for the tribe by the federal government. That income includes royalties, rent, lease payments, and proceeds from the sale of crops and livestock. Indian commercial businesses, such as restaurants and motels, are subject to federal taxes. Legal tribal entities are not subject to the Internal Revenue Code. Finally, Indian tribes and individual Indians are exempt from federal taxation on income derived from protected fishing rights.* When working for off-reservation, non-Indian employers, Indians are subject to federal income taxes.

State and local jurisdictions cannot tax Indian property. In determining state taxing jurisdiction, the federal courts have applied two tests: the infringement test and the preemption test. The infringement test measures whether state authority infringes on tribal sovereignty,* that is, the right of Indian tribes to govern themselves. The preemption test measures whether state authority is preempted by federal law. In essence, state and local governments cannot tax tribal property or tribal income, nor can they tax individual Indian income derived from tribal property. Non-Indians doing business with Indians in Indian country* are exempt from taxation.

Tribes maintain taxing power over Indians and non-Indians living on Indian property. In 1982 Congress passed the Indian Tribal Governmental Tax Status Act. The law, and subsequent amendments to it in 1984 and 1987, awarded the same tax status to tribal governments as enjoyed by state and local political entities. Tribal governments were given the authority to issue tax-exempt bonds to finance private, commercial, and tribal governmental activities. The law also allowed all donations to tribal governments to be deductible from federal income, gift, and estate taxes. It made taxes paid to tribal governments or to tribal political campaigns deductible from federal taxes. The law also authorized the establishment of tax-sheltered annuities for tribal personnel.

Suggested Reading: Russel Lawrence Barsh, "Issues in Federal, State, and Tribal Taxation of Reservation Wealth: A Survey and Economic Critique," *Washington Law Review* 54 (June 1979), 531–86; Felix S. Cohen, *Felix S. Cohen's Handbook of Federal Indian Law*, 1982; *Federal Indian Tax Rules: A Compilation of Internal Revenue Service Rules Relating to Indians*, 1989.

JAMES S. OLSON

TECUMSEH. Tecumseh, the chief of the Shawnee people, was born in 1768 in Old Piqua, Ohio. Because of his personal charisma and oratorical skills, Tecumseh emerged in the early 1800s as a leader of a coalition of Indian tribes in the Ohio Valley, all of whom were concerned about the increased pace of white settlement. As such, he was probably the earliest pan-Indian* leader in U.S. history. Along with his brother, a spiritual leader known as The Prophet, Tecumseh tried to forge a military alliance of Ohio Valley tribes to resist the white onslaught. However, intertribal unity was impossible to achieve. In 1811 Governor William Henry Harrison of the Indiana Territory and a militia army defeated Tecumseh's forces at the Battle of Tippecanoe Creek and went on to destroy the chief's principal camp at Prophetstown. When the War of 1812 erupted between Great Britain and the United States, Tecumseh saw an opportunity to improve the Indian political situation, so he allied with the English. In October 1813, however, Harrison's troops defeated Tecumseh at the Battle of the Thames in Indiana Territory. Tecumseh died in the engagement.

Suggested Reading: R. David Edmunds, *The Shawnee Prophet*, 1983; R. David Edmunds, *Tecumseh and the Quest for Indian Leadership*, 1984.

JAMES S. OLSON

TEE-HIT-TON INDIANS, AN IDENTIFIABLE GROUP OF ALASKA INDIANS v. UNITED STATES (1955). The question of title for lands occupied by Native Americans has been a serious one. The United States throughout its history has taken land from the Indians by treaty or by force. The fact that the land subsequently belonged to the non-Indian population of the United States was not disputed, but some people asked if the Native American population deserved fair compensation* under the Fifth Amendment.* *Tee-Hit-Ton Indians, An Identifiable Group of Alaska Indians v. United States* answered that question.

The majority opinion of the U.S. Supreme Court was delivered by Justice Stanley Reed who declared that the Tee-Hit-Ton Indians, part of the Tlingit tribe of Alaska, had no right to receive compensation for seizure of their lands. The Indians had argued that the Russians, from whom the United States purchased Alaska, had never taken lands from the Indians— as did other European nations. This meant that the United States had not purchased the Tlingit lands from the Russians. The court disagreed, arguing that the Russians took what land they wanted to use—as did the other European nations—and left only what they did not need. Any consideration that the Tee-Hit-Ton Indians were different from the Native Americans in the continental United States was rejected by the court.

Reed went on to say that the U.S. Supreme Court had never ruled that Congress had to compensate Indians for lands seized by the United States. The lands were government lands; Congress could either allow the Indians to use such lands at its pleasure or withdraw their use at any time. Americans were generous people, the court argued, and had and would continue to look after the interests of the American Indians; but such concern was voluntary and not required by law or the Constitution.*

The minority opinion in the case argued that the court overlooked the real meaning of legislation concerning Alaskan Indians. An 1884 law stated that the Indians in Alaska would not be removed from lands they occupied or used without proper methods being devised later by Congress. The U.S. Supreme Court's majority opinion took this to mean that Indian title had not been established; but the minority, including Chief Justice Earl Warren, argued that Indian title had been acknowledged. The question that Congress was to take up later was how to properly allow the purchase of the Indian titles.

Suggested Reading: Russel Lawrence Barsh and James Youngblood Henderson, *The Road: Indian Tribes and Political Liberty*, 1980; Vine Deloria Jr. and Clifford M. Lytle, *American Indians, American Justice*, 1983; H. Barry Holt and Gary Forrester, *Digest of American Indian Law: Cases and Chronology*, 1990; Stephen L. Pevar, *The Rights of Indians and Tribes: The Basic ACLU Guide to Indian and Tribal Rights*, 1992; Wilcomb E. Washburn, *Red Man's Land, White Man's Law: A Study of the Past and Present Status of the American Indian*, 1971; Charles F. Wilkinson, *American Indians, Time and the Law*, 1987; John R. Wun-

der, *"Retained by The People": A History of American Indians and the Bill of Rights*, 1994.

DARREN PIERSON

TERMINATION. The process of termination, or "liquidation" as it was originally named, was proposed during the late 1940s as the best method to solve the "Indian problem" that plagued America. In a post–World War II attempt to "free" the Native American from his or her dependency on the government of the United States, the policy called for the complete termination of all relationships between the Indians and the U.S. government. Native Americans would be treated as all other Americans were, with no special privileges or responsibilities. Tribal relationships would cease to exist. Tribal lands would be parceled out to individual tribe members. Tribal governments would cease to function. With the removal of the special status for the Native Americans, the United States could stop worrying about past inequities and put the problem of the Native American behind the country—or so some argued.

The Bureau of Indian Affairs* (BIA) created a plan that would rate Indian tribes to determine when they could be terminated over a fifty-year period. Although President Harry S Truman supported the concept of termination, it was not put into widespread practice until President Dwight D. Eisenhower's administration took office in 1953. House Concurrent Resolution 108* put the program into law. During the next several years, special congressional termination acts were passed for many tribes, including the Menominees (1954), Klamaths (1954), Western Oregon Indians (1954), Alabama and Coushatta Indians (1954), Utes (1954), Wyandottes (1956), Peorias (1956), and Ottawas (1956).

Many Indian tribes were terminated throughout the United States, but by the early 1960s termination had become increasingly unpopular. The civil rights* movement raised the national consciousness about the problems of America's ethnic minorities, and Indian activists began demanding the restoration of tribal sovereignty.* Termination was not formally reversed until 1970, when the Richard Nixon administration successfully promoted its repeal. It was not until 1988, however, that Congress passed an omnibus measure repealing termination: the Repeal of Termination Act* prohibited Congress from ever terminating or transferring BIA services without the express permission of the tribes involved.

Suggested Reading: Russel Lawrence Barsh and James Youngblood Henderson, *The Road: Indian Tribes and Political Liberty*, 1980; Wilcomb E. Washburn,

Red Man's Land, White Man's Law, 1971; John R. Wunder, *"Retained by The People": A History of American Indians and the Bill of Rights*, 1994.

DARREN PIERSON

TIMBER CULTURE ACT OF 1873. The Timber Culture Act of 1873 was part of the U.S. drive to develop the West and create a fee simple* empire of small landowners. The Homestead Act* of 1862 had allowed individuals to acquire up to 160 acres of public domain land for free, and the Timber Culture Act eleven years later permitted any citizen to do the same for 160 acres of forested land as long as 40 permanent acres of timber were maintained out of the 160 acres; that requirement was reduced to only 10 acres in 1878. The law remained in existence until 1891, when it was repealed. Like other federal legislation encouraging settlement and economic development of the arid lands of the Far West, the Timber Culture Act of 1873 helped bring about the loss of Native American land.

Suggested Reading: Paul Gates, *History of Public Land Law Development*, 1968.

JAMES S. OLSON

TOLEDO ET AL. v. PUEBLO DE JEMEZ ET AL. (1954). One of the more vexing constitutional and civil rights issues involving Native Americans has concerned the civil rights of individual Indians in disputes that call into question the sovereign* rights of a tribe. The *Toledo et al. v. Pueblo de Jemez et al.* case involved such a dispute. Six residents of the Jemez Pueblo in New Mexico, who were practicing Protestants, charged tribal officials of the Jemez Pueblo with religious discrimination. The tribal leaders, who were Roman Catholics, claimed that Catholicism was the official tribal religion and refused to allow the Protestants to construct a chapel on the reservation,* to bury their dead in the tribal cemetery, to hold church services in their homes, or to allow Protestant missionaries to visit the reservation. The Protestants filed a lawsuit against the tribal leaders, asserting violation of their right to freedom of religion. The federal district court in New Mexico decided against the Protestants in 1954, refusing to hear the case and essentially upholding the power of the tribal leaders. The court reasoned that the demands of tribal sovereignty were more compelling than the right of individual Indians to religious freedom.

Suggested Reading: Russel Lawrence Barsh and James Youngblood Henderson, *The Road: Indian Tribes and Political Liberty*, 1980; Vine Deloria Jr. and

Clifford M. Lytle, *American Indians, American Justice*, 1983; H. Barry Holt and Gary Forrester, *Digest of American Indian Law: Cases and Chronology*, 1990; Stephen L. Pevar, *The Rights of Indians and Tribes: The Basic ACLU Guide to Indian and Tribal Rights*, 1992; Wilcomb H. Washburn, *Red Man's Land, White Man's Law: A Study of the Past and Present Status of the American Indian*, 1971; Charles F. Wilkinson, *American Indians, Time and the Law*, 1987; John R. Wunder, *"Retained by The People": A History of American Indians and the Bill of Rights*, 1994.

JAMES S. OLSON

TRAIL OF BROKEN TREATIES. In the summer of 1972, activist leaders including Hank Adams* of the "fish-ins" in Washington and Dennis Banks* and Russell Means* of the American Indian Movement* (AIM) met in Denver to plan the "Trail of Broken Treaties" caravan. A presidential election loomed on the horizon, and Banks, Means, and Adams hoped to generate media support for self-determination* by transporting thousands of Native Americans from the West Coast to Washington, D.C., during the last month of the presidential campaign. In cars, buses, and vans they left in October, stopping at reservations* across the country to pick up more protesters. In Minneapolis, where many Chippewas joined them, the caravan leaders issued their Twenty Points, a series of demands for a complete revival of tribal sovereignty* by repeal of the 1871 ban on future treaties, restoration of treaty-making status to individual tribes, the granting of full government services to the unrecognized eastern tribes, a review of all past treaty violations, complete restitution for those violations, formal recognition of all executive order (created by presidential executive order rather than by acts of Congress) reservations, and admission of the tribal right to interpret all past treaties. They also demanded elimination of all state court jurisdiction over Native American affairs.

From Minneapolis the Trail of Broken Treaties moved on to Washington, where they discovered that their advance people had not made adequate room arrangements. Most of the caravan went to the Bureau of Indian Affairs* (BIA) building, where they demonstrated for several hours. When federal guards in the building tried to push some of the demonstrators outside, the affair became violent. The Native Americans seized the BIA building, blockading all the doors and windows with office furniture. For six days they occupied the building, demanding amnesty and a government pledge to recognize the Twenty Points.

As a basis of negotiation, the Twenty Points constituted the protesters' minimum terms for surrender to federal authorities. Foremost among them was the immediate review and rectification of treaty violations, reestablishment of the treaty relationship formerly in operation between the U.S. government and the various tribes, repeal of termination* laws, reversal of Public Law 280* and any laws executed under its auspices, timely release of some 110 million acres of land for Indian use, tribal jurisdiction over crimes committed by non-Indians on the reservations, substitution of an Office of Federal Indian Relations and Community Reconstruction in place of the Bureau of Indian Affairs, and a variety of measures designed to foster cultural and economic development.

Although the protesters ransacked the BIA offices, destroying BIA files and damaging considerable property, caravan leaders claimed that federal agents had infiltrated the movement and had done most of the damage. The government refrained from an armed attempt at dislodgment and defused the situation by agreeing to consider AIM's demands for reform. On November 8, federal authorities offered the Native American protesters immunity from prosecution and $66,000 for return transportation. The offer was accepted and the crisis was over. But once the threat of violence had evaporated, the federal government resorted to stonewalling tactics and eventually rejected the vast majority of AIM demands. As a result, pan-Indian* activists would renew their violent protests against federal Indian policy.

Suggested Reading: Vine Deloria Jr. *Behind the Trail of Broken Treaties*, 1974; James S. Olson and Raymond Wilson, *Native Americans in the Twentieth Century*, 1984; Francis Paul Prucha, *The Great Father*, Vol. 2, 1984.

MARK BAXTER

TRAIL OF TEARS. The term "Trail of Tears" has been used generally to describe the forcible relocation* of dozens of American Indian tribes in the 1830s and 1840s. The Indian Removal Act* of 1830 provided legislative sanction for the relocation, which assimilationists* and land developers viewed as a way of stimulating economic growth as well as reducing Indian-white violence, because after the American Revolution* so many settlers had crossed the Appalachian Mountains to establish farms in the Ohio and Mississippi river valleys. Eventually, nearly 100,000 Native Americans crossed the Mississippi River under the authority of the Indian Removal Act.

More specifically, the term "Trail of Tears" refers to the removal of the Cherokees. They had resisted removal, exhausting all legal channels until they won the case of *Worcester v. Georgia** (1832). President Andrew Jackson,* however, refused to honor the decision, and in 1838 federal troops evicted the Cherokees. The operation was poorly planned. The troops moved the Cherokees in the dead of winter, and more than 4,000 of them died before reaching the Indian Territory.*

Suggested Reading: Arthur H. DeRosier Jr., *The Removal of the Choctaw Indians*, 1970; John Ehle, *Trail of Tears: The Rise and Fall of the Cherokee Nation*, 1988; Grant Foreman, *Indian Removal: The Emigration of the Five Civilized Tribes of Indians*, 1932; Michael Paul Rogin, *Fathers and Children: Andrew Jackson and the Subjugation of the American Indians*, 1975; Anthony F. Wallace, *The Long Bitter Trail: Andrew Jackson and the Indians*, 1993.

JAMES S. OLSON

TRAPP ET AL. v. DUBOIS ET AL. (1995). The complexity of the religious freedom* issue among Native Americans is revealed by a 1995 decision in the Massachusetts Superior Court. Indian prisoners in the state prison were members of the Native American Spiritual Awareness Council, which met weekly to raise the spiritual consciousness and Indian identity of its members. In the case of *Trapp et al. v. DuBois et al.*, the prisoners charged the prison administration with systematic violation of their First Amendment right to freedom of religion. In particular, prison administrators would only let Indians whose tribes enjoyed federal recognition to participate in the program, and they regularly confiscated such religious articles as pipes, drums, and headbands, labeling them contraband. In its 1995 decision, the Massachusetts Superior Court issued an order allowing the use of these sacred items and permitting any Indian to participate in the Native American Spiritual Awareness Council if he or she secured the approval of "an outside spiritual advisor or sachem [leader]."

Suggested Reading: Elizabeth S. Grobsmith, "The Impact of Litigation on the Religious Revitalization of Native American Inmates in the Nebraska Department of Corrections," *Plains Anthropologist* 34 (1989), 135–47; Charles F. Wilkinson, *American Indians, Time and the Law*, 1987; John R. Wunder, *"Retained by The People": A History of American Indians and the Bill of Rights*, 1994.

JAMES S. OLSON

TREATY RIGHTS. In 1789, when the Constitution* went into effect, the U.S. government decided to approach Indian tribes just as the English had done—by treating them as independent nations and negotiating treaties with them. From 1789 to 1849 the secretary of War was responsible for negotiating those treaties through the Office of Indian Affairs. In 1849 the Office of Indian Affairs was transferred from the Department of War to the Department of the Interior. Between 1789 and 1871 a total of 370 formal, written treaties were negotiated between the United States and various Indian tribes. As far as the United States was concerned, these treaties were no different legally from other treaties negotiated with sovereign nations. The treaties dealt with a variety of concerns, including land cessions, territorial boundaries, hunting* and fishing* rights, trade, rights of way across Indian land, education,* and peace. Approximately 230 of the treaties concerned land cessions; 96 dealt with issues of peace and allegiance; 76 involved removal and resettlement of various tribes; 19 revolved around payment of debts; and 15 established annuity payments for various tribes. Some treaties, of course, dealt with more than one of these issues.

In 1871, Congress passed the Indian Appropriations Act* ending the practice of treating Indian tribes as sovereign* nations and making treaties with them. After 1871, Congress dealt with them as domestic nations, economic organizations, and political interest groups, legislating for them as it did for other entities in American society. For their part, the Indians viewed the pre-1871 treaties as sacred and inviolate agreements between the U.S. government and the tribes, guaranteeing to Indians their lands "for perpetuity" and protecting their rights on those lands from white exploitation. But whereas the Indians viewed the treaties as fixed agreements locked in time and independent of all change, the U.S. government saw them as dynamic political arrangements and evolving legal documents, subject to alteration and renegotiation as political, social, and economic circumstances changed.

Those conflicting interpretations became the source of extraordinary misunderstandings between Indians and whites during the late nineteenth century and first half of the twentieth century. During that time treaty rights negotiated in the past were negated by the allotment,* termination,* and relocation* programs, and in the process the Indians lost tens of millions of acres of land. Through the compensation* program of the 1940s, 1950s, and 1960s the federal government tried to settle many Indian claims about treaty violations through cash payments. The Red Power* movement of the 1960s, 1970s, and 1980s campaigned for tribal sovereignty and self-determination.* In 1972 the Trail of Broken Treaties* protest movement demanded the restoration of tribal sovereignty and of the treaty-making process between the United States and Indian tribes. The federal government refused to accept the proposal, arguing that the Snyder Act* of 1924 had conferred U.S. citizenship* on all Indians and rendered unnecessary any new treaties.

Suggested Reading: Fay G. Cohen, *Treaties on Trial: The Continuing Controversy over Northwest Indian Fishing Rights*, 1986; Henry Fritz, *The Movement for*

Indian Assimilation, 1860–1890, 1963; Robert M. Kvasnicka, "United States Indian Treaties and Agreements," in Wilcomb E. Washburn, ed., *Handbook of American Indians*, Vol. 4: *History of Indian-White Relations*, 1988.

                                                         JAMES S. OLSON

TRIBAL COURTS. For thousands of years most Indian tribes have settled disputes and meted out justice in some form of tribal courts. These tribal courts have continually evolved, especially since white contact. In certain cases this traditional form of tribal government had all but disappeared by the late 1800s, whereas other tribal groups maintained a strong tradition of tribally administered justice. In the late 1800s the Bureau of Indian Affairs* (BIA) became more involved in this area. It encouraged the formation of special courts of Indian offenses on the reservations.* These courts, although often staffed by Indians, were under the local BIA agent's control and were used to enforce white laws. For example, the courts were required to punish Indians for such "forbidden" activities as wearing "Indian" clothes or for practicing most traditional tribal ceremonies.

Major crimes such as murder, rape, assault, and kidnapping that were committed in Indian country* have been under the jurisdiction of the federal government since the Major Crimes Act* of 1885. Until 1934 the states assumed jurisdiction of most other crimes, although this assumption of states' rights was beyond the scope of state jurisdiction. With passage of the Indian Reorganization Act* of 1934, tribal sovereignty* received a major boost. The act allowed tribes to organize their own tribal governments; once organized, they could reassert their control of tribal judicial affairs. Size, resources, and tradition all affected the style and make-up of the courts. Some recognized tribes have relatively informal courts, whereas other larger tribes have sophisticated court systems with appellate and even supreme courts.

The cases they hear also vary by tribal constitution. Some tribal judicial codes address everything from traffic laws to natural resource law; others are more narrowly focused. All tribes are restricted from hearing any cases covered by the Major Crimes Act, and Public Law 280* has further restricted tribes in California, Minnesota, Nebraska, Oregon, and Wisconsin by allowing these states to assume control over some lesser crimes on the reservations. Tribal courts maintain control, if they wish, over areas such as zoning; family relations, including marriage, divorce, and adoption; and civil damage suits. Congress has been willing to increase the jurisdiction of the tribes, as was indicated by the Indian Child Welfare

Act* of 1978, although the Supreme Court has limited their jurisdiction over the regulation of fishing and hunting on non-Indian lands within the reservations.

Tribal courts remain a very effective way to maintain and even extend the tribe's sovereignty. Recognizing their significance, most Indian tribes have invested considerable resources in improving them. Organizations such as the National American Indian Court Judges Association and the National Indian Justice Center have proved very adept at increasing the professionalism of the courts while also preserving the culture of a tribally controlled court.

Suggested Reading: William T. Hagan, *Indian Police and Judges*, 1966; Sharon O'Brien, *American Indian Tribal Governments*, 1989; Charles F. Wilkinson, *American Indians, Time and the Law*, 1987.

JASON M. TETZLOFF

TRIBAL LEASING ACT OF 1938. The debate over tribal sovereignty* for Indian peoples has often revolved around the issue of control of natural resources on the reservations.* Although many reservations were rich in timber, coal, oil, uranium, natural gas, and other mineral resources, non-Indian commercial interests exploited them. Poverty* remained a severe problem on the reservations in spite of those resources. During the Indian New Deal* era, Commissioner of Indian Affairs John Collier* worked to restore tribal sovereignty after the half-century of allotment* and develop the reservations economically.

In 1938, at Collier's urging, the Roosevelt administration supported and Congress passed the Tribal Leasing Act, which required that all tribal leasing arrangements be based on competitive bidding so that the Indians could get the best royalty arrangement possible. The extraction industries would provide jobs for Native Americans and royalty income for the tribes. As it worked out, however, the legislation proved harmful to Native Americans. It was not at all uncommon for the secretary of the Interior to negotiate very long-term leases. Those leases were based on mineral prices as they existed in the depressed economy of the Great Depression during the 1930s. As mineral price levels rose in subsequent years, many tribes found themselves trapped in long-term, unfavorable contracts.

Suggested Reading: Marjane Ambler, *Breaking the Iron Bonds: Indian Control of Energy Development*, 1990; Vine Deloria Jr. and Clifford Lytle, *The Nations Within: The Past and Future of American Indian Sovereignty*, 1984; Roxanne Dunbar Ortiz, *Indians of the Americas: Human Rights and Self-Determination*, 1984; Hurst Hannum, *Autonomy, Self-Determination and Sovereignty: The Ac-*

commodation of Conflicting Rights, 1990; Phyllis Mauch Messenger, ed., *The Ethics of Collecting Cultural Property: Whose Culture? Whose Property?* 1989.

JAMES S. OLSON

TRUDELL, JOHN. John Trudell, a Santee Sioux activist and musician, was born in 1947. During the occupation of Alcatraz Island* by Indians of All Tribes* in 1969, Trudell emerged as the voice of the protest through Radio Free Alcatraz, a station that broadcast news from Berkeley, California. After the evacuation from Alcatraz, Trudell traveled widely, speaking to a variety of groups about Indian needs and demands. He then joined the American Indian Movement,* and within a few months he had become AIM's chief spokesman. In 1972 Trudell joined the Trail of Broken Treaties* caravan that crossed the country and ended in the occupation of the Bureau of Indian Affairs* building in Washington, D.C. In 1973 he was elected co-chair of the American Indian Movement. He was there in 1973 when AIM led the armed occupation of Wounded Knee,* a small town on the Pine Ridge reservation in South Dakota. In 1976, within hours of burning an American flag outside the FBI office in Washington, D.C., his wife, mother-in-law, and three children died in an arson attack on his home in Pine Ridge. More recently, Trudell has released an album—*AKA Graffiti Man*—and acted in the film *Thunderheart*.

Suggested Reading: Duane Champagne, ed., The *Native North American Almanac*, 1994.

JAMES S. OLSON

TRUST RESPONSIBILITY. The term "trust responsibility" refers to a special legal relationship between an Indian tribe and the federal government, in which the tribe is legally separate and independent from state and local political entities. Until 1871 the United States approached the various Indian tribes as individual sovereignties—separate, insular nations independent of federal and state law and subject only to their own tribal laws and customs. According to legal scholar Stephen I. Pevar, "The Indians trust the United States to fulfill the promises which were given in exchange for their land. The federal government's obligation to honor this trust relationship and to fulfill its treaty commitments is known as its *trust responsibility*."

By the 1860s, assimilationists* wanted to incorporate Native Americans into the larger body politic and found the independent legal status of the tribes counterproductive. It guaranteed their long-term separation from

other Americans. In 1871 Congress formally ended the legal sovereignty*
of Indian tribes with the Indian Appropriations Act,* subjecting them to
an array of federal, state, and local laws. When combined with the allotment* program, which Congress launched in 1887, the demise of tribal
sovereignty amounted to a wholesale assault on tribal existence. It was
not until the so-called Indian New Deal* of the 1930s that the tribes
regained their statutory authority as trustees of the federal government
who were free from the powers of state and local governmental entities.
In doing so they protected themselves from non-Indian majorities at the
state and local levels that could threaten Indian land tenure.

After World War II, however, assimilationists again gained the upper
hand in federal Indian policy, and they targeted the federal trust status
of Indian tribes as an anachronism whose relevancy had long since disappeared. The termination* movement of the 1950s and 1960s ended
the trust status of a number of Indian tribes (such as the Menominee of
Wisconsin) and subjected them to state and local laws, as well as state
and local taxes. Native American activists bitterly protested termination,
demanding the preservation of trust protection where it already existed
and its restoration to the tribes who had lost it. The termination program
was formally ended in 1970 by the Richard Nixon administration, and
the trust relationship was restored.

For Indian activists and self-determinationists,* the continuation of the
trust status is central to the survival of Indian culture and the Indian
landed estate. Most Indian leaders are convinced that without that trust
status, Indians will be victimized by the dictates of non-Indian majorities
anxious to assimilate them and seize their land for development. Because
of the existence of the trust status, Native Americans on reservations* are
exempt from state and local taxes, fish and game regulations, and anti-
casino gambling ordinances, all of which have caused controversy in recent years. By the mid-1990s the federal government had a formal trust
responsibility for 510 recognized tribes. That number included 200 village communities in Alaska.

Suggested Reading: Russel Lawrence Barsh and James Youngblood Hender-
son, *The Road: Indian Tribes and Political Liberty*, 1980; Vine Deloria Jr. and
Clifford M. Lytle, *American Indians, American Justice*, 1983; H. Barry Holt and
Gary Forrester, *Digest of American Indian Law: Cases and Chronology*, 1990;
James S. Olson and Raymond Wilson, *Native Americans in the Twentieth Century*,
1984; Stephen L. Pevar, *The Rights of Indians and Tribes: The Basic ACLU Guide
to Indian and Tribal Rights*, 1992; Wilcomb E. Washburn, *Red Man's Land, White
Man's Law: A Study of the Past and Present Status of the American Indian*, 1971;
Charles F. Wilkinson, *American Indians, Time and the Law*, 1987; John R. Wun-

der, *"Retained by The People": A History of American Indians and the Bill of Rights*, 1994.

JAMES S. OLSON

TULEE v. WASHINGTON (1942). Throughout much of the twentieth century, defining the exact nature of Native American hunting* and fishing* rights has been a source of considerable legal and political debate, at both the federal and the state level. Most tribes were considered wards of the federal government and independent of state taxation and judicial authority, and the issue of whether or not they fell under under the jurisdiction of local fish and game laws often surfaced in the halls of state legislatures and courthouses. *Tulee v. Washington* in 1942 was one of the major cases defining those rights. Local fish and game authorities arrested Tulee, a Yakima Indian, for fishing off the reservation* without a license. Tulee claimed that whether he fished on or off the reservation, he was free of the restrictions of local game laws because of his status as an Indian. The state court disagreed and convicted him of the misdemeanor offense. Tulee appealed the conviction. In 1942 the U.S. Supreme Court overturned it, without defining exactly whether licensing regulations were "reasonable and necessary" when applied to American Indians. Nevertheless, in subsequent decades Indian activists have cited *Tulee v. Washington* to prove their independence of state fish and game laws.

Suggested Reading: Russel Lawrence Barsh and James Youngblood Henderson, *The Road: Indian Tribes and Political Liberty*, 1980; Vine Deloria Jr. and Clifford M. Lytle, *American Indians, American Justice*, 1983; H. Barry Holt and Gary Forrester, *Digest of American Indian Law: Cases and Chronology*, 1990; Stephen L. Pevar, *The Rights of Indians and Tribes: The Basic ACLU Guide to Indian and Tribal Rights*, 1992; Wilcomb E. Washburn, *Red Man's Land, White Man's Law: A Study of the Past and Present Status of the American Indian*, 1971; Charles F. Wilkinson, *American Indians, Time and the Law*, 1987; John R. Wunder, *"Retained by The People": A History of American Indians and the Bill of Rights*, 1994.

JAMES S. OLSON

TURNER v. AMERICAN BAPTIST MISSIONARY UNION (1852). Because the legal status of American Indian tribes changed over the centuries, the question of treaty rights* was a constant source of discussion and controversy. When the treaties were first negotiated between the United States and the Indian tribes, the law viewed the tribes as sovereign nations. The treaties were ratified by the U.S. Senate, as were treaties with foreign nations. But as tribes ceded or sold their land, ceased to exist as functional entities, or had their sovereign status compromised by congressional legislation and the citizenship* crusades, many non-Indians hoped to abrogate those treaty arrangements. Over time, however, the federal courts have tended to recognize the level of sovereignty* enjoyed by the Indian tribes at the time of the negotiation of the treaties. The first case to recognize this reality was *Turner v. American Baptist Missionary Union* in 1852. The petitioners tried to argue that a "treaty with Indian tribes has not the same dignity or effect as a treaty with a foreign and independent nation." But a federal circuit court had a clear answer to that argument: "The distinction is not authorized by the Constitution." Ever since then, the *Turner* case has been used to buttress recognition of treaty rights.

Suggested Reading: Wilcomb E. Washburn, *Red Man's Land, White Man's Law: A Study of the Past and Present Status of the American Indian*, 1971; Charles F. Wilkinson, *American Indians, Time and the Law*, 1987; John R. Wunder, *"Retained by The People": A History of American Indians and the Bill of Rights*, 1994.

JAMES S. OLSON

U

UNITED NATIVE AMERICANS. United Native Americans was founded in 1968 by Lehman L. Brightman, who only claims a multitribal heritage, and whose own militancy was an outgrowth of the termination* movement of the 1950s and 1960s. Based in San Francisco, United Native Americans was one of the leading organizations in the Red Power* movement. Brightman was a severe critic of the Bureau of Indian Affairs* (BIA) in particular and federal Indian policy in general, and he also attacked such groups as the National Congress of American Indians,* which he felt was so moderate that its policies amounted to an alliance with the BIA. Brightman demanded Indian control of the BIA, restoration of tribal lands, and complete civil rights* for Native Americans. From 1968 to 1977, United Native Americans published a journal entitled *Warpath*.

Suggested Reading: Armand S. La Potin, *Native American Voluntary Organizations*, 1986.

JAMES S. OLSON

UNITED STATES CITIZENSHIP FOR METLAKATLA INDIANS ACT OF 1934. With passage of the Snyder Act* of 1924, U.S. citizenship* was extended to all American Indians. However, the Metlakatla Indians were a special case. In 1887 nearly eight hundred Metlakatlas left British Columbia in Canada and settled in Alaska. Four years later, in an attempt to protect these Indians from expulsion or exploitation, Congress passed a bill creating the Metlakatla reservation on the Annette Islands. The legislation also placed the Metlakatlans under the supervision of the secretary of the Interior. The question of their citizenship remained unresolved, however, until 1934. The Snyder Act had awarded citizenship to all Indians born in the United States, but some elderly Metlakatlans were natives of Canada. To settle the issue, Congress passed the United States Citizenship for Metlakatla Indians Act in 1934 as part of the Indian New Deal.*

Suggested Reading: Duane Champagne, ed., *Chronology of Native North American History*, 1994.

JAMES S. OLSON

UNITED STATES COMMISSION ON CIVIL RIGHTS. The United States Commission on Civil Rights is an independent, bipartisan agency first established in 1957 and reestablished in 1983. Its primary functions include investigating complaints alleging discrimination in voting,* researching information about legal deprivation of due process, appraising federal antidiscrimination laws, serving as a resource group for information about discrimination or denial of equal protection of the laws, and submitting evaluative reports and recommendations to the president and Congress.

In 1986 the United States Commission on Civil Rights began an evaluative study of the history and enforcement of the Indian Civil Rights Act* (ICRA) of 1968 and submitted its findings and recommendations to Congress. First and foremost, the commission found that the tribes have retained their powers of self-government and, more important, the U.S. government has established and maintained a government-to-government relationship with tribal governments. Complete enforcement of the ICRA resides with tribal governments. The commission's primary criticism was that inadequate funding had slowed the implementation and enforcement of the ICRA; consequently it felt that the lack of funding had for over twenty years placed an unfair procedural and administrative burden on tribal governments.

The commission's recommendations centered around adequate funding, training, and resources for tribal governments. They acknowledged the inherent sovereignty* of tribal governments and suggested that Congress do whatever is necessary and prudent to reinforce this right.

Suggested Reading: Russel Lawrence Barsh and James Youngblood Henderson, *The Road: Indian Tribes and Political Liberty*, 1980; Wilcomb E. Washburn, *Red Man's Land, White Man's Law*, 1971; John R. Wunder, *"Retained by The People": A History of American Indians and the Bill of Rights*, 1994.

CARLOS RAINER

UNITED STATES INDIAN COMMISSION. The United States Indian Commission was founded in 1868 by Peter Cooper, a wealthy inventor and entrepreneur who lived in New York City. Its objective was to protect Indian land and rights and put an end to frontier violence on the Great Plains. The commission's leadership was primarily white religious figures, including Congregationalist minister Henry Ward Beecher. The commission was unequivocal in its belief that the federal government had conspired with white economic interests to deprive the Plains Indians of their lands. The commission organized a nationwide petition campaign and paid for tribal leaders to come to Washington, D.C., Boston, and New York City to promote their demands. By the 1880s the efforts of the U.S. Indian Commission had largely been eclipsed by other reform groups such as the Massachusetts Indian Commission, the New York Indian Peace Commission, and the Lake Mohonk Conferences* of the Friends of the Indian.

Suggested Reading: Frederick E. Hoxie, *A Final Promise: The Campaign to Assimilate the Indians, 1880–1920*, 1984; Armand S. La Potin, *Native American Voluntary Organizations*, 1986.

JAMES S. OLSON

UNITED STATES v. CISNA (1835). The issue of tribal sovereignty* has been at the heart of Indian law cases for two centuries. But as some Indians have assimilated into the larger society, the question arises as to when such individuals become subject to state and local jurisdiction as opposed to federal and tribal jurisdiction. In 1835, Judge John McLean was riding the federal circuit in Ohio and heard the case *United States v. Cisna*. The case involved jurisdiction after a non-Indian stole a horse from an Indian on the Wyandott reservation in Ohio. Although the Indian Trade and Intercourse Act* of 1802 had clearly awarded jurisdiction in such cases to the federal courts, McLean believed that the Wyandott Indians "were surrounded by a dense white population, which have daily intercourse with the Indians. . . . They own property of almost every kind, and enjoy the comforts of life in as high degree as many of their white neighbors." Because the Indians seemed so assimilated, McLean negated the Indian Commerce Clause* of the Constitution* and awarded jurisdiction to Ohio state courts. Over the years, however, the decision in *United States v. Cisna*, which was a blow to notions of tribal sovereignty, did not prevail.

Suggested Reading: Russel Lawrence Barsh and James Youngblood Henderson, *The Road: Indian Tribes and Political Liberty*, 1980; Vine Deloria Jr. and Clifford M. Lytle, *American Indians, American Justice*, 1983; H. Barry Holt and Gary Forrester, *Digest of American Indian Law: Cases and Chronology*, 1990;

Stephen L. Pevar, *The Rights of Indians and Tribes: The Basic ACLU Guide to Indian and Tribal Rights*, 1992; Wilcomb E. Washburn, *Red Man's Land, White Man's Law: A Study of the Past and Present Status of the American Indian*, 1971; Charles F. Wilkinson, *American Indians, Time and the Law*, 1987; John R. Wunder, *"Retained by The People": A History of American Indians and the Bill of Rights*, 1994.

JAMES S. OLSON

UNITED STATES v. DION (1986). The environmental movement often created conflicts with Indian tribes over questions of sovereignty* and individual rights. In 1940, for example, Congress passed the Eagle Protection Act to prohibit the hunting of bald eagles. Under a 1962 amendment to the law, golden eagles were added to the protected list. Indians who wanted to hunt eagles had to acquire a special license from the Department of the Interior. Dwight Dion Sr., a Yankton Sioux, was arrested for violation of the law. Without the appropriate license, Dion had killed four bald eagles. He sued, arguing that his right to hunt eagles was protected by the First Amendment, the Indian Civil Rights Act* of 1968, and the Yankton Sioux Treaty of 1858. Dion also claimed that hunting the bald eagle was necessary to the free exercise of his own religion.

At the federal district level, Dion's conviction was upeld. The court claimed that he had violated the Eagle Protection Act and the Endangered Species Act of 1973. The Court of Appeals reversed the conviction based on the Endangered Species Act but allowed the conviction based on the Eagle Protection Act to stand. But in *United States v. Dion* in 1986, the Supreme Court, in a majority opinion written by Justice Thurgood Marshall, reversed the appellate and restored the federal district court's dual convictions. Marshall argued that the Eagle Protection Act of 1940 and the Endangered Species Act of 1973 both supersede the Yankton Sioux Treaty of 1858. Indian activists considered the decision a blow to Native American rights.

Suggested Reading: H. Barry Holt and Gary Forrester, *Digest of American Indian Law: Cases and Chronology*, 1990; Stephen L. Pevar, *The Rights of Indians and Tribes: The Basic ACLU Guide to Indian and Tribal Rights*, 1992; Wilcomb E. Washburn, *Red Man's Land, White Man's Law: A Study of the Past and Present Status of the American Indian*, 1971; Charles F. Wilkinson, *American Indians, Time and the Law*, 1987; John R. Wunder, *"Retained by The People": A History of American Indians and the Bill of Rights*, 1994.

JAMES S. OLSON

UNITED STATES v. JOHN SMITH (1978). In 1830 the Mississippi Choctaw tribe signed the Treaty of Dancing Rabbit Creek, agreeing to relocate themselves to the Indian Territory.* Although most members of the tribe made the journey, some remained behind, refusing to abandon their ancestral homeland. Congress extended formal recognition to the Mississippi Choctaws, which made them eligible for federal government services and which appropriated funds to purchase land for them. The secretary of the Interior formally proclaimed the existence of the Mississippi Choctaw reservation in 1944, and a year later the Mississippi Choctaws adopted a tribal constitution. At that point, they enjoyed the same level of legal sovereignty* as other federally recognized Indian tribes.

The case of *United States v. John Smith* revolved around the question of federal or state criminal jurisdiction. John Smith, a Mississippi Choctaw, had been convicted in state court of assaulting a non-Indian on the reservation. Smith appealed the conviction on the grounds that the state did not have criminal jurisdiction. However, Mississippi claimed criminal jurisdiction, arguing that since the Mississippi Choctaw reservation was of such recent origin, state law applied. The case went all the way to the U.S. Supreme Court, which decided that although the reservation had been recently established, it was still Indian country* and free of state jurisdiction. Smith was then convicted of assault in a federal court.

Suggested Reading: Russel Lawrence Barsh and James Youngblood Henderson, *The Road: Indian Tribes and Political Liberty*, 1980; Vine Deloria Jr. and Clifford M. Lytle, *American Indians, American Justice*, 1983; H. Barry Holt and Gary Forrester, *Digest of American Indian Law: Cases and Chronology*, 1990; Stephen L. Pevar, *The Rights of Indians and Tribes: The Basic ACLU Guide to Indian and Tribal Rights*, 1992; Wilcomb E. Washburn, *Red Man's Land, White Man's Law: A Study of the Past and Present Status of the American Indian*, 1971; Charles F. Wilkinson, *American Indians, Time and the Law*, 1987; John R. Wunder, *"Retained by The People": A History of American Indians and the Bill of Rights*, 1994.

                                                                                    JAMES S. OLSON

UNITED STATES v. JOSEPH (1876). In 1876 the U.S. Supreme Court heard the case of *United States v. Joseph*. The federal government wanted to apply the Indian Trade and Intercourse Act* of 1834 to the Pueblo Indians of New Mexico, which would prevent them from disposing of their lands as individuals without the consent of the U.S. government. The lands of the Pueblos had become part of the United States after the Mexican American War under the Treaty of Guadalupe Hidalgo,* with the Pueblos choosing to renounce Mexican citizenship in favor of American citizenship.*

The U.S. Supreme Court ruled that the Pueblos could sell their lands as individuals like any other citizen in New Mexico. The fact that the Pueblos had become U.S. citizens under the auspices of the Treaty of Guadalupe Hidalgo, the Supreme Court reasoned, made the Pueblo Indians unique from all other Native Americans living within the boundaries of the United States. The U.S. government had never entered into any treaties with the Pueblo Indians concerning the disposal of Pueblo lands.

Additionally, the Court felt that the Pueblo Indians were unlike any other group of Native Americans because of their lifestyle, manner, and behavior. The Court went so far as to imply that the Pueblos were Indians only in their physical appearance, suggesting patronizingly that the Pueblos were "equal" in intelligence to Europeans. A comparison was made between the Pueblos and the Amish, arguing that as the Amish were not placed under special restrictions, neither should the Pueblos be. The Court's decision temporarily protected the independent status of the Pueblos, only to be overruled in 1913 in the case of *United States v. Sandoval.**

Suggested Reading: Russel Lawrence Barsh and James Youngblood Henderson, *The Road: Indian Tribes and Political Liberty*, 1980; Wilcomb E. Washburn, *Red Man's Land, White Man's Law*, 1971; Charles F. Wilkinson, *American Indians, Time and the Law*, 1987; John R. Wunder, *"Retained by The People": A History of American Indians and the Bill of Rights*, 1994.

DARREN PIERSON

UNITED STATES v. KAGAMA (1886). In 1886 the U.S. Supreme Court heard the case *United States v. Kagama*, in which two Native Americans were accused of murdering another Indian on the Hoopa Valley reservation in California. The Hoopa Indians had become part of the United States after the Mexican American War under the auspices of the Treaty of Guadalupe Hidalgo.* As such, the Hoopa Indians had no treaties with the U.S. government to guide federal action with the Hoopa tribe.

The federal district court that first heard the case issued a certificate of division of opinion, which put the case on the doorstep of the U.S. Supreme Court. The Court had to decide who had jurisdiction in an intratribal criminal case. Could the government of the United States regulate the behavior of Indians within the same tribe on a reservation? The Supreme Court went to great lengths to point out that the U.S. Constitution* did not discuss the regulating of internal tribal matters. The right of Congress to regulate commerce with the Indian tribes was dismissed as a reason for granting the federal government criminal code rights over the reservations.* What the Court did decide, however, was that all Indian reservations resided within the geographical boundaries of the United States. According to American law, there are only two sources of sovereignty*: the state and the United States. Indians did not receive any protection from the states, nor could they expect fair treatment from the states, Miller argued, so the Indians could not be subject to the power of the states. That left only the United States to have power over the Indian tribes. The Court decided that Native Americans depended on the government of the United States for protection, food, and other items of daily survival. This dependency confirmed the right of the United States to rule the Native American population.

If the United States was the only sovereign power over the Indian nations, then obviously, the Court reasoned, Congress and the executive branch could exercise legal power over the reservations. Crimes did not have to involve non-Indians for the United States to have jurisdiction over the events. *United States v. Kagama* upheld the constitutionality of the Major Crimes Act* of 1885 and of Congress's power to legislate on behalf of American Indians.

Suggested Reading: Russel Lawrence Barsh and James Youngblood Henderson, *The Road: Indian Tribes and Political Liberty*, 1980; Wilcomb E. Washburn, *Red Man's Land, White Man's Law*, 1971; Charles F. Wilkinson, *American Indians, Time and the Law*, 1987; John R. Wunder, *"Retained by The People": A History of American Indians and the Bill of Rights*, 1994.

DARREN PIERSON

UNITED STATES v. MAZURIE (1975). In 1971 Robert Mazurie, a non-Indian, purchased land from an Indian on the Wind River Reservation in Wyoming. He then established a liquor store on the parcel. When he applied for a liquor license, however, the tribal council refused to issue it. Instead, Mazurie acquired a state liquor license and began selling alcohol products from his store. He was arrested by Indian police and convicted of illegal liquor sales. Mazurie appealed his conviction, arguing that since he had legally purchased land from an Indian on the reservation, the land was no longer under tribal jurisdiction but rather state jurisdiction. The tribal council, on the other hand, claimed that even if an individual Indian sold his own reservation property, the land remained part of Indian country* and under tribal authority. Mazurie appealed his conviction all the way to the U.S. Supreme Court.

In 1975 the Supreme Court ruled in *United States v. Mazurie* that the Indian Commerce Clause* had empowered Congress to regulate the sale of liquor in Indian country. Hence Congress had acted in accordance with the law by commending the local resolution of the issue to the sovereign* and independent authority of the Indians and their tribal courts.* Based in part on the precedent established in *Williams v. Lee** in 1959, the Court's decision acknowledged the Wind River Tribes' power to regulate the sale and distribution of alcohol and reaffirmed that tribal jurisdiction could lawfully encompass non-Indians.

Suggested Reading: Russel Lawrence Barsh and James Youngblood Henderson, *The Road: Indian Tribes and Political Liberty*, 1980; Wilcomb E. Washburn, *Red Man's Land, White Man's Law*, 1971; Charles F. Wilkinson, *American Indians, Time and the Law*, 1987; John R. Wunder, *"Retained by The People": A History of American Indians and the Bill of Rights*, 1994.

DARREN PIERSON

UNITED STATES v. NICE (1916). The Dawes Act* of 1887 authorized the allotment* of reservation* land to individual Indians. The ostensible purpose of the act was to substitute private land ownership for tribal ownership, on the assumption that private ownership would encourage self-sufficiency and advance the assimilation* of Native Americans into American society—and thereby end the need for the special trust* relationship between the individual Indian and the federal government. The Dawes Act called for the U.S. government to hold the land in trust for the Indian allottee for twenty-five years, at the end of which the land would be conveyed to the individual Indian.

In *United States v. Nice*, however, the U.S. Supreme Court rejected the notion that property ownership and citizenship* terminated the special trust relationship between individual allottees and the federal government. Nice was charged with selling liquor to an allottee, a member of the Sioux tribe in South Dakota, in violation of federal law prohibiting such sales. Nice claimed that because the allottee had been granted citizenship, the U.S. government no longer had a special trust relationship with him and therefore lacked the authority to regulate liquor sales to him. The Supreme Court disagreed, holding that "citizenship is not incompatible with tribal existence or continued guardianship, and so may be conferred without completely emancipating the Indians, or placing them beyond the reach of Congressional regulations adopted for their protection."

The opinion reflected the paternalistic attitude of the Supreme Court of this period toward Indians, who were viewed as dependent on the protection of the U.S. government because their culture was considered inferior.

Suggested Reading: Russel Lawrence Barsh and James Youngblood Henderson, *The Road: Indian Tribes and Political Liberty*, 1980; Vine Deloria Jr. and Clifford M. Lytle, *American Indians, American Justice*, 1983; H. Barry Holt and Gary Forrester, *Digest of American Indian Law: Cases and Chronology*, 1990; Stephen L. Pevar, *The Rights of Indians and Tribes: The Basic ACLU Guide to Indian and Tribal Rights*, 1992; Wilcomb E. Washburn, *Red Man's Land, White Man's Law: A Study of the Past and Present Status of the American Indian*, 1971; Charles F. Wilkinson, *American Indians, Time and the Law*, 1987; John R. Wunder, *"Retained by The People": A History of American Indians and the Bill of Rights*, 1994.

CRAIG HEMMENS

UNITED STATES v. OREGON (1969). For thousands of years, various Native American peoples fished for salmon along the Columbia River. In the 1840s and 1850s, when white settlers began arriving in the Columbia River basin of what is today Washington and Oregon, the tribes ceded land title to the federal government but negotiated treaties* retaining their hunting,* fishing,* and meeting rights at "usual and accustomed places." But in the twentieth century, logging activities and river pollution began to compromise the salmon harvests. Even worse, construction of hydroelectric dams along the Columbia and Snake Rivers inundated traditional fishing sites.

In the 1960s, to protect their fishing rights, a number of tribes sued in the federal courts. One of those cases, *United States v. Oregon*, was decided by the Supreme Court in 1969. It ruled that Native American fishing rights did not come from white people but had originated with Indian peoples. Treaties had guaranteed indigenous peoples the right to fish at their accustomed places and to enjoy jurisdictional control over their own fishing activities. The Court also ordered that the federal government, state governments, and Indian tribes establish cooperative arrangements to manage salmon resources. The decision led to the establishment of the Columbia River Inter-Tribal Fish Commission in 1977 to implement Native American jurisdictional authority and to coordinate fishing activities.

Suggested Reading: Russel Lawrence Barsh and James Youngblood Henderson, *The Road: Indian Tribes and Political Liberty*, 1980; Vine Deloria Jr. and Clifford M. Lytle, *American Indians, American Justice*, 1983; H. Barry Holt and Gary Forrester, *Digest of American Indian Law: Cases and Chronology*, 1990; Stephen L. Pevar, *The Rights of Indians and Tribes: The Basic ACLU Guide to Indian and Tribal Rights*, 1992; Wilcomb E. Washburn, *Red Man's Land, White Man's Law: A Study of the Past and Present Status of the American Indian*, 1971; Charles F. Wilkinson, *American Indians, Time and the Law*, 1987; John R. Wun-

der, *"Retained by The People": A History of American Indians and the Bill of Rights*, 1994.

JAMES S. OLSON

UNITED STATES v. SANDOVAL (1913). "Indian country"* is a phrase used to describe the land set aside for the use of Indians and supervised by the U.S. government. The importance of this designation is that state jurisdiction does not extend to Indian country; instead, federal and tribal law is supreme. The term was first used by Congress in 1790. Today, the outcome of *United States v. Sandoval* defines the term.

Three areas are included in Indian country: (1) all lands within an Indian reservation*; (2) all "trust" and "restricted" allotments* of land regardless of location within or without an Indian reservation; and (3) "all dependent Indian communities" within the United States. This last category was first articulated in *United States v. Sandoval*. A "dependent Indian community" is an Indian tribe for which the U.S. government was responsible. The issue was whether federal law prohibiting liquor sales applied to the New Mexico Pueblos.

A prior U.S. Supreme Court decision, *United States v. Joseph*,* held that the Pueblo Indians of New Mexico were no longer a distinctive Indian community and hence were not subject to federal administration and regulation. They were "Indians only in feature, complexion, and a few of their habits." In other words, they had become assimilated* to such an extent that they no longer needed the protection of the federal government.

In *Sandoval*, a white man named Sandoval had sold liquor to the Pueblos, on their lands, in contravention of federal law prohibiting such sales. Sandoval argued that because the Pueblos were not considered a distinctive Indian community, the Pueblos were not "Indian country" and state rather than federal law applied. A lower court found for Sandoval, but the U.S. Supreme Court effectively overruled *United States v. Joseph* by determining the Pueblos were "essentially a simple, uninformed and inferior people" and as such fell under the protection of the U.S. government. Therefore, the Pueblos were "Indian country" and federal law was paramount.

The opinion displayed the ignorance, racism, and paternalism of white America prevalent at the time. Although the purpose of the statute prohibiting the sale of liquor was to protect the Indians, it was predicated on the assumption that "they are easy victims to the evils and debasing influence of intoxicants." The Supreme Court opinion in *Sandoval* is full of language suggesting that Indians need extra protection because they are less than civilized.

Suggested Reading: Vine Deloria Jr. and Clifford M. Lytle, *American Indians, American Justice*, 1983; Stephen L. Pevar, *The Rights of Indians and Tribes*, 1992; Charles F. Wilkinson, *American Indians, Time and the Law: Native Societies in a Modern Constitutional Democracy*, 1987; Julie Wrend and Clay Smith, *American Indian Law Deskbook: Conference of Western Attorneys General*, 1993; John R. Wunder, *"Retained by The People"*: *A History of American Indians and the Bill of Rights*, 1994.

CRAIG HEMMENS

UNITED STATES v. SEMINOLE INDIANS OF THE STATE OF FLORIDA (1967). As part of its claim against the U.S. government, in which they had lost their ancestral lands in the 1840s under the Indian Removal Act,* the Seminoles demanded, before the Indian Claims Commission,* compensation. Under the terms of the Indian Claims Commission Act of 1946, which allowed tribes to sue the United States government to receive compensation for ancestral lands illegally seized, Indian groups suing for compensation for lost lands were required to prove long-term residency and control of a region before the U.S. government would recognize the existence of their title to the land. But the question of what constituted residency and control became a source of controversy. When the Indian Claims Commission ruled against the Seminoles, claiming that they had not occupied such a large tract, the Seminoles appealed to the Court of Claims. Its 1967 decision in *United States v. Seminole Indians of the State of Florida* found in favor of the Seminoles, arguing that title applies not just to where a tribe might have permanently lived but also to those areas that provided economic sustenance to the tribe, even if their occupation of the land was seasonal. Indian title to land, the court argued, does not depend on actual possession. According to the court, the Indian Claims Commission should consider the nature of land use in determining title.

Suggested Reading: Russel Lawrence Barsh and James Youngblood Henderson, *The Road: Indian Tribes and Political Liberty*, 1980; Vine Deloria Jr. and Clifford M. Lytle, *American Indians, American Justice*, 1983; H. Barry Holt and Gary Forrester, *Digest of American Indian Law: Cases and Chronology*, 1990; Stephen L. Pevar, *The Rights of Indians and Tribes: The Basic ACLU Guide to Indian and Tribal Rights*, 1992; Wilcomb E. Washburn, *Red Man's Land, White Man's Law: A Study of the Past and Present Status of the American Indian*, 1971; Charles F. Wilkinson, *American Indians, Time and the Law*, 1987; John R. Wunder, *"Retained by The People"*: *A History of American Indians and the Bill of Rights*, 1994.

JAMES S. OLSON

UNITED STATES v. SIOUX NATION OF INDIANS (1980). In 1868 the Treaty of Fort Laramie* included the Black Hills* of South Dakota in the Sioux reservation. But in 1877, after discovery of gold in the Black Hills, Congress passed legislation confiscating the land. However, the Black Hills region holds sacred, religious significance in Sioux culture, and on several occasions the tribe has sued for its return. In 1942 the Court of Claims denied the Sioux request, as did the Indian Claims Commission* under its 1946 statutory authority. But in 1978 Congress passed special legislation permitting the Sioux to file a third suit.

The Supreme Court rendered its decision in *United States v. Sioux Nation of Indians* in 1980. The Court decided that Congress had acted in bad faith in 1877 and that the tribe was entitled to more than $100 million in damages—an amount consistent with the land's 1877 value. The Court argued that Congress had confused its role as trustee for the Indian tribes with its power of eminent domain (the right of the government to seize private property for public use, as long as just compensation is paid). Still, the Court did not order the return of the land itself, which the Sioux were demanding; it ordered only monetary damages.

Suggested Reading: Russel Lawrence Barsh and James Youngblood Henderson, *The Road: Indian Tribes and Political Liberty*, 1980; Vine Deloria Jr. and Clifford M. Lytle, *American Indians, American Justice*, 1983; H. Barry Holt and Gary Forrester, *Digest of American Indian Law: Cases and Chronology*, 1990; Stephen L. Pevar, *The Rights of Indians and Tribes: The Basic ACLU Guide to Indian and Tribal Rights*, 1992; Wilcomb E. Washburn, *Red Man's Land, White Man's Law: A Study of the Past and Present Status of the American Indian*, 1971; Charles F. Wilkinson, *American Indians, Time and the Law*, 1987; John R. Wunder, *"Retained by The People": A History of American Indians and the Bill of Rights*, 1994.

JAMES S. OLSON

UNITED STATES v. WHEELER (1978). Before a tribal court, Wheeler, a Navajo, entered a guilty plea to a charge of disorderly conduct and contributing to the delinquency of a minor. Subsequently, as a result of the same episode and under the stipulations of the Major Crimes Act,* a federal court indicted him on the more serious allegation of statutory rape. The question at hand was whether successive prosecution of an individual in tribal and then federal courts violates the Fifth Amendment* protection against double jeopardy (being tried twice for the same crime). The defendant asserted that the federal indictment constituted a breach of the double jeopardy clause in the Fifth Amendment.

Clearly, a decision in favor of Wheeler would have set a precedent by which Indians could plead guilty to lesser charges in tribal court and thereby escape scrutiny at the federal level. Thus the Supreme Court ruled that the federal and tribal courts held what amounted to dual jurisdiction in bringing criminal offenders to justice. It argued that Indian tribes, unlike state and local governments, do not derive their authority from the federal government. They are sovereign entities, and therefore an individual prosecuted for the same crime in federal and tribal courts cannot claim a Fifth Amendment civil rights violation.

Suggested Reading: Russel Lawrence Barsh and James Youngblood Henderson, *The Road: Indian Tribes and Political Liberty*, 1980; Vine Deloria Jr. and Clifford M. Lytle, *American Indians, American Justice*, 1983; H. Barry Holt and Gary Forrester, *Digest of American Indian Law: Cases and Chronology*, 1990; Stephen L. Pevar, *The Rights of Indians and Tribes: The Basic ACLU Guide to Indian and Tribal Rights*, 1992; Wilcomb E. Washburn, *Red Man's Land, White Man's Law: A Study of the Past and Present Status of the American Indian*, 1971; Charles F. Wilkinson, *American Indians, Time and the Law*, 1987; John R. Wunder, *"Retained by The People": A History of American Indians and the Bill of Rights*, 1994.

MARK BAXTER

UNITED STATES v. WINANS (1905). For centuries, the Indians of the Pacific Northwest have fished the Columbia River for salmon and have depended on the migratory runs of these salmon for food and for much of their income. In the late nineteenth century, non-Indians who fished the river began to deny Indians access to it. Fences and guards kept Indians away from many sites that had been used for centuries by the tribes of the region. The Indians—especially the Yakima—protested, for they felt that they had a right of access to the river because of provisions in a treaty signed in 1859. In negotiating this treaty, the Yakima had agreed to sell some of their lands but also reserved the right to fish at "all usual and accustomed places . . . in common with the citizens of Washington."

The resulting 1905 court case, *United States v. Winans*, has become one of the cornerstones of Indian law. In its decision, the Supreme Court ruled that the Yakima tribe could indeed fish at traditional spots along the Columbia River. It reaffirmed several important tenets of Indian law, such as the fact that the treaty has to be interpreted today as the Indians involved in the treaty-making process would have understood it when it was being negotiated. In addition, the Court ruled that the Yakima Indians had not asked for special rights but legal recognition of the rights they had reserved in the treaty negotiations. They had sold their land, but during negotiations they had reserved the right to fish where they had fished for centuries. The Court ruled that these reserved rights were superior to current property owners' rights and even states' rights.

United States v. Winans is an important precedent in hunting* and fishing* rights cases across the country. This confirmation of the concept of reserved rights* forms the basis of court cases involving the Chippewa or Ojibway Indians of Wisconsin, as well as other fishing rights cases in the Pacific Northwest.

Suggested Reading: William C. Canby Jr., *American Indian Law in a Nutshell*, 1988; Fay G. Cohen, *Treaties on Trial: The Continuing Controversy over Northwest Indian Fishing Rights*, 1986; Donald L. Parman, *Indians and the American West in the Twentieth Century*, 1994; Robert H. Ruby and John A. Brown, *Indians of the Pacific Northwest*, 1981; Charles F. Wilkinson, *American Indians, Time and the Law*, 1987.

JASON M. TETZLOFF

UNITED STATES v. WONG KIM ARK (1897). In 1897, the Supreme Court decided this case, in which a man born in the United States was held to be a U.S. citizen even though his parents where Chinese citizens. In the majority decision, the Court took the opportunity to broadly discuss and explain U.S. citizenship* laws, devoting considerable space to the question of the citizenship of Indians born to parents who where members of the native tribes.

Affirming the interpretation made in *Elk v. Wilkins** (1884) of the Fourteenth Amendment* and the Civil Rights Act of 1866, the Court held that Indian tribes were alien nations within the United States and that members of those tribes and their children born within the United States were not U.S. citizens unless naturalized by treaty or act of Congress. The dissenting opinion did not question this point. The Court decided that this denial of citizenship applied only to members of the Indian tribes and not to children born in the United States of foreign parents of Caucasian, African, or Mongolian descent who were not in the diplomatic service of a foreign country. This case held until 1924 when pressure by Indian tribes and several groups, including the American Indian Defense Association,* brought about the Snyder Act* granting full citizenship to all Indians, about one-third of whom had not received such legal status. The law contained provisions specifically to calm the fears of Indians who worried that in gaining citizenship they would lose their tribal rights.

Suggested Reading: *Federal Reporter*, October Term, 1897, p. 649.

J. JEFFERSON MACKINNON

UNMARKED HUMAN BURIAL SITES AND SKELETAL REMAINS PROTECTION ACT OF 1989. During the 1970s and 1980s, Red Power* advocates complained bitterly about the abuse of Indian remains in federal, state, and local museums and historical societies. They demanded repatriation*—the removal from storage and return of the artifacts and remains to the tribes. In 1989 the Nebraska legislature passed the Unmarked Human Burial Sites and Skeletal Remains Protection Act, which established legal protection of unmarked burial sites and ordered the repatriation of human remains and special burial artifacts held in state-supported agencies. Many other states followed suit, as did the federal government when Congress passed the National Museum of the American Indian Act* of 1989 and the Native American Graves Protection and Repatriation Act* of 1990.

Suggested Reading: Michael M. Ames, *Cannibal Tours and Glass Boxes: The Anthropology of Museums*, 1992; Douglas Cole, *Captured Heritage: The Scramble for Northwest Coast Artifacts*, 1985; George P. Horse Capture, *The Concept of Sacred Materials and Their Place in the World*, 1989; Phyllis Mauch Messenger, ed., *The Ethics of Collecting Cultural Property: Whose Culture? Whose Property?* 1989; H. Marcus Price, ed., *Disputing the Dead: U.S. Law on Aboriginal Remains and Grave Goods*, 1991.

JAMES S. OLSON

V

VITORIA, FRANCISCO DE. Francisco de Vitoria was a vociferous critic of Spanish conquest theories and a defender of Indian rights, especially their title to their own land. Vitoria was born in the Basque area of northern Spain in 1480 and raised in Burgos, where he joined the Dominican order. A gifted scholar who spent sixteen years studying in Paris, Vitoria took teaching positions first at the College of San Gregorio in Valladolid and then at the University of Salamanca, where he earned a reputation as one of the fathers of international law. Vitoria focused his attention on colonial questions.

He was perhaps the first European intellectual to apply the idea of natural law to international law. In his book *On the Indians Lately Discovered*, Vitoria argued that Spain had no right to forcibly convert Indians to Christianity and that their refusal to convert was no justification for taking their land. But he did argue that when Indians themselves violated natural law, Spaniards were justified in making war on them. Spaniards, of course, readily used that loophole to justify violent assaults on the indigenous peoples of the New World. Nevertheless, Vitoria was one of the earliest European figures to address the question of Native American rights. He died in 1560.

Suggested Reading: Bernice Hamilton, *Political Thought in Sixteenth-Century Spain: A Study of the Political Ideas of Vitoria, Soto, Suárez, and Molina*, 1963.
JAMES S. OLSON

VOTING RIGHTS. Until 1871, U.S. authorities treated American Indians as citizens of foreign nations and, therefore, considered them ineligible to vote in national and local elections. But on January 1, 1872, after Congress passed the Indian Appropriations Act* of 1871, the United

States no longer recognized Indian tribes as sovereign nations, and a movement to assimilate Indians into American society—culturally, economically, and politically—gained momentum. Voting rights was perceived as one form of assimilation.* The Dawes Act* of 1887, which provided for the allotment* of tribal lands to individual Indians once the tribe was deemed "ready" for the process, awarded U.S. citizenship* to each Indian receiving an allotment. During the next thirty years, tens of thousands of American Indians received citizenship under the Dawes Act. All Native Americans gained citizenship with the Snyder Act* of 1924. Presumably, with citizenship came the right to vote.

However, citizenship did not always translate into the right to vote. Like African Americans in the South and Mexican Americans in the Southwest, American Indians' voting rights were often compromised by local prejudice and discrimination. In 1940 in the Selective Service Act, Congress once again designated American Indians to be American citizens and subjected them to Selective Service* registration for World War II. Despite impressive achievements in the military, in the defense industry, and on the home front by Native Americans, six states continued to deny the vote to tribal members. State constitutions in North Carolina, Utah, Washington, Idaho, New Mexico, and Arizona cited illiteracy, residency, nontaxation, and wardship status as legitimate factors in denying Native Americans access to the ballot.

After World War II, a civil rights movement began to address the problem of Native American voting rights. A powerful coalition—consisting of Commissioner of Indian Affairs John Collier,* Native American veterans groups, missionaries, and the Civil Rights Commission appointed in 1946 by President Harry Truman—lobbied to effect political reform in these states. In 1948, Arizona's restrictions against Native American voting were declared unconstitutional when the U.S. Supreme Court, in the *Harrison* v. Laveen case, enfranchised 40,000 Indian voters. Idaho in 1957 and New Mexico in 1962 completed the reform movement when they withdrew all restrictions against Indian voters.

But in many parts of the West, the right of Indian people was worth little more than the paper on which it was written. Local election officials continued to raise obstacles to voting, either through cumbersome registration and voting procedures or through outright intimidation. The Lyndon Johnson administration, as part of its Great Society program of civil rights and anti-poverty legislation, passed the Voting Rights Act of 1965 to protect the right to vote of African Americans in the South and Hispanics in the Southwest. Federal marshals were stationed at polling places throughout the South and Southwest to make sure that all people were allowed to vote. Native Americans, especially in Arizona and New Mexico, were beneficiaries of the legislation. Under the Voting Rights Act, individuals are protected from having to pay a fee or pass a literacy test in order to vote. Amendments to the legislation in 1975 also prohibited discrimination against individuals, including Indians, whose primary language is other than English.

Suggested Reading: Stephen L. Pevar, *The Rights of Indians and Tribes: The Basic ACLU Guide to Indian and Tribal Rights*, 1992.

JERE' FRANCO

VOTING RIGHTS ACT OF 1965. See **VOTING RIGHTS.**

W

WALK FOR JUSTICE. In 1994, Dennis Banks* and Mary Jane Wilson-Medrano of the American Indian Movement* (AIM) sponsored the "Walk for Justice" march. They demanded clemency for Leonard Peltier* (an imprisoned AIM leader), the end of police brutality,* and equal treatment before the law for Native Americans. They also protested construction of the James Bay Great Whale Project, a hydroelectric dam that threatens Cree and Ojibway fishing rights*; demanded the return of the Black Hills* to the Sioux; and opposed the government's attempts to settle the Navajo-Hopi land dispute. The march began at Alcatraz Island* on February 11, 1994, and ended in Washington, D.C., on July 15, 1994.

Suggested Reading: Duane Champagne, ed., *Chronology of Native North American History*, 1994.

JAMES S. OLSON

WARREN TRADING POST CO. v. ARIZONA TAX COMMISSION (1965). In 1961 the state of Arizona implemented a 2 percent sales tax for items sold by traders on Indian reservations.* This action was contested by the non-Indian operator of the Warren Trading Post, who claimed that the Arizona statute violated the congressional right to regulate Indian commerce. The Arizona Supreme Court ruled that the tax was perfectly legal and did not violate federal law.

The case was appealed to the U.S. Supreme Court in 1965. The Court ruled that Arizona had no right to impose taxes on the reservation to be paid by Indians; the state of Arizona could not levy taxes on both Indians and non-Indians on the reservation, only the non-Indians. The sales tax that Arizona tried to implement for the reservation would be a burden for the Indian population, the Court felt, and such burdens could be imposed by Congress but not by the states. The Court also argued that prior agreements between the United States and the Navajos prohibited Arizona from taxing the reservation. In addition, Justice Hugo Black argued that the state of Arizona had no responsibilities for the reservation and, therefore, had no right to collect monies there.

Suggested Reading: Monroe E. Price, *Law and the American Indian: Readings, Notes and Cases*, 1973; John R. Wunder, *"Retained by The People": A History of American Indians and the Bill of Rights*, 1994.

DARREN PIERSON

WASHINGTON v. WASHINGTON STATE COMMERCIAL PASSENGER FISHING VESSEL ASSOCIATION (1979). A bitter difference of opinion between Indians and non-Indians over fishing rights* has continued for years in the Pacific Northwest. In the 1850s, when most of the treaties* with the Indians of Washington State were negotiated, the Indians fished the rivers with hand-held dip nets, wooden traps, and a variety of hooks, spears, and arrows. By the mid-twentieth century, however, Indian commercial fishermen had switched to highly efficient monofilament gillnets, which can be stretched across most rivers and catch fish in huge numbers. Non-Indian sports fishermen especially resented the use of monofilament gillnets to catch steelhead, which is the most prized sports fish in the Pacific Northwest. They feared that Indian commercial interests would overfish the rivers and endanger the supply of steelheads. Sports fishermen interest groups successfully convinced the legislatures of Washington, Oregon, and California to outlaw the use of monofilament gillnets in all commercial steelhead operations, regardless of whether the fishermen were Indians.

However, Indian commercial fishermen regarded the laws as violations of sacred, treaty-based fishing rights. They sued in state courts, but the state judges upheld the legislation. The Washington State court claimed that the protected fishing rights the Indians enjoyed encompassed only those technologies in use in 1854. Indians appealed the decision, and in 1979 the U.S. Supreme Court rendered its decision in *Washington v. Washington State Commercial Passenger Fishing Vessel Association*. The Court sided with the Indians, upholding their treaty-based fishing rights and allowing them to adapt their fishing techniques to the most recent, efficient technologies.

Suggested Reading: Russel Lawrence Barsh and James Youngblood Henderson, *The Road: Indian Tribes and Political Liberty*, 1980; Vine Deloria Jr. and Clifford M. Lytle, *American Indians, American Justice*, 1983; H. Barry Holt and

Gary Forrester, *Digest of American Indian Law: Cases and Chronology*, 1990; Stephen L. Pevar, *The Rights of Indians and Tribes: The Basic ACLU Guide to Indian and Tribal Rights*, 1992; Wilcomb E. Washburn, *Red Man's Land, White Man's Law: A Study of the Past and Present Status of the American Indian*, 1971; Charles F. Wilkinson, *American Indians, Time and the Law*, 1987; John R. Wunder, *"Retained by The People": A History of American Indians and the Bill of Rights*, 1994.

JAMES S. OLSON

WATER RIGHTS. Disputes over Indian water rights have been long-standing and often bitter. In the water-scarce states of the West, a system of water rights has developed that often is contrary to the needs and practices of the Indians. Appropriative water rights give the priority or senior water rights to the first user of the water who puts it to "beneficial" use. Examples of beneficial use include the use of water for domestic needs and especially for agriculture. Thus in the West, large-scale irrigated agriculture often claims most of the available water rights. Although many of the major irrigation and water use projects were federally funded, Indian tribes generally were excluded by active discrimination from participating in many of these projects. This allowed non-Indians who did benefit to claim the first-user rights.

Indian claims to senior water rights, however, have considerable legal basis. In 1908 the Supreme Court ruled in *Winters v. United States** that Indian water rights were reserved by "necessary implication." The so-called Winters Doctrine meant that if the government placed a tribe on a reservation* so that its members would become farmers, it also implied that the tribe would have all the water necessary to farm. The Court reasoned that it made no sense for the federal government to adopt a reservation policy that required tribes to become farmers if it did not intend that the tribes would have priority or senior rights that superseded any white claim to available water supplies. In addition, the tribe could not lose these senior rights just because it had not exercised them.

Despite this very strong ruling, which virtually guaranteed tribes all the water they needed or would ever need, the federal government did little to assert these rights on the tribes' behalf. For much of the twentieth century, the federal government essentially distributed most of the West's water to non-Indian farmers and ranchers and to rapidly growing western cities. The Supreme Court, however, continued to strengthen Indian water rights. In its 1963 ruling in *Arizona v. California*,* it reaffirmed the tribes' senior water rights. In this case the Court ruled that the tribes of the Lower Colorado River Basin had senior and superior claims to water from the Colorado River. In its 1976 ruling in *Cappaert v. United States*, the Court expanded the concept of senior rights to include available groundwater under or near federally recognized reservations.

Despite these strong precedents, the question of Indian tribes' senior water rights has not been completely resolved. Tribes throughout the West have found it difficult to convert "paper" water rights granted them under the Winters Doctrine into real, or "wet," water. An increasingly conservative federal court system in the 1980s and 1990s has favored more state control of water rights, a defeat for tribes who have often been victims of state-level discrimination. Congress has tried to define Indian water rights clearly but has consistently been blocked by the western legislative coalition. In addition, demands for water from both Indian and non-Indian sources have increased dramatically as population has swelled in the West. Many tribes in the West have turned to negotiating or trading their sometimes theoretical water rights in return for real supplies of water or for money for economic development. As the need for more water increases, Indian water rights will continue to be a major political and economic issue in the West.

Suggested Reading: Lloyd Burton, *American Indian Water Rights and the Limits of the Law*, 1993; William C. Canby Jr., *American Indian Law in a Nutshell*, 1988; William L. Kahrl, *Water and Power: The Conflict over Los Angeles' Water Supply in the Owens Valley*, 1982; Donald L. Parman, *Indians and the American West in the Twentieth Century*, 1994; Charles F. Wilkinson, *American Indians, Time and the Law*, 1987.

JASON M. TETZLOFF

WHEELER-HOWARD ACT OF 1934. See INDIAN REORGANIZATION ACT OF 1934.

WHITE MOUNTAIN APACHE TRIBE v. BRACKER (1980).

In 1973 the state of Arizona tried to levy a motor carrier license and fuel use tax on non-Indian contractors who were carrying out logging operations on the reservation land of the White Mountain Apaches. The White Mountain Apaches sued in federal court, arguing that tribal sovereignty* prohibited the state from imposing such a tax. In 1980 the Supreme Court decided the *White Mountain Apache Tribe v. Bracker* case, agreeing with the Indians and invalidating the tax.

Suggested Reading: Stephen L. Pevar, *The Rights of Indians and Tribes: The Basic ACLU Guide to Indian and Tribal Rights*, 1992.

JAMES S. OLSON

WILLIAMS v. LEE (1958). In 1955 a non-Indian sued to collect monies owed to him by Navajo Indians in Arizona. The man operated a general store on the Navajo reservation and had entered into the contract on the Navajo reservation. In order to collect his money, however, he sued in an Arizona state court and not in the Navajo tribal court system. Over the objections of the Navajo couple being sued, the Arizona Superior Court ruled that the case could be tried in a state court because the U.S. Congress had not specifically prohibited non-Indians from filing civil suits against Indians in state courts.

The U.S. Supreme Court heard the case in 1958. The argument that Arizona courts could hear the case was rejected in the decision written by Justice Hugo Black. Black stated that Public Law 280,* which had given certain states the right to claim jurisdiction over reservation legal affairs, had not been properly implemented by the state of Arizona. As such, Arizona could not claim Public Law 280 as a rationale for hearing the case.

The Court held that states could not pass laws that would significantly interfere with the ability of tribal courts* to handle reservation legal matters. This ruling, however, was limited to the states and did not apply to the U.S. Congress or the executive branch. Congress could still limit Native American legal power on the reservations,* but the states did not enjoy the same power. Many constitutional scholars believe that *Williams v. Lee* inaugurated the modern era of federal Indian law by enhancing the power of tribal governments and restricting the jurisdiction of state and local legislative and judicial institutions.

Suggested Reading: Monroe E. Price, ed., *Law and the American Indian: Readings, Notes and Cases*, 1973; Charles F. Wilkinson, *American Indians, Time and the Law*, 1987; John R. Wunder, *"Retained by The People": A History of American Indians and the Bill of Rights*, 1994.

DARREN PIERSON

WILLIAMS, ROGER. Founder of the settlement of Providence, Rhode Island, and a negotiator between colonists and Indians. The son of a London merchant, Roger Williams was born in 1603. He reeived a B.A. from Pembroke Hall, Cambridge, in 1627, after which he went into law briefly and then into theology. Opposing the Church of England, he migrated to New England in 1630.

A learned, eloquent preacher, Williams proved uncompromising in his principles. He became assistant pastor of a Separatist church in Plymouth; but being dissatisfied with its standards, he moved to Salem and became pastor there in 1635. After quarreling with John Winthrop and other leaders of the Bay Colony, mainly over the issue of church-state relations, Williams fled Massachusetts in 1636. He bought land from the Indians and formed the settlement of Providence, Rhode Island. He served as governor of the colony from 1654 to 1657.

While still in Plymouth, Williams began to study Indian languages and later lived at times among the Narragansetts, Pequots, and Wampanoags. Although he stressed just dealings with them, Williams did not romanticize the natives. He referred to them as heathens and barbarians, yet he believed them open to divine grace. In a letter dated 1643, Williams noted: "I have acknowledged amongst them an heart sensible of kindness and have reaped kindness again from many." He greatly admired native hospitality: "a man shall generally find more free entertainment and refreshing amongst these barbarians than amongst thousands who call themselves Christians."

Williams urged the colonists to act with justice and mercy toward the Indians and to be respectful of their culture. He questioned English claims to Indian land, proposing that "it be not only possible but very easy to live and die in peace with all the natives of this country." He condemned what he called unjust wars and "cruel destruction of the Indians in New England."

Williams's interest and insight into Indian culture was rare for his time. He tried to be a liaison between colonists and Indians. During the Pequot War (1636) and King Philip's War* (1675–1676), he negotiated between the sides. As a missionary, he avoided cultural imperialism. He was open to what the Indians could teach him. What he learned of their beliefs, systems, and past history he published in a work entitled *A Key to the Language of America*. Maintaining friendly relations with them to the end, Williams died in 1683.

Suggested Reading: John Garret, *Roger Williams*, 1970; Perry Miller, *Roger Williams*, 1965.

S. CAROL BERG

WILSON v. BLOCK (1983). One of the main concerns of Red Power* advocates over the years has been the protection of the Indian landed estate. Indians have lost their land or its use has been compromised because of economic development. This has often been a critical issue to Indian religious practitioners, because for many tribes the ancestral lands possess sacred, religious significance. The *Wilson v. Block* case of 1983 involved such a dispute. The San Francisco peaks in Arizona hold great religious significance for both Hopi and Navajo peoples. Both tribes wanted to stop the development of a ski resort in the San Francisco peaks, arguing that construction of the resort would bring a flood of white tourists to the region who would inevitably pollute the area. The Indians argued that construction of the resort would constitute a violation of their religious rights. But in *Wilson v. Block*, decided in 1983, the U.S. Supreme Court disallowed the Indians' claim and allowed construction of the ski resort. The Court reasoned that since the ski development was on land that had been the private property of non-Indians for decades, Indian religious values could not be considered to have priority over non-Indian property rights.

Suggested Reading: Vine Deloria Jr., "Sacred Lands and Religious Freedom," *NARF Law Review* 16 (Spring/Summer 1991), 1–6.

JAMES S. OLSON

WINNEMUCA, SARAH. Sarah Winnemuca, a Northern Paiute, was an advocate of better treatment for American Indians and Paiutes in particular. Born in western Nevada near the Humboldt River in 1844, in the mid-1850s she moved with her family to San Jose, California. In 1858 Winnemuca lived for a time with a non-Indian family and learned English. She returned home in 1860. Winnemuca attended a Roman Catholic school for only a month before non-Indian students demanded her removal. She then went to work as a servant. Shortly after the Paiute War of 1860, Winnemuca, along with other Paiutes in Nevada and California, was forcibly relocated to a reservation* outside of Reno. Because of her English-speaking skills she soon found work as an interpreter, laboring as a liaison between U.S. Army officials and Paiute and Shoshoni Indians. Along with many Paiutes, Winnemuca was relocated to the Malheur reservation in Oregon in 1872. In 1878, during the Bannock War, she again served as an interpreter. After 1879 she spent the rest of her life touring the country advocating improved conditions for American Indians. She died of tuberculosis in 1891.

Suggested Reading: Gae Whitney Canfield, *Sarah Winnemuca of the Northern Paiutes*, 1982.

JAMES S. OLSON

WINTERS DOCTRINE. See **WATER RIGHTS; *WINTERS v. UNITED STATES*.**

WINTERS v. UNITED STATES (1908). *In Winters v. United States* (1908) the issue before the U.S. Supreme Court was that of water rights.* Farmers upstream of the Indians on the Milk River in Montana were disputing the federal government's decision to use water for irrigation projects on the Fort Belknap reservation. Western water law stipulated that precedence be given to the water needs of those upstream over any users downstream. The needs of the Fort Belknap reservation—home of the Gros Ventres, Piegans, Bloods, Blackfeet, and River Crows—were such that the total water supplies would be insufficient for both the farmers and the Indians.

The Court ruled that the reservation* was entitled to acquire necessary amounts of water from the Milk River for irrigation purposes. It reasoned that the Indians had given up their lands to become civilized peoples, and that refusing necessary water supplies to the Indians would make their attempts at settled agriculture futile. Native Americans were entitled to use water as necessary to maintain their survival, and water rights had not been given up by the Indians when they had moved onto the smaller reservation. The decision established what became known as the Winters Doctrine.

Additionally, the Court rejected the claim that the admission of Montana to statehood had terminated any agreements between the federal government and the Native Americans within the boundaries of Montana. The Supreme Court ruled that Congress had recognized the future water needs of the Indians and had reserved future water rights when it created the Fort Belknap reservation. The admission of Montana into the Union as a state had done nothing to limit those reserved rights.* The water rights of the Indians living on reservations were equal to all other claims unless competing claims had existed before the creation of the reservation.

Suggested Reading: Monroe E. Price, ed., *Law and the American Indian: Readings, Notes and Cases*, 1973; Harold A. Ranquist, "The *Winters* Doctrine and How it Grew: Federal Reservation of Rights to the Use of Water," *Brigham Young University Law Review* 4 (1975), 639–724; John R. Wunder, *"Retained by The People": A History of American Indians and the Bill of Rights*, 1994.

DARREN PIERSON

WOMEN OF ALL RED NATIONS. In 1974 a number of women Indian activists formed the Women of All Red Nations organization (WARN). Among the founders were Lorelei Means (Minneconjou Lakota), Madonna Thunderhawk (Hunkpapa Lakota), and Phyllis Young (Hunkpapa

Lakota). They are active in the American Indian Movement,* but they also realize the gender dimension of Indian activism, primarily because of the violence so often directed at male demonstrators. WARN demands an end to police brutality* and full civil rights for American Indians.

Suggested Reading: Duane Champagne, ed., *Chronology of Native North American History*, 1994.

JAMES S. OLSON

WOMEN'S NATIONAL INDIAN ASSOCIATION. During the period after the Civil War* when U.S. economic and governmental policy was extremely conservative, some important reform agencies originated that were collectively known as the Friends of the Indians. These included the federal government's Board of Indian Commissioners,* set up in 1869; the Boston Indian Citizenship Commission (1879); and the Women's National Indian Association (1881). These were followed in the early 1880s by the Indian Rights Association* and the National Indian Defense Association.*

The Women's National Indian Association was set up in 1879 by a group of Protestant churchwomen in Philadelphia under the leadership of Mrs. Amelia Quinton. Although all the agencies known as Friends of the Indians had women members, this was the only one led by women. From the beginning, the association strongly supported the allotment* program. The association also had a strong educational emphasis, petitioning Congress to increase the number of Indian schools and to improve the quality of instruction. It strongly backed citizenship* for Indians and urged the government to honor all treaty obligations to the tribes with "scrupulous fidelity." Through its monthly publication, *The Indian's Friend*, it exposed corruption in the Bureau of Indian Affairs,* protested mistreatment of the Indians, and strongly urged reform in governmental handling of Indian affairs.

The Women's National Indian Association was associated from the first with the annual Lake Mohonk Conferences* on the American Indian. Its members also attended the annual meeting of the Board of Indian Commissioners. At such meetings, they coordinated their efforts with the other Friends of the Indians. With some eighty-three branches in cities around the country, the association was the most widespread agency.

Like many other civil rights groups, the Women's National Indian Association had mixed results in helping the Indian. It was able to increase the number of schools available, although quality of instruction remained a problem. Eventually citizenship was granted to all Indians in 1924 through the Snyder Act,* but it had reached many of them earlier. On the other hand, the association had little success in influencing the honoring of treaties.* Unfortunately, it was closely associated with all the agencies in supporting passage of the Dawes Act.* Considered a reform by all groups except the National Indian Defense Association, this act was eventually a major disaster for the Indians because it resulted in the loss of millions of acres of tribal land.

Suggested Reading: Armand S. La Potin, *Native American Voluntary Organizations*, 1986; James S. Olson and Raymond Wilson, *Native Americans in the Twentieth Century*, 1984.

FRED S. ROLATER

WORCESTER v. GEORGIA (1832). This case identified federal, not state, regulation over Indian affairs. It was preceded by the case *Cherokee Nation v. State of Georgia** of 1831, which determined that Indian nations were dependent on the United States for commerce and protection. This dependency* meant that Indian nations were not true foreign nations capable of being plaintiffs in the U.S. Supreme Court while suing a state. In 1832, *Worcester v. Georgia* again raised the issue of state and federal authority regarding Indians.

Samuel Worcester was a missionary living on the Cherokee reservation in Georgia in violation of a Georgia statute prohibiting whites from living on the reservation. Worcester, who was originally from Vermont, sued the state of Georgia after being arrested by Georgia officials. Although the Cherokees were not actually participants in the case, the right of the Cherokees to control their own land was the real issue.

Worcester lost in state court and appealed the case to the U.S. Supreme Court in 1832, arguing that the state of Georgia had no right to pass laws concerning the Cherokee reservation. Such laws violated the U.S. Constitution,* Worcester argued, and various treaties* approved by the U.S. Senate. The Court ruled that Georgia did not have the right to regulate the Cherokee reservation, holding that the duty and responsibility to control Indian affairs had been given solely to the United States when the Constitution was ratified. The individual states were not given any power to regulate Indian affairs, and the Georgia statute was struck down by the Court.

Unfortunately for Worcester, he had to serve his entire four-year sentence of hard labor imposed by the state court. Bureaucratic delays and the refusal by President Andrew Jackson,* who had little sympathy for the plight of the Cherokee, to actively enforce the U.S. Supreme Court's rulings made the outcome of the appeal irrelevant to Worcester. The case itself did have a major impact on future Indian law. The supremacy of the federal government when dealing with Native Americans would be jealously guarded.

Suggested Reading: Monroe E. Price, ed., *Law and the American Indian: Readings, Notes and Cases*, 1973; Wilcomb E. Washburn, *Red Man's Land, White Man's Law*, 1971; John R. Wunder, *"Retained by The People": A History of American Indians and the Bill of Rights*, 1994.

DARREN PIERSON

WORLD WARS I AND II. For three reasons, World War I and World War II had a dramatic impact on minority affairs in the United States. First, large numbers of African Americans, Native Americans, and Latinos served in the military and were transferred overseas to Europe, where racism did not seem as deeply entrenched as it was in the United States. There, they were often treated with more acceptance and respect than in the United States; when they returned home, the prejudice and discrimination endemic to American life seemed more acute and much less tolerable. That experience raised the political consciousness of tens of thousands of minority servicemen, and after the wars they were less willing than before to tolerate racial and ethnic abuse.

Second, the rhetoric of both wars revolved around the struggle between democracy and dictatorship, with the United States viewed as the "home of the free and the brave." During World War II, for example, the rhetoric of American democratic virtue and fascist oppression raised the nation's consciousness about race, ethnicity, and equality and helped promote the civil rights movement. Among Native Americans, the National Congress of American Indians* was formed in 1944 to promote the rights of Indian people.

Third, thousands of Native Americans served their country during both wars, and many of them made the ultimate sacrifice. When those who survived returned home, many non-Indians were willing to accept the argument that men who had risked their lives for the flag deserved equal treatment before the law. The best example of that sentiment was the Indian Veteran Citizenship Act* of 1919, which awarded U.S. citizenship to Indian veterans.

Suggested Reading: Alison R. Bernstein, *American Indians and World War II*, 1991; James S. Olson and Raymond Wilson, *Native Americans in the Twentieth Century*, 1984.

JAMES S. OLSON

WOUNDED KNEE (1890). Historians are divided about what to call the bloody confrontation at Wounded Knee Creek in 1890. Some call it a massacre, others a battle; but in any event, it was the last significant military confrontation between whites and Indians in U.S. history. Wounded Knee is located on the Pine Ridge reservation in South Dakota. The Ghost Dance religion had swept through the Sioux community in the late 1880s, and its predictions of white decline and Indian triumph disturbed a number of non-Indian officials on the reservation.* The Ghost Dance did not advocate an Indian uprising. It simply promised those Indians who performed the Ghost Dance that they would be pro- tected from the white man's bullets. The religion also promised a divine apocalypse that would sweep all white people from the earth and res- urrect all dead Indians. In December 1890 a government agent panicked and called in federal troops to suppress the Ghost Dance religion. Certain that Sitting Bull* was behind the movement, the federal government sent Indian police* to arrest him, but they killed him instead. His death es- calated fear and tension among both Sioux and non-Indians. When U.S. soldiers tried to disarm a group of Sioux at Wounded Knee Creek, the Indians, angry about reservation conditions and the death of Sitting Bull, resisted the soldiers. Armed with rapid-fire Hotchkiss guns, the troops opened fire on the assembled Native Americans, slaughtering more than 150 men, women, and children. Photographs of the death scene and news stories circulated widely and created political support for Indian policy reform.

Suggested Reading: Ralph K. Andrist, *The Long Death: The Last Days of the Plains Indians*, 1964; Roxanne Dunbar Ortiz, "Wounded Knee 1890 to Wounded Knee 1973: A Study in United States Colonialism," *Journal of Ethnic Studies* 8 (Summer 1980); Weston LaBarre, *The Ghost Dance*, 1970; James Mooney, *The Ghost Dance Religion and the Sioux Outbreak of 1890*, 1965.

JAMES S. OLSON

WOUNDED KNEE (1973). After American Indian Movement* (AIM) mil- itants seized the symbolic site of Wounded Knee, situated on the Pine Ridge reservation in South Dakota, where U.S. troops had slaughtered more than 150 Sioux men, women, and children in 1890, federal agents descended on the scene. Thus commenced an armed stand-off that at- tracted international attention. The actions of the pan-Indian* activists were partially motivated by claims that the duly elected tribal leader at Pine Ridge, Richard Wilson, and his Indian police* force were the pliant surrogates of the Bureau of Indian Affairs.* The ensuing confrontation, which lasted for more than seventy days, fueled a media blitz that did much to publicize and dramatize the plight of the American Indian. In the process, the militant Indians declared the sovereign independence of the Oglala Sioux Nation in accordance with the boundaries established by the Treaty of Fort Laramie* of 1868. Having achieved a substantial propaganda victory, AIM leaders negotiated a peaceful withdrawal and vacated their stronghold at Wounded Knee.

Although the incident at Wounded Knee succeeded in making Indian grievances front-page news, AIM tactics elicited a mixed response from the Native American community. Many Indians objected to the violent actions and inflammatory rhetoric of Oglala Sioux spokesman Russell Means* and AIM. Moreover, in most instances American Indian militancy had little or no effect on the direction of federal Indian policy and in some respects proved self-defeating by alienating formerly sympathetic whites.

Suggested Reading: Robert Burnette and John Koster, *The Road to Wounded Knee*, 1974; Roxanne Dunbar Ortiz, "Wounded Knee 1890 to Wounded Knee 1973: A Study in United States Colonialism," *Journal of Ethnic Studies* 8 (Summer 1980); James S. Olson and Raymond Wilson, *Native Americans in the Twentieth Century*, 1984; Francis Paul Prucha, *The Great Father*, Vol. 2, 1994.

MARK BAXTER

WOVOKA. Wovoka, also known as Jack Wilson, was the founder of the Ghost Dance religion. Born around 1856 in Mason Valley, Nevada, to a Paiute Indian family, Wovoka was adopted, when his father died, by the local Wilson family, who renamed him Jack. Sometime in the late 1880s Wovoka fell ill with a high fever, and during his sickness he had a dream or vision that eventually led to the development of the Ghost Dance religion. In the vision, Wovoka claimed to have received a revelation from the Great Spirit, which told him to pass on a simple message to his people: avoid fighting and stealing, love one another, and perform the Ghost Dance. If the Indians were obedient, the Great Spirit would soon restore all their lands, revive the buffalo herds, resurrect dead Indians, and kill all white people in a great flood.

Consisting of five days of physically exhausting dancing, complete with a series of other rituals, the Ghost Dance offered hope and redemption to Indian peoples, and it spread rapidly throughout the Great Basin and onto the Great Plains. Whites, of course, found its prophecy of their demise quite threatening. Although the religion became an important phenomenon among late nineteenth-century Native Americans, its spread was spontaneous. Wovoka himself never traveled much beyond the region of what is today the Walker Lake reservation. He died in 1932.

Suggested Reading: James Mooney, *The Ghost Dance Religion and the Sioux Outbreak of 1890*, 1896; James S. Olson and Raymond Wilson, *Native Americans in the Twentieth Century*, 1984.

JAMES S. OLSON

Z

ZAH, PETER. Peter Zah, a leader of the Navajo Nation, was born in 1928 on the Window Rock Navajo reservation in Arizona. He attended the Phoenix Indian School of the Bureau of Indian Affairs* and then won a basketball scholarship to Arizona State University in Tempe. In 1963 he graduated with a degree in education. Zah then returned to Window Rock, where he taught carpentry skills to Indian children. He later went to work for the Volunteers in Service to America (VISTA), a Peace Corps–like federal agency serving communities in the United States. He headed the VISTA training center at Arizona State University. A year later Zah took a position with Navajo People's Legal Services, a state-chartered agency dedicated to establishing Native American civil rights and tribal sovereignty* through legal action.

Zah's success as a leader with (DNA) gave him a high profile in the Navajo community. In 1987 he became the primary fund-raiser for the Navajo Education and Scholarship Foundation. Three years later he was elected president of the Navajo Nation. In 1992 Zah was elected chairman of the Navajo Nation and remains the only man to be elected to both positions.

Suggested Reading: Duane Champagne, ed., *Chronology of Native North American History*, 1994.

JAMES S. OLSON

APPENDIX: MAJOR INDIAN CIVIL RIGHTS COURT CASES

CITIZENSHIP

Elk v. Wilkins (1884)

McKay v. Campbell (1870)

Standing Bear v. Crook (1879)

Swift v. Leach (1920)

United States v. Wong Kim Ark (1897)

CIVIL JURISDICTION

Fisher v. District Court of Montana (1976)

Kennerly v. District Court (1971)

National Farmers Union Insurance Company v. Crow Tribe (1985)

United States v. Nice (1916)

Williams v. Lee (1958)

CIVIL LIBERTIES

Allen v. Merrill (1957)

Colliflower v. Garland (1965)

Dodge v. Nakai (1969)

Elk v. Wilkins (1884)

Harrison v. Laveen (1948)

Iron Crow v. Oglala Sioux Tribe (1956)

Mississippi Band of Choctaw Indians v. Holyfield et al. (1989)

Morton v. Mancari (1974)

Piper v. Big Pine School District (1924)

Standing Bear v. Crook (1879)

Swift v. Leach (1920)

United States v. Nice (1916)

United States v. Wheeler (1978)

CRIMINAL JURISDICTION

Duro v. Reina (1990)

Ex Parte Crow Dog (1883)

Gerber v. United States (1993)

McBratney v. United States (1882)

Oliphant v. Suquamish Indian Tribe (1978)

Talton v. Mayes (1896)

United States v. John Smith (1978)

United States v. Kagama (1886)

United States v. Wheeler (1978)

FISHING AND HUNTING RIGHTS

Antoine v. Washington (1974)

Kimball v. Callahan (1974)

Metlakatla Indian Community v. Egan (1961)

New Mexico v. Mescalero Apache Tribe (1983)

Organized Village of Kake v. Egan (1962)

Puyallup Tribe v. Department of Game (Puyallup I) (1968)

Puyallup Tribe v. Department of Game (Puyallup II) (1973)

Puyallup Tribe v. Department of Game (Puyallup III) (1977)

Tulee v. Washington (1942)

United States v. Oregon (1969)

Washington v. Washington State Commercial Passenger Fishing Vessel Association (1979)

GAMING OPERATIONS

Cabazon Band of Mission Indians v. California (1987)

Seminole Tribe of Florida v. Butterworth (1981)

Seminole Tribe v. Florida (1996)

LAND TITLE AND COMPENSATION

Barker v. Harvey (1901)

Caddo Tribe of Oklahoma, et al. v. United States (1961)

Confederated Tribes of the Warm Springs Reservation of Oregon v. United States (1966)

County of Oneida v. Oneida Indian Nation (1985)

Fletcher v. Peck (1810)

Georgia v. Tassel (1830)

Johnson's and Graham's Lessee v. M'Intosh (1823)

The Kansas Indians (1866)

Lipan Apache Tribe, etc., Mescalero Apache Tribe, etc., and the Apache Tribe of the Mescalero Reservation, etc. v. the United States (1967)

Lone Wolf v. Hitchcock (1903)

New Jersey v. Wilson (1812)

Seneca Nation of Indians v. United States (1965)

Turner v. American Baptist Missionary Union (1852)

United States v. Joseph (1876)

United States v. Sioux Nation of Indians (1980)

RELIGIOUS FREEDOM

Badoni v. Higginson (1980)

Employment Division, Department of Human Resources of Oregon, et al. v. Alfred L. Smith (1990)

Fools Crow v. Gullet (1983)

Lyng v. Northwest Indian Cemetery Protective Association (1988)

Native American Church v. Navajo Tribal Council (1959)

People v. Woody (1964)

Quick Bear v. Leupp (1908)

Sequoyah v. Tennessee Valley Authority (1980)

Toledo et al. v. Pueblo de Jemez et al. (1954)

Trapp et al. v. DuBois et al. (1995)

United States v. Dion (1986)

United States v. Wheeler (1978)

Wilson v. Block (1983)

TAXATION

Central Machinery Co. v. Arizona State Tax Commission (1980)

Choate v. Trapp (1911)

Department of Taxation and Finance of New York State v. Milhelm Attea & Bros. (1994)

Iron Crow v. Oglala Sioux Tribe (1956)

The Kansas Indians (1866)

Kerr-McGee Corp. v. Navajo Tribe (1985)

McClanahan v. Arizona State Tax Commission (1973)

Merrion v. Jicarilla Apache Tribe (1982)

Mescalero Apache Tribe v. Jones (1973)

Moe v. Confederated Salish & Kootenai Tribes (1976)

Montana v. Blackfeet Tribe (1985)

Oklahoma Tax Commission v. Citizen Band Potawatomi Indian Tribe (1991)

Squire v. Capoeman (1956)

Warren Trading Post Co. v. Arizona Tax Commission (1965)

White Mountain Apache Tribe v. Bracker (1980)

TRIBAL SOVEREIGNTY

Brendale v. Confederated Tribes and Bands of the Yakima Indian Nation (1989)

Cherokee Nation v. State of Georgia (1831)

Colliflower v. Garland (1965)

Dodge v. Nakai (1969)

Ex Parte Crow Dog (1883)

Fisher v. District Court of Montana (1976)

Georgia v. Tassel (1830)

Iron Crow v. Oglala Sioux Tribe (1956)

Kerr-McGee Corp. v. Navajo Tribe (1985)

Lac Courte Oreilles Band of Lake Superior Chippewa Indians et al. v. State of Wisconsin (1991)

Lone Wolf v. Hitchcock (1903)

Martinez v. Santa Clara Pueblo (1978)

Martinez v. Southern Ute Tribe (1955)

Menominee Tribe of Indians v. United States (1968)

Merrion v. Jicarilla Apache Tribe (1982)

Mississippi Band of Choctaw Indians v. Holyfield et al. (1989)

Missouri, Kansas and Texas Railway Company v. Roberts (1894)

Native American Church v. Navajo Tribal Council (1959)

Oklahoma Tax Commission v. Citizen Band Potawatomi Indian Tribe (1991)

Seminole Tribe of Florida v. Butterworth (1981)

Talton v. Mayes (1896)

United States v. Cisna (1835)

United States v. Mazurie (1975)

United States v. Wheeler (1978)

Worcester v. Georgia (1832)

TRUST RELATIONSHIP

Fisher v. District Court of Montana (1976)

United States v. Sandoval (1913)
Worcester v. Georgia (1832)

WATER RIGHTS

Ahtanum Irrigation District v. United States (1956)
Arizona v. California (1963)
Colorado River Water Conservation District v. United States (1976)
Kansas v. Colorado (1907)
Metlakatla Indian Community v. Egan (1961)
Montana v. United States (1981)
Nevada v. United States (1983)
Skeem v. United States (1921)
United States v. Winans (1905)
Winters v. United States (1908)

SELECT
BIBLIOGRAPHY

Aberle, David F. *The Peyote Religion among the Navajo*. 1966.

Ambler, Marjane. *Breaking the Iron Bonds: Indian Control of Energy Development*. 1990.

Ames, Michael M. *Cannibal Tours and Glass Boxes: The Anthropology of Museums*. 1992.

Anderson, Edward F. *Peyote: The Divine Cactus*. 1980.

Anderson, Terry I. *Property Rights, Constitutions and Indian Economies*. 1992.

Arnold, Robert D. *Alaska Native Land Claims*. 1978.

Barsh, Russel Lawrence, and James Youngblood Henderson. *The Road: Indian Tribes and Political Liberty*. 1980.

Bataille, Gretchen M., and Charles L. P. Silet, eds. *The Pretend Indians: Images of Native Americans in the Movies*. 1980.

Bee, Robert L. *The Politics of American Indian Policy*. 1982.

Berkhofer, Robert E., Jr. *Salvation and the Savage: An Analysis of Protestant Missions and American Indian Response, 1787–1862*. 1965.

———. *The White Man's Indian: Images of the Indian from Columbus to the Present*. 1978.

Bernstein, Alison R. *American Indians and World War II: Towards a New Era in Indian Affairs*. 1991.

Boldt, Menno. *Surviving as Indians: The Challenge of Self-Government*. 1994.

Bowden, Henry Warner. *American Indians and Christian Missions: Studies in Cultural Conflict*. 1981.

Boyer, Ernest L. *Tribal Colleges: Shaping the Future of Native America*. 1989.

Brodeur, Paul. *Restitution: The Land Claims of the Mashpee, Passamaquoddy, and Penobscot Indians of New England*. 1985.

Brophy, William A., and Sophie D. Aberle. *The Indian, America's Unfinished Business: Report of the Commission on the Rights, Liberties and Responsibilities of the American Indian*. 1966.

Burnette, Robert, and John Koster. *The Road to Wounded Knee*. 1974.

Burt, Larry W. *Tribalism in Crisis: Federal Indian Policy, 1953–1961*. 1982.

Burton, Lloyd. *American Indian Water Rights and the Limits of the Law*. 1991.
Cadwalader, Sandra A., and Vine Deloria Jr., eds. *The Aggressions of Civilization: Federal Indian Policy since the 1880s*. 1984.
Cahn, Edgar S., ed. *Our Brother's Keeper: The Indian in White America*. 1969.
Calloway, Colin B. *The American Revolution in Indian Country: Crisis and Diversity in Native American Communities*. 1995.
Canby, William C., Jr. *American Indian Law in a Nutshell*. 1988.
Carlson, Leonard A. *Indians, Bureaucrats, and Land: The Dawes Act and the Decline of Indian Farming*. 1981.
Case, David S. *Alaska Natives and American Laws*. 1984.
Castille, George Pierre, and Robert L. Bee., eds. *State and Reservation: New Perspectives on Federal Indian Policy*. 1992.
Chamberlain, J. E. *The Harrowing of Eden: White Attitudes toward North American Natives*. 1975.
Champagne, Duane, ed. *Chronology of Native North American History*. 1994.
———. *The Native North American Almanac*. 1994.
Churchill, Ward. *Struggle for the Land: Indigenous Resistance to Genocide, Ecocide, and Expropriation in Contemporary North America*. 1992.
Churchill, Ward, and Jim Vander Wall. *Agents of Repression: The FBI's Secret Wars against the Black Panther Party and the American Indian Movement*. 1988.
Cleman, Michael C. *American Indian Children at School, 1850–1930*. 1993.
Clinon, Robert N., Nell Jessup Newton, and Monroe E. Price. *American Indian Law: Cases and Materials*. 1991.
Cohen, Fay G. *Treaties on Trial: The Continuing Controversy over Northwest Indian Fishing Rights*. 1986.
Cohen, Felix S. *Felix S. Cohen's Handbook of Federal Indian Law*. 1982.
Cole, Douglas. *Captured Heritage: The Scramble for Northwest Coast Artifacts*. 1985.
Collier, John. *From Every Zenith: A Memoir and Some Essays on Life and Thought*. 1963.
Cornell, Stephen. *The Return of the Native: American Indian Political Resurgence*. 1988.
Davis, Mary B., ed. *Native Americans in the Twentieth Century: An Encyclopedia*. 1994.
Debo, Angie. *And the Waters Still Run*. 1941.
———. *A History of the Indians of the United States*. 1970.
Dejong, David H. *Promises of the Past: A History of Indian Education in the United States*. 1993.
Deloria, Vine, Jr. *American Indian Policy in the Twentieth Century*. 1985.
———. *Behind the Trail of Broken Treaties: An Indian Declaration of Independence*. 1974.
———. *Custer Died for Your Sins: An Indian Manifesto*. 1969.
———. *God Is Red*. 1973.
———. *We Talk, You Listen: New Tribes, New Turf*. 1970.
Deloria, Vine, Jr., and Clifford Lytle. *American Indians, American Justice*. 1983.
———. *The Nations Within: The Past and Future of American Indian Sovereignty*. 1984.

Dippie, Brian W. *The Vanishing American: White Attitudes and U.S. Indian Policy*. 1982.

Drinnon, Richard. *Facing West: The Metaphysics of Indian-Hating and Empire Building*. 1980.

DuMars, Charles T., Marilyn O'Leary, and Albert E. Utton. *Pueblo Indian Water Rights: Struggle for a Precious Resource*. 1984.

Dunbar Ortiz, Roxanne. *The Great Sioux Nation: Sitting in Judgment on America. An Oral History of the Sioux Nation and Its Struggle for Sovereignty*. 1977.

———. *Indians of the Americas: Human Rights and Self-Determination*. 1984.

Falkowski, James E. *Indian Law/Race Law: A Five Hundred Year History*. 1992.

Fey, Harold E., and D'Arcy McNickle. *Indians and Other Americans: Two Ways of Life Meet*. 1970.

Fixico, Donald L. *Termination and Relocation: Federal Indian Policy, 1945–1960*. 1986.

Forbes, Jack D. *The Indians in America's Past*. 1964.

———. *Native American Higher Education: The Struggle for the Creation of D-Q University, 1960–1971*. 1985.

———. *Native Americans and Nixon: Presidential Politics and Minority Self-Determination, 1969–1972*. 1981.

Foreman, Grant. *Indian Removal: The Emigration of the Five Civilized Tribes of Indians*. 1932.

Fortunate Eagle, Adam. *Alcatraz! Alcatraz! The Indian Occupation of 1969–1971*. 1992.

Friesen, Carol. *Disputed Jurisdiction and Recognition of Judgments between Tribal and State Courts*. 1990.

Fritz, Henry. *The Movement for Indian Assimilation, 1860–1890*. 1963.

Fuchs, Estelle, and Robert J. Havighurst. *To Live on This Earth: American Indian Education*. 1983.

Gedicks, Al. *New Resource Wars: Native and Environmental Struggles against Multinational Corporations*. 1993.

Getches, David H., and Charles F. Wilkinson. *Cases and Materials on Federal Indian Law*. 1993.

Gibson, Arrell Morgan. *The American Indian: Prehistory to the Present*. 1980.

———. *Between Two Worlds*. 1986.

Green, Donald E., and Thomas V. Tonnesen, eds. *American Indians: Social Justice and Public Policy*. 1991.

Green, L. C., and Olive P. Dickson, *The Law of Nations and the New World*. 1989.

Greenberg, Pam, and Jody Zelio. *States and the Indian Gaming Regulatory Act*. 1992.

Grinde, Donald A., Jr., and Bruce E. Johansen. *Exemplar of Liberty: Native America and the Evolution of Democracy*. 1991.

Gross, Emma R. *Contemporary Federal Policy toward American Indians*. 1989.

Guillemin, Jeanne. *Urban Renegades: The Cultural Strategy of the American Indians*. 1975.

Hagan, William T. *American Indians*. 1993.

———. *Indian Police and Judges: Experiments in Acculturation and Control*. 1966.

————. *The Indian Rights Association: The Herbert Welsh Years, 1882–1904*. 1985.

Hannum, Hurst. *Autonomy, Self-Determination and Sovereignty: The Accommodation of Conflicting Rights*. 1990.

Harring, Sidney L. *Crow Dog's Case: American Indian Sovereignty, Tribal Law, and United States Law in the Nineteenth Century*. 1994.

Hart, Richard E. *Zuni and the Courts: A Struggle for Sovereign Land Rights*. 1995.

Harvey, Karen D., and Lisa D. Harjo. *Indian Country: A History of Native People in America*. 1994.

Hauptman, Laurence M. *The Iroquois and the New Deal*. 1981.

————. *The Iroquois Struggle for Survival: World War II to Red Power*. 1986.

————. *Tribes and Tribulations: Misconceptions about American Indians*. 1995.

Hertzberg, Hazel W. *The Search for an American Indian Identity: Modern Pan-Indian Movements*. 1971.

Hill, Tom, and Richard W. Hill, eds. *Creation's Journey: Native American Identity and Belief*. 1994.

Hoebel, E. Adamson. *The Law of Primitive Man: A Study in Comparative Legal Dynamics*. 1954.

Hoebel, E. Adamson, and Karl N. Llewellyn. *The Cheyenne Way: Conflict and Case Law in Primitive Jurisprudence*. 1941.

Holt, H. Barry, and Gary Forrester. *Digest of American Indian Law: Cases and Chronology*. 1990.

Horse Capture, George P. *The Concept of Sacred Materials and Their Place in the World*. 1989.

Horsman, Reginald. *Expansion and American Indian Policy, 1783–1812*. 1967.

Hoxie, Frederick. *A Final Promise: The Campaign to Assimilate the Indians, 1880–1920*. 1984.

Huddleston, Lee E. *Origins of the American Indians: European Concepts, 1492–1729*. 1967.

Hundley, Norris. *Water and the West*. 1981.

Iverson, Peter. *Carlos Montezuma and the Changing World of American Indians*. 1982.

Jacobs, Wilbur R. *Dispossessing the American Indian: Indians and Whites on the Colonial Frontier*. 1972.

Jennings, Francis. *The Founders of America: From the Earliest Migrations to the Present*. 1993.

Johansen, Bruce, and Roberto Maestas. *Wasi'chu: The Continuing Indian Wars*. 1979.

Johnson, Troy R. *The Occupation of Alcatraz Island: Indian Self-Determination and the Rise of Indian Activism*. 1996.

Johnston, Basil H. *Indian School Days*. 1989.

Jones, Dorothy V. *License for Empire: Colonialism by Treaty in Early America*. 1982.

Josephy, Alvin M., Jr. *The Indian Heritage of America*. 1970.

————. *Now That the Buffalo's Gone: A Study of Today's American Indians*. 1984.

————. *Red Power: The American Indians' Fight for Freedom*. 1971.

Kappler, Charles J. *Indian Affairs: Laws and Treaties*. 5 vols. 1904–1941.

Keller, Robert H. *American Protestantism and United States Indian Policy, 1869–1882*. 1983.

Kelly, Lawrence C. *The Assault on Assimilation: John Collier and the Origins of Indian Policy Reform*. 1983.

———. *The Navajo Indians and Federal Indian Policy, 1900–1935*. 1968.

LaBarre, Weston. *The Peyote Culture*. 1975.

La Potin, Armand S. *Native American Voluntary Organizations*. 1986.

Layton, Robert, ed. *Conflict in the Archaeology of Living Traditions*. 1989.

Lazarus, Edward. *Black Hills, White Justice: The Sioux Nation versus the United States, 1775 to the Present*. 1991.

Levitan, Sar A., and Barbara Hetrick. *Big Brother's Indian Programs, with Reservations*. 1971.

Levitan, Sar A., and William B. Johnson. *Indian Giving: Federal Programs for Native Americans*. 1979.

Levy, Jerrold E., and S. J. Kunitz. *Indian Drinking: Navajo Practices and Anglo-American Theories*. 1974.

Lewellen, Ted C. *Political Anthropology: An Introduction*. 1983.

Limerick, Patricia Nelson. *The Legacy of Conquest: The Unbroken Past of the American West*. 1987.

Lincoln, Kenneth. *Native American Renaissance*. 1983.

Lyden, Fremont J., and Lyman H. Legters, eds. *Native Americans and Public Policy*. 1992.

Lyons, Oren. *Exiled in the Land of the Free: Democracy, Indian Nations, and the U.S. Constitution*. 1992.

Mardock, Robert W. *The Reformers and the American Indian*. 1971.

Matthiessen, Peter. *In the Spirit of Crazy Horse*. 1991.

———. *Indian Country*. 1984.

McCool, Daniel. *Command of the Waters*. 1987.

McDonnell, Janet A. *The Dispossession of the American Indian, 1887–1934*. 1991.

McLoughlin, William G. *After the Trail of Tears: The Choctaw Struggle for Sovereignty, 1839–1880*. 1994.

McNickle, D'Arcy. *Native American Tribalism: Indian Survivals and Renewals*. 1973.

Meriam, Lewis. *The Problem of Indian Administration*. 1928.

Messenger, Phyllis Mauch, ed. *The Ethics of Collecting Cultural Property: Whose Culture? Whose Property?* 1989.

Meyer, William. *Native Americans: The New Indian Resistance*. 1971.

Miner, H. Craig. *The Corporation and the Indian: Tribal Sovereignty and Industrial Civilization in Indian Territory, 1865–1907*. 1976.

Nagel, Joane. *American Indian Ethnic Renewal: Red Power and the Resurgence of Identity and Culture*. 1995.

Neils, Elaine M. *Reservation to City: Indian Migration and Federal Relocation*. 1971.

O'Brien, Sharon. *American Indian Tribal Governments*. 1989.

Orfield, Gary. *A Study of the Termination Policy*. 1965.

Otis, D. S. *The Dawes Act and the Allotment of Indian Lands*. 1973.

Parman, Donald L. *Indians and the American West in the Twentieth Century*. 1994.

———. *The Navajos and the New Deal*. 1976.

Pearce, Roy H. *Savagism and Civilization: A Study of the Indian and the American Mind*. 1965.

Peroff, Nicholas C. *Menominee Drums: Tribal Termination and Restoration, 1954–1974*. 1982.

Perry, Richard J. *Apache Reservation: Indigenous Peoples and the American State*. 1993.

Pevar, Stephen L. *The Rights of Indians and Tribes: The Basic ACLU Guide to Indian and Tribal Rights*. 1992.

Philp, Kenneth R. *John Collier's Crusade for Indian Reform, 1920–1954*. 1977.

Philp, Kenneth R., ed. *Indian Self-Rule: First-Hand Accounts of Indian-White Relations from Roosevelt to Reagan*. 1986.

Pommershein, Frank. *Braid of Feathers: American Indian Law and Contemporary Tribal Life*. 1995.

Price, H. Marcus, ed. *Disputing the Dead: U.S. Law on Aboriginal Remains and Grave Goods*. 1991.

Price, Monroe E. *Law and the American Indian: Readings, Notes and Cases*. 1973.

Priest, Loring Benson. *Uncle Sam's Stepchildren: The Reformation of United States Indian Policy, 1865–1887*. 1942.

Prucha, Francis Paul. *American Indian Policy in Crisis: Christian Reformers and the Indian, 1865–1900*. 1976.

———. *American Indian Policy in the Formative Years: The Indian Trade and Intercourse Acts, 1790–1834*. 1962.

———. *American Indian Treaties*. 1994.

———. *The Great Father: The United States Government and the American Indians*. 2 vols. 1984.

Query, Ron. *Native American Struggle for Equality*. 1992.

Reid, John Phillip. *A Better Kind of Hatchet: Law, Trade, and Diplomacy in the Cherokee Nation during the Early Years of European Contact*. 1976.

———. *A Law of Blood: The Primitive Law of the Cherokee*. 1970.

Reno, Philip. *Mother Earth, Father Sky, and Economic Development: Navajo Resources and Their Use*. 1981.

Reyner, John, and Jeanne Eder. *A History of Indian Education*. 1989.

Richardson, Jane. *Law and Status among the Kiowa Indians*. 1940.

Rosenthal, Harvey D. *Their Day in Court: A History of the Indian Claims Commission*. 1990.

Schrader, Robert Fay. *The Indian Arts and Crafts Board: An Aspect of New Deal Indian Policy*. 1983.

Sckolnick, Lewis B. *American Indians*. 1994.

Senese, Guy B. *Self-Determination and the Social Education of Native Americans*. 1991.

Shattuck, Peter T., and Jill Norgren. *Partial Justice: Federal Indian Law in a Liberal Constitutional System*. 1991.

Sheehan, Bernard W. *Seeds of Extinction: Jeffersonian Philanthropy and the American Indian*. 1973.

Slotkin, Sydney J. *The Peyote Religion: A Study in Indian-White Relations*. 1956.

Snipp, C. Matthew. *American Indians: The First of This Land*. 1989.

Sorkin, Alan L. *American Indians and Federal Aid*. 1971.

———. *The Urban American Indian*. 1978.

Spaeth, Nicholas J. *American Indian Law Deskbook*. 1993.

Spicer, Edward H. *Cycles of Conquest: The Impact of Spain, Mexico, and the United States on the Indians of the Southwest, 1533–1960*. 1962.

Starr, June, and Jane F. Collier, eds. *History and Power in the Study of Law: New Directions in Legal Anthropology*. 1989.

Steiner, Stan. *The New Indians*. 1968.

Stern, Kenneth S. *Loud Hawk: The United States versus the American Indian Movement*. 1994.

Stewart, Omer C. *Peyote Religion: A History*. 1987.

Strickland, Rennard. *Fire and Spirits: Cherokee Laws from Clan to Court*. 1975.

Sutton, Imre, ed. *Irredeemable America: The Indians' Estate and Land Claims*. 1985.

Szasz, Margaret Connell. *Education and the American Indian: The Road to Self-Determination since 1928*. 1977.

Taylor, Graham D. *The New Deal and American Indian Tribalism: The Administration of the Indian Reorganization Act, 1934–1945*. 1980.

Taylor, Theodore W. *The Bureau of Indian Affairs*. 1984.

Thomson, Judith Jarvis. *The Realm of Rights*. 1990.

Thornton, Russell. *American Indian Holocaust and Survival: A Population History since 1492*. 1987.

Trennert, Robert A., Jr. *Alternative to Extinction: Federal Indian Policy and the Beginnings of the Reservation System, 1846–1851*. 1975.

Tyler, S. Lyman. *A History of Indian Policy*. 1973.

Utley, Robert. *The Indian Frontier of the American West, 1846–1890*. 1984.

Vecsey, Christopher. *Handbook of American Indian Religious Freedom*. 1991.

Vecsey, Christopher, and William A. Starna, eds. *Iroquois Land Claims*. 1988.

Viola, Herman J. *After Columbus: The Smithsonian Chronicle of the North American Indians*. 1990.

Vizenor, Gerald. *Manifest Manners: Postindian Warriors of Survivance*. 1994.

Waddell, Jack O., and Michael W. Everett, eds. *Drinking Behavior among Southwestern Indians: An Anthropological Perspective*. 1980.

Waddell, Jack O., and O. Michael Watson, eds. *The American Indian in Urban Society*. 1971.

Walker, Hans, Jr. *Federal Indian Tax Rules: A Compilation of Internal Revenue Service Rules Relating to Indians*. 1989.

Washburn, Wilcomb E. *The Assault on Indian Tribalism: The General Allotment Law (Dawes Act) of 1887*. 1975.

———. *The Indian in America*. 1975.

———. *Red Man's Land, White Man's Law: A Study of the Past and Present Status of the American Indian*. 1971.

Wells, Robert N., Jr., ed. *Native American Resurgence and Renewal*. 1994.

Weyler, Rex. *Blood of the Land: The Government and Corporate War against the American Indian Movement*. 1982.

White, Richard. *Roots of Dependency: Subsistence, Environment, and Social Change among the Choctaws, Pawnees, and Navajos*. 1983.

White, Robert H. *Tribal Assets: The Rebirth of Native America*. 1991.

Wilkinson, Charles F. *American Indians, Time and the Law: Native Societies in a Modern Constitutional Democracy*. 1987.

———. *Crossing the Next Meridian*. 1992.

Williams, Robert A. *The American Indian in Western Legal Thought: The Discourses of Conquest*. 1990.

Wise, Jennings C. *The Red Man in the New World Drama: A Politico-Legal Study with a Pageantry of American Indian History*. 1971.

Wunder, John R. *"Retained by The People": A History of American Indians and the Bill of Rights*. 1994.

Zimmerman, Bill. *Airlift to Wounded Knee*. 1976.

INDEX

Page numbers for main entries in the dictionary are set in **boldface** type.

ABOUT THE EDITOR
AND CONTRIBUTORS

MARK BAXTER is a graduate student at the University of Colorado in Boulder.

S. CAROL BERG is a member of the history department at the College of Saint Benedict in St. Joseph, Minnesota.

JENNIFER BERTOLET lives and writes in Arlington, Virginia.

JEFFREY D. CARLISLE is completing the Ph.D. in history at the University of North Texas in Denton, Texas.

JERE' FRANCO is a member of the history department at the University of Texas at El Paso.

EMILY GREENWALD teaches history at the University of Nebraska in Lincoln, Nebraska.

ANTHONY GULIG teaches history at Western Washington University in Bellingham, Washington.

CRAIG HEMMENS is a faculty member in the Department of Criminal Justice at Boise State University in Boise, Idaho.

PHILIP HUCKINS is an assistant professor of education at New England College in Henniker, New Hampshire.

TROY JOHNSON is a historian at California State University in Long Beach, California.

JERRY LARSON recently graduated from Sam Houston State University and is planning a career as an attorney. He is currently a student at the University of Houston Law School.

PAULEENA M. MACDOUGALL is an anthropologist with the Maine Folklife Center at the University of Maine at Orono.

J. JEFFERSON MACKINNON teaches at the Collin County Community College campus in Plano, Texas.

TIMOTHY MORGAN is a member of the history department at Christopher Newport University in Newport News, Virginia.

JAMES S. OLSON is a historian at Sam Houston State University in Huntsville, Texas. He coedited, with Robert Shadle, *Historical Dictionary of the British Empire* (2 volumes) (Greenwood, 1996).

JUDITH E. OLSON teaches bilingual education and English-as-a-second-language at Sam Houston State University in Huntsville, Texas.

DARREN PIERSON is a graduate student in history at Texas A&M University in College Station, Texas.

CARLOS RAINER recently graduated from Sam Houston State University and is planning a career as an attorney.

DAVID RITCHEY teaches at Collin County Community College in Frisco, Texas.

FRED S. ROLATER teaches history at Middle Tennessee State University in Murfreesboro, Tennessee.

JOSEPH M. ROWE JR. is professor of history at Sam Houston State University in Huntsville, Texas.

MARA RUTTEN lives and writes in Murphysboro, Illinois.

JASON M. TETZLOFF, a graduate student at Purdue University, is now teaching history at Western Washington University in Bellingham, Washington.

RAYMOND WILSON is professor of history at Fort Hays State University in Fort Hays, Kansas.

ROY WORTMAN is a historian at Kenyon College in Gambier, Ohio.